SCANDINAVIA

Michael's

SCANDINAVIA

Series editor:
Michael Shichor

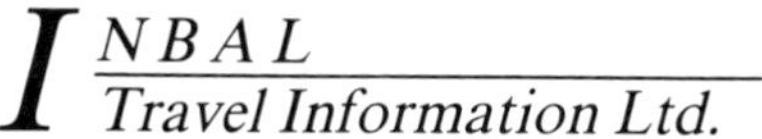
INBAL
Travel Information Ltd.

Inbal Travel Information Ltd.
P.O. Box 1870 Ramat Gan 52117

Intl. ISBN 965-288-103-1

The publishers have done their best to ensure the accuracy and updating of all information contained in this guide; however, they can accept no responsibility for any errors and/or inaccuracies found in this edition.

Text: Eliezer Sachs

Distributed in the United Kingdom by:
Kuperard (London) Ltd.
9, Hampstead West
224 Iverson Road
West Hampstead
London NW6 2HL

U.K. ISBN 1-870668-44-8

CONTENTS

FINLAND 311

INDEX 384

TABLE OF MAPS

Preface

In a sense Scandinavia is geographically, historically and culturally a separate region within the European continent. The variety of its settings offers the tourist an incomparable array of attractions, sights and experiences. The most distant as well as the least frequented (and most expensive) region of Europe, its inhabitants are among the most sophisticated and progressive in the world. With this in mind we have designed a very detailed guide, with lots of information, suggestions and hints tailored to the needs and tastes of most visitors both, young or old.

We have subdivided this volume into separate sections for each of the Scandinavian countries. We shall invite you to pedal leisurely side by side with the Danes, to join the Norwegians on their world-famous ski-slopes, and to follow the Swedes and the Finns along the ancient paths of their forests. We shall also recommend sea, road and railway routes through some of Europe's most spectacular sceneries.

Special thanks to Eliezer Sachs, who wrote this guide, and to the entire staff of Inbal Travel Information (1983) Ltd. We are also grateful to the courteous personnel of the Tourist Offices and the embassies of the Scandinavian countries, for their warm assistance and tireless help. Beautiful Scandinavia has recently opened its doors to international tourism, making an effort to bring down its prices, and is today one of the major and most popular destinations of the tourist world.

Michael Shichor

Using this Guide

The information we have collected for you in this volume is designed to assist you throughout your visit, and to assure that you make maximum advantage of your time, effort and money.

Our basic guideline, here as in all "Michael's Guides" publications, is to provide you with practical information make you feel at home in Scandinavia as soon as you arrive.

Along with the basic background data (historical notes, climate, populations etc.) you'll find in the introduction many valuable suggestions about what to wear and carry, as well as information on documents, customs, transports, accommodation etc.

The itineraries in this guide are organized by the country, and take you to some of the most exciting and least known sites in the region.

Each section of the book is provided with a general map. On the city maps you'll find marked all major sites covered by our local itineraries and walks. Lists of recommended restaurants and lodgings are provided for all major stopovers. A short list of emergency phones and addresses can be found at the end of each chapter. Maps and information will make it easy for you to prepare a detailed plan of your visit even before your departure.

At the end of the book you'll find an index of all the sites mentioned throughout the volume.

As you know, each Scandinavian nation has its own language — or languages — and alphabet. This is why we have enclosed, a very short glossary and phonetic guide at the end of the book.

A tourist guide must always strive for accuracy with regard to visiting hours, timetables etc. Some of the data, however, may already have become outdated. We apologize for any inconvenience incurred; confirm opening schedules obtainable at any local Tourist Information Office, upon arrival in each town.

To help us keep as up-to-date as possible, we would appreciate your assistance. If you discover any changes in information provided by this guide, please fill out the questionnaire printed at the end of this volume. A complimentary copy of the new edition will be forwarded to those of you whose contribution will appear in the next edition of this Guide.

Have a pleasant and exciting trip — Bon voyage!

SCANDINAVIA

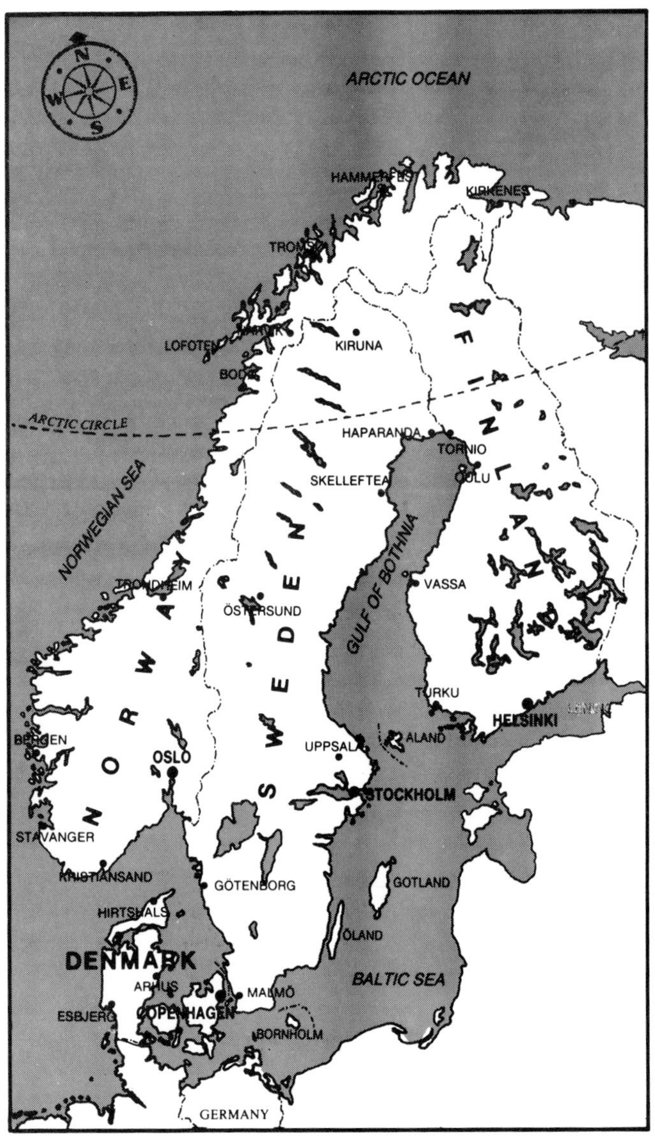

INTRODUCTION

Scandinavia — brings to mind images of ice and snow, of foreboding peaks dropping precipitously into the deep waters of dark fjords. This is true of Norway's northern coasts; but Scandinavia, in fact, has much more to offer beyond its gloomy stereotyped images of ice and winter. You are in for many unexpected sights — anything but the Sahara sands...

The Scandinavian countries which are today a paragon of human progress, especially in the field of social welfare, have a long and proud history. Before the end of the first millennium, their courageous seafaring forefathers, the Vikings, were absolute masters of the northern seas. Later, the great kings of Denmark and of Sweden brought their countries into the limelight of European history, and introduced their peoples to the art and culture of the Renaissance. Many Scandinavian towns date from Medieval times and their old buildings preserve the aura and the awe of bygone. Behind their snow-capped peaks, in the shadow of their ancient warrior lore, live some of the most openminded and friendly peoples on Earth.

Today, Scandinavia is an integral part of the Western World; its borders are wide open and the strife of the past has long been forgotten. Daily life is free of the hustle of a modern metropolis. The streets are a paragon of neatness; there are no crowds or pushing queues at the entrance of the subways; even in the middle of a morning traffic jam you'll feel free of any sense of stress. Dog-owners clean up after their pets; cigarette butts are properly disposed of, and do not end up in the gutters. Here the earth is beautiful, and so is man.

English is willingly and fluently spoken by a large majority of Scandinavians. Hospitality seems to be the Scandinavians' eleventh commandment. Service is outstanding throughout the region — in hotels, offices, restaurants, trains, banks and ferries.

The only drawback is the cost of living. Scandinavia is still one of the most expensive regions in the world, in spite of the recent efforts of the tourist establishment. There are, during the summer, several relatively attractive package deals, discounted train tickets and other reduced travel rates. Still, prices remain on the whole higher than elsewhere in Europe (with a growing number of welcomed exceptions...). A Scandinavian tour, in any case, will always prove to be well worth its price!

Part One — Getting to know Scandinavia

As we have already said, Scandinavia is a subcontinent of its own. Its peoples — the Danes, the Swedes, the Norwegians and the Finns — have so much in common that they seem to belong to a single tribe. Even their languages often sound similar and in fact, they will be able to communicate with one another, without having to resort to sign language (with the exception of the Finns).

However, in order to make your life easier, our Guide deals with each country separately. This introduction deals with the common aspects of the whole region, its history, its culture, its services and transportation facilities.

History

While feasting your eyes on pastoral scenes and the cultural harmony of the land, it may seem hard to believe that for many centuries Scandinavia was riddled by almost uninterrupted warring and strife. Kings and barons, bishops and priests battled here for centuries, striving for supremacy, at the expense of their peoples.

5000-1500 B.C. — Archaeological findings indicate the existence of hunting tribes and other nomadic groups in the northern wastes of Finland and Sweden.

1500-500 B.C. — In the Bronze Age many nomads settled in small agricultural villages. Among the finds are burial grounds, and thousands of tools, jewels, pots and ornaments. Some of the objects point at the beginning of trade between local tribes and more advanced travellers from the south.

500 B.C.-800 A.D. — Trading expanded as far as the Mediterranean. Various groups of local tribes formed the first local quasi-national units — the Danes and the Svear — getting their first taste of what was to become the Scandinavian taste to war, which was to last some thousand years.

INTRODUCTION

800-1050 A.D. — The Vikings settled along the southern shores of the peninsula, building scores of townships, tilling the land and squabbling among themselves for trading rights. Having mastered the art of shipbuilding, they turned seaward, scourging the coasts of the British Isles and all Western Europe.

The Vikings, organised in local tribes, swarmed out of their respective territories into Europe to loot and conquer, exploiting the fall of the great European empires of that epoch.

The Svear (Swede) tribe turned eastward to Russia, reaching as far as the Black Sea, Persia and Byzantium. The Norwegian tribes sailed westward and southward, conquering northern Scotland, Ireland, the Shetlands, the Orkneys and the Hebrides. Towards the end of the 10th century they reached as far as Greenland, Labrador and Nova Scotia.

The Danes conquered Northern England, setting up their capital at York. Crossing the Channel, they invaded Normandy (=Land of the Northerners). Trade prospered between the Vikings and the Franks, in spite of all their fighting, and many Viking sailors brought their wives the newest of the sophisticated Frank fashions.

The Viking era was doomed; their quick expansion brought them into contact with Christianity. The new religion conquered the hearts of the northen warriors, and shipbuilding was replaced by churchbuilding.

1050-1300 A.D. — Christianity — This is indeed the era of the "Stave Churches", pagoda-like wood structures, whose carved crosses are often enhanced by pagan ornaments and symbols. Christianity expanded slowly but surely, progressing gradually northward, with the cross and the sword, until all Scandinavia adopted the new faith.

1300-1500 A.D. — Somewhat belatedly, Scandinavia entered the arena of the struggle between the Crown and the Church. The trade wars carried on as usual. The Black Death of 1349 devoured one-third of the population. Enfeebled Scandinavia fell prey to the guiles of the Hanseatic League, and all major ports were monopolized by Hanseatic traders from Hamburg and Lübeck.

In 1397, the Kalmar Treaty of Union brought the whole of Scandinavia under Danish rule, creating an empire which was to last for 130 years.

1500-1700 A.D. — Sweden set up its own kingdom under Gustavus Vasa, expanding gradually northwards. With the Treaty of Roskilde (1657) the whole of Sweden freed itself from Danish supremacy.

The Danish kings, however, still ruled Norway, and under Christian IV — the Architect King — many new towns and castles, most of which have remained to this day, were built throughout the Danish empire.

1700-1900 A.D. — An age of revolution, industry and cultural growth, Scandinavia became a full-fledged member of the European civilization: the French Revolution, the Napoleonic Wars and the industrial revolution brought the spirit of liberalism to all northern shores. Norway and Finland fought for their independence, Denmark and Sweden returned to their relatively modest original dimensions. Tired of strife and wars, the people of Scandinavia set themselves to rebuilding their life, having achieved peace among themselves and with their neighbours.

The Twentieth Century — Norway and Finland won their independence. In Finland, political strife turned into bloody civil war. The First World War bypassed Scandinavia, whose countries remained strictly neutral, and prospered. In the Second World War, Hitler invaded Denmark and Norway, while Finland became his ally. Only Sweden was able to maintain its neutrality. During the German retreat, the Nazis left northern Norway scorched.

The second half of the century has been an era of great prosperity, when the Scandinavian countries have become the paragon of the Welfare State. Standards of living have reached unprecedented highs. The Scandinavian democracies have focused their attention on global problems, like ecology and nuclear disarmament.

Population and Culture

The homogeneity of the cultures and peoples of Scandinavia surprises even the experts. The only exception to the Viking-Scandinavian model is the Sami, a small tribe, still jealously maintaining its ancient customs at the northern fringes of the subcontinent. Yet, the brilliant, explosive Vikings disappeared totally from history in less than ten generations, while the daily life of the Sami shepherds has gone on undisturbed and practically unchanged for millennia.

The Vikings

The Scandinavians of today look back upon the model of the

tall, strong, blonde Viking warriors, bent on their conquest of the seas, as the prototype of their forefathers. Indeed, this stereotype has found considerable support in archaeological findings and in many ancient legends and poems.

The origins of the Vikings are not clear ("Vik" means a small watercourse or cove). They made their first appearance at the beginning of the ninth century in Norway, Denmark and Sweden. Accustomed to harsh living conditions, they sought strengh in tribal groups, and expanded, mainly seaward, from their desolate fjord hamlets to all the Atlantic coastal towns, down to the Iberian Peninsula, In the year 800 the Danish Vikings forced the hitherto unvanquished armies of Charlemagne to retreat. Later, Danish and Norwegian Vikings jointly invaded the British Isles. In 1033 the Vikings ruled most of England and French Normandy, and their ships were absolute masters of the northern seas. The Norwegians ruled northern Scotland, the Shetlands, the Hebrides and the Orkneys. We even find their remains on the western coast of Ireland.

In 836, the Norwegians founded Dublin, which became their main base for further conquests of the Faröes and of Iceland. In 985 their ships reached Greenland, and in the year 1000 they landed in Labrador. To the east, the Swedish Vikings were masters of the Baltic and of most of its ports, and reached the Caspian and the Black Sea by land. The Swedes settled and built wherever they conquered, and in the East the local Slav tribes gave them the name of **Rus** ("Swedes" in ancient Russian) — the origin of the name "Russia".

The union enforced in 1035 by Knut the Great brought together under his rule Danes and Norwegians, and little later the Viking empire reached the height of its short lived expansion. The causes of its sudden fall are unclear; the main cause could possibly have been the recurrence of internecine strife, as a result the rapid infiltration of Christianity. Viking rule, as such, had practically disappeared by 1050.

Their cultural influence, however, survived for centuries. Much has been learned about their life and customs from archaeological research and especially from the retrieval of several sunken ships, some which had been ceremonially "buried at sea" with "all hands on board".

The Viking Ships — The mystery of the Vikings' prowess at sea is at least partly explained by the quality of their shipbuilding, revealed in full, thanks to the retrieval of several ships from the bottom of the Norwegian fjords. The Vikings built merchant ships as well as men-of-war. The successful digs at the Roskilde Fjord in 1962 brought to light several different models of Viking ships. There are two types of merchant ships, two of warships and one ferry-type boat. The warships were 30 meters long, the merchant ships 16.5 and the ferryboat 10. The merchant ships could hoist an 86 square meter sail and its hold could take in 20 ton of cargo. The wood is clearly recognizable as Norwegian pine, and, in fact, the same wood was identified in Viking ship fragments as far north as Baltic Sea and Greenland. A recently reconstructed Viking ship sailed (1984-86) around the Earth twice. Modern research into the seafaring prowess of the Vikings points clearly to their masterful navigational achievements.

You might find it difficult to associate these sophisticated seafarers with the barbarous custom of the ceremonial burial of ships and sailors, as displayed in the Oslo Museum of Viking Ships. There are also written eyewitness reports on the burial ceremonies of Viking barons, interred with all their personal belongings, including at least one of their maids, "honoured" by all the local gentry course of rich banquets and orgies before being buried. The final execution was carried out in the bloodiest manner by the high priestess of the clan.

The awesome descriptions of villagers and townpeople subjugated by "yellow-bearded" giants do not fit the norms of their own daily life customs. According to the *Havamal* epic, the Vikings considered life a passing stage toward a better world, and demanded norms not unlike those of the Ten Commandments. Another unusual Viking custom was that of the *Ting*, a quasi democratic periodical assembly of the tribe.

Many attempts have been made to rationalize the "Viking phenomenon", often on the basis of the ethos of their idolatrous religion. Their many gods required believers to prove their faith by means of sacrifices, in the bleak climate of their daily life, that often resulted in violence and death.

The Sami Tribes

The origins of the Sami — or Lapp — tribes is still a subject of controversy among anthropologists. Their migration to Scandinavia and Lappland is not well documented, though all agree that it must have taken place at least ten centuries ago.

Today, the Sami amount to about 40,000 souls. 15,000 live in Sweden, 20,000 in Norway, 2,500 in Finland and 2,000 in Russia.

Though their past is still a riddle, they are identifiable by their language, and by their traditional occupation as reindeer shepherds.

INTRODUCTION

In the Stone Age, the Lapps were mainly hunters and fishermen, and only later they took to shepherding local reindeer herds, still one of the mainstays of their economy and culture. The reindeer owes its "status" to its ability to survive in the rugged arctic climate of the region. The natural pastures, which were recently very seriously endangered by the Chernobyl disaster, provide all its needs; in winter, the reindeer feed on the so-called "reindeer moss", which grows under the winter blanket of snow. This moss was most severely polluted by the radioactive ashes carried by the wind from Chernobyl, and level of pollution, ten times higher than the average level of other organisms, remained high over several years, poisoning thousands of reindeer and depriving the Sami of their livelihood. This tragedy, together with the crisis of modernization at the beginning of our century, has undermined the original tribal structure of the Sami.

The **Sami village** is comprised of living quarters and the surrounding lakes, woods and pastures used by the community. It is generally long and narrow, situated at the bottom of a well sheltered valley. There are, summer pastures on the mountainsides, while spring and autumn pastures are found lower down, among the birch trees. Winter pastures are under the cover of the evergreens, mostly larch trees, at the bottom of the valley. When the reindeer are in heat, the Sami set up their tents, *visten*, which serve them also in other seasons. In spring and summer, the Sami follow their herds to the higher slopes, living in their traditional *köta*. In several regions today the seasonal migration of the herds is monitored by helicopter, and the young calves are often fed from the air with additional fodder.

Up to the beginning of this century, the Sami lived according to their ancient customs, and their regular diet consisted exclusively of reindeer meat and milk. Gradually more of them were forced to abandond their pastoral life, adopting, more modern occupations. With the growth of local tourism, Sami arts and crafts have become increasingly popular. In response to increasing demand, this has become an industry of growing importance. The Sami (Lapp) language is now taught regularly in all Sami schools. Christianity, which was introduced in Lappland only in the 17th century, has made only relatively litlle inroads.

The nomadic character of the Sami tribes has brought them in contact with several different cultures, and many Samis are fluent in three or even four different languages. Ancient Sami traditions are transmitted orally, mostly through the troubadour-like *Yoiking*, and includes hundreds of old legends and proverbs, published in 1910 under the name of *Muitalus Samiidbirra*.

INTRODUCTION

During the Second World War the Sami tribesmen were of great assistance to the Norwegian resistance fighters in their struggle against the Nazis. In spite of recent (rather feeble, according to the Sami themselves) attempts to rehabilitate Sami traditions, intercultural contacts take place even today almost exclusively along the highways, where small groups of Samis entice the passing tourists, with their traditional handicrafts.

We remind you to call them **Sami** — never Lapps. Also, be careful not to enquire into the number of heads in their herds; for them it is a matter of pride, and a very private matter!

Part Two — First Steps

The size of Scandinavia and its very high cost of living require careful planning of your time and budget, making use of the information available at the Tourist Information Offices of Norway, Denmark, Sweden and Finland.

The Scandinavian Tourist

In spite of the sedate "family image" of Scandinavia, there are also thousands of attractions for the younger visitor. Hitchhiking has become obsolete thanks to the considerably discounted tariffs of railways and airlines for travellers under 26 years of age.

Tour groups, families, students, pensioners and schoolclasses will be able to take advantage of attractive bargains and special offers for their Scandinavian tours. The information is generally available at most travel agencies and in all Scandinavian Tourist Information Offices.

How to travel

The easiest (and often also the cheapest) alternative is, of course, an **organised tour**. Most tours offer interesting itineraries, superficial but comprehensive, covering most popular sites. Those who prefer to make their own plans, even at an additional cost in time and money, can rent a car, buy road maps and set out, assisted by this guide. The **rented (or private) car tour** may be planned to the last detail; if you're addicted to camping, you'd do well to make reservations by phone. In the major cities, especially in the summer, accommodation is scarse: here too, reservations are a must.

Younger travellers will find Scandinavia a land of surprises. Trains, ferries, buses and airlines offer very attractive bargains of all types. Many spectacular parks and mountaintops are found along the itinerary of fascinating walks through valleys and fjords, glaciers and lakes — and between tours there are activities of all sorts, from fishing to boating to skiing. Trains and ferries stop at most tourist sites. You are free to make your own choices. Youth hostels, camp sites and alpine refuges are at your disposal, comfortable and convenient in prices.

The more staid tourist may prefer a good hotel, conveniently located for short outings within a predetermined radius. This alternative is probably the best in the "Fjord Region". Others might prefer to hire their own transportation and make their overnight stops at preselected centres, returning the hired car as soon as they reach a major city.

Business people, who are traditionally short of time, will prefer to ask their travel agent, to provide them with detailed plans, including all accommodation and travel reservations.

Families travelling with children will find a true paradise in Scandinavia. Just follow in the footsteps of the natives.

Where to go

When touring, Scandinavia (like other regions), has two aspects: nature and people. Norway is mainly nature, Sweden and Finland are both, and Denmark is mainly people. One of your first considerations in planning your trip might be how many, and which, countries to visit. Other considerations, of course, are time and money. This guide describes, in detail, all four countries, indicating border crossings. Each country has its own travelling tradition: in Norway it's mostly walks and sea-tours, hence the guide presents two special chapters, one on walking tours, the other on a coastal cruise. Denmark is a bicycle-addicted nation; therefore we added a chapter on bicycling.

The tourist has many alternative choices: a selection of seaside, fjordside or lakeside resorts; fishing trips, winter sports, sea cruises to the "fjord region", to the far north or east; or a leisurely stay in Copenhagen or Stockholm. The sky (or the North Pole) is the limit.

If you are thinking in terms of a 15-30 days visit, you probably will select one of three major alternatives. **The first** begins with Copenhagen, then to Hälsingborg in Sweden, then to Oslo, Bergen and the Fjord region, northward to Trondheim and back south to Malmö and Denmark.

The second starts at Stockholm, then to Helsinki in Finland, northward by train or by air to Lappland or to the Nord Kapp in Norway; then by air or train or car or boat to Trondheim and the fjords; then Oslo and finally Denmark.

The third begins at Oslo, then to Bergen and the fjords, Trondheim and northward along the coast; southward to Helsinki, then to Stockholm, Malmö, Helsingborg and Copenhagen.

Of course one may also make other choices. Some may elect to spend most of the time in Norway, with one or two brief trips to Stockholm and Copenhagen; others may feel drawn to the great forest parks of the mountains. Choose what you wish.

When to come and for how long

In Scandinavia the four seasons are extremely varied. The best season is spring and early summer, when the snow melts and the flowers bloom. In summer all tourist sites are open; in the far north you will enjoy the sight of the midnight sun (and many attractive package deals). In the fall it is not too crowded; the forests are at their best and the weather at its worst; quite a few resorts close rather early. Winter is for winter-sports people and for the young in heart.

Don't come for less than ten days, not even just to Norway; one or two months are more satisfactory — and six months are a dream!

How much does it cost

Scandinavia is costly, but with careful planning one will be able to keep the cost down to reasonable European standards. Make the best possible use of seasonal bargains, and you might even come out ahead!

If you rent a car ($20-$25 a day), you will spend an additional $20 in gasoline. Bed and breakfast accommodation will cost $30. Meals (one daily restaurant meal and a supermarket dinner) will account for $20-$30; add museums and other spots for a total of $100-$140 a day for two.

If you choose to spend nights at a 3-4 star hotel ($50-$60), you will spend the same amount again for meals, and end up with a daily budget of $140-$200.

A single student using a pre-purchased *Eurail* ticket will spend $10-$20 a day for transportation,$5-$15 for a hostel, or camping bed and $10-$15 for food; a total of $30-$50 a day.

INTRODUCTION

Planning details

Careful planning will ensure a successful visit at the best possible rates in the shortest possible time.

Documents

Norway and Denmark are EEC member states, and as such are open to all holders of European Identity Cards; the other two countries require a valid passport.

International Driving Permits are valid in all Scandinavia; while driving, don't forget to keep to the right!

For further information, call the Scandinavian embassies in your home country.

A **Student Card** entitles the bearer to considerable discounts on transportation fares and many other fees. This may be obtained at your college or university administration office.

The **Youth Hostel Card** entitles you to special accommodation rates in hostels. Health and baggage insurance should be taken out through your travel agent or your insurance agency.

Insurance: in EEC countries, EEC mores (green card recommended for cars).

Financial details

Credit cards (*Visa*, *Mastercard-Eurocard*, *Diner's* and *American Express*) and *Travelers' Cheques* are welcome in many hotels, restaurants and shops. In the smaller towns and beyond, however, only cash counts. One should always keep at least a small sum of cash in local currency: Scandinavian banknotes may be changed in most banks, but of course for a price.

SAS airline offices are generally very helpful — both in your home country and on your arrival in Scandinavia.

What to take

Backpackers are advised to use a medium-sized pack, to which they may attach a double-walled tent, a portable mattress, a warm but compact sleeping-bag and comfortable walking shoes; one might want to add a gas-burner and other cooking paraphernalia, warm clothes, a good raincoat and, for use during shorter walks, a smaller pack.

Cameras and film are very expensive in Scandinavia.

Medical Services are excellent, efficient and... expensive. In the non-EEC countries, come provided with your basic needs: first aid, aspirins, a second pair of glasses, etc.

Part Three — Where Have We Landed?

How to get there

Scandinavia is serviced by *SAS* and all the major international airlines. Updated information is available at any travel agency in your home town or anywhere else.

At Copenhagen airport there are daily flights to most Scandinavian destinations (for timetables, rates and eventual package deals — inquire at your agency). Scheduled flights with stopovers in other Europe cities are considerably more expensive.

Scandinavia may also be reached by railway, road or sea. There are several ferry lines from England and Scotland and there are express train lines to Stockholm from London, Paris, Rome and Istanbul.

Car hire is cheapest in Denmark — but gasoline is more expensive there than in any of the three other countries.

Public transportation

In Scandinavia most major cities are also sea ports. They are at considerable distance from each other, and the difficult topographical conditions (specially in Norway) often require multiple means of transportation.

Maritime lines have, until very recently, been the most common means of transportation throughout Scandinavia. Ferries and small motor boats are still a vital component of the transportation network, — and often the most comfortable of all. All ferries are equipped to carry cars and even whole trains.

The rail system of Scandinavia is comprehensive, and "ignores" borders; thanks to local ferries, the trains often cross fjords and other waterways.

INTRODUCTION

Tourists will find it convenient to enquire at their travel agency about special cumulative railway tickets. The *Nordturist* ticket, for instance, costs about $200 and provides free passage on all trains and ferryboats in Scandinavia. For travellers under 25, the cost is only about $150. The *Eurail Pass* and the *Eurail Youth Pass* are valid in Western Europe, including Scandinavia.

The *Eurail Pass* is valid outside the British Isles and costs about $500. For information, inquire at the Railway Information Offices of any major railway station in Europe.

The Fjord Region is not wholly covered by the rail system, and other means of transportation must be used.

The **bus network** covers mainly the interior areas only partially serviced by the railway. The buses generally connect with passing trains, and updated information is available at the railway stations.

There is a sizable network of inland *SAS* and *Finnair* flights, with connections to all major Scandinavian centres. Here too, one may find some very advantageous cumulative tickets and other package deals. In view of the size of Scandinavia, this means of transportation is rapidly becoming more popular.

Compulsive **car** drivers will find in Scandinavia an excellent system of highways. In spite of the high price of fuel, a motor car remains the best means of transportation. It will take you anywhere. Seat belts and day-lights are compulsory.

All major **car-rental agencies** are represented throughout Scandinavia. However, it is probably more convenient to make your reservation and arrangements beforehand.

The **bicycle** is still the most popular means of transportation in most of Scandinavia; the bike is often used for long week-end and even longer family and group outings. Recently the bike has been adapted by tourists, especially for shorter, panoramic tours.

Bicycle hire agencies may be found in most tourist centres and also in many provincial towns, often attached to local Tourist Information Centres or to the larger youth hostels. Prices vary according to the bicycle requested (regular, sports, mountain, competition etc.) and to the terms. Generally a refundable deposit is requested.

Hitchhiking is frowned upon in Scandinavia, and we strongly

advice you not to plan your vacation around this means of transportation.

Tourist services

The standards and availability of Scandinavian tourist services are simply outstanding. In all Tourist Information Centres you'll be offered a heap of maps, leaflets, cards, programmes, timetables, hotel lists, tours, bicycle rentals etc. You ought to start your Scandinavian tour with a visit to the first Tourist Information Centre you see where, among other things, you will find a complete list of the Tourist Information Centres you'll find along your itinerary.

In many towns you'll be able to buy a "Tourist Card", entitling you to discounts on transportation fares, museum tickets and even hotel rooms. The purchase of a Tourist Card is particularly convenient if you intend to visit a certain number of tourist sites, as in all the major cities.

Discounts

Scandinavian prices are so high that discounts should always be taken advantage of. Student cards, senior citizen cards and other tourist cards are all valuable documents. The Railway Card (*Scandinavian Bonus Pass*) costs about $25, and entitles its bearer to discounts of 15-40% in summer and on winter week-ends in many Scandinavian hotels.

Accommodation

Scandinavian **hotels** are of very high standards (and prices — unless you know how to make the most of tourist opportunities). The most popular are the medium-priced hotels (2-4 stars), the B&Bs and motels. Prices vary by location and category, from $40 to $80, per double bedroom.

The cheapest (and perhaps also the most attractive) choice is a room in a private residence. Such accommodation is available only at the local Tourist Information Centre, even by phone, upon your arrival. Prices range between $20 and $40 a night.

There are hundreds of **youth hostels** in all corners of Scandinavia; they cater to thousands of young in age and in spirit. They are always very clean and orderly, and they often offer a choice of double or multiple-bed (family) rooms.

Travelling by car or by backpack you'll probably appreciate the net of **camp sites** conveniently situated all around the major cities and most conveniently priced according to services required.

Note: in the Scandinavian hoteliers' lingo *hitter* means an overnight room in a private residence, or a hut or camping bungalow; *zimmer* or *rom* both mean a room in a private residence or chalêt.

Food and drinks

The two most striking peculiarities of the Scandinavian cuisine are: the *smørebrød* — a variety of cold cuts, cheeses and other staples on slices of limitless kinds of bread, served at most hotels and restaurants at almost all hours of the day and night; and the outrageous prices of all alcoholic beverages.

Otherwise, Scandinavian cooking does not differ from what is found throughout continental Europe, except for the almost daily presence of fish on the menu. The fact that a large majority of the population lives along the coast, together with the sophisticated standards of the dairy sector, have left a pleasurable imprint upon Scandinavian menus. The long and icy winters have also encouraged the refinement of a home cuisine that does honour to the most demanding of diners.

Communications

The post and the telecommunication network is, as might be expected, among the most efficient in the world. English speakers will find very little difficulty in communicating — either at the post office or with the generally very kind telephone operators. Public phones are equipped with clear instructions in English.

The Main Post Office of every major town has at least one *Poste Restante* counter.

Weights and measures

All Scandinavian countries use the metric system.

Clothes and footwear are sold by European sizes.

INTRODUCTION

Voltage: 220V.

Time zone GMT+1 in Norway, Sweden and Denmark; GMT+2 in Finland.

DENMARK

"Something is rotten in the state of Denmark" to quote Prince Hamlet. (Hard to believe?) Denmark, the most ancient kingdom in the continent, with its nobleminded people and its glorious history, is one of the most attractive and inviting countries in Europe.

Its location and climate, its beaches, its islands and its verdant plains form a background of such refreshing harmony that even the most troubled soul must perforce relax.

"Wonderful wonderful Copenhagen" with the pastoral villages of the province, create a unique scenery that never fails to fascinate even the most seasoned traveller.

History

Denmark has a long and troubled history. The first signs of human settlement date from before the last Ice Age, which covered the region with a thick mantle of impenetrable ice. After the retreat of the great glaciers, Man reappeared, leaving his imprint on the land for the next ten millennia, after long centuries of nomadic life. Four thousand years ago the first agricultural settlements appeared.

Archaeological digs of Bronze and Iron Age settlements have uncovered tools and ornaments in silver, bronze and glass, and point at a series of migratory waves coming from the south-east.

At the time of the Roman Empire, Denmark was inhabited by teutonic tribes, often threatened by Viking incursions from the north. The necessity to form a united front in time of emergency contributed to the establishment, toward the end of the ninth century, of a United Kingdom of Denmark. The new entity was soon forced to defend itself also from the incoming armies of the great Empires born following the fall of Rome: the Kingdom of the Franks and later the Holy Roman Empire. This was the reason for the erection of the *Danvirke*, the defensive wall crossing southern Yutland from east to west. The two foremost rulers of that time were King Gorm and his son Harald Blaatand (Blueteeth).

DENMARK

During the tenth century the Danes and the Vikings joined in a series of raids against the British Isles, completing their conquest in 1013. King Knut the Great, who had already "annexed" Norway, was now King of Denmark, Norway and England.

In the wake of his military conquests, Knut dedicated himself to agriculture and trade, making Denmark one of the most prosperous countries of his times in Northern Europe.

Knut's triumphs brought Denmark to the attention of the Church, and scores of missionaries soon undertook the conquest of Denmark to the new faith.

The waves of Barbarian hordes coming from the Asian steppes reached Denmark at the beginning of the eleventh century, bringing havoc to the country and plunging it back into anarchy and strife. After two centuries of local and regional conflicts with the neighbouring German states, Margrete, wife of Haakon VI of Norway, was crowned Queen of Denmark in 1376. Upon her husband's death, she became queen of Norway, and in 1397, with the Union of Kalmar, Margrete found herself sole ruler of Scandinavia — Sweden (which included present day Finland), Norway and Denmark, as well as Iceland and Greenland. Copenhagen became the capital of the new empire. The Union survived for little more than a century after Margrete's death (1412), under the gradually weakening sceptres of the first two Christians (King Christian I and II). At the end of the Seven Years War, in 1523, Sweden regained its independence; the Danish predominance in Scandinavia had come to its end.

The rigid absolutism of the Monarchy, its feudal structure and the advent of Luteranism brought to Denmark a long period of unrest, rebellion and civil war.

Christian IV became King of Denmark in 1596, and his many military debacles in the Thirty Years War against Sweden, together with his passion for urban growth and architecture, made of Denmark a small, militarily weak but magnificent provincial state.

Repeated Danish attempts to avenge the debacle of the Thirty Year War failed again and again, until Denmark reconciled itself to its modest political and military status, avoiding, whenever possible being drawn into its neighbours' wars. No longer able to remain neutral, Denmark joined Napoleon's armies against the united European front, and lost all its Norwegian lands (which were annexed by Sweden) as well as Helgoland (which went to Great Britain).

The wave of liberal unrest that swept through Europe toward

the middle of the last century forced King Frederik VII to grant a Constitution that put an end to Danish absolutism. The new legislation voted by the two chambers of the new Parliament made of Denmark one of the most liberal states in Europe.

During the First World War Denmark was able to maintain its traditional neutrality. After the war the Versailles treaty sanctioned a plebiscite for the territory of Schleswig-Holstein (that for centuries had been the object of controversy between Denmark and Germany), and its people voted for annexation to Denmark.

In April 1940, only a few months after the beginning of the Second World War, Hitler invaded Denmark. The great majority of Danes, faithful to their proud history and to their democratic ideals, did not surrender and carried on a long-drawn, clandestine struggle that lasted until Hitler's final fall.

Denmark became a charter member of the UN in 1945, and a full-fledged member of NATO in 1949. The Marshall Plan for European Reconstruction assisted Denmark in its rapid economic and social recovery, toward attaining a life of peace and prosperity, envied throughout Europe.

Geography

The territory of Denmark is compromised of the Jutland Peninsula and an archipelago of more than 100 inhabited islands and 383 barren rocks and islets. The archipelago extends north-eastward from the peninsula, and it forms the Skagerrak and Kattegat straits between the Northern and the Baltic Sea, with Sweden on the north-eastern side and Denmark on the south-western side. The southern end of the Jutland is Denmark's border with Germany.

The Jutland represents 70% of the total territory of Denmark (43,025 km^2); it extends for 320 km from north to south, and its maximum width is 150 km from east to west.

The **Sjælland** Island, with the capital, Copenhagen, is the most developed and populated region of Denmark, and is closer to the Swedish coast than to the Danish mainland of the Jutland. South of the Sjælland are the three islands of Lolland, Falster and Møn.

Denmark is a mountainless plain, whose modest hills rise to no more than 177 m in height. The western coast of the Jutland is barren and sandy, but the soil of the rest of the country is very fertile and very intensely cultivated.

Climate

Thanks to its seas, Denmark enjoys a very moderate climate. The annual average temperature is 6°-8°C (summer average 16°C, winter average is 0°C). Annual precipitation amounts to 400-800 mm; a mantle of snow covers the country from December to the beginning of February.

Flora and fauna

The Danish flora is surprisingly rich, in spite of its often unchanging appearance.

Many islands are covered with coniferous forest, in several cases the product of modern afforestation projects.

Wildlife has been practically exterminated by man from most of the country — and replaced with domestic animals — mostly cattle and poultry.

The people

The population of Denmark amounts to 5.2 million people, most of whom are urban dwellers. The capital, Copenhagen, is a city of about 1.5 million people.

There are several ethnic minorities: the German communities of Schleswig-Holstein and immigrant groups from Third World countries. 92% of the population belongs to the Luteran faith.

Education

Education is compulsory to the age of 15. About 90% of the pupils continue their high school studies, and most of them go on to college. The oldest university is the University of Copenhagen, founded 1479.

Perhaps the most popular type of high school education is the *Falkehojskole*, a chain modern, liberal, open schools, established before the end of the last century; it boasts more than 100 campuses.

English is the most common second language in Denmark.

Traditions and culture

The cultural standards of Denmark are best reflected in the architectural monuments of its cities.

The best known Danish authors are Ludvig Holberg (an 18th century playwright — often considered the father of Danish literature), Hans Christian Andersen (with his world-famous tales), and the philosopher Søren Kirkegård.

Danish figurative arts, music and dance are of the highest standards, as witnessed in the scores of art museums and frequent performances in Copenhagen.

Sports

The two most popular sports are soccer and sailing. The national soccer team has thousands of fans, who, unlike their counterparts in many countries, know how to keep their cool even under the worst conditions.

Economy

Denmark is a small country, poor in mineral resources; nevertheless, its standards of living are among the highest in the world. The secret of its achievements is in the quality of Danish manpower. Their products are famous throughout the world for quality. Industry, agriculture, trade and services are organised with efficiency and expertise.

Danish farmers are great innovators and all their branches are always up-to-date with the most recent scientific discoveries. Danish fishermen sail a fleet of 8000 boats; the total average annual catch amounts to more than 100,000 ton of fish — for export, local consumption and industry.

The main industries include dairy products, agriculture, and some of the best shipyards in the western world.

Social and medical services are second to none in the world.

The administration

Queen Margrete II was crowned in 1972. The Danish monarchy is more than ten centuries old, an unparalleled world record. Constitution Day — June 5, 1849 — has become a national holiday.

The Danish Parliament (*Falketing*) has 179 members. Elections are regional, and all citizens are eligible to vote from the age of 18. The multi-party system makes it difficult for any Danish government to survive its entire four-year tenure. The five major parties — Social-Democrat, Conservative, Liberal, Radical and Socialist — must often form more or less stable governative coalitions.

DENMARK

The language

Danish is a Scandinavian language with considerable Germanic influence. Its alphabet includes several dyphtongs and consonant groups that may cause considerable trouble to unprepared foreigners. To assist you in your first steps, here is a simplified phonetic guide:

æ — is pronounced like "a" in "bad"
ø — "o" in "Rome"
å — "e" in "egg"
hv — "v"
hj — "e" in "he"
k — "g" (hard)
sj — "sh"
g as an initial letter — "g" (hard)
g as an end letter — "y" or "h"
t — if between two vowels — "d"

General information

When to come

Copenhagen is an all-year round city; the rest of the country is at its best in spring and early summer.

Holidays
New Year
Easter
May Day
Constitution Day — June 5
Ascension Day
Christmas

How long to stay;

How much does it cost

Denmark is a small country; in a week you'll be able to see most of it; even for an in-depth visit, including the archipelago, a fortnight is ample.

Although Denmark is less expensive than the other Scandinavian countries, you'll find its prices quite steep. Even the least demanding tourist will spend not less than $25-$50 a day, and a couple will need $40-$80. If you want comfort, be ready to spend up to $100 a day.

Denmark

How to get there

The main port of entrance is Copenhagen Airport. It's possible, of course, to arrive by road, by train, or by boat as well.

By air

All major international airlines maintain regular Copenhagen flights, landing at **Kastrup** international airport. *SAS* flights connect Copenhagen with all major Scandinavian airports, with all European capitals and with major overseas centres. There are hundreds of seasonal charter flights, and discounted rates are offered throughout the year to students and to senior citizens, mainly by *SAS* and *Finnair*.

By sea

Several ferry lines connect Denmark with the rest of Scandinavia. Other lines connect Denmark with various British and Central European ports. Timetables and tariffs vary from month to month; for updated details contact the closest Tourist Information Office or your Travel Agent.

From Great Britain: The regular *Harwich-Esbjerg* line, with rail connection for Copenhagen, functions throughout the year. It's a 27 hour crossing; a ticket costs £90 (£55 for minors). The London-Copenhagen train (London-Dover-ferry-Ostende-Copenhagen) is faster and costs the same.

From Sweden: The fastest and cheapest ferry crosses from Helsingør to Hälsingborg in 20 minutes. Other lines connect Göteborg with Frederickshavn, Grenå with Varberg and Malmö with Copenhagen.

From Norway: The only Oslo-Copenhagen connection is the **DFDS**, which is rather expensive. As an alternative, you may ferry to Frederickshavn and proceed to Copenhagen by train. Other lines connect Bergen and other Norwegian ports with the Jutland (Frederickshavn, Hirtshals and Hantsholm).

From Germany: There are regular ferry lines between Copenhagen and Lübeck and Kiel.

From Finland: There is one regular line, the Helsinki-Copenhagen line.

By car

All ferry lines offer vehicle transportation facilities. Tariffs vary according to sizes and categories. The only two overland highway entrances to Denmark are from Germany, through the Jutland.

By rail
Copenhagen is the main railway junction connecting Western Europe to Scandinavia, with scores of daily international, regional and local arrivals, departures and transit flights. In many cases the trains cross the straits between Denmark and Sweden by ferry.

By bus
Bus lines are very efficient and comfortable, relatively inexpensive and often rely upon ferry crossings.

Tourist services

Practically all Danish towns have their local Tourist Information Centre (their total number is over 170!); there you'll find regional and local maps, leaflets and lots of information on cultural, artistic and sport events of the current week. There is always a desk for hotel, pension and B&B reservations. Also on sale are discounted tickets for the urban and national transportation lines and for local sites and museums, and a registration desk for organised tours and rental of cars and bicycles.

The major car rental agencies, like *Avis*, *Hertz* and *Budget* have several branches in Denmark; car returns can be made at any branch of the same agency.

Domestic transportation

Trains: Denmark boasts an excellent railway network, the *DSB* (Danish State Railways). In Denmark trains always run on time. *Eurail*, *Inter Rail*, *BIJ* and *Nordtourist* cards are valid practically everywhere. The most remote corners of the country can be reached by means of private rail or bus lines. In the high season, for the longer runs, it's advisable to make sure of a seat by prior reservation.

Buses: In Denmark bus lines are not very common, except for direct lines between Copenhagen and the other major centres. Inquire at the Tourist Information Centres or at Travel Agencies.

Ferries: There are several ferry lines connecting the main islands to the Jutland. Crossings are fast and frequent; prices are based upon railway tariffs. Ferrying your car from Korsar (Sjælland) to Nyborg (Fyn) will cost you 135DKR (for two persons and one car).

National flights: Even though Denmark is so small a country, there are quite a few regular national flights. You may inquire at the Tourist Information Centres or at the *SAS* branches.

Bicycles: The bicycle is the most popular national means of transportation. Bicycle rides are pleasant, leisurely and safe: along all main motorways exclusive bicycle paths run. Rental agencies are at your disposal practically everywhere — near the Tourist Information Centres, the Railway Stations, Youth Hostels etc. Tariffs vary between 25-40DKR daily — plus a cash deposit that will be refunded on the bike's return (s. **Bicycles**).

Car hire: The high price of fuel, and the relatively inexpensive rate of railway transports tend to discourage car rental. The weekly rental rate for an economy class car is about 930DKR to holders of an international driving licence who are over age 20.

Speed limits are 50 and 80 kmh (in urban and interurban zones respectively); 100 kmh on highways. Be very careful: cyclists have the right of way!

Hitchhiking: This is not an easy way of getting around. Look for *Use It* posters at the exits of some highways. Potential hitchhikers may sign their name on one of the cards left there by a driver seeking companions for a trip abroad.

Accommodation

Denmark offers a wide range of hotels and other tourist accommodation. Copenhagen prices are generally very steep throughout the year, and in high season they go even higher. In most cases you'll probably be able to find more convenient alternatives in the suburbs. In the smaller urban centres prices are less forbidding: from 300DKR in economy class to 1000 in luxury hotels. The Danish Ministry of Tourism sponsors a number of attractive package deals and organised tours, based either on the cheaper chain of camp sites and hostels, or on excellent hotels.

For stays of at least one week, it's strongly advised to ask, upon arrival, if any of these deals are available.

Danish Youth Hostels (similar to those of the other Scandinavian countries) are excellent. Thanks to the **YHA** (Youth Hostels Union), many establishments have been recently refurbished and are equipped with family rooms, with bath and kitchenette. Most hostels close their doors after sunset — only a few remain open until midnight.

Hostel beds can cost from 30 to 45DKR per night; in summer

you should reserve your bed ahead of time. The use of sleeping-bags is forbidden: only blankets are allowed in hostels.

At the Tourist Information Centres you may sometimes find offers to *sleep in* in a large hall equipped with beds and mattresses. This service might be free of charge, or cost up to 45 DKR, and the company is generally young, and fun.

Camp Sites — The rural regions of Denmark are rich of *Campingplads* (camp sites); most of them are open only from April to September.

Entrance tickets to the camp sites are on sale at the entrance desk for 16-30DKR, according to category: 3 stars for camp sites equipped with bar, restaurant and TV services; 2 stars for camp sites with kitchen, showers and minimarket; 1 star for places equipped only with running water and toilets. For a full list of camp sites, apply to the Tourist Information Centres or directly to *Campingradet*, Skjolsgade 10, Copenhagen, DK-2100, tel. 33 32 32 22.

The Danish Cuisine

Denmark's cattle farms and fishing boats have left their imprint upon the Danish cuisine. Local farming and international trade contribute a rich selection of vegetables and fruit. Restaurant prices are (surprised?) high, although you will also find in most cases a relatively convenient *Dan Menu* (Menu of the Day). Danish beer is famous throughout the world, but it will cost you twice as much as outside the country.

The traditional *morgenmad* (breakfast) can fill you up for the whole day: cold cuts, cheeses, fish and vegetables, a selection of breads, fruit juices, coffee or tea.

For lunch try a *smørbrød* — a meal of cold cuts and other goodies, to spread on thin slices of appetizing breads. You'll find a smørbrød at most restaurants as well as in many groceries and supermarkets.

There are also a number of international eateries, mainly Chinese, French and Italian.

Among the most popular traditional fares we recommend:

Bollery Karry: curried meatballs with rice.
Flæksesteg: roast pork with red cabbage and potatoes.
Hakkebøf: meatballs fried in onion sauce.
Medisterpølse: sausages and vegetables.
Sildykarry: curried herrings.

Ølstegmedstuvede Kartofler: fried snails with potatoes in white sauce.
Æbleflæsk: smoked pork steaks in apple and onion sauce.

The two most popular brands of beer are *Tuborg* and *Carlesborg*. The *Lys Pilsner* is a light ale, while the *Guldøl* is much stronger. Also popular is the *dram* — a local brand of alcoholic drink.

Currency

The Danish currency is the *Krone* (DKR.; 1$ = 6.25DKR), subdivided in 100 Øre. The smallest coin is 5 Øre.

All bank branches accept and change most foreign currencies; there are also a number of Change Agencies, mainly at railway stations, post offices and many Tourist Information Centres. Credit Cards, like *Visa*, *Eurocard*, *Mastercard*, *Diners* and *American Express* are welcome in most shops, restaurants and hotels.

Office and shopping hours

Banks are open Mon.-Fri. 9.30am-4pm; Thursday 9.30am-6pm.

Most shops are open Mon.-Thu. 9am-5.30pm, Fri. until 7pm and Sat. only until 2pm.

The Post Office is open Mon.-Fri., 10am-5pm; airport and railway station branches remain open until late evening, seven days a week.

Shopping

We'll say it again: Denmark is expensive — but with a little luck one may find some very good bargains. The Copenhagen clothing net of *Stroget* offers a wide range of apparel, from the simplest and cheapest articles to the most exclusive designer fashion. In many cases your VAT (as high as 20-22%!) will be refunded to you when you leave the country.

Telephones

Telephone booths are equipped with clear instructions (in Danish and English) for local, interurban and international use. The phones are coin operated, and accept the following coins: 25 and 50 Øre, 1, 5 and 10DKR. For international calls dial 009. For additional information, call 0033.

Suggested itinerary for Denmark

Copenhagen is a fast city, with a rhythm quite different from that of rural Denmark. If you have a week to spend in the country, use at least half of it in the capital; for the rest of Denmark, 2-3 days will be ample.

Copenhagen — København

Don't be surprised if you find yourself singing Danny Kaye's melody "Wonderful wonderful Copenhagen" when you get off the plane... The sight of its streets, majestic palaces, shopwindows, and the unique fusing of town and people will probably send you straight into the centre of town, without taking time to freshen up or plan your walk. But don't worry: Copenhagen's days are long: its lights never go out, and life goes on, even into the wee hours of the night.

History

In the early Middle Ages, Copenhagen was a small Viking hamlet. In 1167, Bishop Absalon, who was passing through, liked what he saw and established his bishopric there. On the site of present day Christianborg he built a small but strong walled fort, thus opening a new era for the village. As the people of the country converted to Christianity, more and more of them sought to build their homes under the bishop's protection. The old village soon became the town of Køpmannaehafn (= Trade Port). In 1443 the Royal Family took up residence in town, and Copenhagen became the capital of the kingdom. Soon it had its own university. Christian IV (1588-1648) transformed it into a modern European capital, with its new edifices, among them the Rosenborg Fort, the Round Tower, the Stock Exchange, the Wharf and the Arsenal.

When Gustav Adolph of Sweden invaded Denmark in 1659, besieging its capital, the people rallied around its beloved souvereign Frederick III, and in a heroic struggle, forced the superior Swedish army to retreat. Ten years later (in 1669), King Frederick built the new Amalienborg Royal Palace for his wife Sophia Amalia.

The Old City, made up, like most medieval towns, of primarily wooden structures, was repeatedly destroyed by fire, first in 1725 and again in 1795. The British Navy bombed the town twice, in 1801 and 1807, during the Napoleonic Wars. In the 19th century, Copenhagen grew rapidly, expanding well beyond its ancient walls. The shipyards, the distilleries, the harbour and many industries brought great prosperity to Copenhagen.

DENMARK

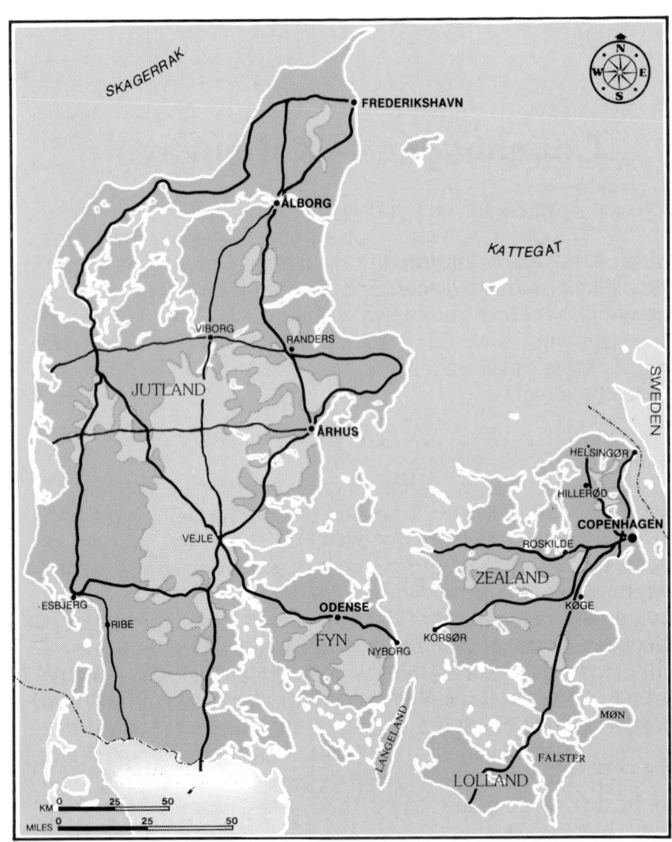

The urban structure

With a metropolitan population of close to 1.5 million people, the historic centre of town, enclosed by its two main canals, is today closed off to motor and even bicycle traffic. A quarter of a million people use their bikes for their daily ride to and from work — and a bike is a must even for most tourists. In the city centre, however, distances are so small that you'll be able to see most of the sights in a few unhurried short walks.

DENMARK

How to get there

Copenhagen is the main gate to Denmark, and to all Scandinavia.

By air: *SAS* and all major international airlines have regular flights to *Kastrup* Airport, conveniently situated only 10 kilometres south of town. You will find also many charter flights and even a few internal ones. The airport has been practically surrounded the metropolis, and it is very well equipped with services, like information desks, banks, car-hire agencies, restaurants, day hotels and shopping.

Bus lines 32 and 33 service the airport; tickets cost only 12DKR, much less than the Airport Bus Service (20DKR) and private taxis (80DKR).

By sea: The regular ferry line from Malmö (Sweden) makes two daily 90 minutes crossings. The crossing from Norway takes 16 hours. The ferry and hydrofoil pier from Oslo is near Nyhavn, in the centre of town. Regular ferries land at Dragør, 15 kilometers south of town.

By rail: Copenhagen is the main railway junction of Western Europe and Scandinavia, and many international trains from north and south stop at the Copenhagen Station. The lines of the national railways, the *DBS*, which connect the whole of the country to its capital, branch out from the same station. The Central Station is situated behind the Tivoli Gardens, facing Bernstorffsgade. At the station you'll find several bank branches, a post office, the *Kiosk P* for hotel reservations and a number of shops and restaurants.

By car: The E4 Highway runs through Copenhagen from north to south, and the E66 runs westward from the city. Copenhagen is an insular city (on the Sjælland), and motor traffic reaches it by ferry, from the east and the south-west (Korsør).

Tourist services

Copenhagen tourist services are faultless. There are Tourist Information Centres at all the city entries. The Main Office is downtown, near the Tivoli Gardens and the City Hall (Hans Christian Andersen Ave. 22; tel. 33 11 13 25). At the Central Train Station you'll find the very efficient *Kiosk P*, with its outstanding desk for hotel reservations.

The **Use It**, an Information Office and Culture Centre (whose English name is a pun on the Danish *huset*, which means "house") is at Rådhusstræde 13 (tel. 33 15 65 18). In 1969, this was the main base of the young homeless rebels, who were later ousted and housed in the Christiana "free state". In 1972, the building was restored and transformed into an imposing Community Centre, complete with art galleries, theatre, cinema hall, coffee bar and restaurant. At the Information Office, you'll find maps, leaflets and other material, and you may also register for outings and organised tours, reserve inexpensive rooms and even arrange to hitchhike a ride to your next destination. Two free English language weeklies keep you informed of the cultural and night life of Copenhagen: *Copenhagen This Week* and *Playtime*. They are distributed at all Tourist Information Centres and at the best hotels.

A three-day ticket for all urban transport entitles you to free tickets to most local museums. It costs only 120-250DKR — a very convenient bargain indeed.

Public transportation

A visit to downtown Copenhagen requires no transportation other than walking or bicycle riding. The choice residential areas are connected with the city centre by the urban transportation network. The trams (trolleycars = *S-tram-tog)* run 22 hours a day. When they stop, between 3.00 and 5.00, they are replaced by the night buses. Tickets remain valid for any number of trips within 60, 90 or 120 minutes (according to the various zones). The zone map is on sale at all stops. The metropolitan tram network is complemented by the bus lines. Prices vary from 8 to 32DKR. A ticket for 10 trips costs 70, 125 or 190DKR.

The **S-tog** network of regional electric trains connects the centre with the suburbs and beyond. If you plan to use public transportation frequently we recommend the *Rabatkort*, a packet of ten 60-minute tickets for a specific urban zone. Two tickets are good for 90 minutes and 3 for 2 hours. The *Grundbillet* is good for one hour in two adjoining zones. For further details, call tel. 36 45 45 45 or 33 14 17 01.

The *EuRail* cards are valid also for the *S-Tog* lines.

Taxis: When free, taxis show a green-lighted **FRI** sign. Taxis may be ordered at tel. 31 35 35 35. The minimum tariff is 12DKR, plus 7DKR per km. Tips are not customary.

Bicycle hire: The rate is 30-40DKR per day, plus a refundable deposit of 100DKR.

Hire agencies are found all around the city centre; the most popular one is near the Central Station, at Gothersgade 157, tel. 33 14 07 17.

Car hire: All major agencies have a branch in Copenhagen:
Avis: Kampsmannsgade 1, tel. 33 15 22 99.
Hertz: Ved Vesterport 3, tel. 33 12 77 00.
InterRent: Jernbanegade 6, tel. 33 11 62 00.

Accommodation

Copenhagen begins to be crowded with tourists in the beginning of spring. Reservations are needed and should be made prior to arrival or at one of the Tourist Information Offices at the earliest opportunity.

Luxury Hotels

D'Angleterre: One of the best in Europe. Kongens Nytorv 34, very central, tel. 33 12 00 95.
SAS Royal: A monumental structure, furnished in modern Danish style. Hammerichsgade, tel. 33 14 14 12.

Tourist Hotels

Vestersøhus: Vester Søgade 58, tel. 33 11 38 70. Discounts for prolonged family visits.
Alexandra: H.C. Andersen Ave., tel. 33 14 22 00. Central, but not too noisy.

Pensions

Those who plan to stay for a week or more will find it more convenient to stay at one of the following pensions:
Esplanadan: Bredgade 78, tel. 33 13 21 75. The weekly rate is 900DKR for singles, 1100DKR for doubles.
Bruuns: Store Kongesgade 40, tel. 33 13 53 80. Rooms w. kitchenette, weekly rates 850-1000DKR.
Store Triangel: tel. 33 38 59 25. 700-800DKR.

Economy Class Pensions

Basic accommodation, sometimes without breakfast; weekly prices run from 180 to 500DKR.
Jorgensens: Rømersgade 11, tel. 33 13 81 88; 200DKR, + 50 for each breakfast.
Ibsens: Vendersgade 25, tel. 33 13 19 13, 480DKR for two, including breakfast.

Bargains

An updated list of bargains is printed on the back of the *Use It* map.

Private Residence Beds
Reservations can be made at the *Kiosk P*, at the Central Station. Ideal way to get acquainted with local people. Prices are around 220DKR for two.

Youth Hostels
Copenhagen: Sjællandsbroen 55, tel. 33 52 29 08. Two and four beds to a room. Basic services, open all night. Bus 46 or line C to Valby and bus 37.
Bellahøj: Herbergvejen 8, tel. 33 28 97 15. Eight, twelve and sixteen bed dormitories. Locks up at 1.30am; buses 2, 8, 63 and 68 during the day, 902 at night.

Other Hostels
Sleep-In: Henrik Lings Alle 6, tel. 33 26 50 59. Summers only. A wide dormitory subdivided in four-bed units. A pleasant youth centre. Sleeping bags allowed. Blankets for rent (10DKR each). Noisy but colorful. Excellent railway connection with downtown (10 minutes). Price 60DKR, breakfast included.
International University: Olfert Fischersgade 40, tel. 33 15 61 75. Close to the centre. Very crowded in summer, but cheap: 30DKR. Locks up at 1am.

Camp Sites
The camp sites are all out of town, and are open only to members of the Camping Association. Membership on sale at the entrance (45DKR per year) to the grounds.

Strandmøllen: tel. 42 80 38 83; 14 km north of Copenhagen; 35DKR.
Bellahøj: tel. 31 10 11 50, 5 km from town (lines 2, 8), 35DKR.
Absalon: tel. 31 41 06 00, 9 km from town (S-tog or line B), 35DKR.

Food
Restaurants are somewhat cheaper than in the rest of Scandinavia; still, prices are rather high. Several restaurants have a *Dan Menu*, a fixed price menu at only 70DKR. It's generally advertised on the window or by the door. *Playtime* publishes a detailed list of restaurants, including economy-class eateries.

Luxury restaurants are to be found downtown and in the luxury hotels; their service and elegance are world-famous.

Luxury
L'Alsace: Ny Østergade 9, tel. 33 14 57 43. In an ancient courtyard; classic French cuisine, fish specialities.
Reine Pedaugue: at the Hotel d'Angleterre. Wine included in the price of the meal.

Tourist
Café Nikolaj: Danish cuisine served in an awe-inspiring church.
Ida Davidsen: Store Kongensgade 70, tel. 33 91 36 55. Traditional Danish cuisine and buffet.

Dan Menu
Axelborg Bodega: Axeltorv 1, tel. 33 11 06 68.
Frederiksberg Rådhuskælder: Smallegade 12-21, tel. 31 86 66 66.
Kirsten Piils Kilde: Dryehaven 18, tel. 31 63 15 82.

In view of the prices (and other considerations), we recommend, for lunch, the *smørbrød*. Try it at Vesterbrogade 6c, Kattesundet 18, or at the corner of Mastræde and Rådhusstræde.

Inexpensive Vegetarian Restaurant
Urten: Lars Bjørnsstræde 18, tel. 33 15 03 52.

There are many simple Italian eateries, several Chinese and international restaurants and 2 Jewish restaurants. You'll find them listed in *Playtime* and in the information leaflets distributed by the Tourist Information Centres.

The City, Step by Step

In Copenhagen, the adventurous tourist will be able to design personalized itineraries with the help of the complimentary brochures and kind staff of the Tourist Information Centres. At *Use It* you'll find a map of a summer bicycle tour and a selection of daily guided tours. On the following pages you'll find some itineraries that cover the principal downtown sites: the markets, the public parks, the churches and museums of Copenhagen.

The city centre is situated between the two great canals of Inderhavnen and Sortedams Sø. The traditional starting point is the wide Rådhuspladsen (City Hall Square). The **Rådhus** (City Hall) is an impressive 17th century palace. There is a splendid view of the city centre from its tower. A lift will take you to the top. Visiting hours: 11am-2pm.

Tha major attraction of City Hall is the **Astronomic Clock** by Jans Olsen, which, with its sophisticated machinery, gives the exact time anywhere on the Earth, the Moon, the solar system or anywhere else in the Universe. The clock claims to be precise within one millionth of a second. It should continue to give the exact time for no less than 5000 centuries.

Behind the City Hall are the famous Tivoli Gardens.

Indre By — Downtown
The **Strøget** is the main downtown pedestrian mall; its sidestreets are also part of the traffic free complex of the centre. On the Strøget you'll see some of the most inviting and luxurious galleries and shop windows in town.

Weather permitting, you can sit at the open air tables of several cafés, enjoying the view of the passing crowds, or you can stroll past the attractive shop windows, stopping from time to time to admire some monuments or to listen to the tunes of the everpresent street musicians.

As you reach **Torv** Square, turn right onto Råhusstræde, where you'll find, at No. 15, the **Use It.**

Further on you'll see at your left the Vor Fruekirke Cathedral (1829), which was built on the site of an old 11th century church, destroyed by the British in 1807. You are at the gates of the Old City, facing the buildings that used to belong to the University of Copenhagen.

Proceeding from the Fiolstræde to the Kristalgade you'll come across the elegant **Central Synagogue** (open to visitors per appointment, tel. 33 12 88 68).

The pleasant café and pub across the street is the evening meeting grounds of hundreds of students.

Turning back toward Kultorvet Square you'll see the **Museum of Musical Instruments** of Åbenrå (open summers 10am-4pm; closed on Monday). Further on you'll come to Trinity Church and the **Runde Tårn** (Round Tower), built by King Christian IV in the 17th century. Climb the tower's winding staircase to the upper platform of the Observatory (open 10am-8pm).

Turn back to the old Post Office building, and soon you'll reach the Amagetorv. At No. 10 you'll see the **Illum Bolighus** (a museum and sales centre of various knick-knacks in modern Danish style). The most ancient church of Copenhagen, **Helligånds** (14th century) is not far from here. Carry on to **Skt. Nikolai Kirkke**, another church with on the upper floor frequent interesting exhibitions, and on the ground floor an inviting café. Proceeding along the alleys of the pedestrian mall you'll come across many attractive shop windows: old and new books, objets-d'art, second hand clothing, antiquariat and other curios.

The Østergade ends at the majestic *Hotel d'Angleterre*, described earlier.

Coming to the ancient **Kongens Nytorv** Square you'll find yourself at the exit of the pedestrian mall. On your right you'll see the palaces of the National Theatre and the Charlottenborg. This is where we start our next four walks:

— To the Christianborg Fortress
— To Little Amsterdam and Christiana
— To the Amalienborg Palace and its surroundings
— To Rosenborg and the Botanic Gardens.

The Christianborg Fortress
Turn right on Torden just beyond the National Theatre, then again right on Heibersgade. Proceed along Holmens Kanal (which is not a canal, but an avenue), crossing the bridge. In the **Holman Church** (1619 — also known as the Seamen's Church) are buried two Danish national heroes of the Swedish wars: Niels Juel and Tordenskjold. Now you'll find yourself on the island of **Slotsholmen**, enclosed within four man-made canals. On your left you'll see the **Bursen** Palace, an impressive 17th century Renaissance building. As the name indicates, it used to house the Stock Exchange, but today it has become a complex of international trade offices. The four dragons decorating the corners of the palace were designed by King Christian IV in the 17th century.

Before entering the Christianborg Fortress, follow its wall to the right, cross the bridge and you'll come to the **Thorvaldsen Museum** (open 10am-4pm), named after the sculptor (1770-1844) whose remains are buried here; his tomb is surrounded by a collection of his major works, including the statues of several famous figures of his times. Proceed along the canal until you reach the **Nationalmuseet**, a museum of history and archeology dedicated to the Danish pre-Christian eras, from the Stone Age to the days of the Vikings. Its collection of pagan art is outstanding; the ethnographic department is much less interesting (open 10am-4pm; closed on Monday).

You are now at the main entrance of the **Christiansborg Slot** (Slot = Fortress), seat of the Danish *Folketing* (Parliament) and of the Supreme Court. That is where, in 1167, Bishop Absalon set the cornerstone of his castle, whose ruins can still be seen within the yard of the fortress. Today's fortress was constructed

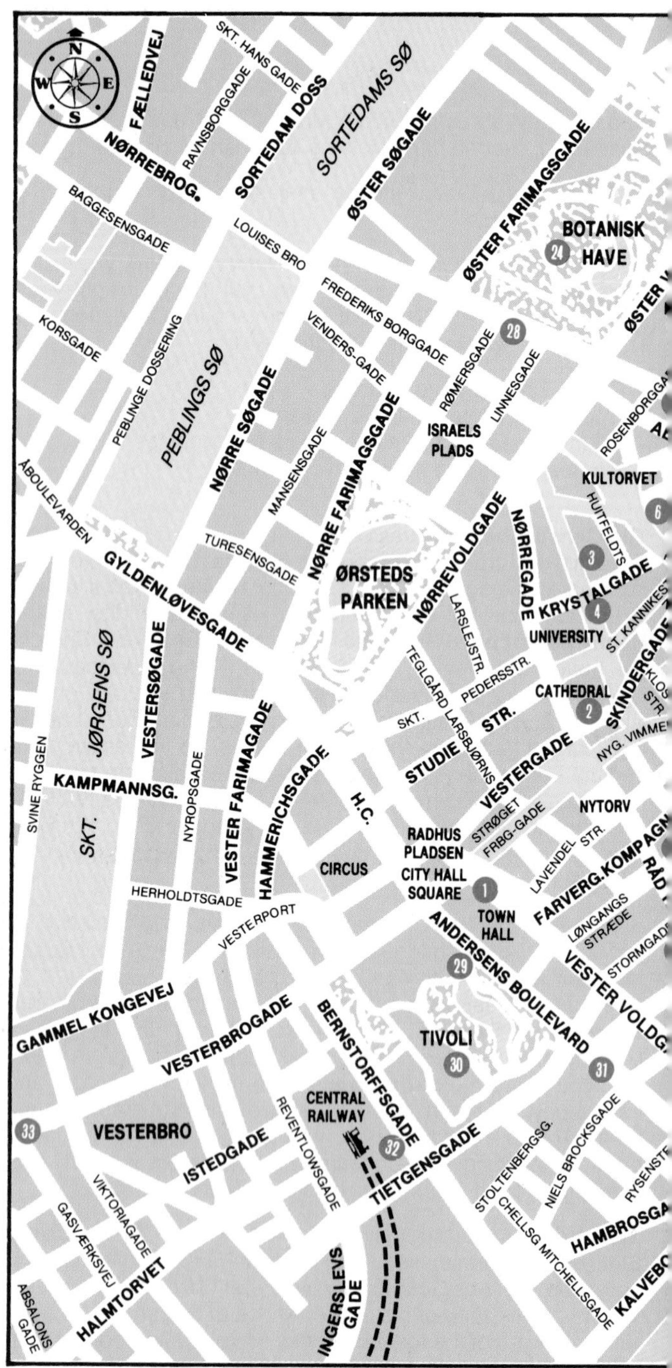
N
S
E
W
FÆLLEDVEJ
SKT. HANS GADE
RAVNSBORGGADE
SORTEDAM DOSS
SORTEDAMS SØ
ØSTER SØGADE
ØSTER FARIMAGSGADE
BOTANISK
HAVE
NØRREBROG.
BAGGESENSGADE
LOUISES BRO
FREDERIKS BORGGADE
VENDERS-GADE
KORSGADE
PEBLINGE DOSSERING
PEBLINGS SØ
NØRRE SØGADE
MANSENSGADE
NØRRE FARIMAGSGADE
RØMERSGADE
LINNESGADE
ISRAELS
PLADS
ROSENBORGG
KULTORVET
HUITFELDTS
ÅBOULEVARDEN
TURESENSGADE
ØRSTEDS
PARKEN
NØRREVOLDGADE
NØRREGADE
KRYSTALGADE
UNIVERSITY
ST. KANNIKEST
GYLDENLØVESGADE
JØRGENS SØ
VESTERSØGADE
LARSLEJSTR.
TEGLGÅRD
PEDERSSTR.
CATHEDRAL
SKINDERGADE
KLOS
STR.
SKT.
LARSBJØRNS
STR.
STUDIE
VESTERGADE
NYG.
VIMME
SVINE RYGGEN
KAMPMANNSG.
SKT.
NYROPSGADE
VESTER FARIMAGADE
HAMMERICHSGADE
H.C.
STRØGET
FRBG-GADE
NYTORV
RADHUS
PLADSEN
LAVENDEL STR.
CIRCUS
CITY HALL
SQUARE
FARVERG.
KOMPAGN
RÅD
HERHOLDTSGADE
VESTERPORT
TOWN
HALL
LØNGANGS
STRÆDE
STORMGADE
ANDERSENS BOULEVARD
VESTER VOLDG.
GAMMEL KONGEVEJ
VESTERBROGADE
BERNSTORFFSGADE
TIVOLI
CENTRAL
RAILWAY
VESTERBRO
REVENTLOWSGADE
ISTEDGADE
TIETGENSGADE
STOLTENBERGSG.
NIELS BROCKSGADE
RYSENSTE
CHELLSG MITCHELLSGADE
HAMBROSGA
VIKTORIAGADE
GASVÆRKSVEJ
HALMTORVET
ABSALONS
GADE
INGERSLEVS
GADE
KALVEBO
ØSTER V
24
28
6
3
4
2
1
29
30
31
32
33

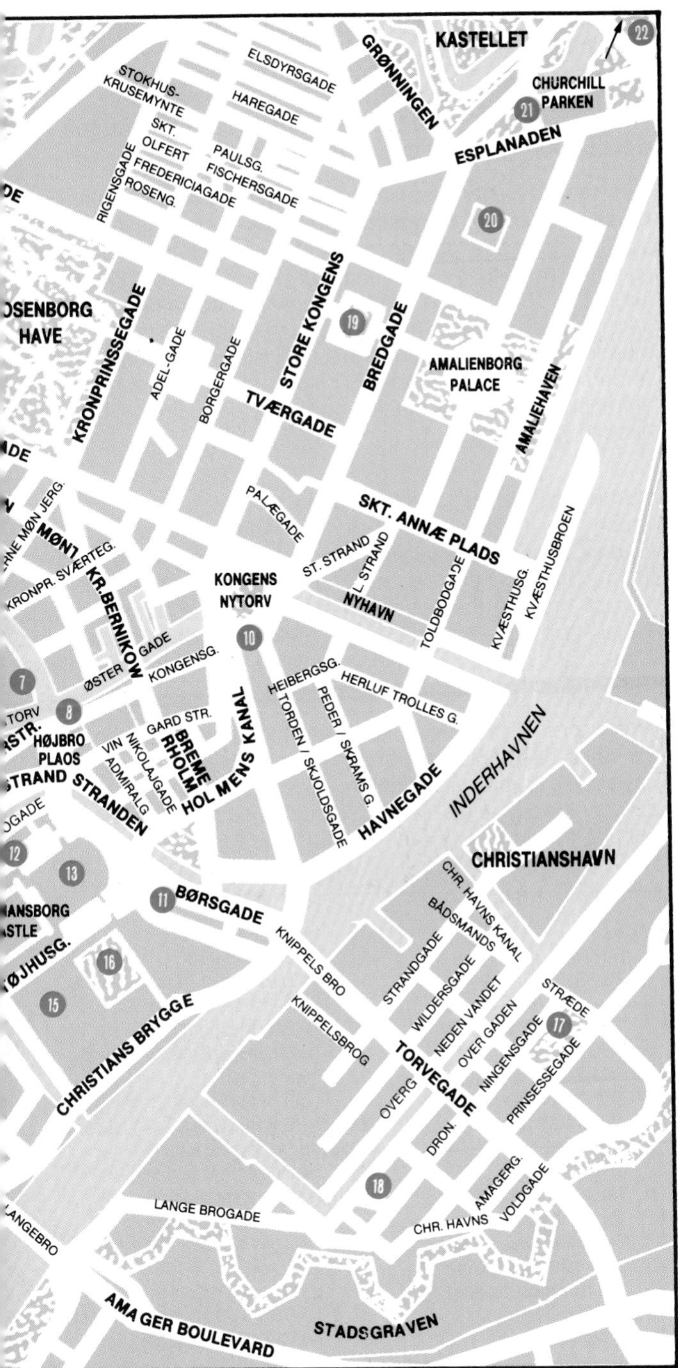

KASTELLET
CHURCHILL PARKEN
GRØNNINGEN
ELSDYRSGADE
STOKHUS-
KRUSEMYNTE
HAREGADE
SKT.
OLFERT
PAULSG.
FREDERICIAGADE
FISCHERSGADE
RIGENSGADE
ROSENG.
ESPLANADEN
OSENBORG HAVE
KRONPRINSSEGADE
ADEL-GADE
BORGERGADE
STORE KONGENS
BREDGADE
AMALIENBORG PALACE
AMALIEHAVEN
TVÆRGADE
PALÆGADE
SKT. ANNÆ PLADS
ST. STRAND
L. STRAND
NYHAVN
TOLDBODGADE
KVÆSTHUSG.
KVÆSTHUSBROEN
KONGENS NYTORV
MØNT
KRONPR. SVÆRTEG.
KR.BERNIKOW
ØSTER GADE
KONGENSG.
HEIBERGSG.
HERLUF TROLLES G.
TORDEN / SKJOLDSGADE
PEDER / SKRAMS G.
GARD STR.
BREME RHOLM
HOL MENS KANAL
HØJBRO PLAOS
VIN
NIKOLAJGADE
ADMIRALG
STRAND
STRANDEN
HAVNEGADE
INDERHAVNEN
CHRISTIANSHAVN
CHR. HAVNS KANAL
BØRSGADE
KNIPPELS BRO
KNIPPELSBROG
BÅDSMANDS
STRANDGADE
WILDERSGADE
NEDEN VANDET
OVER GADEN
NINGENSGADE
STRÆDE
PRINSESSEGADE
TORVEGADE
OVERG
DRON.
CHRISTIANS BRYGGE
LANGE BROGADE
LANGEBRO
AMAGERG.
VOLDGADE
CHR. HAVNS
AMAGER BOULEVARD
STADSGRAVEN

in 1916, and it rises on the ruins of five earlier fortresses, that were razed repeatedly by fire and war.

Near the fort are three museums (the **Theatre Museum**, the **Arms Museum** and **Det Kongelige Bibliotek** — the Royal Library). You'll find in the garden an excellent spot for a short rest (weather permitting) and wonderful view. The Royal Library, the largest in Denmark, contains excellent documentation of the Viking expeditions to Greenland and to America, several original manuscripts of the Danish philosopher Kirkegård, Hans Christian Andersen and Karen Bliksen. You may stop for a moment at the entrance of the Royal Stables and carry on to the next walk (or back to your rooms).

"Little Amsterdam" and Christiana

Cross the Inderhavnen Canal on the Knipples bridge to reach **Christianshavn** Island; proceed along Torvegade Ave. to the main canal, and, as if by magic, you'll see yourself transported into the heart of Amsterdam. The narrow canals, the old buildings, the waterside streets and side alleys, and the boathouses moored along the canals do not fit in with downtown Copenhagen!

This is one of the few spots where the original atmosphere of the days of the Builder King has been preserved as it must have been in the 17th century, when Christian IV decided to build a new residential section, modeled on one of Amsterdam's popular quarters.

Index

1. City Hall
2. The Cathedral
3. The Great Synagogue
4. The University
5. The Museum of Musical Instruments
6. The Round Tower
7. The Design Centre
8. St. Nicholas
9. Use It
10. The National Theatre
11. The Exchange
12. The Thorvaldsen Museum
13. Christiansborg Palace
14. The National Museum
15. The Royal Museum of Weapons
16. The National Library
17. Saviour's Church
18. The Museum of Danish Cinema
19. Marble Church
20. The Arts Museum
21. The Museum of the Partisan Struggle
22. The Mermaid
23. Rosenborg Palace
24. The Botanic Gardens
25. The Geological Museum
26. The Fine Arts Museum
27. The Hirschsprung Collection
28. The Workers' Museum
29. Tourist Information Centre
30. The Tivoli
31. The Gkyptotek Collection
32. The Railway Station and the Kiosk P.
33. The Municipal Museum

Like in Amsterdam, it is best here to walk and lose yourself in the labyrinth of alleys that meander between old buildings. The **Filmhuset** (the Museum of Cinema, not far from here, on Store Søndervolstræde) will give you an idea of the first steps of the Danish film industry.

At the corner of Skt. Annæ Gade and Dronningensgade stands **Vor Frelsers** (the Church of the Saviour), whose tower is clearly recognizable from afar by the winding staircase that runs up its outside walls; daring climbers will enjoy the outstanding view they'll get from the upper platform, one of the best observation points of the Bohemian Quarter of **Christiana**, your next stop. The official entry gate to Christiana is at the "Galopperiet" House, at the corner of Prinsessegade and Bådsmandsstræde.

Christiana was an abandoned military camp, until it was invaded and occupied by small groups of homeless youngsters. In September 1971, the neighbourhood was declared public property, free of the regular urban regulations and statutes. There were talks of "autonomy", a "free state" or an "open city", leading to a lengthy dispute on the measure of freedom allowed citizens by a state or local government. The liberal outlook of the Danish authorities has given the people of Christiana a wide margin of freedom, and the statistics of local crime quoted by more conservative factions cannot be taken at face value. After the neatness, law and order of downtown Copenhagen, visitors will be shocked at the chaotic climate of Christiana. However, it is worth seeing. Moreover, restaurants here are surprisingly cheap (since Christiana's residents don't pay taxes) and the food is excellent. Even the poorest sections are picturesque and interesting. Please don't bring with you your camera — or at least do not use it without prior permission. Do not even think of spending the night here in your tent or sleeping-bag.

The Amalienborg Palace

Walk back to the Knippels Bridge, crossing the wide square to the **Nyhavn** quarter, where Copenhagen's seafolk once lived. Today it has been restored, and boasts some of the city's most pleasant cafés, restaurants and antique shops. At the southern end of the cove is the hydrofoil pier for the Malmö fast ferries. At the northern end is the pier used by the Norway ferries. Turn right into Bredgade, and on your left you'll see the **Marmorkirkken** (Marble Church), with the monumental marble memorial of Frederick V.

To the right of the memorial is the entrance to the **Amalienborg** palace. In the middle of the small entrance square there is a statue of Frederick V, who built the palace as a present to his beloved consort. The complex consists of a series of

The impressive Bursen Palace

The Christiansborg Slot

"Little Amsterdam", in downtown Copenhagen

impressive structures, two of which serve today as residence of Queen Margrete and her family. When the Royal Family is in residence, the Palace Guard holds the daily ceremony of the Changing of the Guard at noon. The elegant Amaliehavn Gardens, which extend from the palace to the gulf, form a dream-like background to the whole complex.

Return to Bredgade and turn right toward the **Museum of Medical History** (guided tours on Tuesday, Thursday and Saturday at 2pm), a suitable ending to this pastoral tour. Near the museum stands a church, and behind the church is the **Kunstindustrimuseet** (Museum of Applied Arts), with interesting shows of art objects and handicrafts from all over the world (open 1-4pm, closed on Monday).

Now turn right into Esplanaden St., to Churchill Park and to the **Frihedsmuseet** (Museum of the Danish Resistance Fighters), where you'll find a convincing documentation of the Danish partisan struggle against the Nazis, including the daring smuggling of Denmark's Jews to Sweden, and the story of the heroic Ålborg youngsters who defied the Nazi invaders. The museum is open 10am-4pm; closed on Monday.

Proceeding along the park you'll see the **Kastellet**, yet another Christian IV architectural project, built as a defensive bulwark at the time of the Swedish wars. This small fortress stands upon an islet, surrounded by parkland, waterways, piers and the open sea — and **Den Lille Havfrue** (The Sea Maiden), an Andersen legend brought to life, has become a symbol of Copenhagen. It's strange that such a modest statue could become the object of so many legends and folk tales.

Turn back toward the city centre, crossing **Nyboder**, a small quarter of dark alleys and old houses dating also from the days of Christian IV, who built them as a shelter for sailors. Over the centuries the quarter changed into a slum, and was finally restored as an exclusive residential zone.

The Rosenborg Palace and the Botanic Gardens

There are at least four ways to reach the Botanic Gardens; we will start from the Kongens Nytorv and continue along the Gothersgade. You will come to the back entrance of the **Rosenborg Gardens**, and crossing the parkland, the statuary, the canal and the private gardens, you'll end up yourself at the Øster Voldgade main entrance.

The Rosenborg Palace is one of the major renaissance works of Christian IV, who probably fell in love with his new work of art, and decided to use it as his own royal residence. The visit to the royal palace is a splendid beginning of this tour (the palace is open to the public 10am-3pm).

Proceed across the street to the gate of the **Botanisk Have** (Botanic Gardens) quite a few hours. The variety of plants, the watercourse with its ducks, and especially the hothouse complex, make this garden one of the best in the world. Within the garden itself, the **Geologiskmuseet** (Geological Museum) displays some very interesting and rare meteorites, a selection of minerals and fossils, and even a small fragment of moon stone, donated to this museum by NASA.

Across the Solvgade stands the **Statenkunstmuseet** (National Art Museum), with some very good works by great artists from the Renaissance to today (open 10am-5pm, closed on Monday). In the same garden you'll find also **Den Hirschsprungske Samling**, a collection of Danish works of art that used to belong to Baron Heinrich Hirschsprung (open 1-5pm, closed on Monday and Tuesday). The final stop of this rather strenuous walk is the **Workers' Museum**, on Rømersgade downtown, documenting the history of the Danish Workers' Movement from 1850 to our days.

Copenhagen for the young

This is a walk dedicated to the young in body and in mind. It starts, of course, with a visit to the famous **Tivoli Gardens**.

The Tivoli Gardens are Scandinavia's Disneyland. Founded in 1847, they still remain one of the best loved entertainment grounds anywhere. Long before Walt Disney's "original" project, this was the model upon which scores of entertainment grounds were based. Even after one and a half centuries of technological sophistication, this forerunner of the modern fair-grounds still attracts more than 40,000 persons a day.

The Tivoli Gardens open every year on May Day with an impressive opening ceremony that has almost become Copenhagen's spring rite. The gardens are open fourteen hours a day, 10am-12pm, until the first week of September, when they close down for the winter. The programmes and performances are of great variety: ballet, theatre, mime, games and competitions, carousels, love tunnels and all the gimmicks found at the worlds best fairs. What makes Tivoli so special is the harmonious blend of culture, entertainment and relaxation in splendid grounds — and the dynamic pulse of scores of attractions, unruffled cafés and spirited nightclubs, as well as **Louis Toussaud's Wax Museum** and the **Holography Museum**.

Every year the Tivoli management introduces new ideas and programmes, like the **March of the Tivoli Children Guards Parade**.

During the season the whole complex remains open (and crowded) until midnight: tents, halls, restaurants, carousels and all. Many shows have their own ticket desks; prices are relatively modest, ranging from 20 to 40DKR; some attractions are free of charge.

Because Tivoli had become so overcrowded, a newer, smaller, not less attractive and much less crowded entertainment centre was opened — **Bakkan** — about 12 km out of town, conveniently connected to the city centre by the *S* trains and regular bus lines (timetables and other details at any Tourist Information Centre).

The information desks at Tivoli (tel. 33 15 10 01) and Bakkan (tel. 33 63 73 00) will provide details of daily programmes, transportation timetables, etc. Near Tivoli is the **Circus** (one of the best in the world, founded 1887). Programmes are available at the entrance gate and at the Tivoli information desk. The very young will enjoy the **Zoologisk Have** (Zoo and Zoologic Museum, open 9am-4pm). The Zoo is the largest and oldest (1859) in Scandinavia.

Rosenburg Palace

DENMARK

The Tivoli Gardens

The weekly *City Guide* lists all major entertainment and cultural programmes in town, complete with show times and ticket prices.

Additional Copenhagen Attractions
Copenhagen is such a busy town that we can bring you only a small sample of its activities, leaving the rest to your own spur-of-the-moment decisions.

Københavns Bymuseum — The City Museum: Vesterbrogade 59. A detailed documentation of Copenhagen's history, with emphasis on Christian IV's building projects and on Kirkegård's works.

The Carlesberg Distilleries: Ny Carlesberg; guided tours (including free beer tasting) Mon.-Fri. at exactly 9am, 11am and 2.30pm.

The Glyptotek: near Dantes Plads; a classic exhibition of ancient Egyptian, Etruscan, Greek, Roman, European and Danish art — sponsored by the nearby distillery.

Den Permanente: The Danish Centre of Arts and Crafts, facing the Central Station. With a very well-stocked sales department (furniture, home and kitchen knick-knacks and other decorative objects, mostly handmade in the provinces).

Asistens Kirkegård: the charming cemetery at Nørrebro Park, with the tombs of Hans Christian Andersen and Kirkegård. A map of the grounds, that mark the site of the VIP tombs, may be obtained at the gates.

Around Copenhagen

Not far from the capital are additional sites worthy of a visit.

Louisiana: A Museum of Modern Art surrounded by statues and parkland of breathtaking beauty along the seashore. Its location along the E4 highway, near the town of Humlebæk makes it easily accessible to travellers in private cars on their way to Helsingør (also connected to Copenhagen by *S Train*).

The harmony of form and content — between the grounds and the museum — is a major achievement of the planners of this outstanding museum, which offers concerts, plays, films and temporary shows, as well as an attractive cafeteria and restaurant.

The Tuborg Distilleries: If the Carlesberg distillery is closed and you are thirsty for a good beer, join a tour of the Tuborg Cellars (8.30am and 2.30pm, Mon.-Fri.). Board bus lines 1 or 21, alighting at Strandejen 54.

Dragør: a medieval fishermen's village not far from the airport where the ferries to Sweden dock. Bus connections: lines 30 and 33 from downtown.

Entertainment

Copenhagen is the merriest of Scandinavian cities, as you can tell from the pages of *Copenhagen This Week* and of *Playtime*. Cosmopolitan in character but modest in size, there is a little of everything, for all tastes and ages and pockets: nightclubs and theatres, pubs and cafés, shows and concerts.

Theatre and classic music: plays are generally presented in Danish; the *Mermaid* (N.Y. Vestergade 7) is the only English language theatre.

Den Kongelige Theater (Royal Theatre) offers mostly operas, ballet and some plays. The **Kongelige Theater Orchestra** is one of the best in Western Europe; its programmes are regularly listed in the weeklies.

Discounted tickets for tourists are often available at most travel agencies and Tourist Information Centres. We recommend the *Wilhelm Hansen* Agency, tel. 33 15 54 47.

Most cinemas are to be found around the Rådhuspladsen; films are generally screened without dubbing. Art films are shown at half price at several Cinemateques: the *Klaptræt* at Koltorvet 11, the *Delta Bio* at Kompagnistræde 19 and a third one at the *Use It* centre. Regular tickets cost 30-50DKR.

Light entertainment is rich and varied. The *Playtime* weekly magazine will provide you with a comprehensive list of bars, nightclubs, rock and jazz spots, discoteques, concert halls and gay bars.

Here is a modest selection:

Bars and cafés
Krasnapolsky: Vestergade 10. A very fashionable VIP bar and café.
Andy Bar: Gothersgade 33b.
Biograf & Café: Kultorvet 11-13. Trendy and bohemian.
Café Sommersko: Kronprinsensgade 6.
Universitetscafen: Fiolstræde 2. The last two are students' bars, not unlike the *Use It* bar.

Live music clubs
Montmartre: Nørregade 41. Light music of all trends; week-end disco.
Musikcafe'n: on the 3rd floor of the *Use It* Centre. Jazz, blues, rock et al.
De Tre Musketerer: Nikolaj Plads 25.

Discos
Woodstock: Vestergade 12.
Bar Bue: on the 1st floor of the *Use It*.

Shopping

The Strøget complex of pedestrian malls is a rich shopper's heaven. A prudent word of warning: in view of the prices, leave this type of entertainment for the end of your stay — and in the meanwhile, do some shopper's homework. The great department stores — like *Magasin* — are of the highest international standards, and often add also a taste of strictly Danish fares: furs, silverware, ceramics and glass, designer's furniture and art objects.

The local weeklies double up as a well informed shopper's guide.

Louisiana — Modern Art

Communication

Telephone: Public phones use 25 Øre and 1DKR coins. Come armed with a pocketful of change. The Copenhagen exchange is 01, and 02 in the suburbs.

Public phones accept also international and interurban calls. The Europe prefix is 0015 and the overseas prefix 0016. International calls are operator assisted. For information call 0030 or 0039. The Main Post Office, with its Poste Restante desk, is at Tietsensgade 37.

Telegrams may be phoned in at tel. 0028 — or sent out from any post office.

Important addresses and phone numbers

SAS: Hammerichsgade 1-5, tel. 31 54 17 01.
Lost and Found: tel. 31 74 88 22.

DENMARK

Medical assistance: tel. 33 93 63 00 or 31 22 00 41.
Emergencies: tel. 112; calls free from any public phone.
Sauna: Borgergade 12, Frankrigsgade 35 — and many others.

Embassies
United States: Dag Hammerskjölds Allé 24, tel. 31 42 31 44.
Britain: Kastelsvej 40, tel. 35 26 46 00.
Australia: Kristianiagade 21, tel. 35 26 22 44.

Sjælland

When you arrive in Copenhagen you have, in fact, reached the Sjælland. However, we hope to show you that the Sjælland has more to offer besides the capital.

The North

Coming from Sweden, you almost certainly will have passed through the northern Sjælland. If you're travelling on the E4, take any one of the exits, slow down, and look around; you won't regret it.

Near the Hørsholm exit, is the residence of Karen Bliksen, author of the best-selling novel and Oscar-winning film *Out of Africa*. Past the Helsingør exit, at **Humlebæk** is Louisiana (see previous chapter: Around Copenhagen).

Helsingør

The northern Sjælland end of the E4 is at Helsingør, 47 km north of Copenhagen. The **Kronberg Slot** (Slot = Fort) was, according to tradition, the home of Prince Hamlet of Shakespearian fame, and, as such, is visited by thousands of tourists. The fort (open 10am-4pm) overlooks the whole town, offering a splendid view of the Kattegat. The fortress walls date from the 16th century — the days of Frederick III; having nothing to do with Prince Hamlet, who lived, according to legend, many centuries earlier. In one of the inner courts stands the statue of Holgar Dansk, the famous national hero. Inside the fort, the halls house two interesting museums: Museum of Architecture and the Museum of the Navy. In the summer evenings, weather permitting, the garden is used as an open-air theatre, mostly presenting Shakespeare of course. For information, call tel. 49 21 13 33.

Walking along the Old City streets, be sure not to miss the Town Hall, the Church and the spectacular Railway Station, where you'll also find a Tourist Information Centre.

Not far from there, an excellent golf course and other seaside resorts are located.

Hotels are very expensive. Try the *Hamlet* (tel. 49 21 52 20) and the *Scandia* (tel. 49 21 09 02). Half an hour west of town, by car, or by bus no. 340, there is a pleasant Youth Hostel (tel. 49 21 16 40). The camp sites are conveniently close to town (tel. 49 21 58 56).

You can visit Sweden (Helsingborg) by ferry during the day, and return to Denmark in the late afternoon. If you're travelling by bike, you'll be able to take it with you.

Hillerød

Hillerød can be reached by rail or by road (a 20 minute ride on Road 6). It's a pleasant ride, passing through **Tisvildeleje**, a gorgeous seaside resort with the exclusive attraction of a nudist colony.

Hillerød is the native town of the Architect King. **Frederiksborg Slot**, where he was born, is a majestic royal residence, whose splendid rooms are full of art treasures. The complex is undoubtedly one of the most beautiful in ali Scandinavia: its Dutch Renaissance style, so dear to King Christian IV, is enriched and enhanced by later additions in different styles, presented in a series of restorations following repeated outbreaks of fire.

The castle is the seat of the **Nationalhistoriskmuseet** (National Museum of History), a Carlberg Beer enterprise. It houses historic documents, side by side with art treasures and epoch furniture. In the summer, frequent classical music concerts are held in its beautiful chapel. Seen from the northern slopes of the park, the castle is simply majestic. Its grounds and halls are open to visitors 10am-4pm. A map and other material is available at the local Tourist Information Centre (tel. 42 26 28 52).

Roskilde

About 40 kilometers west of Copenhagen is **Roskilde**, a pleasant medieval town nestling on the shore of the awe-inspiring fjord.

Roskilde is one of the oldest towns in the region. According to legend, it owes its name to some very interesting origins. Before the end of the first millennium, King Harold (with the blue teeth) built his kingdom's first church here (a wooden one, razed by fire many centuries ago); later the town became a major Viking port, with an impressive cathedral and a monumental seawall more than three kilometres long. In the 14th century Roskilde was one of the main centres of the region, with 14 churches and 5 monasteries.

After the Reformation, and with the rapid growth of Copenhagen, Roskilde was neglected and gradually abandoned.

EASTERN DENMARK

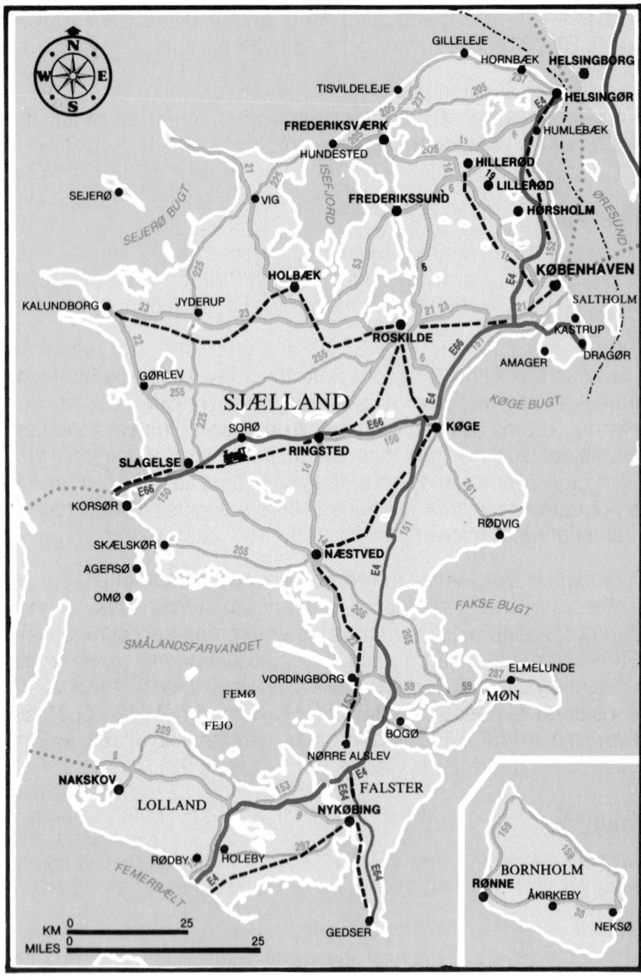

The natural resources of its port were exploited once again toward the middle of the last century, and a new railway line was built to connect it with the capital. Today Roskilde is a small but modern industrial centre, equipped with ultra-modern research facilities.

Tourism brought the **Roskilde Festival** to Roskilde, which has become the main annual jazz event in northern Europe. During the festival you'll have a hard time finding accommodation (unless by previous booking through the local Tourist Information Centre, tel. 42 35 27 00).

The visit begins at the **Cathedral**, a red brick structure erected in 1170 by Bishop Absalon. Later expansion and restoration works added several chapels and decorations in many styles to the original building. Thirty-seven Kings of Denmark, including Christian IV, are buried in this cathedral. The **Roskilde Museum**, dedicated to the history of the town, is of considerable interest. Also worth a visit is the **Vikingskibshallemuseet** (Museum of Viking Ships). It contains five ancient ships, raised from the muddy bottom of the fjord. Back in town, stop at the **Spilkammeret**, a small museum of card games, with a splendid collection of old playing cards.

Two daily guided tours start from the Tourist Information Centre in the afternoon and evening; price 5DKR. During the summer the town fills with tourists, and there is not a single bed available. Early bookings are an absolute must, either at the *SR Hotel* (tel. 42 35 66 88) or at the *Prindsen* (tel. 42 35 80 10) — or at the considerably cheaper hostel of *Hørgården* (tel. 42 35 21 84, lines 601 and 604) or at the camp site (tel. 42 75 79 96, line 602).

Younger people, coming to Roskilde at the beginning of July for the Festival often spend the late night hours recuperating for the next day on the grounds of the enormous parking space of the Festival.

Western Sjælland

Western Sjælland is a resort area, rich in white beaches, forest paths and picturesque farmland. The adventurous may perhaps find it rather boring, but nature lovers will discover a perfect pastoral background.

Road 21 reaches the ancient town of **Holbæk**, a rare jewel hidden on the coast of the fjord and surrounded by hilly farmland, forests and lakes. In the vicinity are several interesting villages.

Tveje Meriøsa, one of them, is famous for its church — the oldest in Denmark. In this region are scores of attractions, old ruins and museums. Holbæk's pier is the gate to the island of Orø and its golden sands is only a 30 minute ferry crossing away.

Road 23 reaches **Kalundborg**, a seaside resort famous for its white sands and its ancient tombs and millennary runic stones. The church, with its singular five towers, dates from the 12th century. At Kalundborg you may board the ferry that goes to the summer resort island of Samsø and to the Jutland.

Road 22 turns southward, crossing the pleasant town of **Gørlev**, to **Slagelse**, one of the major towns in western Sjælland. Slagelse is a very old town indeed: in fact, it was known as the site of an important mint before the end of the 10th century. About 6 km west of the town stands the restored Viking castle of Trellborg (built 980) and the Maltese monastery (1164). Regrettably, this old city has been repeatedly destroyed by fire, and therefore its ancient history remains a mystery.

From Slagelsee the E66 proceeds westward to **Korsør**, another summer resort that seems to have been able to preserve its medieval aura, thanks to its picturesque market malls and its miniature gardens. Its shimmering white sands are among the most attractive and the cleanest in the region. Another exceptional seaside resort is not far from here, 12 km southeast of Korsør, at **Skælskør**: white sands, old farms and several medieval churches.

Now follow one of the narrow roads that lead north-eastward, through several timeless hamlets, to **Sorø**, a medieval hunting retreat that in 1683 was granted a town's statute. In its old church the remains of Bishop Absalon, founder of the Danish church are buried as well as those of the great Danish playwright Ludwig Holberg. The church often hosts good summer organ recitals.

Turn back on E66 toward Copenhagen to reach the town of **Ringsted**, another living museum of medieval history: churches, ramparts and old palaces galore; within the church of Skt. Bendt several kings and queens of Denmark are buried.

Southern Sjælland

Køge

Leaving Copenhagen southward on E4, you'll come to **Køge**, infamous for its contribution of industrial waste to the Baltic waters in recent years. But the incident is already a thing of the past, and all damages have been fully repaired. Køge is the terminus of the S-Train, and has become a popular week-end resort, frequented in summertime by tens of thousands of Copenhagenians, who flock to its pubs and open-air cafés; the streets are crowed with scores of street musicians and folk singers.

Køge was branded in the past as the hometown of executioners, witches and exorcists. This dark fame has surrounded Køge with a mantle of horror stories and macabrous humour. This aspect of local 17th century life is illustrated for the tourist at the Tourist Information Centre (Vestergade 1, tel. 53 65 58 00) and at the Town Museum (Nøregade 4).

The Old City streets are paved in stone; its wooden houses are grouped around the central **Torvet Square**, with **S. Nicholas** on one side and the **City Gallery** of contemporary art on the other.

There are several attractive summer camp sites, all along the gulf beaches: *Vallø* (tel. 53 65 28 51) is one of the best. There is also a youth hostel (tel. 53 65 14 74).

Another pleasant Southern Sjælland centre is **Næstved**, an ideal starting point for day-long nature walks and canoe trips. At the local Tourist Information Centre (tel. 53 72 11 22) and at the youth hostel (tel. 53 72 20 91) you'll find maps and other useful material. Canoeing is a very popular sport in Denmark; further information on these activities can be obtained at the local canoe rental agencies (tel. 53 64 61 44).

The Southern Islands

There are four main islands south of the Sjælland. The E4 and the railway cross two of them on the way from Copenhagen to Germany. The largest is Lolland, the second is Falster, the third, and much smaller, is Møn and the last is a long strip of farmland, rightly called Langeland.

The southbound trains stop at Nykøbing (Falster) and turn westward to Nakskov (Lolland). The islands may also be reached by ferry from Germany.

Møn

Road 59 and bus 64 from **Vordingborg** reach the charming island of Møn. with its shining white calcareous cliffs. **Stege**, the first town you cross, is an excellent starting point for your tour of the island. Just wandering about in any direction will bring

you in sight of some of its many Neolithic tombs (just follow the arrows found along the main roads). Bus 51 — or your own car — will take you to **Elmelunde**, to the eastern beaches and the cliff of **Møns Klint**. At its feet you'll find the parking grounds of the camp site, though a stopover at Stege will probably be more comfortable. Road 287 will take you back to the E4.

Falster

Although the island of Falster is larger than Møn, the only site worth a short visit is the town of **Nykøbing**, and this only because of its medieval quarter. It has, of course, a Tourist Information Centre, a camp site and a youth hostel. Its western beaches, near the village of Marielyst, are often overcrowded.

Proceeding through Falster on the E4 you will cross over to Lolland.

Lolland

Lolland is the largest of the 4 islands in this southern group. Its two main centres are well worth a visit, **Maribo** and **Nakskov**, and travelling through the island you might also stop at some of the old villages you cross (see "Denmark by bike"). A ferry will then take you from Nakskov to the next island, Langeland.

Helsingør's Kronborg Slot

Bornholm

"The Pearl of the Baltic Islands", "the Isle of Nightingales", "Cherry Island" are three of the many names given to this captivating island. In spite of its proximity to Sweden, Bornholm belongs to Denmark, and it is a true treasure trove for historians, for nature lovers — and for gold diggers too.

In fact, in 1986 a small archaeological dig uncovered, in an area of less than 100 square metres, no less than 100 perfectly preserved 8th century gold bars, duly stamped and embossed with human figures. This is but the most recent of several findings: todate more than 2,000 gold bars have been recovered here — while in all the rest of Scandinavia only 150 bars have ever been found. Truly a real Treasure Island!

Little is known of the origins of such a monumental treasure. One of the less wild scenarios takes us back to 1255, when during a bitter war between church and king, the Archbishop of Lund built fortress of **Hammershus** here in Bornholm. The ruins of this fort and of its church seem to indicate a very rich, princely stronghold, one of the largest and most impressive in Northern Europe.

Bornholm is full of historic sites; some of them are but ruins, while others are still inhabited by the islanders, who often lead their daily life in farms and houses that were built several centuries ago.

Due to its picturesque views, Bornholm has become a Mecca of Danish artists in the last century. At first painters and sculptors, and then scores of actors and musicians, come to seek their inspiration in the magic backdrop of this island.

Situated as it is at the gates of the Baltic, Bornholm is also a natural stopover for many species of migrating birds, who, crossing over it on their annual voyages, have developed a habit of stopping for a while to visit its forests and prairies. The **Almindingen**, for instance, is the third largest forest in Denmark, and it covers a large section of the island, its valleys and mountains.

Bornholm's Medieval Alleys

How to get there

Bornholm is regularly connected with the mainland both by air and by sea. The main airport is at Rønne, the capital, and it is serviced by regular flights from Copenhagen and from Ystad (Sweden).

A 7 hour daily ferry crosses over from Copenhagen; other ferries reach Bornholm from Malmö in Sweden and from Germany. During the summer the ferry service is considerably more frequent.

What to see

All tours of Bornholm start from Rønne — an ancient market town, founded seven centuries ago, with about 15,000 inhabitants. It is a comfortable centre, pleasant and with good tourist services. The Tourist Information Centre (tel. 56 95 08 10) is particularly helpful for accommodation and bicycle hires.

The impressive church that meets the eye of incoming tourists upon their arrival by ferry was built in 1918, but the back streets are at least two centuries older. A short walk through the stone-paved alleys of the small town will take you to the **Forsvarsmuseum** (Museum of Defence), which is situated within the fortress and documents the island's wars against Sweden.

One of the most picturesque local events are the traditional chariot races, held during the summer. Rønne is mainly a tourist centre, and the whole island life revolves around tourism: guided tours, sport activities, sailing, fishing etc. Families and small groups of tourists often cycle over the entire island, in a matter of 3 or 4 days (s. "Denmark by bike"). By car, two days at most will suffice.

Rønne has several (expensive) hotels, a youth hostel (Søndre Alle 22, tel. 56 95 13 40) and a camp site (Strandvejen 4, tel. 56 95 23 20).

The visit to Bornholm includes nature walks, visits to some of the older villages and perhaps a longer stay at one of its many beaches. The following itinerary runs mostly along the seashore, but there are also many interesting side roads leading to the inland.

Leave Rønne northward to **Hasle**, an old market town with beautiful wooden houses. The church (1600) dominates both the town and the fishermen's harbour. Further north you'll come to Helligpeder and then to **Jons Kepel**, where, according to a legend, that holy man, Jon, (who, of course, lived in a cave), used to preach to the townfolk from the height of a towering peak.

North of Jons Kepel you'll come to **Hammershus**, a very old (13th century) stone fortress. Here, in 1648, Danish national hero Jans Kopend slew the Swedish governor of the island. On the northern tip of the island there is a lighthouse, whose tower is an outstanding observatory, commanding the sea strait and the neighbouring twin towns of **Sandvig** and **Allinge** with their wooden farms and narrow alleys. The hotels and the small harbour, with its scores of fishing vessels and leisure yachts, add local colour to the view. In summer the white **Sandkås** beach, sheltered as it is by its boulders, attracts large crowds of tourists; indeed, the north-eastern coast of Bornholm is rightly called the "Danish Riviera".

If the seaside is beginning to bore you, you'll find four round churches of the 12th century in the neighbourhood. These round churches, built so close to the **Olsker** fortress, served a vital defense purpose for quite a few centuries. Next you may proceed to **Rø**, with its spectacular natural rockeries.

If you like round churches, in **Østerlars**, you'll find one of the most impressive of that type, with an inner diametre of 18 metres.

Turning back to the "Danish Riviera", the small village of **Gudhjem** is probably the most attractive of its resorts. Its houses, perched high on the towering cliffs of the gulf, seem to wave over the blue waters, frequented by scores of local fishing boats. The Riviera extends along the white sands of the beaches and their inviting rocky coves to **Svaneke** and **Neksø**, two ancient villages recently declared national monuments, and as such are preserved for future generations, with the special attractions of their past. They are two fishermen villages, who have taken the best care of their abodes and, not less, of their boats for centuries.

The visit to Bornholm won't be complete without the sights of the southern beaches, the **Almindingen** Park and the ancient religious centre of **Åkirkeby** (12th century). Åkirkeby's old church is the largest on the island and its walls are covered with several interesting frescoes. The best way to reenter Rønne is through the majestic forest of the hilly region.

Accommodation

Bornholm offers a wide choice of accommodation: more than 40 hotels, several B&Bs, more than 20 hostels and 17 camp sites. Quite a few hotels have at least some large family rooms; details are available at the Tourist Information Centre.

Some hotels offer seasonal bargains:
Rønne: *Ryttergården*, Strandvejen 79, tel. 56 95 19 13.
Sandvig: *Holiday*, Strandvejen 82, tel. 56 98 02 16.
Gudhjem: *Pension Koch*, Melstedvej 15, tel. 54 98 50 72.
Svaneke: *Munken*, Storegade 12, tel. 56 99 61 12.
Åkirkeby: *Rosengården*, Bodernevej 28, tel. 56 97 49 50.

Six of the hostels are affiliated to the Youth Hostel Association; they charge about 55DKR and are only open in the spring and summer. They are at **Rønne** (tel. 56951340), **Allinge** (tel. 56964175), **Gudhjem** (tel. 56985035), **Svaneke** (tel. 56996242) and **Neksø** (tel. 54988119).

The Island of Fyn (Funen)

This charming island, so often selected by Hans Christian Andersen (himself a son of Odense), as site of his tales, is the perfect resting stop before — or after — the visit to the capital. The Danes have nicknamed it "The Garden Island" or "Denmark's Park", and even a short stopover will suffice to justify its fame.

The E66 crosses the island from east to west, passing very close to the island capital and its center, Odense. However, the island beaches are also full of attractions, and you shouldn't miss the pleasant coastal roads, that lead to the island's eight major sea resorts.

The Korsør (Sjælland) ferry docks at **Nyborg** is situated, on the east coast of Fyn. The local Tourist Information Centre is at Torvet 9 (tel. 65 31 02 80) and it will provide you with ample information on the island and its attractions.

After the visit to the restored 12th century fort, follow road 165 northward to **Kerterminde**, a tourist resort restored as a Viking stronghold. The history of the town is attractively presented at the local **City Museum** (open daily, 10am-4pm). Here the artist **Johannes Larsen** lived, and his home has been transformed to a museum in memory of his life and work (open 10am-4pm, closed on Monday). At the Tourist Information Centre (Strandgate 5A, tel. 65 32 11 21) and at the youth hostel there are bicycle hire agencies; a bike is the perfect means for an outing to the peninsula of **Hindsholm**. The *Tornøes* hotel in Kerterminde (tel. 65 32 16 05) is not too expensive, and neither is the *Kro* restaurant (and rooms, tel. 65 97 40 30) by the roadside.

The south-western road crosses **Munkebo** and its shipyards and proceeds to Odense, the capital.

Odense

In 1988 Odense celebrated its millennium: its name is mentioned in a message sent on 16 March of the year 988 by German Emperor Otto II. It is a relatively large town of 170,000 inhabitants), the third largest in Denmark.

WESTERN DENMARK

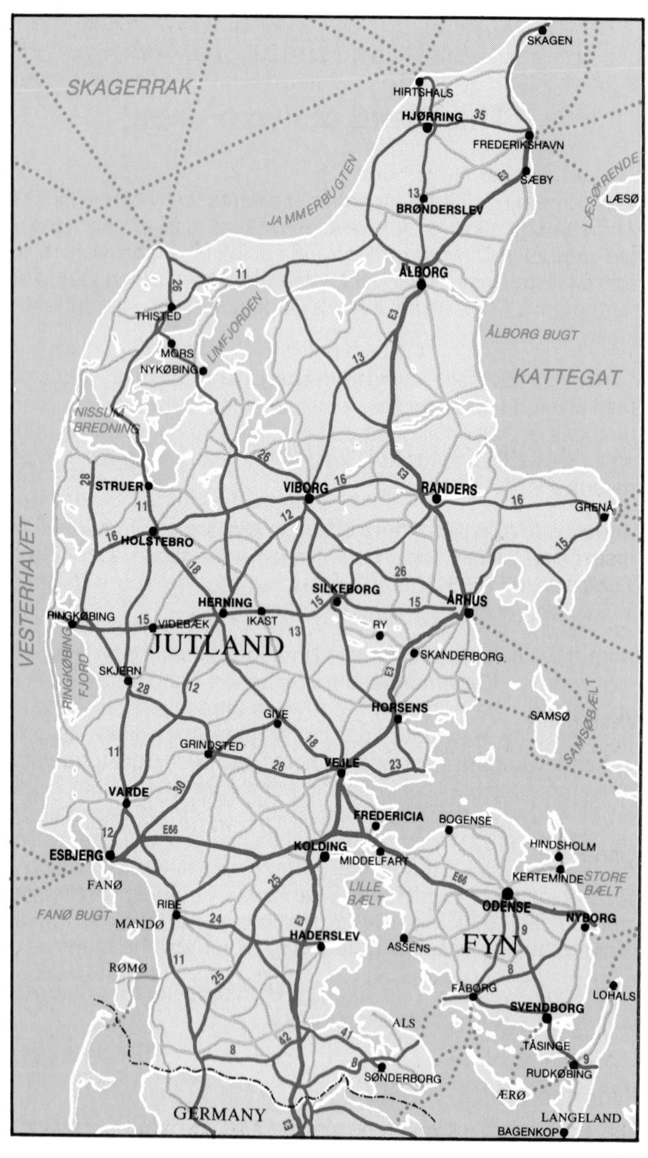

The Tourist Information Centre (tel. 66 12 75 20) is in the **Rådhuset** (City Hall) building. During the summer (June-August) it's open daily from 9am-7pm; in other seasons, Mon.-Fri. from 9am-5pm and Saturday from 9am-12am. It will assist you with accommodation, cheap transportation and theatre tickets, maps and other information.

Food and Accommodation

Odense is quite well provided with eateries of all types. We'll mention two of the best (not inexpensive, of course): *Franck A* (Jernbanegade 4, tel. 66 12 27 57) and *Den Gamle Kro* (Overgade 23, tel. 66 12 14 33). Much cheaper are the pizzerias and the junk-food spots.

There is also a wide choice of hotels, from luxury establishment to the really cheap youth hostel (Kragsbjerggården 121, tel. 66 13 04 25).

The most exclusive hotel is the *H.C. Handersen* (Claus Bergs Gade 7, tel. 66 14 78 00). Slightly cheaper is the *Odense* (Ø. Stationsvej 24, tel. 66 11 77 45). Much cheaper but situated 11 km out of town, is the *Mørkenborg Kro* (tel. 66 83 10 51). The closest camp sites are the *DCU* (bus 1, tel. 66 11 47 02) and the *Blommenslyst* (tel. 66 96 76 41).

The tiny *Kahema* hotel (Dronningensgade 5, tel. 66 12 28 21) charges only 280DKR for a double room, including breakfast.

What to see

Odense is known to all Danes as Hans Christian Andersen's town. His home has been transformed into a museum that documents his life and times in a most refreshing and sincere style. Another great son of Odense, Carl Nielsen has been also honoured with a personal museum.

Odense is a prosperous industrial centre; it developed further after the opening (in the last century) of the canal joining it to the deep water fjord that cuts into the island from the north. The industrial area has been kept strictly separated from the historic centre, which remains to this day an attractive tourist resort. Its many museums especially the Andersen museum with its appeal for younger guests, who simply love the Tivoli gardens and Zoo, attract tens of thousands of tourists to the town.

After visiting the **Andersen** and the **Nielsen Museums**, you'll enjoy walking through the old streets and squares of the centre, that have been perfectly preserved for several centuries. The **St. Knud Cathedral** was built in the 12th century on the foundations of the former Church of King Knud II, the king that was murdered in 1086 during a peasants' uprising and later canonized by Rome. King Knud and his brother Benedikt, another local Saint, are buried in the Cathedral. **Møntegårdenie**, the old City Hall building, has been fully restored and its majestic front graces the main street of the town, Vestergade.

At the crossing of Vestergade with Overgade you'll see some very interesting old buildings. Mønterstæde is a street of 16th century houses, many of which have been transformed into small museums, such as the **Stiftmuseet** (pre-historic artifacts and local art). The Railway Museum and the Fire Brigade Museum are in the same neighbourhood.

There are three main forms of entertainment: lovers of classic theatre, ballet and concerts will often find interesting programmes; lighter entertainment is well represented in the Brandt Passage cultural centre, with the *Café Biografen* on the first floor and the *Undergraduate Ice Cream* on the second. Pubs, bars and cafés are scattered throughout the centre, among them are Duffy's Bills' Pub and *Café Kløverstik*.

Southern Fyn

Road 9 turns south to **Svendborg**, a small seaport with an attractive marina. From its pier the local ferry service to Ærø, sails and the road itself crosses to Langeland by bridge. The **Valdemar** Slot and museum on the Island of **Tåsinge**, is well worth a visit.

Road 9 runs through **Langeland** straight to the capital, **Rudkøbing**. The town is a classic tourist resort, from which one may select a choice of beaches — northward or southward, on the east or the west coast of this elongated island.

Ærø is further out; its main centre, **Ærøskøbing**, is connected to Rudkøbing (Langeland) and to Svendborg (Fyn) by a frequent ferry service (75 minutes, five daily crossings).

The Ærøskøbing Tourist Information Centre (in the square, tel. 62 52 13 00) offers maps, accommodation information and guided tours to the ancient tombs of the island. The youth hostel (tel. 62 52 19 44) and the camp sites (tel. 62 52 18 54) are only open in summer.

Follow Road 44 to **Fåborg** , a small provincial town perfect as a starting point for bicycle and walking tours of the island. The **Egeskov Slot** (1554), one of the best preserved and most beautiful Danish Renaissance forts, stands proudly on a hill, north-west of the town. Its halls house a collection of firearms.

Don't miss Fåborg's **Fyn Museum of Painting**, with a rich collection of local artists. Near the museum stands the most ancient Danish youth hostel (tel. 62 61 12 03, summers only) and a camp site (tel. 62 61 90 04), tents and bungalows.

The next town is **Assens**. From here, climb into the hills along Road 329 to the crossing with 168, and turn westward, into a spectacular region of medieval farms.

Assens itself has little to offer, except for the legendary lore of a youngster, who allegedly led Copenhagen's defence that saved the city from the British naval bombardment of 1801. According to some, Admiral Nelson congratulated the child on his inventive strategy. His birthplace has become a national sanctuary.

The last town on the way to the Jutland is **Middelfart**. Its proud suspension bridge connects the island to the Jutland mainland.

The Jutland

The Jutland peninsula (Jylland to the Danes) has a very long settlement history. It is in a sense a natural bridge between Europe and Scandinavia, a fact that caused many Danish kings a lot of substantial headaches. The Jutland is a practically uninterrupted agricultural plain. Most tourists avoid it, driving through as fast as possible on their way to Fyn or to Frederikshavn in the north, hurrying to Sweden or to Norway.

A visit to the Jutland is an intermittent visit through city and village, through intensely cultivated farmland. It is a cyclist's paradise (s. Denmark by bike). Our itinerary starts at Fredericia, on the east coast, proceeding northward to Skagen, then westward and back south along the western coast. Arriving by road from Germany or by ferry to Esbjerg will change only the starting point of the trip.

The history of the Jutland is well reflected in all its towns and hamlets. Here in the peninsula the first Christian conquest of Scandinavia took place over 1,000 years ago, in an atmosphere of constant bloodshed and even mass murder.

Road 66 and the Copenhagen railway reach the Jutland from Fyn through the Middelfart bridge. The E3 cuts northward through the whole length of the Jutland, while roads 13 and 18 cross it from east to west. The Jutland railway net reaches practically all the centres.

Fredericia

Fredericia is the natural gateway to the peninsula. King Frederick built a great castle for his alternative capital here in 1650. The inhabitants of three old villages were ousted from their homes, and the villages themselves were razed to the ground to make place for the king's new city. Around his town the king built 15 metre walls, that stand to this day and provide the itinerary of a spectacular walk above the roofs of the town's houses. "Fredericia Day" is celebrated on July 6, commemorating the heroic resistence of the town against the Prussian armies in July 1849. The Landsoldatan monument was erected to honour the memory of the fallen soldiers and civilian fighters of that battle. The remains of those revered heroes are buried in the

Jutland's Windmills

Trinitatis church, and their feats are documented with great pride at the City Museum and in several pamphlets, available at the local Tourist Information Centre (Brotorvet 1, tel. 75 92 13 77).

Follow the E66 to **Kolding**. This is a modern town, built around the ruins of a 13th century royal residence, surrounded by a moat. The building was destroyed by the Spaniards in 1808, and only a century later it was restored in full. There is a rather interesting Botanic Garden beside the villa.

Vejle

After Kolding the E3 climbs northward to Vejle, a medieval town nestling at the end of a deep fjord, whose mouth opens toward the Kattegat Straits. The **Church of St. Nicolai**, on the main square, has two major attractions. The first is a transparent sarcophagus which contains the corpse of a woman, whose shape is surprisingly well preserved in... mud. For many years this was believed to be the remains of the Viking Queen Gonhilde (a.k.a. "Gonni"), but later research dated it back much further: the lady appears to have been embalmed a full millennium before Gonni's times, in 490 B.C. The second attraction, no less morbid than the first, is provided by 23 human skulls, buried in the northern wall of the church; according to a local legend they belonged to the bodies of 23 thieves, known to have been publicly executed in 1630. The Tourist Information Centre (also on the square, tel. 75 82 19 55) and the youth hostel (tel. 75 82 51 88) will help you to find accommodation and to arrange visits to Jelling and to Legoland.

The *Grejsdalens* (tel. 75 85 30 04) is a pleasant hotel, with a beautiful view.

After Vejle you may proceed on the E3 to **Århus**, or turn to the lake district through **Jelling** or **Billund**, with its famous **Legoland** park.

Since distances are not too great, one may combine both alternatives in a single day; however, you should plan to arrive to Legoland before noon.

Both the railway and Road 18 reach Jelling, an ancient burial ground and the pagan sanctuary of King Gorm (s. "History") and his queen, who lived toward the end of the first millennium. King Gorm's burial site is unknown; some claim that his remains are buried here; others maintain that they were transported by his son, King Harald the Blueteeth, to Roskilde, for a somewhat delayed Christian burial. At the railway station there are trains for Herning, and a local old and rather slow railway line for Jelling.

Legoland

Near the small provincial town of Billund, about 20 km west of Vejle on Road 28, you'll find the largest Legoland park in the world, loved dearly by all Danish children. It's a dreamland park, built of no less than 30 million Lego bricks. It attracts thousands of children, their parents and other adults daily. The park includes villages and towns, forests and roads, trains and cows, and even real restaurants, gardens, and roundabouts. The Legoland Park is open from May to September, 10am-8pm.

The Lake District

Silkeborg is a pastoral town surrounded by scores of small lakes. It cannot be reached by train, but its buses connect with most railway lines. It has the highest peak of the Jutland, the Ejer Baunderhøj (a 171 m tall giant) in its vicinity.

Travelling along the E3 to the lake district, take the **Skanderborg** exit and follow Road 445 through **Ry** and **Them** to **Silkeborg**. At Ry there are canoe-hiring agencies, and from there one may row from lake to lake, through a network of connecting waterways. Coming from the south, you'll probably use Road 52 or 13.

Westward from Ry the road crosses some of the most beautiful woodland in the region and comes to **Silkeborg**, with its Tourist Information Centre (Torvet 9, tel. 86 82 19 11) and two interesting museums: the **Art Museum** (Gudenåvej 7-9, open 10am-5pm), mostly dedicated to the work of Asger Jorn, a local artist, and the **Town Museum**, whose main exhibits are the Tollund Man and Woman — two surprisingly well preserved mommies more than 2,000 years old (open 10am-5pm). In town, by lake Julsø, one may hire canoes, sailboats and bicycles.

Århus

With its 250,000 inhabitants, Århus is the second largest city in Denmark — and the Jutland's major centre. Its wide deepwater harbour and large industrial area have been wisely developed away from the city centre. This excellent natural port was discovered by the Vikings, who built it up as one of their major regional strongholds. Some of the old buildings and churches still stand in what has become the centre of a large provincial town. Its climate, its colleges and its gardens make any visitor feel comfortably at home immediately on arrival. There are also several interesting sights to see, and at night it's a very lively town indeed. A lot of good reasons to come, see, and stay overnight.

The Tourist Information Centre (City Hall, tel. 86 12 16 00) provides all the usual services. It has on sale a *Tourist Card* and quite a few bicycles for hire. Two-hour long guided tours of the town (15DKR) leave the Tourist Information Centre regularly every Thursday at 2pm during summer.

Food and Accommodation

There are expensive hotels, like the *Atlantic* (on the gulf, tel. 86 13 11 11) or the *Marselis* (tel. 86 14 44 11). The *Ritz* (by the Railway Station, tel. 86 13 44 44) and the *Royal* (central, tel. 86 12 00 11) are also quite good. Among the relatively cheaper hotels, there is the *Park* (Søndre Alle 3, tel. 86 12 32 31) and the *Eriksens* (Banegådsgade 6-8, tel. 86 13 62 96). At the Tourist

Information Centre you'll find the addresses of several rooming offers.

The youth hostel is 3 km from the centre of town (buses 1, 2 and 8, tel. 86 16 72 98).

Camp sites: *Blommenhavn* (7 km away, buses 6 and 19, tel. 86 27 02 07) and *Århus Nord* (8 km north of the town, buses 118 and 117, tel. 86 23 11 13).

There are scores of restaurants and eateries of all types and prices. The luxury hotels also have luxury restaurants, but the pride of the town goes to the *De 4 Årstider* (The Four Seasons, Åboulevarden), an internationally renowned culinary attraction. The *Hereford Beefstouw* chain of eateries is good and not too expensive; the most popular is at Skolegade 5 (tel. 86 13 53 25). Also cheap are the Chinese and Italian eateries. The University mess is of course the cheapest; its only competitors are the cafeterias of the centre. At Vester Alle 15 there is a vegetarian restaurant.

What to see

The **Rådhuset** (City Hall) is the starting point of our itinerary, and perhaps also its main site. The Norwegian marble front was completed in 1941, but the main attraction is within the halls. Here two young architects let their imagination soar, and it is worthwhile joining the (free) guided tour of the building (in English), in order to be able to grasp and appreciate it as a whole. On the walls of most rooms you'll find many outstanding works of art, such as several paintings by A. Naur, who worked here, in hiding, during the Nazi occupation.

A short crossing of the gulf or a walk along Sondergade will take you to the **Skt. Klement Domkirken**, a 15th century gothic style cathedral, built upon the foundations of two earlier churches. With its 93 metres, it is the longest church in Denmark, and it contains a number of outstanding works of art. Behind the cathedral, within an old police station, is the **Kvindemuseet** (the Ladies' Museum). Across the square from the cathedral is the **Vikingemuseet**, with some interesting artifacts and fragments recovered during local building works.

Next turn now to Studsgade and left into Nørrebrogade, to the **Kunstmuseum** (Arts Museum), with its collection of Danish paintings of the 18th, 19th and 20th centuries, and some very good specimens of international contemporary art. Above the museum, in the middle of a large public garden, is the campus of the Århus University, one of the most dynamic colleges in Denmark.

Den Gamle By (the Old City) is Århus' greatest pride. It comprises 63 old wooden houses, carefully transported here from all over Denmark (for obvious reasons, most come from Jutland sites), forming a giant market, neatly arranged according to trades of the original owners. Enter and lose yourself in its medieval atmosphere, stopping from door to door to admire the variety and quality of hundreds of old artifacts (open 10am-5pm, entrance 20DKR).

Another interesting site is the **Forhistorisk Museum** (Prehistoric Museum) of Moesgård, south of the city centre. It contains several interesting collections dating from the Stone Age to the days of the Vikings. The mommy preserved in mud within its glass case is 2,000 years old, and the neat wound evident on her neck seems to indicate that the young lady was sacrificed on the altar of a fertility goddess. Was she perhaps a close relation of the Silkeborg mommies?

We'll end with a mention of several other local museums: the Natural Museum, the Museum of Firefighting, the Science Museum, the Press Museum, the Museum of Medicine and the Aquarium.

Entertainment

Århus' cultural life is rich but rather dull. The local theatre presents a few regular performances, the local symphonic orchestra offers a few regular concerts of classical music. There is even an Opera House. The new Concert Hall and its foyer double up as a cultural centre. Early in September there is a week long international jazz festival, which branches out to folkmusic, reggae, rock and other bands. Several cafés hold daily or weekly performances; their programmes are listed in the *Århus This Week* sheet.

In Århus you'll find the traditional programme of "Meet the Dane", through which future visitors may write to the Tourist Information Centre, telling about themselves and their family, and upon their arrival they will be introduced to a suitable local family. Address: Århus Tourist Information Centre, Town Hall, Århus, Denmark DK-8000.

The E3 proceeds from Århus to **Randers** — but you might prefer to leave by Road 15 to Grenå or by Road 31 to Ebeltoft and Mols.

Grenå is the Jutland gateway to the Sjælland. **Ebeltoft** is a small medieval town, in which time seems to have stood still. **Randers** is a pleasant provincial town, rich in ancient monuments, among which the 15th century **Skt. Mortens** church, and the so-called **Heligåndshuset** (House of the Holy Ghost, at the Erik Menveds Plads), where the monks used to exorcize ghosts to deliver the poor and the sick from their ills. On the roof of the House of the Holy Ghost, the storks take temporary residence, on their annual voyage to and from warmer shores. Randers is the seat of one of the main branches of the World Society for the Protection of Storks.

The E3 runs on northward, through land and sea straits; but you may also wish to leave it for a short visit to the Langerak fjord and to the town of Ålborg.

Ålborg

This rather large town is situated on the shores of the **Limfjord**, the fjord cuts across the Jutland, forming the island of Vendsyssel. Ålborg the fourth town of Denmark, and is at the same time a dynamic industrial centre and a tourist resort.

Food and Accommodation

Ålborg is very well endowed with accommodation, eateries and entertainment for tourists. There are several central luxury hotels, like the Phoenix (tel. 98 12 00 11, Danish cuisine and music) and the *Scheelsminder* (tel. 98 18 32 33). The *Central* (tel. 98 12 69 33) and the *Park* (tel. 98 12 31 33) are slightly more modest. The *Hafnia* (tel. 98 13 19 00) is one of the cheapest. The youth hostel (tel. 98 13 00 48) is situated west of the town, and not far from it is the camp site (tel. 98 12 76 29).

What to see

Ålborg was once one of the richest towns in Denmark, thanks to its role as the main fish market of the region. It gradually became a large cultural centre as well. Walking through the alleys of the Old City you'll often recognize the remains of those past glories. As in many other Danish towns, here too great efforts were made to harmonize the old with the new. At the local Tourist Information Centre (Åsterå 8, tel. 98 12 60 22) you'll find an excellent town map and a long list of accommodation. Across the street is the **Jens Bangs** building, a majestic renaissance residence built by the formidable rich trader in 1624. Today it houses a drugstore and a restaurant. The richly decorated front of the residence has often raised the curiosity of passers-by; according to legend, the human figures engraved in the walls represent the city elders who excommunicated Jens Bengs, while the central figure, whose tongue points brazenly at City Hall, is that of the owner himself.

On Algade you'll see the **Budolfi Cathedral**, that was dedicated in the 16th century to the British St. Budolph. This impressive Gothic building stands on the ruins of an older Romanesque church. The Concerts and Exhibitions Centre of **Aalborghallen** is a very modern work by world-famous architect Alvar Aalto. The **Ålborg Historisk Museum** (Algade 42, open 10am-5pm) documents the history of the town and exhibits hundreds of Viking artifacts, recovered at the Lindhølm Hoje digs from no less than 642 tombs. Across the street is the **Helligåndsklosteret**, a 15th century monastery, that made history at the time by allowing monks and nuns to eat together at the same table. Today the building serves as a rest home for the aged. There is much more to be seen, and a comprehensive tour will require at least one whole day.

Do not miss, in any case, the narrow alley of **Jomfru Ane Gade**, with its shopwindows, cafés and restaurants. This is the highlight of Ålborg's night life, and, last but not least, there's *Pepe's Pizza*, substantial, tasty and cheap, at the end of the alley on Obel's Plads.

You might also take time for a small detour to Lindholm Høje, just across the fjord. A one hour walk, or a few minutes on bus 4 through the bridge, will take you to a very impressive Viking burial site; rather interesting is the grouping of sarcophagi arranged as if to suggest the shape of a ship — and therefore duly called "the ship".

North of Ålborg

Ålborg is the starting base for a visit to the northern Jutland. The E3 will take you as far as **Fredrikshavn**, where you'll board the Norway ferry. If you happen to have missed the ferry, or wish to spend a last night on Danish soil, the local Tourist Information Centre (Brotorvet 1, tel. 98 42 14 75) will provide you with ferry and train timetables and with a list of accommodation for the night.

On the northernmost tip of the Jutland, which separates the Skagerrak from the Kattegat, is **Skagen**. The unusual contrast of colours between the Baltic and the North Sea waters has often attracted many painters, and several of their works are exhibited at the **Skagen Museum**. You'll be able to experience the artists' inspirations from the museum observatory, that was used by Anna and Michael Ancher for their work. But Skagen's appeal is not only due to the unusual shades of blue and green of those northern waters; and the local Tourist Information Centre (Skt. Laurentiivej 18, tel. 98 44 13 77) will point out to you its main architectural attractions and assist you in your choice of accommodation for the night, from 3-star hotels to B&Bs, to the youth hostel (tel. 98 44 13 56) and the camp site (tel. 98 44 14 70).

Turning southward along the western coast of the peninsula, you'll come to **Hirtshals**, a small sea port, frequented by the ferry crossing to Norway. Roads 55 and 11 lead to one of the most popular resorts in the Jutland, a district of small fishermen's villages and picturesque hamlets, sandy beaches, old churches and ancient tombs and other ruins. Even the smallest centre boasts its own historic museum.

Viborg

Situated in the heart of the Jutland, Viborg has been an important road junction for more than 12 centuries. Proof of this is provided by the ancient Hærvejeh road, which was used by travellers and traders as early as the 8th Century. For more than a century, Viborg was the coronation site of the first Kings of Denmark, and the residential seat of King Knut the Great, conqueror of England (1027). With the rise and growth of Copenhagen, and the transfer of power to the Sjælland, Viborg lost most of its former splendour.

The Tourist Information Centre (Nytorv 5, tel. 86 62 16 17) has excellent town maps — and of course all the usual information. Take your map and start your walk at the **Domkirke**, an impressive granite church, whose foundations date from the beginning of the 12th century. In 1726 the cathedral was completely destroyed by fire, to be restored in Barock style only 150 years later, toward the end of the 19th century. The frescoes inside are the works of Joachim Skovgaard and his pupils. At the **Skovgaard Museum** (open daily, 10am-5pm), you'll see a rare collection of Skovgaard's works. The **District Museum** (open daily, 11am-5pm) presents clearly and attractively the history of the district from prehistoric times to this day.

South of the town, approaching the **lake district**, you'll find yourself in quite another world. You've left behind the echoes of past history, to find yourself immersed in nature's kingdom: prairies, meadows and lakes, that are perhaps even too plentiful in fish for self-respecting fishermen.

The garden district of **Haldege** lies west of the town, and here nature is combined with memories of war: this is the site of the bloody peasants' rebellion of 1351.

Crossing the Lake District from north to south you'll find yourself

Ribe's Medieval Charm

at **Holstebro**, a modern town, proud of its well ordered and well kept avenues and of its **Giacometti Museum**.

18 kilometres south-east of Holstebro is the town of **Herning**, a centre of Danish textile industry and a popular convention town. It boasts several museums and even a small zoo.

The West Coast of the Jutland

Ringkøbing, one of the oldest towns in Denmark, lies on the west coast of the Jutland, well protected from the ire of the North Sea by a long series of dykes. According to archaeological research, the town was founded in 1250, and it has maintained most of its original character to this day. In the summer its sand dunes and its natural port contribute to the charm of its old buildings and alleys.

Road 28 leads southward, crossing the **Skjern**, whose banks are lined with numerous 13th century buildings. The Skjern itself is known throughout Denmark as a fisherman's paradise.

Road 12 runs southward to another ancient town, **Varde**, whose 11th century church has been restored time after time to its present shape. In addition to the customary local museums, Varde has also a city model, depicting the town as it was in 1800.

Road 12 proceeds to **Esbjerg**, with the British ferries landing pier. Its fishermen's harbour vaunts the largest local fleet in Denmark, and moreover Esbjerg is the one and only deep sea harbour in Western Jutland. The early morning fish market is smelly but very picturesque.

The port of Esbjerg connects the mainland with the islands of Fanø and Mandø. These islands are simply a must for any self-respecting fisherman — or even for ambitious amateurs, who will have the opportunity to follow in the steps of local masters of the art.

Tides are very spectacular in this region, and the crossing to Mandø is by car, is during the ebb tide.

Ribe

Ribe is the oldest town in Denmark, and also the best preserved of all medieval centres. In its charming streets the lights go off — and the whole city retires — as early as 10.30pm.

Ribe was founded around the year 800 as a regional Viking market town. In 850 a missionary monk built the first round church in northen Europe, and brought Ribe to Christianity. The Cathedral, built in 1117-25, underwent frequent restoration works; several religious orders built their seats around the honoured cathedral, and some of them are still active. Many centuries ago the Kings of Denmark granted Ribe a privileged status, but during the Reformation Ribe suffered grave setbacks, from which it never recovered. Its nine monasteries, thirteen churches and other religious institutions closed their doors forever. Then came a series of fires, floods and wars. Ribe was barely able to survive, as a sort of life-size history museum.

It was only at the beginning of our century that a sort of revival began to take shape; today Ribe is one of Denmark's prosperous tourist resorts.

The Tourist Information Centre (Torvet 3-5, tel. 75 42 15 00) is, as usual, of great assistance as well as a good starting point for a tour of the town. An outstanding guided tour takes off on summer nights at 10pm from Torver Sq., near the old **Weis Stu** pub. The tour guide is a well known elderly Ribian, and he leads his flock with a lantern held aloft, not unlike the candle bearing time-callers of old ("ten o'clock and all's well, no fires are burning...). All around is the silence of deep sleep — sleeping people and sleeping walls. The guide stops at each and every building, and for each of them he has a bonny tale of past glories and awes. Another daytime tour by minibus crosses the river Ribe, passing though the town's charming park, to reach at low tide the island of Rømø (crossing forbidden in private cars!).

The island is an unusual nature reserve, particularly attractive in summer thanks to its bird colonies, its sea-lions and its... nudist beach. The visit to Rømø must follow the timetable of the tides.

There is a wide choice of restaurants and eateries of all types; as for accommodation, it's advisable to book hotel rooms ahead.

An overnight stay at the inexpensive *Weis' Stu* (tel. 75 42 07 00) is an unforgettable experience (regardless of the fact that its rooms have no private toilets!). If no rooms are available there, try next door, at the *Dagmar* (rather more expensive, tel. 75 42 00 33).

Two camp sites are comfortably close to the town: Ribe (2 km from town, tel. 75 42 08 87) and *Villebøl Kongeå* (not far from the first, tel. 75 43 71 04). The youth hostel (tel. 75 42 06 20) is in the same nieghbourhood and has also family rooms.

Denmark by Bike

In recent years bicycling in Denmark has become increasingly popular — and the pedalled fleet of this small country has grown and grown until it numbers more than two and a half million bikes of all types. First there are the "daily pedallers", who commute daily by bike. On the week end, they join the crowds of the "weekenders", streaming bike after bike to the parks of suburbia. Now to those two legions we must add the tourist tribes, wandering through Denmark's cycling paths from spring to fall.

The **Dansk Cyklist Forbund** (Association of Danish Cyclists, Langes Gade 14, Copenhagen, tel. 33 14 42 12) distributes maps on request as well as itineraries and lists of hire agencies throughout the country. Additional information is available at all the Tourist Information Centres, at the information desks of the railway stations and elsewhere. Hiring prices range from 20-40DKR a day (80-200DKR a week).

Denmark is not really a flat country, as you will soon learn while pedalling through its lanes. It is not too strenuous, however the variety of topography makes for very pleasant rides; as a tip, it's worth while hiring a bike equipped with some sort of sports gear.

Bicycle transportation

While Denmark is not a large country, here and there you'll find yourself pedalling for hours through seemingly endless and featureless plains. In such cases, the right place for your bike is on some train or bus rack, while you sit comfortably in the same transportation.

Trains: The railway network maintains regular bicycle transportation services. The passage must be booked several days ahead and the tariff is about 30DKR per 100 km. Bikes may be sent on separately, but it's generally better to keep them in sight, boarding the same train. For further information, call tel. 33 14 17 01, or inquire at the Railway Station.

Buses: Most buses can accommodate at least 3-4 bicycles. Some of the interurban buses are equipped with a special cargo

Biking through Denmark

section for bikes. Advance booking is absolutely necessary. Bikes are not allowed on urban lines.

Ferries: On most ferries bike transportation is free, even for the longer crossings (to and from Sweden and Germany).

National flights: Air bike transportation costs 65-75DKR. In some cases your bike will have to fly separately, in a cargo plane. For further details, inquire at the *SAS* offices.

Bicycle regulations

Bikes

According to Danish law, bikes must be equipped with a bell, they must have light reflectors on both pedals or above the back wheel — and a "red eye" reflector behind the seat. From dusk to sunrise two lights are compulsory: a white front light above the front wheel, and a red back light above the back wheel, bright enough to be seen from a distance of 150 m. Regular bikes must be equipped with hand or pedal brakes; tandem (double) bikes must have brakes on both wheels.

Bicycle thieves are common, therefore all bicycles come equipped with a security lock or chain.

Many Danes often carry on their bikes, various loads and even babies in baskets. There are specially designed carry-alls, duly registered as infant carriers for children under 6 years of age; the rider's age must be above 15. Infants may be carried either on the bike itself or in the carry-all, never on both. The carry-all must be equipped with two back red lights, two white reflectors and two "red eyes" on the back, and a yellow reflectors on each side. The carry-all must also be equipped with safety belts and its metal parts must be padded with soft material.

Traffic laws

Wherever and whenever possible, all bicycle traffic must make use of the special paths that run parallel to most Danish roads — where such paths don't exist, bicycles must keep to the right shoulders.

Bicycles are allowed to run on the road itself only if and when this does not interfere with other traffic. Bicycle riding is forbidden on all international highways and expressways. To signal a left turn, raise your hand and stop; when you move on you'll signal again, this time with your right hand. A signal made with the left hand indicates a right turn. Danish drivers are very familiar with these regulations.

Punctures and other repairs

Denmark has no less than 800 bicycle shops, and most of them are well equipped for road repairs. Very often you'll also have the help of some other pedalling passer-by. However, you should carry your own repair kit with you, equipped at least with brake cables, irons, patches, rubber and pump.

Further information

Maps, books and pamphlets are available at the *DCF* and at most Tourist Information Centres.

The *DCF* maps offer three types of bicycle tours:

Blue itineraries, along exclusive bicycle paths.
Yellow itineraries follow the bicycle paths that run along most major motorways.
Brown itineraries follow other roads.

Most large urban centres have clearly indicated bicycle-path networks; and everywhere in the country cyclists are given absolute right of way.

DENMARK

We won't encourage you to plan your bicycle tour for the colder season, between October and March.

The Itineraries

Copenhagen

The *Use it* distributes several excellent maps of bicycle tours of the metropolis. A 1:50,000 map for cyclists is on sale (45DKR) at the *DCF* offices and in the best bookshops.

The three following routes have been designed to fill up a whole day of pedalling; but using the map, you may add your own variations if you so wish.

Route 1 — to Dyrehaven, Møllæen, Fredriksdal and Furesøen (50 km). Leave the city with ease, pedalling northward along the Peblinge Sø waterway, and turn left on Østerbrogade. Follow Strandvejen along the Øresund coast; the bicycle path will bring you to the beautiful **Dyrehaven Park**, with its aviary and deer reserve. Proceed westward to Lake Lyngby, Fredriksdal and the spectacular Lake Furesø. Turn back to Copenhagen through Harreskovvej.

Route 2 — to Amager Park, Kongelunden and Dragør (45 km). Leave town at Christiana, crossing the **Amager Fælled** and its many paths. Follow one of the seaside lanes, proceeding southward, and cross Kongelunden to reach the medieval village of Dragør. The return route may be either through the airport or along the eastern borders of the great park.

Route 3 — to Utterselv Mose (25 km). Follow Gyldenløvesgade, Åbovlevard, Ågade, Borups Alle and Hareskorvvej — and you'll come to **Utterselv Mose**, only 10 km north-west of Copenhagen. It's a splendid park, with several small lakes and the ruins of ancien city ramparts. Its close proximity to the capital and its picturesque sights make it one of the most popular week-end havens.

For most of the way, except for the city exits, all three routes belong to the "yellow" or "blue" categories.

Sjælland

The best bicycle lanes in **Northern Sjælland** lead to the **Grib Skov**, the forest-covered hills above Hillerod and the white cliffs of Stevns. In the **Central Sjælland** the best route goes to the Tystrup-Bavelse lakes and **Sorø**, between Roskilde and Kalundborg; in **Southern Sjælland** it's best to pedal from farm to farm, along the coastal road.

DENMARK

Bornholm

The one and only cyclist's paradise. The local roads "belong" almost exclusively to thousands of cyclists; there are few climbs — and they are never too strenuous, but the view is always superb: canyons and forests, cliffs and white beaches.

The **Klemensker-Rø** route is only 8 km long — but it is simply breathtaking in beauty. Don't miss it!

Fyn

The southern reaches and hilly districts of the "Garden Island" attract thousands of cyclists throughout the summer. The southern islands of Tåsinge, Ærø and Langeland are connected to the main island by bridges, and are also frequented by many cyclists. The island ferries are also used by cyclists to cross over from Fyn to the Jutland, to Sjælland and Lolland. At the Tourist Information Centre you'll find a 1:50,000 map of Fyn, with it you'll be able to plan your own most suitable routes, far from the motorways and from the more crowded Odense district.

Jutland

This is where the network of bicycle paths is thickest (especially in the south-west). Sometimes you may leave beautiful Ribe toward Varde and the Legoland Park without meeting even a single motor car.

The Lake District, around Silkeborg, requires good leg muscles, but also provides quite a few restful breaks by the lakeside, meadow or on board a local sailing boat.

The ancient **Ox-Drover** road goes from Viborg to Kruså (at the German border), passing through some of the most picturesque sites in the peninsula. An annotated diagram of this route along the "Ancient Military Road" is available at the *DCF* offices and the Tourist Information Centres.

At the **Ringkøbing Fjord** of Tipperne Island you'll find an interesting sea-bird reserve.

Northern Jutland has some of the most spectacular bicycle routes in Denmark, along white calcareous cliffs and through medieval fishermen's villages; their starting point is the village of **Skagen**.

Before embarking on a bicycle ride in Denmark, don't forget to visit the Copenhagen *DCF* offices!

SWEDEN

Sweden is for many synonymous with economic prosperity, peace, law and order. It's the country of Volvos — and of tall, blue-eyed and blonde young men and women.

But Sweden is also the land of the Vikings, short but dramatic history left its traces not only on Sweden's towns and hamlets but on thousands of miles of the Northern Atlantic coastline.

History

The earliest human settlements in the region date from the 2nd or 3rd century B.C. Roman coins recovered here and there from several sites indicate the existence of trade contacts with Central Europe and Britain. According to Tacitus' Annals, the northern Svear tribes were a nation of warriors, strong, well armed and proficient at sea. The vast ruins discovered on the island of Gotland seem to have been at one time a large trading centre, often frequented by the Roman legions.

Toward the beginning of the 9th century, Sweden was already a feudal monarchy of sorts, firmly led by the tribe of the Svears. While Viking ships scourged the Atlantic waters, reaching as far as Greenland and America, Christianity was rapidly conquering the whole of Scandinavia, causing a long series of bitter local wars between the followers of the old idolatrous religions and the advocates of the new faith. Finally, in 1164, after the whole country had been won over to Christianity, a new Archbishopric was established in Uppsala (the very nest of the ancient gods...). The only compromise accorded by the Church to the local tribal barons was the creation of a Crown Council, composed of the major chieftains of all tribes.

During all the 12th century, the Swedes conducted a long series of wars of conquest, directed mainly against Denmark and Russia. Toward the end of that century, Sweden built its new capital, Stockholm.

SWEDEN

The Black Death of 1349 brought Sweden to its knees: one third of the population died, and anarchy reigned among the impoverished survivors.

In addition to the age-long strife between church and crown, there was now impending danger from the South. The Sacred Roman Empire was on the march, and Sweden was forced to join arms with Queen Margrete of Denmark; in 1397 Denmark, Sweden and Norway formed a single kingdom, within the Union of Kalmar.

The new Scandinavian empire lasted little more than a century. The bellicose character of the Swedes caused a long series of rebellions, and finally, when most tribes rallied under the flag of Gustavus Vasa, the Swedes confronted the Danes in open battle and won their independence from Denmark. In 1523 Gustavus Vasa became Gustavus I of Sweden.

Even in such hectic times Sweden didn't neglect its cultural growth, and in 1477 the University of Uppsala was founded, the first of several great Swedish centres of study.

Under Gustavus I the new Lutheran cult became the official religion of the country. Gustavus reorganized the civil administration, encouraged trade and industry and created a large and powerful army.

Toward the end of the 16th century Sweden was once again at war with Denmark and Russia. The Thirty Year War, from which Sweden emerged victorious, brought under its rule the whole of Finland and of the Baltic coastal lands. Sweden was now a major European power.

Carl XII, who reigned at the end of the 17th and the beginning of the 18th centuries, wanted to carry on the traditions of Swedish conquest, but in 1709 his armies were defeated by Peter the Great, Czar of all Russias, and Sweden was forced to abandon all the territories it had won south-east of the Scandinavian peninsula.

The new, and increasingly powerful middle classes exploited the chaotic situation of the kingdom following the death of Charles XII (1718), and after two years of squabbling a new Constitution was finally approved (1720). Sweden was now a constitutional kingdom, whose Parliament was divided in two main parties, the Mercantilists (the "Homburgs") and the Liberals (the "Berets"). But only half a century later, after another unlucky war against

Germany, King Gustavus III repealed the Constitution, setting himself up as absolute ruler of his country.

In 1805 Sweden joined the anti-Napoleonic alliance, and after the fall of the French Emperor (to whose fortunes the Danes had allied themselves), all of Norway, that had priorly been a Danish province, was annexed to Sweden.

After the Napoleonic Wars, Swedish Parliament gradually won back many of its original powers, and by mid-century Sweden had again become a prosperous constitutional monarchy. Within few years, four new universities opened their gates, several daily newspapers were founded and industries made gigantic steps in all major ports and urban centres.

In our century, due to its firm neutrality during both great World Wars, Sweden became one of the richest countries in Europe, and set the guidelines and policies for the modern Welfare State.

In 1974, after a series of vast social reforms, the Swedish Parliament voted and approved a new Constitution, that makes of Sweden one of the most democratic countries in the world.

To this day Sweden maintains its strict neutrality, and has not joined the EEC community, preferring to head the less demanding and much less political-minded *EFTA* European grouping.

Geography

Sweden is a large country, covering an area of almost 450,000 square kilometres. On the west it borders with Norway; Finland is to the north-east, and the Baltic Sea encloses it from the east. Thousands of lakes cover some 12% of its total area.

The coastal regions form an uninterrupted 1,500 km-long plain, crossed by a series of rivers, whose cold waters run from the glaciers of the Norwegian Alps and through a chain of mountain lakes, to end at the Baltic Sea, where they create small fjords, estuaries and natural harbours.

Sweden may be subdivided into three main geographic regions:

The **Norrland** (Land of the North), which accounts for about 60% of the total territory, a land of tundras, forests, lakes, rivers and ice.

SWEDEN

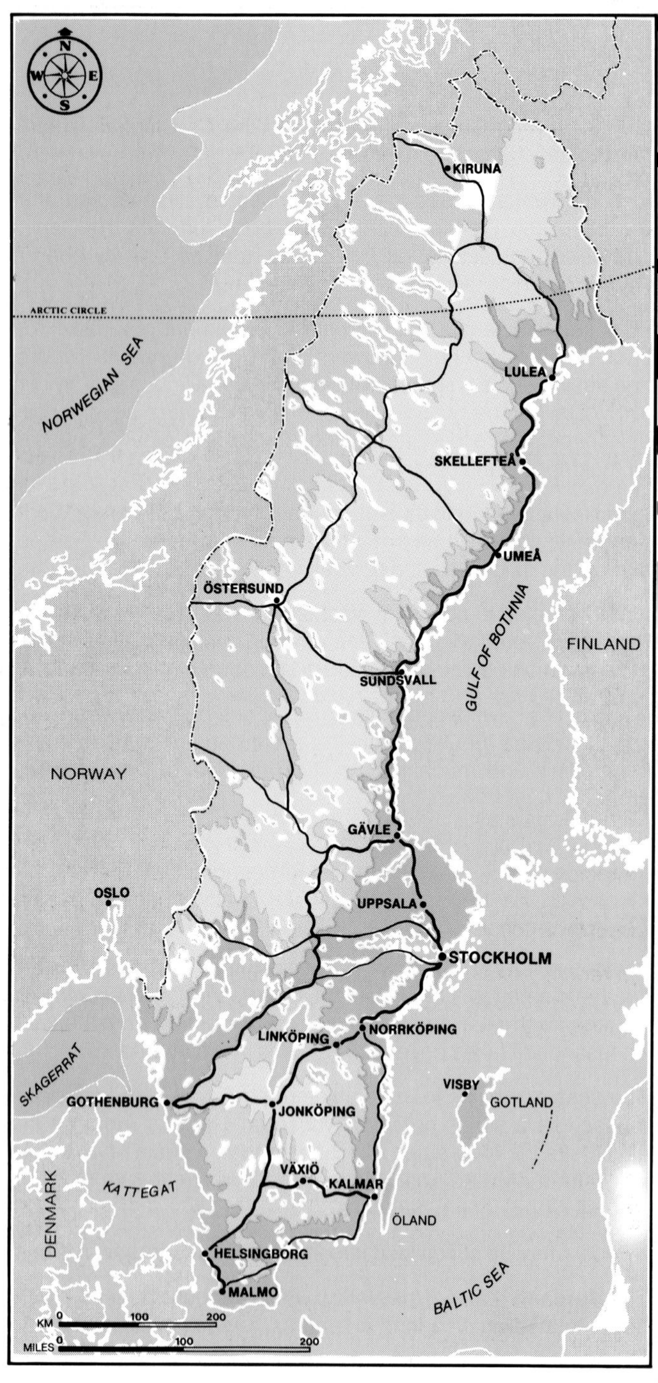
N
W
E
S
KIRUNA
ARCTIC CIRCLE
NORWEGIAN SEA
LULEA
SKELLEFTEÅ
UMEÅ
ÖSTERSUND
GULF OF BOTHNIA
FINLAND
SUNDSVALL
NORWAY
GÄVLE
OSLO
UPPSALA
STOCKHOLM
NORRKÖPING
LINKÖPING
SKAGERRAT
VISBY
GOTLAND
GOTHENBURG
JONKÖPING
VÄXIÖ
KALMAR
DENMARK
KATTEGAT
ÖLAND
HELSINGBORG
MALMO
BALTIC SEA
KM 0 100 200
MILES 0 100 200

The **Svealand**, or Land of the Svears, which occupies the central regions of Sweden: a coastal plain and its hilly interior, with Sweden's three great lakes: the Vänern (5,546 km^2), the Mäleren (1,158 km^2) and the Vättern (1,911 km^2).

The **Göteland**, or land ot the Gotes, a highland rich of forests, lakes and swamps, situated at the extreme southern tip of the country. East of Göteland, in the Baltic, are the two major islands of Gotland and Öland.

Climate
The influence of the Gulf Stream reaches the coasts of southern Sweden; however, 15% of the country is north of the Arctic Circle, where it gets quite cold indeed, at least during the long polar nights off December and January. Even in June and July, under the midnight sun, it remains quite cool.

Average February temperatures range from -3°C in the extreme south to -14°C up in the Norrland. The August averages are 18°C in Göteland, 17°C in Stockholm and 14°C in Norrland. Precipitations are rather modest: 400 mm in the far north and 650 in the south. The Norrland remains covered by snow for about 8 months. The northern Baltic is riddled with dangerous icebergs from November to May.

Flora and fauna
Almost half of the Swedish territory is forestland (mostly larch forests), one of the main industrial resources of Sweden. The rest of the country is agricultural soil, swamplands and pastures (mostly along the coastal plain and around the lakes).

In recent years, thanks mainly to the endeavours of the Greens, nineteen forests have been declared ecological reserves, where hunting and deforestation are forbidden.

The people

Sweden today has a population of about 8.4 million people — about 20 people per km^2 (very very low by European standards!). One third of the population lives in the three major urban centres: Stockholm 1.4 m, Göteborg 800,000 and Malmö 450,000.

After the Second World War an uninterrupted stream of migrants settled in Sweden, putting an end to the thousand-year-old ethnic unity of the nation. During the same period urban development assumed new, hectic dimensions. Medical and social progress joined to bring about a demographic revolution: today more than 18% of the Swedish population is above the age of 65!

Religion

95% of all Swedes belongs to the Lutheran faith. Thousands of old churches, often shaped like stalwarth defensive forts, record the progress of the Christian conquest. Less than two centuries after the complete conversion of Sweden to Christianity, the Reformation caused new strife and conflicts — between various Christian churches, and between the Church and local gentry. Today a large majority of the population joins in prayer every Sunday within the gates of the churches.

Culture

Cultural progress is one of the explicit goals of the Swedish administration, in a very liberal climate of full respect of human rights, traditions and beliefs. The government encourages frequent cultural projects of local, ethnic and regional character: libraries, study centres, theatres, community centres, music halls etc.

Regional entities are also encouraged to maintain and preserve old traditions and customs — a factor of great value in such a wide and underpopulated country.

Swedish schools are among the best in the world; compulsory education includes all stages of formal study, from kindergarten to college.

While all schools (including local centres of higher studies) are administered by the local authorities, the Universities come under the aegis of the central Ministry of Education, and attract hundreds of foreign students.

The two major sports are tennis and winter-sports. Recently soccer, athletics and swimming have become more and more popular, and several Swedish athletes have achieved considerable international fame.

The administration

Sweden is a constitutional monarchy. Its *Riksdagen* (Parliament) is composed of 349 members; they are elected every three years, together with the local and regional administrations.

Voting rights are universal from the age of 18; King Gustav XVI fulfills only ceremonial functions, but is loved and revered by his people.

Swedish feminism has a history of considerable achievements, and roughly one third of the Parliament members belong to the "weaker" sex.

Economy

Swedish prosperity is proverbial throughout the world. This is due not only to a century of political neutrality, but also, and perhaps more, to the qualities of its people and to the considerable natural resources of its soil.

Under these favourable conditions, the Swedish Government has been able to achieve the major goals of social liberalism, setting up a vast and comprehensive net of welfare institutions and services that make Sweden one of the most progressive countries in the world. Practically all Swedish industry is in private hands. In order to maintain its very high standards of life and of welfare services, the Swedes submit to a very high income taxation.

Swedish industry is at the vanguard of the world in the fields of motors, hydro-electricity, automobile production (Saab and Volvo), shipbuilding, architecture and wood production. About 40% of Swedish manpower is employed by industry.

Agricultural produce amounts to 4% of the NGP; the major branch is milk production. Agriculture developed mainly along the southern coastal plain; however, even there the soil is poor and the government does not encourage agricultural enterprises.

Holidays

New Year
Epiphany
Easter
May Day
Ascension Day
Whitsunday
Summer Festival (25 June)
All Saints Day
Christmas

The language

Swedish, like all Nordic tongues, is rich in diphtongs and special phonetic signs, that could cause problems while asking for a given address or reading a road sign.

ej — sounds like "a" in "any"
å — sounds like "who" in "whole"
ä — sounds like "a" in "arrow"
pj, gj, øj, j — sound like "eo" in "people":
tj, kä, kö, ky, ke, kl — sound like "ha" in "hand".
z — sounds like "s" in "sound".

How and when to come

The best season to visit Sweden is late spring and early summer when the climate is most temperate and all resorts are open. Autumn is often cold and rainy; winter is the first choice of winter-sport fans.

How long to stay

Sweden is costly; there are, however, many bargains to be found, which bring prices down to average European standards. By travelling by rail, with a *Eurail Pass*, a *Nordic Railpass*, or a *Reslustkart*, making do with only one daily restaurant meal and sleeping in hostels or camp sites, $30 a day will be sufficient. A couple settling for cheap B&B accommodation will spend as much as $80 a day. In short, if a couple wishes to plan a week long tour of Sweden they will require a budget of about $600.

We advise you to dedicate at least 3 days to Stockholm and its region (up to Uppsala). You'll need at least a whole week if you plan to see northern and central Sweden — and 3-4 days for the south. For a thorough visit to all Sweden, you'll need at least three weeks. If you have only one month for all of Scandinavia, we suggest two weeks in Norway, one in Sweden, and 3-4 days each in Denmark and Finland.

How to get there

The proverbial efficiency and order of the Swedes are of great help to the incoming tourist. The railway network is vast; the road system is excellent. There are also some very good sea and air connections.

SWEDEN

By rail: The great international European railways cross the Kattegat by ferry (crossing price included in train tickets) to Malmö, Stockholm and the rest of Sweden. Two other ferries connect Denmark with Sweden: the Helsingør-Hälsingborg line and the Fridrikshavn-Göteborg line. There are three main Norwegian rail connections: from Oslo, Trondheim and Narvik.

By air: Many international airlines have regular Stockholm flights; *SAS* has several daily Stockholm flights, transatlantic and European ones as well as regional and national ones. The Göteborg and Malmö airports also service several *SAS* European flights.

By sea: There is, as we have already mentioned, regular ferry crossings that connect Sweden with the rest of northern Europe. Timetables are available at any Tourist Information Centre. The major seaport in Sweden is Göteborg; it is visited by hundreds of commercial ships from all over the world. The ferry crossings are vital also to road transportation.

By bus: The Lisbon-Stockholm bus line is an interesting alternative to railway travel, and makes short stops at all principal centres. There are also regular lines between Norway and Sweden.

By car: Here too, the way to enter is by ferry. The Swedish road system is directly connected with Finland and with Norway.

Tourist services

Even the smaller provincial centres have their own Tourist Information Centre: in all there are in Sweden 380 such centres; a list of their phone numbers and addresses is available at the main Stockholm Tourist Information Centre. They are an invaluable source of information regarding accommodation, tours, cultural and artistic programmes etc. They also distribute free maps, pamphlets and other informational material. You'll often find a list of bicycle hire agencies. In all offices you'll be able to communicate comfortably in English or in German.

Transportation services

The more densely populated regions of Sweden have very good and frequent rail and road transportation services. The north is serviced by two mail railways. Even the most desolate hamlet in the far north is connected to the railways by a daily bus line. Timetables are always available at the Tourist Information Centre.

Trains: The **S.J.** (State Railways Administration) administers the whole national railway system. *Eurail* tickets are valid throughout the country. Inquire about eventual discounted cumulative tickets, and other possible discounts you may be entitled to as a tourist, a student, a senior citizen etc. An updated timetable, available at all the main railway stations and at the Tourist Information Centres, should be obtained as soon as possible.

Bus lines: All public bus lines are also administered by the **S.J.**; they complement the railway, making it possible to reach with relative ease any destination in the country. Bus lines generally depart from the railway station, and are always connect with stopping trains. Some of the most isolated villages may be reached only by one daily run — that of the "Mail Bus".

Urban and suburban lines are frequent and fast; tickets are valid for any number of rides within one hour or more.

Before you buy your ticket, ask for cumulative discounted cards. The personnel of any Tourist Information Centre will be happy to assist you.

National flights: The size of the country often requires the use of national flights. Thanks to the special tariffs adopted by *SAS* and *Lin*, air travel has become a very popular means of transportation in Sweden, used frequently by local people and tourists. Tourists under the age of 26 and senior citizens enjoy special discounts; there are often very convenient tickets for families travelling together and for larger groups. Again, ask about available flights at the Tourist Information Centre.

Interior waterways: Sweden's great lakes are not fully exploited as an inland transportation route. A boat line connects Stockholm with Göteborg by means of the Göta Canal, crossing the two great lakes of Vänern and Vättern. The two major Swedish islands off the Baltic shores, Gotland and Öland, are connected to the mainland by excellent ferry services.

The road net: Swedish roads are very well kept. Slower vehicles are encouraged to use the right-hand lane. Headlights are compulsory throughout the day.

Car hire: All major agencies are well represented in Sweden. There are discounted tariffs for week-end (and longer) hires; local tariffs encourage the hire of small economy cars.

Hitchhiking: is neither popular nor advisable.

Bicycles: In Southern Sweden and in Uppsala the bicycle is the most popular means of transportation, and not only within the larger cities. Many hostels and Tourist Information Centres have also a bicycle-hire desk. Prices range between 20-30SEK.

Accommodation

Stockholm hotels compete with Tokyo and New York for stiffness of prices. In August, the peak of the high season, many top hotels offer special bargains at considerable discounts — as much as 50%! — putting even the luxury establishments within the reach of many tourists. On the other side, their regular rates are simply forbidding: bed and breakfast for two will cost 650SEK (the special bargains may bring this down to 350SEK).

Tourist class accommodation include also a number of B&B and private residence rooms. Here bed and breakfast for two will cost you about 200-300SEK.

There are also, of course, cheaper choices. There is a national network of 280 hostels (two beds — and sometime more than 2 — for only 100SEK); a camping bungalow (with 4 or 6 beds) will cost about 200SEK; trailers and tent space are even cheaper, and they provide toilets, electricity and a minimarket.

The *Bilturlogi* is an organisation that offers bed and breakfast at very convenient prices — 100-150SEK. At the Tourist Information Centre you'll find also a number of other opportunities. For general information, call tel. 0247.50040.

The Swedish Cuisine

The Swedish cuisine has two main characteristics in common with all Scandinavia: its taste (outstanding) and its prices (exhorbitant). Restaurant service is at least invariably good.

Breakfast: is served 7am-10am and is not too costly: about 40SEK. It includes a selection of cold cuts, cheeses, fish, eggs and cereals, several types of breads and lots of (rather indifferent) coffee or tea.

Lunch: In many restaurants between 11am and 2.30pm for the modest sum of 35-50SEK you'll find the *Dagens Rägens*

Rätt (fixed price menu). It includes a generous plate of meat or fish, a side dish of vegetables, bread and a soft drink. One of the most popular dishes is *Pytt i Panna* (fried eggs with meat and potato chips). Another superb choice is the traditional *Smörgasbörd* — an enticing buffet with a rich choice of meats, cheeses and seafood, to be spread on gigantic bread slices or buns. Also try to get acquainted with *Köttbular* (meatballs in berry sauce), and *Bruna Bönor* (pork cutlets with beans); don't miss *Torsk* (cod), the everpresent fish of the day. But these dishes will inflate your bill to as much as 100SEK.

Dinner: There are no "fixed price menus" for dinner. This is when prices go sky-high and you might be presented with a bill for as much as 700SEK per person at the end of your meal.

Drinks: All of Scandinavia has decided to fight alcoholism by the simple means of increasing the price of drinks to unparalleled heights. The price of different brands of beer, for instance, is determined by its alcohol contents: a half-pint of the stronger beer — *Starköl* — costs not less than 25SEK; the lighter ones, like *Fölkol* or *Rättol* cost about 12SEK.

Other alcoholic drinks — wine and *Aquavit* — are also terribly expensive.

General information

Currency

The Swedish currency is the Krone (SEK), subdivided in 100 Øre. There are banknotes (10, 50, 100, 500, 1000 and 10,000SEK) and coins (10 and 50 Øre, 1 and 5SEK.

The rate of exchange is currently 1$ = 7.2SEK.

Foreign currency may be imported freely; export of local currency is limited to 6,000SEK in cash and 25,000 in travelers' cheques.

All major credit cards (*Visa, Eurocard, Mastercard, Diners*) are welcome in many shops, hotels and restaurants. Your foreign currency will be changed at any bank, at the Post Office, at the Change Agencies and at many railway stations and Tourist Information Centres.

Working hours

Banks are open Mon.-Fri. 9.30am-3pm (Thursdays also 4-5.30pm). At the airport and at railway stations bank branches remain open until long after dark.

Post Offices open Mon.-Fri., 9am-6pm; Saturdays 9am-1pm. Shops open Mon.-Sat., 9.30am-6pm.

Shopping

If the prices of most local products are high, their quality is even higher. VAT may be refunded to tourists after their departures either upon exit or by mail. Swedish glass and crystal objects are world famous for their beauty and style; at the factory outlets prices are often reasonable.

When you see a *REA* sign on an attractive shopwindow, it means that a bargain sale is on; it may be worth your while to step in...

Tips

Hotel and restaurant bills include a 15% service charge. Therefore tips are not required. Cab drivers expect a 10-15% tip; the hotel porter will accept a 5SEK coin.

Telecommunication

Public phones use 1SEK coins (the cost of a local call). For inter-urban calls we recommend using 50 Ore coins (most phones do not return small change). The international dialing prefix is 009; for the international operator, call 0011 or 0015. Public phones are equipped with English instructions.

At most post offices you'll also find facilites for direct international calls. Hotel calls are much more expensive.

Health services

Your hotel's information desk — or of course the local Tourist Information Centre — will have names and addresses of physicians on call and 24-hour pharmacies. Emergency calls may be made from any public phone, free of charge, directly or through the operator.

Entertainment

Sweden is a modern western country, and in all major towns you'll find good entertainment. For full details, visit the local Tourist Information Centre, where you'll be able to obtain listings of theatre programmes, concerts, films, discos, pubs and night clubs.

Films are never dubbed; TV programmes are also presented in their original language. Nightclubs are generally respectable; their prices range from expensive to forbiddingly expensive. Discos are often very crowded and noisy. There are age limits, strictly enforced by the bouncer at the gate.

Suggested itineraries for Sweden

Before your arrival you may have read some introductory material or (hopefully) this guide. For further details, inquire at your closest Swedish Consulate; the information will most probably be of use during your visit.

Sweden is a country of wide open spaces and great variety, from the alpine glaciers of the far north to the steppes of the centre and the forests of the south. It's difficult terrain and, it could even be boring, to go through all of it. Try to focus your interest on some of its more attractive aspects: the spectacular north or the picturesque south, with its great cities, lakes and forests. Coming from Finland, it will be easy to start from Uppsala and Stockholm, proceeding to Göteborg and Denmark. Coming from Oslo, it is best to start at the extreme north, proceeding either to Stockholm or to Lappland (in Finland).

But there are many other possibilities; arm yourself with a good map of the region, seek the advice of an experienced friend and plan your tour with the assistance of your local Travel Agent or local Tourist Office.

On the following pages we'll present you with two itineraries. Both of them begin in Stockholm, but after visiting the capital, they turn in opposite directions: the first aims for the northern ice, the second for the southern forests.

We'll stress again that anywhere in Sweden you'll find great help at the everpresent Tourist Information Centres. In the summer, you should always make prior bookings for your first stop; further reservations should be made at the earliest opportunity, before moving on.

SWEDEN

As we have already pointed out, to get acquainted with Sweden if you have only of a few days, you shouldn't try to "see it all", but rather limit yourself to one of its many facets.

Stockholm

If everything you know about Stockholm comes from the occasional postcards you may have received from some of your luckier friends or acquaintences — you're in for a real surprise! Stockholm is one of the most beautiful cities of the world. — Downtown and suburbs, great green parks and ancient palaces and churches; then, when you think you've seen it all, at the next corner a narrow alley beckons, opening on to some surprising, unexpected marvel. You'll also find a long list of "musts": more than 50 museums, some of the most pleasant avenues in Europe, and some of the most eye-catching shop-windows in the world; Enormous department stores, hundreds of restaurants, cafés, night clubs; And wherever you turn, you take in and are taken into the aura of a great civilization, born of a long proud history and secure in its present day achievements and prosperity. All this is reflected in your first impression of the city, the obvious great care with which its streets and parks are so carefully maintained.

History

The strategic importance of the archipelago that protects Lake Mälaren from the Baltic waters was recognized by the Vikings as early as the 11th century, when they built one of their regional fortified ports on those islets. Two centuries later, in 1252, King Birger Jarl made that small town his capital. When the Union of Kalmar brought all of Scandinavia under the sceptre of Queen Margrete of Denmark, Stockholm continued to develop as a seaport, until Gustavus Vasa freed Sweden from the Danish yoke and restored to Stockholm its former status of capital city. In the 17th century during the Swedish wars of conquest, which made of it one of the major powers in Europe, Stockholm assumed the splendour, tastes and size of a great metropolis. Its population increased tenfold in less than one century. The next century was the golden age of building, and many great European architects competed for the honour of building ever grander and more sophisticated palaces in the Swedish capital. During the last two centuries, Stockholm has continued to grow and flourish — today it's a city of more than 1,400,000 people.

SWEDEN

Gamla Stan, the Old City, is eight hundred years old. The Royal Palace stands on the ruins of the old Coronation Palace that was destroyed by fire in 1697.

Topography

Stockholm is built on 14 islands and islets that form the eastern tip of an archipelago composed of no less than 20,000 isles. The main island is Stora Fjäderholmen. The easternmost island, on Lake Mälaren, is the site of Gamla Stan, Stockholm's Old City, and is connected by bridges to the islands of Skeppsholmen and Skansen. The new centre begins at the corner of Kungsgatan and Drotininggatan, crosses the island of Helgeandjholmen to Gamla Stan and to the island of Södermalm.

How to get there

By air: Most of the major international airlines have regular direct flights to Stockholm. The international airport is at Arlanda, about 45 minutes from downtown. The city terminal is at Vasagatan 6-8 (airport buses leave every 10 minutes; the 50 minute ride costs 30SEK). Special *SAS* airport taxis will take you to any address in town for 170-200SEK.

By rail: The Railway Station has train connections to many European capitals and with most major Scandinavian cities. The main entrance is on Vasagatan. At the information desks you may ask for a complete timetable of all Swedish trains, with details of distances, departures and arrivals.

By bus: Several trans-European lines connect Stockholm with all major European capitals. Although the buses are very fast, modern and well equipped, most tourists prefer air or rail travel.

By sea: Two daily ferry crossings connect Stockholm with Helsinki (a 15 hour crossing); another line sails for Turku (also in Finland — 13 hours) and two daily ferries cross to the island of Öland.

The *Viking* line ferries land at the Södermalen pier, south of Gamla Stan. The *Silja* ferries land at Gärdet. Remember that *EuRail* tickets are valid also for the Finish ferries.

A bus line connects Stockholm with Nynäshamm, the landing port of the Gdansk (Poland) ferries (price 380SEK).

By car: All ferry lines carry private vehicles also. The main two

Stockholm highways are the E3 and E4 (north-south bound), the E12 and E18 (east-west bound) and Road 73.

Stockholm's phone prefix is 08.

Tourist services

On the ground floor of the *Sverigehuset*, just opposite the Nordiska department store, is the Main Tourist Information Centre of Stockholm. Here you will find a good map of the city and *Stockholm this Week*, an English publication with lots of tourist information. The staff will assist you with problems like hotel bookings and currency change. The office is open daily, 8am-5pm; tel. 7892000. For specialized information, climb one floor to the Swedish Institute Library where your queries will be answered by the staff. The Tourist Information Centre has branches at the *Stadshuset* (City Hall), at the *Arlanda* Airport, at the railway station and at the TV Tower of the *Djurgården Park*. The *Stockholm Card*, on sale at all Tourist Information Centres entitles you to free transportation on all public urban lines, free entrance tickets to all museums and several other interesting discounts (very convenient at 70SEK for 24 hours, 12 for two days, 175 for three and 230 for four). There might also be other discounted cards or tickets; ask the Tourist Information Centre staff!

The Information Centre for Youth is at Valhallvågen 14 (tel. 6634389). For two months in summer (June 15 to August 15) the centre doubles as a hostel, in addition to its regular information services.

Urban transportation

Convenient cumulative tickets are available at all train, bus and *Tunnelbana* (underground; in short *T-Bana*) stations. The T-Bana is very popular and fast. The stations are marked by large posts, with a blue "T" on a white field. There are three T-Bana lines, and they reach almost all parts of the city. The stations often serve also as modern art galleries — each station has its own style. A map of all three lines and their stops is available at all station entrances and at the Tourist Information Centres; for timetable information, call tel. 236000.

Buses: Bus transportation is considerably slower than the T-Bana; but bus routes are of course much more interesting to the tourist. There is also a special *Touristlinjen*, a circle line with stops at all major tourist sites. Daily cumulative tickets for all bus lines are on sale for 35SEK.

Car hire: Stockholm's three main car-hire agencies are:
Avis: Sveavägen 21, tel. 349910.
Hertz: Master Samuelsgatan 67, tel. 240720.
Europcar: Birger Jarlsgatan 59, tel. 231070.

Taxi: Taxis may be flagged down on route, or called at tel. 150000. They are far from inexpensive, and the driver will expect a 15% tip. The average price of a city trip is around 40SEK.

Bicycle hire: Urban traffic is quite heavy and will generally frighten off most unexperienced cyclists; however, more expert and daring pedallers will be able to make the most of this popular transportation means. Bikes are available at the *Cykelspecialisten Ho.*, Karlsbergsvågen 55, tel. 345758.

Parkings: Car parking is strictly regulated; the instructions are clearly written on the parking posts; parking hours are 8am-6pm. Night parking is forbidden (while the street cleaners get on their job). Illegally parked vehicles are towed to municipal lots (in the suburbs); the fine for releasing them (tel. 542120) is quite stiff. From June to August holders of the **Stockholm Card** are entitled to free (daylight only!) parking in all *Parkeringsbalaget* or *Gatukontoret* zones.

Accommodation

During the summer, Stockholm is not an easy city to find accommodation in, in spite of its many hotels. Do not neglect to book your rooms on time, especially in the high season.

Luxury Hotels — Very Costly
Amaranten: Kungshumsgatan 31, tel. 6541060.
Mälardrottningen: Riddarholmen, tel. 243600, on a luxury yacht.
Royal Viking: Vasagatan 1, tel. 141000; splendid view of Gamla Stan.

Tourist Class Hotels — Costly
Gamla Stan: Lilla Nygatan 25, tel. 244450.
Bema: Upplandsgatan 13B, tel. 232675.
Kom: Döbelnsgatan 17, tel. 235630.
Klara: Gamla Brugatan 25, tel. 112936.

STOCKHOLM

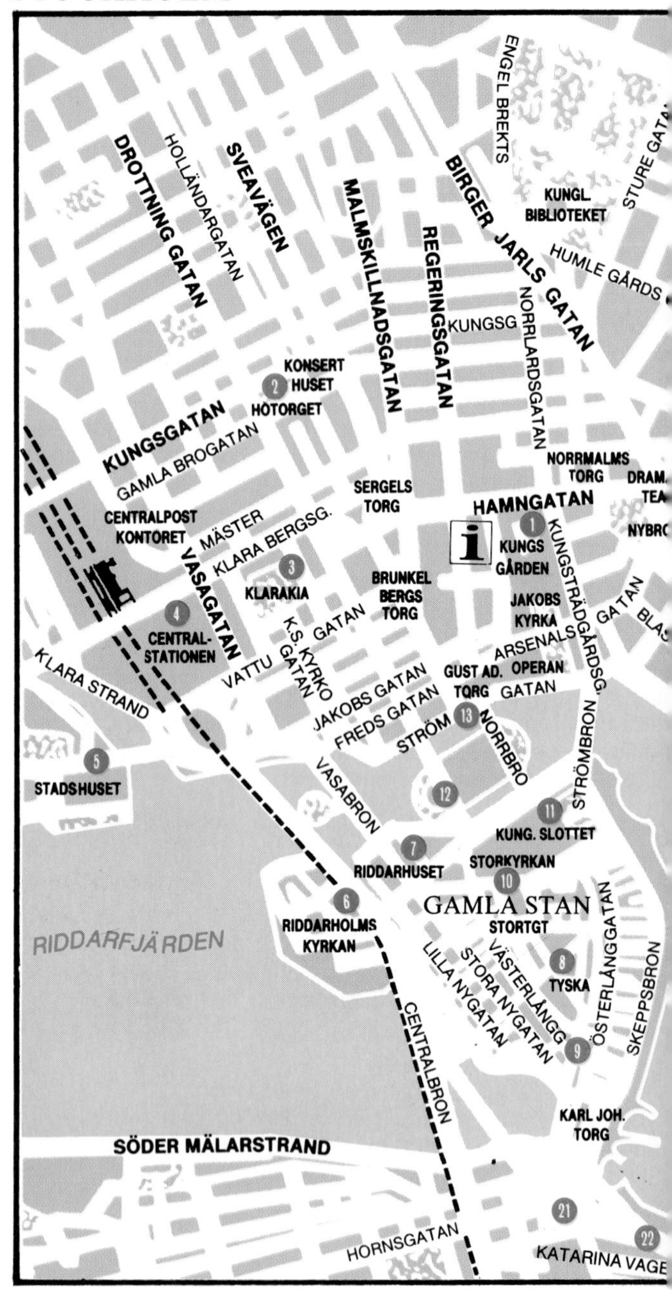

ENGEL BREKTS
STURE GATAN
KUNGL. BIBLIOTEKET
HUMLE GÅRDS
BIRGER JARLS GATAN
DROTTNING GATAN
HOLLÄNDARGATAN
SVEAVÄGEN
MALMSKILLNADSGATAN
REGERINGSGATAN
NORRLARDSGATAN
KUNGSG
KONSERT HUSET
HÖTORGET
KUNGSGATAN
GAMLA BROGATAN
NORRMALMS TORG
SERGELS TORG
HAMNGATAN
CENTRALPOST KONTORET
MÄSTER
KLARA BERGSG.
VASAGATAN
KLARAKIA
BRUNKEL BERGS TORG
KUNGS GÅRDEN
KUNGSTRÄDGÅRDSG.
JAKOBS KYRKA
CENTRAL-STATIONEN
VATTU GATAN
K.S. KYRKO GATAN
ARSENALS GATAN
GUST AD. TORG
OPERAN
GATAN
KLARA STRAND
JAKOBS GATAN
FREDS GATAN
STRÖM
NORRBRO
STRÖMBRON
STADSHUSET
VASABRON
KUNG. SLOTTET
RIDDARHUSET
STORKYRKAN
GAMLA STAN
STORTGT
RIDDARHOLMS KYRKAN
RIDDARFJÄRDEN
LILLA NYGATAN
STORA NYGATAN
VÄSTERLÅNGG
TYSKA
ÖSTERLÅNGGATAN
SKEPPSBRON
CENTRALBRON
KARL JOH. TORG
SÖDER MÄLARSTRAND
HORNSGATAN
KATARINA VAGE

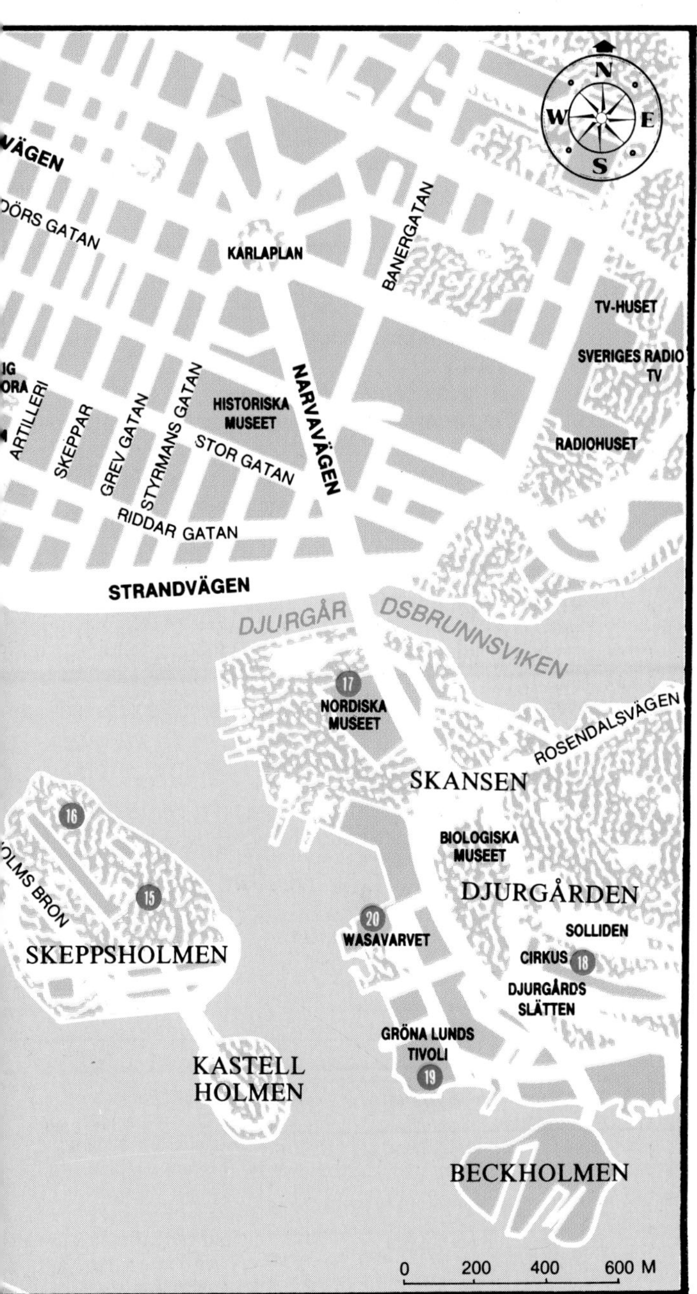
N
W
E
S
VÄGEN
DÖRS GATAN
KARLAPLAN
BANERGATAN
TV-HUSET
SVERIGES RADIO
TV
ARTILLERI
SKEPPAR
GREV GATAN
STYRMANS GATAN
HISTORISKA
MUSEET
NARVAVÄGEN
STOR GATAN
RADIOHUSET
RIDDAR GATAN
STRANDVÄGEN
DJURGÅRDSBRUNNSVIKEN
17
NORDISKA
MUSEET
ROSENDALSVÄGEN
SKANSEN
16
BIOLOGISKA
MUSEET
DJURGÅRDEN
15
20
WASAVARVET
SOLLIDEN
SKEPPSHOLMEN
CIRKUS
18
DJURGÅRDS
SLÄTTEN
GRÖNA LUNDS
TIVOLI
19
KASTELL
HOLMEN
BECKHOLMEN
0
200
400
600 M

SWEDEN

There are hundreds of B&Bs and private residence rooms (prices around 200-250SEK), all listed at the Tourist Information Centres. Some very convenient accommodation are on the Södermalm Island, south of Gamla Stan.

Hostels
Chapman: very pleasant and popular, situated on Skeppsholmen Island, on a ship at anchor not far from the centre. Bookings a must! Tel. 6795015.
Hantverkhuset: in the same neighbourhood, tel. 202506.
Zinken: on Södermalm Island, Pipmakargrand 2, tel. 103107. T-Bana to Zinkensdamn.
Columbus Hotel: an hotel functioning as hostel. Tjärhovsgatan 11, tel. 6441717. T-Bana to Medborgplatsen.

Camp sites
The closest is 10 km out of town.
Bredängs: a seaside camping, south-east of the city, open throughout the year. Trains 13 and 14. Price 40SEK per tent. Tel. 977071.
Flatens: 15 km south-east of the city. Bus 401 to Slussen, tel. 7730100.

There are two campers' parks in town:
Östermalms Idrottsplats, behind the stadium, tel. 102903.
Södermalen: near Eriksdalsbadet, tel. 439118.

Index
1. Tourist Information Centre
2. Foods Market
3. Clara Church
4. The Railway Station
5. City Hall
6. Riddarholmen Church
7. The High Courts of Justice
8. Tyska German Church
9. Järntorget Square
10. The Storkyrkan (Cathedral)
11. The Royal Palace
12. The House of Parliament
13. The Mediterraneum Museum
14. The National Museum
15. The Museum of Modern Art
16. The Far East Museum
17. The Nordic Museum
18. The Skansen Open Air Museum
19. The Tivoli
20. The Vasa Museum
21. The Municipal Museum
22. Catherine Church

The Hotellcentralen (Hotel Booking Centre) is at the Railway Station and it has hundreds of listings at very convenient prices. Often during the summer and at most week-ends there are some very interesting bargains. For more details, call tel. 240880.

Food

Food is quite good, but also very expensive. The best restaurants are downtown. There are also a good number of cafés, pizza-counters and sausage stands where the food is unpretentious but decent. The price of a full restaurant meal varies according to the main dish: a meat dish will cost 100-150SEK; fish "only" 80-120. A spaghetti lunch will limit the damage to 50-80SEK. A half pint of beer costs 35SEK and a bottle of table wine 120SEK.

Luxury Restaurants

Stortorgskällaren: in Gamla Stan, Stortorget 7, tel. 105533. Don't miss it: get in, look around; you'll probably take flight at the sight of the prices on the menu...
Den Gyldene Freden: the oldest restaurant in Sweden: founded eight centuries ago. Of course, in Gamla Stan, Österlånggatan 51, tel. 101259.
Backahästen: Hamngatan 2, tel. 206136. Closed on Monday.
Vau-de-Ville: Hamngatan 17, tel. 212522. French cuisine.

Cheaper Restaurants

Rodolfina: Stora Nygatan 1, tel. 1184971; a rather good Italian eatery.
Zum Franziskaner: Skeppsbron 44, tel. 118330; German cuisine.

Many restaurants offer a fixed price menu (50SEK); look for the *Dagens Rätt* sign.

At the Östermalmshallen market there are several small delicatessen, often equipped also with lunch counters and tables. At *Gerdas*, a fish store, they also offer excellent fried fish dishes. Above *Gerdas*, on the second floor, there is a quite pleasant vegetarian buffet.

There are at least two other vegetarian restaurants: at Lilla Nygatan 12 and at Mäster Samuelsgatan 10 (tel. 112790).

The University cafeteria is open throughout the year.

Stockholm from the Air

Sightseeing in Stockholm

Sightseeing in Stockholm may be divided in two main parts: the (new and old) city — and the suburbs.

You will most probably start from the **Sverigshuset**, at the Main Tourist Information Centre, the right place to equip yourself with maps, pamphlets and other information. Now turn left on Hamngatan, to Sergels Torg, with its glass obelisk and its fountain.

Cross the street and proceed along the pedestrian mall of Drottningatan, where you'll see the **Åhléns** department store. Now you come to the **Hötorget**, Saturday morning's open market. Across the square is also the covered market of

Hötorgetshallen, where you can pause for a cup of coffee or even a snack. On Saturday, of course, both square and market are crowded, and along the street you'll see several street artists and musicians.

Turn back to the Klarabergsgatan corner, and follow that street to **Clara Kyrka** (Clare Church), a characteristic 18th century structure. The statue that stands before the church, and the tomb in its courtyard honour the memory of two Swedish poets.

Next, on Vasagatan, you'll see the Railway Station. Your next, stop, past the station and across the bridge, is the **Stadshuset** Palace (City Hall, built 1923), an outstanding example of modern architecture, from which you'll enjoy a splendid view of the gulf and of Gamla Stan.

Recross the bridge. On your left you'll see the pier used by the tourist motorboats sailing for the Drottningholm Royal Palace and other Lake Mäleren sites.

Proceed to Vasabron, a pedestrian bridge not far from the pier, and you'll find yourself on Riddarholmen (Knights Island). On your right stands the **Riddarsholmkyrkan**, an ancient 14th century church, that was once the chapel of a Franciscan monastery and the burial ground of the Kings of Sweden. Turn your eyes toward City Hall for a view of the sites you have just seen, but from a different perspective.

Gamla Stan (The Old City)

The next bridge takes you to Gamla Stan. The palace on your left is the **Riddarhuset** (Noble House), undoubtedly one of the most beautiful palaces in Stockholm. This 17th century Dutch Barock palace is today the seat of the Supreme Court but houses also a permanent exhibiton of 2,000 ancient armours (open Mon.-Fri., 11.30am-12.30pm).

Follow the main street of the Gamla Stan, **Västerlånggatan**, with its elegant cafés, luxury shops and night clubs (you'll be able to appreciate them more fully during a night tour). The side streets you'll cross along the Västerlånggatan are very inviting, and well worth a detour; and don't worry, there is no risk of getting lost.

During these detours you'll find the **Post Museum** and the **Tyska Kyrkan** (a church). This is the centre of Stockholm's luxury shopping, around Gamla Stan main streets. If the weather is good, you'll hear the sounds of various musical instruments from the open windows of several palaces; after school hours, the neighbourhood children come to play in the Cathedral gardens. The main street ends at **Järntorget** Square, with the statue of Sweden's national poet, Evert Taube.

Make a U-turn to the **Österlånggatan**, near St. George's monument (a replica of the original, which is in the Storkyrkan). Follow Köpmangatan to **Stortorget** Square. This is the site of the famous "Stockholm Blood Bath" of 1520 that gave Gustavus Vasa the final motive to rebel against the Danish yoke. The square is a characteristic example of Medieval architecture, to be admired conveniently (weather pemitting) from one of the tables of its open-air café.

Proceed now along Trångsund St., to admire briefly the

Storkyrkan, the church where the Royal Family celebrates its wedding and coronation ceremonies. Originally built in 1306, this church was completely restored toward the end of the 15th century; its Barock style is, of course, much later and was completed in 1730. Its interiors are more impressive and elegant than its exterior, and along its walls are several important art works.

After crossing the parking space reserved for tourist buses you'll find yourself at the **Kungliga Slottet** (Royal Palace). The ceremony of the **Changing of the Guard** takes place at midday; when members of the Royal Family are in residence, the ceremony is conducted with great pomp. The palace itself is a splendid example of the Northern style charcteristic of the 18th century. It was built in 1760 by Tessin the younger, on the site of the ancient **Tre Kroner** (Three Crowns) fortress, that was destroyed by fire during the reign of Carl XII. Its interiors are in obvious Baroque and Rococo styles, and in its halls there are several museums and exhibits (entrance free to *Stockholm Card* owners). Opening hours vary from season to season and sometimes even from day to day; but if you find it locked, most probably the guard will open for you at least the Hall of Arms.

In this hall the assassination of King Gustav III is commemorated, and among the exhibits you'll see the assassin's weapons and the King's blood-stained tunic. The best chance to find everything open is midday — when you'll also be able to enjoy the Change of the Guard: at that hour it's a fair bet that both museums and the Hall of Arms will be open. In any case, try to keep some energy for the rest of the itinerary, and stop for at least a brief rest to take in the view of the lake, with the reflection of the palaces in its waters.

Having rested your legs, you'll be ready for another round in Gamla Stan's alleys, coming gradually closer to the lake; particularly after sunset, the view of the lake, the lighted palaces and the captivating shop windows form an unforgettable harmonious unity.

Reenter the New City crossing the **Norrbro** Bridge. On your left you'll see the **Riksdagshuset** (House of Parliament, daily guided visits at noon). On your right you'll have the **Stromparterren** Gardens.

The Norrbro Bridge ends at Gustav Adolph Square, with the Foreign Ministry building and the **Medelhausmuseet** (Museum of the Mediterranean), where you'll find a rich collection of

Egyptian objects and relics from Cyprus, Greece and other Middle Eastern regions; opening hours 11am-4pm; closed on Monday and Tuesday, entrance 10SEK.

Further on to your right stands the Opera House, with its attractive garden café.

If you're not too tired, turn right, following Stromgatan, the lakeside lane, to the **Nationalmuseet** (National Museum), where you'll find quite a few Rembrandts, Renoirs, and many other great names from the last five centuries. Its halls are decorated with period furniture belonging to the Royal Family. Another attraction is the vast collection of ancient Russian icons. Opening hours are 10am-4pm; during the summer there are frequent free concerts. The bridge you'll see beyond the museum crosses over to **Skeppsholman Island**.

Skeppsholman

Along the pier leading from downtown Stockholm to Skeppsholman is moored a sailing ship, which is in fact a vast youth hostel. Passing the ship, you'll reach the museums for which that island is famous. In front of the **Moderna Museet** (Museum of Modern Art) is a spacious statuary, sided by an attractive café and an open-air summer restaurant. Most of the museum is dedicated to Picasso and his Swedish students. Other schools are also represented, and a few halls are reserved for different temporary exhibitions. The building is an interesting example of modern architecture, so that the form reflects the value of the contents. The regular summer concerts at the Museum are one of the major musical attractions in Stockholm; at lunchtime scores of local artists leave their Skeppsholman ateliers, to get together in the bohemian museum restaurant. The museum is open Tues.-Fri. 11am-9pm, and on week-ends 11am-5pm; closed on Monday. Entrance 20SEK (students 10SEK; free under 16) on Thursday the entrance is free.

There are several other museums on the island; we'll mention two of them: the **Östasiatiska** (Museum of Far Eastern Antiquities), with its rare Chinese and Indian collections (open 12am-4.30pm; Tuesday until 9pm; closed on Monday; entrance 10SEK) — and the **Arts Museum**, situated just across the Royal Palace, near the National Museum, on the island side of the bridge (open 10am-4pm; Tuesday until 9pm; closed on Monday; entrance 20SEK).

Metropolitan Stockholm

You'll begin this itinerary by boarding a motorboat for a tour of the lake. Its leisurely pace will let you enjoy some of the best views of the city, while you keep your strength for the visit to the sites, parks and museums that follow.

Start your walk from **Djurgården** (the Garden Islånd), situated south of Gamla Stan. It may be reached by the 44 bus from Karlaplan, or by the 47 from Nybroplan.

The commercial centres of Normalm and Ostermalm may be either the first or the last step of your walk. The neighbouring parks can only be visited on foot; take your time and follow your instincts.

Djurgården

If you've crossed the bridge to the island, you'll be standing in front of the **Nordiska Museet** (Nordic Museum), whose halls contain several collections of art objects characteristic of the northern civilizations; it is probably the only museum to deciate one of its halls exclusively to the history of the **Sami** tribes (s. p. 22, "The Sami Tribes"). The museum is open Mondays and Tuesdays 10am-4pm, and on week-ends 12am-5pm.

Follow Djurgårdenvagen Avenue to the **Museum of Biology** (open 10am-4pm) and to the **Skansen**, the vast open air museum that is the island's major attraction. It contains 150 buildings reproducing faithfully the daily life, traditions and national customs of Sweden: old windmills and farms, ancient pubs and the timeless **kota** (tents) of the Sami. Other buildings serve as handiwork centres, where the visitor is invited to see the artisans at work (and, to buy their artistic creations). Finally, there is also a small zoo, whose main attractions are the monkeys and snakes — and its vast aquarium. If after a few hours of wandering through the Skansen you feel the need to rest your legs, you could enjoy its restaurant and café. The museum is open from May to the end of August, 8am-11.30pm; from September to the end of April, only until 6pm. Entrance 12SEK.

Cross the avenue, and here is the **Gröna Lunds Tivoli** a well equipped amusement park, whose attractions are almost never as crowded as those of the Tivolis of Copenhagen or Göteborg. It opens daily 11am-5pm; during the summer, from May to September, it remains open until midnight. Entrance 20SEK.

If you'd rather have a change of atmosphere to something more restful and quiet, follow the arrows to **Villa Rosendals**, an elegant villa built in 1823 for Queen Desirée, with a splendid view of the lake; for information about its opening hours, inquire at the Tourist Information Centre.

Your next stop will be at the **Wasavarvet** (Wasa Museum), just behind the Tivoli, at the western end of the island. At its entrance are the 44 bus stop and the landing of the Skeppsbron and the (summer only) Nybroplan ferries.

The history of this museum is no less enticing than its collections: the admiral ship, Wasa, had barely left harbour for her maiden voyage in 1628 when she suddenly and shamelessly sank in the middle of the Gulf of Stockholm. For three centuries the misfortunate admiral ship enjoyed an undisturbed if undeserved rest on the muddy bottom of the gulf, until in 1961 King Adolph II had it recovered, refloated and transformed in a museum. Thus, the Wasa stands today at its pier, recovering at least some of its glory from the homage paid by thousands of daily visitors of all ages. It's open throughout the year, 10am-6pm. Entrance 15SEK.

About one kilometre north of the island, on the Frihamn islet, close by its piers, is the **Jewish Museum** of the Jewish Community of Stockholm. Open Wednesday and Sunday, 12am-5pm.

On the way to the Jewish Museum you'll see the **Kaknästornet** (TV Tower) — the tallest building in Sweden (155 m high). From its upper terrace there is an incomparable view of the city and even of the whole archipelago. The terrace has, of course, its own café and restaurant, a souvenir shop and a small branch of the Tourist Information Centre (open 9am-12pm).

Södermalm

The next island on your route is Södermalm, easily reached from Gamla Stan, through a bridge leading to **Södermalmstorg** Square and the **Stadsmuseet** (Towns Museum). This Baroque style palace (1685) by Tessin used to be the seat of the local aministration for the quarter. Today it houses the museum of Stockholm's history. Open 11am-5pm; entrance 10SEK. The majestic church adjacent to the museum is the **Katarina Kyrka**, that was restored two centuries ago in Renaissance style. It contains the remains of the victims of the "Stockholm Blood Bath". This is one of the poorest neighbourhoods of Stockholm, and in its homes there are hundred of rooms to let for very convenient prices (details at the Tourist Information Centre).

Other sites

Here is a list of several museums well worthy of a visit:

Museum of Architecture: Skeppsholmen, entrance 15SEK.
Dance Museum: Laboratoriegatan 14, near the Anglican Church. With filmed documentaries. Bus 68; entrance 10SEK.
Carl Aldo Museum: An exclusive gallery of Aldo's works. Lögebodvägen 10; buses 43 or 53; entrance 10SEK.
Ethnografic Museum: Djygårdjbrunnsvägen, bus 68; entrance 10SEK.
Hallwyll Museum: The private collection of the Duchess of Hallwyll; guided visits; Hamngatan 4, entrance 12SEK.
Lljevalch Art Gallery: Djugården, a modern art gallery with transient shows. Inquire at the Tourist Information Centre. 15SEK.
Puppet Theatre Museum: Kungstådgarden; a collection of 4,000 puppets.

If you wish to have a longer list of various Stockholm museums, ask for it at the Tourist Information Centre.

Entertainment

Stockholm is indeed a metropolitan city, and in the *Stockholm This Week* magazine you'll find long lists of all types of evening shows, entertainment and cultural programmes. Tickets may be purchased through the Tourist Information Centres, at the cash boots or at the Norrmalstorg square kiosk. For gala spectacles and for the most popular shows tickets should be booked at the earliest opportunity. Inquire about discounted tickets (for students, senior citizens or just any tourist).

There are scores of cafés, nightclubs and pubs all throughout the city; they are thickest, of course, at Gamla Stan. There are several spots where you may combine entertainment with supper, for instance, at the *Café Art* of Våsterlanggatan and at the *Stampen*, of Stora Nygatan, both easily found by following the sounds and streams of hurrying youth, or at the more sedate *Daily News Café* or across the square, at the *Vau-de-Ville*.

Stockholm summer nights are most lively around the Skansen and the Tivoli, or in Södermalm, with its many eateries (e.g.

the *Fryshuset* of Tegelviksvägen 19-23 and the *Café Pan* of Götagatan 27).

Cinema: Films are a very popular form of entertainment, although rather costly (45SEK). There are several cinemas along the Kungsgatan; the programmes are listed in all dailies and in *Stockholm This Week*.

Shopping

The centre of the New Town is a shopper's paradise — and a challenge to the addicted to department stores. There are incomparable collections of modern furniture and crystal objects (two mainstays of Swedish consumer industries). Shopwindows are always very attractive and meticulously organised. Prices, alas, are what they are. Even accounting for VAT returns (10-15%) at the end of your visit, they remain very high indeed.

The best department stores are the *Nordiska Companiet* (across the street from the Tourist Information Centre). But don't disregard also the *Gallerian* or the *Åhléns*, both also on Sergels Torg.

On Hötorget Square there is a flea-market, just opposite a very attractive roofed market. The luxury shops of Gamla Stan will probably frighten you off with their prices.

A 20 minute ride by car or on T-Bana will take you to the **Loppmarknaden**, the vastest flea-market in all Scandinavia. Prices are moderate, and there is just about everything in the world; in any case, markets hounds will enjoy several hours of leisurely sightseeing, and perhaps also unearth some unexpected bargain.

The Suburbs

After several days of energetic walks, you will probably enjoy the ease of a... sitting tour.

Drottningholm

Drottingholm's Royal Palace, 11 km out of town, is one of the most spectacular works of the Tessin dinasty of 17th century architects. It dates from the second half of that century, and

Downtown Stockholm's busy pedestrian mall

was built by Queen Eleanor, Carl X's widow. Tessin the Elder designed a Versailles of the North for her; Tessin the Younger introduced, in his father's designs, elements of British style. This mélange is reflected also in the gardens, and the result pleased the royal family so well that they made of this palace their permanent residence.

One of the great halls of the palace is sometimes open to the public as a concert and theatre hall (for information, ask at the Tourist Information Centre).

The palace may be reached by ferry (from the City Hall piers) or by rail (alighting at Brommaplan and proceeding by bus 301). We strongly recommend the alternative of a guided tour (inquire at the Tourist Information Centres) that will lead you throughout the interiors and the wonderful grounds of the palace. Open May-September 11am-4.30pm, week-ends 12am-3pm.

The Archipelago

Many archipelago islands and islets become during the summer and on week-ends crowded resorts, frequented by thousands of Stockholmites. The *Inter Skerries Card* is a cumulative travel ticket, valid for 16 days of wandering among the isles of the archipelago. It costs barely 130SEK, and is on sale at all Tourist Information Centres, where one can also get a selection of pamphlets and other information material about the region.

For a one-day tour, start at the **Vaxholm** Fort, which in earlier centuries served as a fortress defending the entrance to Stockholm harbour. Today it houses a museum.

Then you might go on to the 13th century iron mines of Utö, to the village of Norrtälje and to the fishermen's cove of Grisslehamn. You might then cross to Birka, Sweden's oldest town, built upon a 10th century Viking fort.

To really enjoy this tour you'll need the luck of a sunny day; in any case, don't forget to get, before embarking, a full timetable of all ferries and opening hours of the sites you'll want to see.

In the archipelago there are also several accommodation opportunities: in hostels, camp sites and also some private residences.

Important addresses and phone numbers

Red Cross emergency: tel. 6449200.
24 hours pharmacy: *Scheele*, Klarabergsgatan 64, tel. 248280.
Police, Ambulance and Firemen, tel. 90000.
Laundries: Sturegatan 4 and St. Eriksgatan 97.
Lost and Found: in train, tel. 7622000; police, tel. 7693075.
Poste Restante: Vasagatan 28-34, tel. 7812055.
International Phone Calls: Skeppsbron 2, tel. 100939 — or at the Railway Station, tel. 106439.

Embassies

United States: Stranvågen 101, tel. 7835300.
Britain: Skarpögatan 6-8, tel. 6670140.
Australia: Sergels Torg 12, tel. 6132900.

North of Stockholm

While many tourists tend to neglect Stockholm's northern approaches, preferring to turn to the more civilized, westernized forests and beaches of the south, it's worth making at least one brief dash northward, to **Uppsala** — less than one hour away from the capital.

There are also a few sights to be seen on the Uppsala road. The first is **Sigtuna**, founded almost a thousand years ago by King Olof Skötkonung, Sweden's first Christian king. Sigtuna's glory was short-lived, and only two centuries later, in 1187, Sigtuna was razed to the ground — walls, fortified churches and houses — by the Vikings.

Fifteen kilometres north of Sigtuna you'll see **Skokloster**, a Baroque 17th century castle, that finally became State property after changing hands several times. It houses the Swedish Imperial Art Museum, a collection of vintage cars and a recreation centre. Near the castle there is also a 14th century chapel.

The castle may be reached from Uppsala by ferry. In the summer, after landing, you'll be invited to join one of the hourly guided tours that begin at the parking lot before moving to the castle itself.

Uppsala

The approaches to Uppsala, either by road or by train, are spectacular: you will never forget the first sight of its skyline: palaces, the cathedral, the University campus, the canal, the crowds of students on their bikes and the winding alleys of this old aristocratic town.

At the Tourist Information Centre (Frystorg 8, tel. 018-274820) you'll find a wide selection of maps and written material, a list of accommodation, booking services and a bicycle hire desk.

Uppsala hosts various summer cultural programmes and

The interior of Uppsala's Cathedral

conventions; all details are available at the Tourist Information Centre.

History

Uppsala's history and its origins are a mixture of history and legend. The Svear tribe settled here almost twenty centuries ago. One of its chieftains, the legendary Aun, claimed in the 5th century to have signed a pact with his gods, by which he would live forever, as long as he sacrificed, every nine years, one of his sons to the gods (a sacrifice which very conveniently eliminated also the direct claimants to his throne...). Be as it may, the poor man finally ran out of sons, and thus ended his life.

Ancient Uppsala was in fact one of the main religious centres of the Svear, and its people used to regularly attend its two major sanctuaries of Frö and Njord (the two father-gods of the king, and vassals of the father-god of all gods, Thor).

The tombs of the ancient Svear kings are at Gamla, north of the centre of the city.

The pagan sanctuaries and temples of Uppsala were razed to the ground at the beginning of the 13th century, after the whole tribe converted to Christianity. Upon their ruins rose Sweden's first great Cathedral, and Uppsala became the seat of a new Archbishopric. In 1245 the wooden cathedral was destroyed by fire, and the famous French architect Bonneuill was charged with construction of a new cathedral, much wider and richer than the former.

The great fire of 1543 destroyed the whole of the Old Town on the east side of the river. King Gustavus Vasa undertook the rebuilding of the town, around a new, even more prestigious cathedral, and all Uppsala's citizens joined in the effort. The new cathedral was consecrated to St. Eric, the national saint, Patron of Sweden.

King Gustavus Vasa also built, in 1549, the Red Fortress, erected as a defensive rampart, close to the cathedral. After the king's death, in 1567, all members of the royal family were put to death within the Red Fortress. Barely a century later, in 1654, Queen Christina celebrated in Uppsala's cathedral her return to the Catholic Church.

The famous University of Uppsala was founded in 1620, together with the Gustavianuin Palace, with its onion shaped dome. Uppsala was the alma mater of many famous 17th century scientists, including Olaf Rudbeck, the anatomist who discovered the lymphatic system and its functions. The Uppsala University Library, which was at one of the most important libraries in Europe, survived miraculously the great fire of 1702. Rudbeck himself was among the library's rescuers. This legendary Renaissance man was, in fact, not only an outstanding anatomist, but also an architect (creator of the onion shaped dome of the Gustavianuin) and captain of Uppsala's fire brigade. After this second fire, the reconstruction of Uppsala was a long affair that took more than a century. The majority of Uppsala's present day buildings belong to the second half of the last century.

Uppsala has a population of close to 150,000 people. It is mainly a university town, with several ancillary research establishments in its suburbs.

What to see

A superficial visit to Uppsala requires only a few hours on foot or by bike. The first step, as usual, will be at the local Tourist Information Centre. The second is the **Domkyrkan** (the Cathedral), a structure in French Gothic style, very similar to the Trondheim Basilica (in Norway) but considerably larger. The statues and the frescoes of the interior describe the life of St. Eric, whose remains are buried in the central chapel, not far from the royal tombs of Gustavus Vasa and his son Johannes III, and that of the famous botanist Linnaeus.

At the **Textiles Museum** there is a rare collection of ancient fabrics; in one of its halls are preserved the garments of the members of the royal family who were slain in 1567 at the Red Castle Massacre of Sture.

Facing the Cathedral is the onion shaped dome of the **Gustavianuin**, with, on its upper floor, the old 17th century **Operating Theatre**.

The lower floors house no less than three museums: the Museum of Ancient Egypt, the Archeology Museum and the Ancient History Museum. A little further on you'll see the **University Building**, a Renaissance style palace. It is always crowded with students, but in May, during the graduation ceremonies, it attracts thousands and thousands of people. Within its walls there is a University dining room and a vast gallery of sculptures and portraits.

Behind the University gardens you'll see the impressive **Carolina Rediviva Palace**, the seat of the great Uppsala University Library, with more than 80,000 metres of bookshelves, covered with several million volumes, including the famous **Silver Bible** (handwritten in gold ink in a Gothic translation in the year 520), the original Mozart manuscript of the Magic Flute and a great number of outstanding old maps.

Follow the riverside lane, crossing the river to Linnegatan, and you'll reach the **Linnaeus Gardens** (which are at their best toward the end of July). These are the University's first botanical gardens, extablished by the great Linn*us himself.

Turn back toward the centre, passing through what is today mostly a students' quarter. The ancient Red Castle is not open to visitors, and neither are its grounds.

Wandering along the alleys of Uppsala, don't forget to visit some of its colourful old cafés and student eateries; if you are the bearer of a *student card*, this is the right place to put it to good use.

The *Sagan* motorboat provides ferry service to and from the Skokloster Castle. At the castle you'll be able to return to Stockholm by rail, or to board the Stockholm boat, that stops also at Sigtuna.

The 700 bus goes from the centre of Uppsala to **Gamla Uppsala**, the Old City with the burial grounds of the Svea Kings (6th century v.e.). The little chapel was erected upon the site of the ancient altar of the Svear human sacrifices.

Food and accommodation

The restaurants in the luxury hotels are particularly expensive, but all through town you'll be able to find many good and convenient eateries. *Barnowick* is an excellent vegetarian restaurant, very close to the castle. On the riverside lanes there are several cafés and restaurants.

Near St. Eric's Square is the renowned *Åkanten* restaurant.

For overnight accommodation, inquire at the Tourist Information Centre. Should you prefer to make your bookings in advance, here is a brief list of recommended hotels:
Hotel Svea: central; a double room for 300-500SEK. Tel. 018-130030.
Hotel Elit: pleasant and inexpensive: 250-300SEK only. Tel. 018-130345.

There are two hostels:

Sunnersta Herrgård: 6 km south of town, summers only, tel. 018-324220.
Fritidsgarden Gläntan: 2 km south of town, tel. 018-108060.

Both hostels are serviced by buses 6 and 7.

SWEDEN

NORTHERN SWEDEN

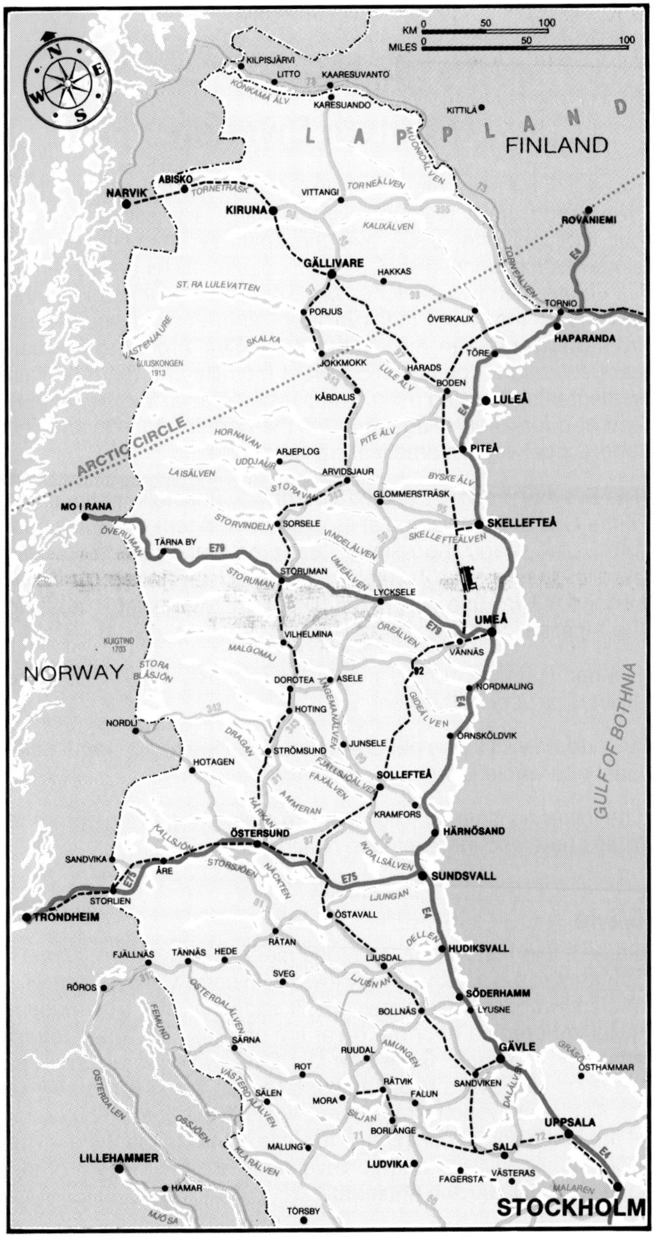

To the Norrland — Northern Sweden

Sweden's northern regions, from Gävle to the extreme north of Haparanda, have uniform characteristics: a relatively densely populated coastal plain, and the sparsely inhabited eastern slopes of the Norwegian Alps. The coastal towns are generally little more than two centuries old. The major centres are at the mouths of the rivers that run from north-east to south-west, from the Norwegian Alps to the Baltic Sea. From those urban centres several roads climb toward the hills and the mountain settlements, crossing rivers and passing glacial lakes until they end at a forsaken village or cross the border into Norway. The tundra inbetween is practically a wasteland.

The two major arteries are the E4 highway (that follows the coast of the Gulf of Bothnia and at its extreme northern end turns east into Finland) and the railway (that runs along a more or less parallel line, into the hinterland, about 20 km from the sea). A second railway line covers the lake district northward, crossing the Alps into Norway, to Narvik.

Sweden is a big country, and the *EuRail Pass*, which is valid for all lines, is very convenient.

An indepth visit to the parks and forests of the region requires at least one whole week.

The following itinerary follows the E4 coastal highway, with short forays here and there into the hinterland.

Gävle

Gävle is the first sizable town one meets along the E4, north of Stockholm. It is a 15th century town, with narrow alleys lined with ancient wooden residences, you'll suddenly see two modern buildings erected after the great fire of 1869. The main tourist attraction is **Gamle Gefle** (the Old City), which is a replica of the original. Gävle's most famous son was Joe Hill, a martyr of the American workers' movement, who left this town in his teens at the beginning of our century to settle in the United States. The story of his odyssey and achievements are the subject of the local **Joe Hill Gården Museum**.

Gävle has several other museums: **Silvanum** is a museum of afforestation; the **Railway Museum** documents the history of Swedish railways. At the Tourist Information Centre (Stortorget, tel. 026-101600) you'll find lots of detailed information, including lists of rooms in private residences and in hotels. The hostel (tel. 026-121745) is in the heart of the Old City.

Dalarna

Road 80 leaves Gävle toward the west, crossing the picturesque Dalarna region.

The road crosses **Falun**, an old copper mining town. Then it comes to **Rättvik**, a small cultural centre, rich of local history museums. It has a Tourist Information Centre (tel. 0248-10916), a hostel (tel. 0248-10566) and a camp site (tel. 0248-11691). Rättvik is situated on the western coast of the charming **Siljan Lake**, a very popular summer resort famous for several cultural events, based in the **Leksand** village (Tourist Information Centre, tel. 0247-80300).

East of the lake is the district capital of **Mora**, situated on the railway line that runs northward to the great parks and national forests.

Söderham

The E4 proceeds northward, crossing **Ljusne** — a local salmon fishing centre — and comes to **Söderham**, a town built by King Gustav Adolph in the 17th century. For more than a century, Söderham was considered an important strategic centre, and its **Ulrika Eleonora Church** is one of the most beautiful in all Sweden. From the upper platform of the **Oskarborg Tower** you'll have an outstanding sight of the whole town and its picturesque countryside. Kvarnen, once an important milling center, is today a small tourist resort, built around its exhibition centre and restaurant.

Hudiksvall

Further northward you'll come to **Hudiksvall**, a small 16th century town, which for three centuries has been one the country's major centres of the wood industry. Its church still bears the signs of a naval bombardment launched by the Russian navy at the beginning ot the 18th century. The Old City is very well preserved; its alleys lead to several wooden bridges, crossing the canal to end at the fishermen's piers and the regional fish market.

The Dalarna Lakes

At the Tourist Information Centre (tel. 0650-13920) you'll find all the usual information and assistance. The **Halsingland Museum** is deep in Fiskarstan (the fishermen's quarter), behind the Stadshotellet (Town Hall).

During the first week in July, Hudiksvall hosts a Music Festival, when accommodation is considerably **cheaper**: Bed and breakfast at the best hotels costs little more than a night at the hostel. However, the hotel rooms must be booked in advance!

Sundsvall

Going northward, 82 km past Hudiksvall on the E4 you'll reach **Sundsvall**, a small modern model town, rebuilt on the ruins of its old wooden houses, destroyed by fire in 1888. In fact, the greatest innovator in northern Swedish building has been fire; of course, there has been much human suffering in the process and much of the original charm of the old towns has been lost forever.

This process is well evidenced here, along **Storgatan Avenue** and in **Stortorget Square**, with their neat, elegant residential condos and the attractive shopwindows that open along the pedestrian malls. Even the Sundsvall Civic Museum is dedicated mostly to the rebuilding of the town after the fire that consumed it almost one hundred years ago. Even the **Gustav Adolf Kyrkan**, the proudest church in town, was subject to the same process.

The local Tourist Information Centre is, of course, on the main square (tel. 060-114235). Sundsvall is an important railway and road junction and the Vaasa (Finland) ferries land.

The *Sundsvall Hotel* (Esplanaden 29, tel. 060-171600) is probably the best in town, and is equipped with restaurant, dance hall and sauna. There are two hostels: *Norra Stadsberg* (tel. 060-112119, with camp sites) and the *YMCA* (tel. 060-113535), situated near the church.

West of Sundsvall

Östersund

Highway E14 and a railway line start westward from Sundsvall, to cross the Norwegian Alps, ending at Trondheim, in Norway. About 185 km off Sundsvall, both the highway and the railway reach Östersund, the major centre in this back country. Östersund lies along the coast of **Lake Storsjön**, one of the richest fishing grounds in Sweden. All around the lake there are several small resorts and fishermen's hamlets, very easily reached from Östersund. In the great **Jamtli Park** you'll find a charming open-air museum of the local fauna, traditions and daily life (open 11am-6pm, entrance 15SEK). Within the park there is a hostel, and along the lake you'll find several B&Bs and camp sites.

Beyond the lake, along the E14, you'll come to **Åre**, one of Sweden's most popular winter sport centres. Wintersport buffs will be happy to learn that its hotels often offer attractive discounts.

In fact the winter resort also functions also during the summer; take a ride on one of its cable cars for a breathtaking view from the mountaintops. The local Tourist Information Centre (tel. 0647-50010) will provide you with the usual information and services. The hostel (tel. 0647-70138) and the camp site (tel. 0647-51100) are very good.

From Sundsvall to Umeå

Back in Sundsvall, follow the E4 northward for 30 km to **Härnösänd** (you'll be able to reach Härnösänd also from

Östersund, following Road 87). Coming from the hinterland, on Lake Ångerman, you'll find **Sollefteå**, a small tourist lakeside resort. You'll find little else of interest until you come to Umeå.

Umeå

Umeå is immediately recognized as by its hordes of young people busily pedalling along on their bicycles. The local Tourist Information Centre is at Remmarkstorget Square (tel. 090-161616) and it has all the usual services, including accommodation lists and, next door, a bicycle hire agency.

The **Ume Ålv** River is Umeå's lifeline and the main local tourist attraction. The **Gammlia** is a centre of museums and exhibition halls; its open-air museum has about 20 very interesting ancient residences. At the **Västerbotten**, near the open-air museum, the history of the region is presented by means of a pleasant audio-visual programme. The complex is open Mon.-Fri. 9am-6pm and on week-ends 12am-6pm. You'll need at least three hours to see and enjoy it all.

The town's most interesting sites are City Hall, the church and the university campus. A not very comfortable dirt lane leads to a rocky wall decorated with some interesting 30-century old graffiti, and to an impressive hydro-electric complex. The route is indicated on the Tourist Information Centre maps.

Food and accommodation

The best accommodation is to be found in private residences through the Tourist Information Centre. The hostel (tel. 090-194300, summer only) is close to the university campus' Alidhem Centrum. The closest camp site is 5 km from town, on the E4 (tel. 090-161660, bus 2). The best, but rather expensive hotel is the *Blå Dragonen* (Norrlandsgatan 5, tel. 090-132380).

On the main street there are several pizza and sausage counters; the vegetable and fruit market is in the City Hall Square.

Local night life is strictly connected with college life. The best spots are *Kafe Postell* (Renmarkstorget) and *Scharinska Villan*, near the church. The *Krogan Disco* of the hostel remains open all night long.

A ferry service joins Umeå with Vaasa, in Finland.

Westward on E79, the "Bla Vagen" (Blue Road)

Turn westward once again from the E4, climbing along the River

Ume on the E79, to the Vasterbotten, a colourful region of Alpine lakes. The folklore of its people is no less fascinating than its lakes.

The E79 leaves Umeå to Vännas and to **Lycksele**, with its polar zoo and its open-air museum, the **Gammelplatsen**. Then it proceeds to **Storuman**, where you'll find a Tourist Information Centre (tel. 0951-10500) and a hostel (tel. 0951-11358).

Further on is **Tärnaby**, a winter-sports resort and the starting point of several outstanding summer alpine walks. The **Samegården** museum provides a good introduction to the whole region. Both museum and hostel (tel. 0954-10420) are open only during the summer, 11am-6pm.

Here the E79 crosses the border into Norway, to Mo-i-rana.

Skellefteå

Don't give in to the temptation to proceed northward by rail or by Road 343 (from Storuman), and turn back to Umeå and the E4 to Skellefteå. Passing through **Lövanger**, observe the little wooden residences along the beach — 300-year old summer bungalows (some of which are still available for rent to tourists). 40 km north of Lövanger, on the river bank, rises Skellefteå, one of the major tourist attractions in Northern Sweden. This town has a rather curious origin: it was founded by King Magnus Erikson in 1324, to serve as a compulsory retreat for Christians. Soon, around the local church grew a pleasant and prosperous little town.

The Tourist Information Centre is on Storgatan 46 (tel. 0910-58880). The **church** is very interesting, because of its contents and because of its age. Pace along the town's winding alleys until you happen to reach the open-air museum, which reproduces the first century of the town's life; at one of the riverbank piers you'll be able to hire a canoe, and row up and down to some of the river islets.

Skellefteå is very well equipped to provide every tourist's whim all year long. Its hotels often offer very attractive discounts. The hostel (tel. 0910-37283) has several convenient family bungalows. A second hostel (tel. 0914-10944) is rather far out of town; the camp site (tel. 0910-18855) is much closer.

Skellefteå is an important road and railway junction, with ferry connections for Finland. Road 95 leads through parks and forests toward the north-west, while the E4 goes on along the seashore to Luleå.

Luleå

Luleå grew gradually around its old medieval church and its open-air market of **Gammelstad** (the Old City), until it was granted urban status in 1621. Later the town expanded toward its harbour, 10 km east of the Old City. However, the people of Luleå refused to abandon their old homes and turned their backs to the New City. Repeated fires and Cossack incursions made things even more difficult for the New City. The exciting history of the town during the last three centuries is illustrated at the local museum.

Today Luleå has overcome most of its old problems, and is a lively university town. At the end of July the whole population partakes in the student festival, that ends in a great parade along the Storgatan. For guidance, bikes and information, turn to the Tourist Information Centre (tel. 0920-93746). The new Cathedral has replaced various earlier structures, repeatedly gutted by fire. Weather permitting, in the summer you might make the most of the spectacular Gültzauudden beach.

Gammelstad

Gammelstad may be reached from Luleå by bus 22 (last run, 9.30pm). Its ancient church is still surrounded by several old wooden houses — and by 15 museums. The site gets particularly crowded at the time of its frequent religious ceremonies. The old harbour, in the Gulf of Gammelstad (at 3 km from the village), has been transformed in a seabird reserve, that often attracts hundreds of bird-watchers.

Food and accommodation

Luxury hotels

SAS Hotel: Storgatan 17, tel. 0920-94000.
Scandic Hotel: Mjölkudden — tel. 0920-28360.

Economy Hotels

Aveny: tel. 0920-21820.
Park: tel. 0920-11149.

A hostel (tel. 0920-93264) and a camp site are located north of the village.

Approaching Finland

The E4 proceeds north-eastward to the Finnish border, not far from the town of Haparanda. The border follows the course of the River Torne, and after crossing the bridge you'll find yourself in Northern Finland. This is what many Swedes do in order to buy alcoholic beverages at the relatively less expensive Finnish markets. The **Tornio** (Finland) bars are also frequented by crowds of thirsty Swedes. The Tourist Information Centre (tel. 0992-11801) will provide you with a list of accommodation and with the routes of some colourful tours, like for instance:

The island of **Seskarö** (5 km from town), and Kukkolaforsen, site of the end of July *Festival of the White Fish* (Sikfesten), a picturesque and very tasty traditional festival. Kukkolaforsen is 15 km. north of Haparanda and it offers several other tourist attractions, all connected with its river-life.

165 km west of Haparanda is the 17th century Sami village of **Jokkmokk**, known to the tourists as one of the centers of the Sami handicraft industry. The local Sami Museum is by the church, on the market square. The "Winter Market" is held in February, and in spite of temperatures that often go below -30°C, it attracts thousands of visitors. The local Tourist Information Centre (tel. 0971-11977) is as useful and well organised as all the others.

Lapland and the Far North

From Luleå Road 97 goes on, along the banks of the Lule, to **Boden**.

Gällivare

From Boden, the road and the railway continue northward to Gällivare, an important iron mining centre. Local iron-rich ore layers are estimated at more than 400 million tons. The Tourist Information Centre (tel. 0970-18663) has vital information for all tours of the neighbouring national parks. Near the Tourist Information Centre is a café restaurant and the Sami Museum.

Gällivare is situated north of the Arctic Circle; therefore, in high summer, it's a good spot to experience the midnight sun. A two hour walk will take you to **Bornfäallen**, where, for almost two months (from half-June to the end of July) the sun never sets, the sky often assumes spectacular hues.

The Malmberget mines, 6 km out of town, were once in the heart of an old Sami village; all that remains of it today are two ancient churches: the Läppharbärget (Sami Church) and the Ettoveskyrkan (Iron Church).

Should you wish to stay overnight, book your rooms through the Tourist Information Centre or directly, upon arrival, phoning the local hostel (tel. 0970-14380) or the camp sites (tel. 0970-18679).

The 500-km^2-wide **Muddus Park**, south-west of Gällivare, is a centuries old forest, that was granted parkland status in 1942 to protect it. Road 97 follows the north-western limits of the park. The forest paths lead to several very spectacular sites; the park map is available at the Tourist Information Centre.

Kiruna

Road 98 and the railway go from Gällivare to Kiruna, a "town" whose 25,000 people are spread over 4,800 km^2, making it the vastest urban centre in the whole world. It's a town of iron miners; the ore mined here is carried by rail to Narvik, in Norway.

The Tourist Information Centre (tel. 0980-18880) and the local authorities provide well for their visitors, including guided tours of the mines (40SEK) and organised tours of the region and its parkland. Thousands of people reach Kiruna by special tourist trains, direct from Stockholm; they alight here for a short visit to the town and its neighbouring park, before proceeding to their next stop, in Norway. At Kiruna you'll find several hotels, restaurants and shopping centres.

East and south of Kiruna there are several picturesque Sami villages; the most interesting is **Jukkasjärvi**, 25 km east of Kiruna, on the other bank of the **Torne**, with its outstanding Sami Museum (open in summer, 10am-9pm). Another pleasant Sami village, **Kaitum**, is 24 km south of Kiruna.

Kebnekajse Mountain (21123 m, Sweden's highest peak) is the goal of a rather difficult mountain route, starting from Kiruna with a 30 km bus ride, continuing with a 40 km motorboat crossing and ending with a steep 24 km mountain walk. For additional details, inquire at the Tourist Information Centre.

The Abisko Park

Road 98 and the Narvik railway pass very close to Sweden's most famous National Park, **Abisko**, established in 1903 to preserve the unique natural parkland and to undertake a series of ecological studies. After the Vassaijaure Research Centre was gutted by fire, it was restored with considerable improvements and today the Park and its Centre have become a very popular attraction for thousands of tourists.

"Abisko", in the Sami language, means "ocean-forest", probably hinting at the spread of that enormous forest westward, toward the sea. Five centuries of reindeer grazing have caused very serious damage to the vegetation, and monumental reclamation works have been undertaken since the beginning of our century; compounding the problem, to many Samis the reindeer is not unlike the Hindu cow, not to be touched dead or alive.

The park covers 75 km^2 on both banks of the River Abiskojokk. Along the park paths there are several mountain shelters, equipped for overnight visits. At the park entrance you'll be offered maps and instructions for your visit to the park; don't neglect to come prepared for the unavoidable onslaught of mosquitoes: a good insect-repellent is an absolute must!

The **Kungsleden** ("Kings' path") is the most popular parkland route. It begins at Abisko and covers about 500 km, ending at Hemavan (near Tärnaby, in the south). It's not an easy route, and requires careful preparations and the assistance of the Tourist Information Centres.

The Vadvetjåkka Park

Not far from Abisko, this minor National Park offers some spectacular sights that attract hundreds of tourists (mostly Swedes). It's not very easily accessible, has a very rainy climate (its precipitations are fivefold those of Abisko), and has practically no provisions for tourists.

The Hinterland Railway Line — Inlandsbanen

The Inlandsbanen Railway, inaugurated in 1937, is 1,300 km long and goes from Stockholm to Gällivare, with train connections to Narvik, in Norway.

It is an outstanding tourist route, crossing many isolated but spectacular regions. The train stops at each and every hamlet on its route — even the most desolate and small. During the summer a special cumulative ticket is on sale, valid for 14 days of unlimited travel along the line. The ticket costs 350SEK, and entitles its owner to considerable discounts at many hotels, restaurants and museums of the region. The train travels only during the day, and in order to plan your itinerary you'll have to familiarize yourself with its detailed timetable, available at the Railway Stations and at most Tourist Information Centres. *EuRail* tickets are also valid.

The Abisko Forest

The first stop, travelling northward from the capital, is **Kristinehamn**, a leisurely town on the coast of Lake Vänern, with at its gates a statue of Picasso. For a brief visit to the town (and lake) call the Tourist Information Centre, tel. 0550-10573.

The second stop is **Filipstad**; the third is **Långban**, a mining centre in the Värmland, with an outstanding Museum of Mining.

Further on is the railway junction of **Mora**, the best strategic centre for a visit to Lake Siljan. **Orsa**, on Lake Orsasjön, is famous throughout Sweden for its brown bears: visit the splendid *Grönklitt*, the bear's reserve, situated 13 km off town (open from May to September), where you'll be wheeled about within a cage, while the brown bears roam around in freedom.

Then the train reaches the **Härjedalen** region and its main township of **Sveg**, with its hostel (tel. 0680-10338) and camp sites (tel. 0680-10881); at the local Tourist Information Centre you'll find details of walks, routes, and visits to the winter-sport resorts of **Åsarna** and **Klövsjö**. The next stop is at **Östersund** (see p. 149 above). Then the train crosses several small hamlets, like **Sorsele** on the Vindel river and **Arvidsjaur**, **Jokkmokk** and, before reaching the end of the line at Gällivare, **Porjus**, with its spectacular waterfalls. At **Vuollerim**, a little village on the river Lule, where the ruins of a 6000 years old prehistoric settlement were discovered.

Southern Sweden

The region is big enough to deal with in two separate itineraries, one to the south-east and one to the south-west. Starting from Stockholm, follow the coast in a southerly direction, taking time now and again to make a digression into the interior. Of course, one might also invert the itinerary, crossing first westward to Göteborg, through the great lake district, and southward, to end finally in the capital.

Norrköping

Norrköping is about 100 km south-west of Stockholm. It is a modern industrial centre, situated in an outstanding natural harbour. It has a population of 120,000 people (which make it the fourth largest town in Sweden). It is little more than 300 years old (the oldest building in town is the Edwigkyrkan, a church built in 1675). Don't miss the **Kolmårdens Djurpark** — a 55 acre zoo and safari park, with a dolphin pool and a tourist beach.

The Göta Canal

The first route starts along the E4 to **Jönköping**; the second moves along the E66 to the **Söderköping** junction, at the mouth of the Göta Canal, that connects Göteborg with the eastern coast of Sweden. This canal was dug at the beginning of the 19th century, to avoid the Danish customs barriers. It crosses two of the great lakes, the Vänern and the Vättern, as well as several other minor ones.

The gradiation made it necessary to build, along its course, not less than 65 closes. The canal was completed in 1823, and for more than a century it remained a navigational artery of vital importance to Swedish trade and industry; today, after the inauguration of the Stockholm-Göteborg railway, the canal is only a tourist attraction, frequented by thousands of lake lovers and fishing enthusiasts. In the summer, the lanes that run along the canal banks are crowded with bicycle riders, who board the boats only to cross the wider lakes. Boat ticket prices vary accordingly; a full Stockholm-Göteborg trip costs as much as 1,200SEK (deckside) and three times as much in a first class double-bed cabin. For further details, inquire at the Tourist Information Centres.

Linköping

The E4 will take you to Linköping, the home town of the *SAAB* industries; however, it also boasts a great Cathedral, built in the 16th century on much older foundations.

In the middle of the main square, not far from the cathedral, stands the **Miles Fountain**, a monument erected in honour of the **Folkunga** dynasty. Opposite the cathedral you'll see the Museum of Architecture.

Jönköping

Jönköping is the capital of the province — and since the end of the last century it is also the world capital of kitchen matches. It goes without saying that one of its major attractions is the Museum of Matches.

At the Tourist Information Centre (tel. 036-169050) you'll find maps of the region and of the town, and information about accommodation. The hostel (tel. 036-61448) is rather far from the town.

Växjö

The Småland is probably the most interesting region in Sweden. The **Småland Museum** will introduce you with great pride to the region's 2500 lakes and 6000 km^2 of forests, to its picturesque villages and its quasi-alpine peaks. For those who are just passing through, there are the E4 to Hälsingborg and Denmark, or Road 40 to Göteborg. However, we'd rather have you take Road 30 to **Växjö**, an ancient Viking market town that is today one of the major centres of Sweden's glass industry.

The ancient Cathedral was restored in 1960 and doesn't merit much more than a passing glance; much more interesting are two of the town's museums: the **Museum of Småland**, with a unique collection of crystal glass from all the world, and the **Utvandrarnas Hus** (Museum of Emigration), which documents the rise and the fall of the Swedes' Great American Dream. At the Tourist Information Centre (tel. 0470-41410) you'll find, as usual, all the answers to your questions.

SOUTHERN SWEDEN

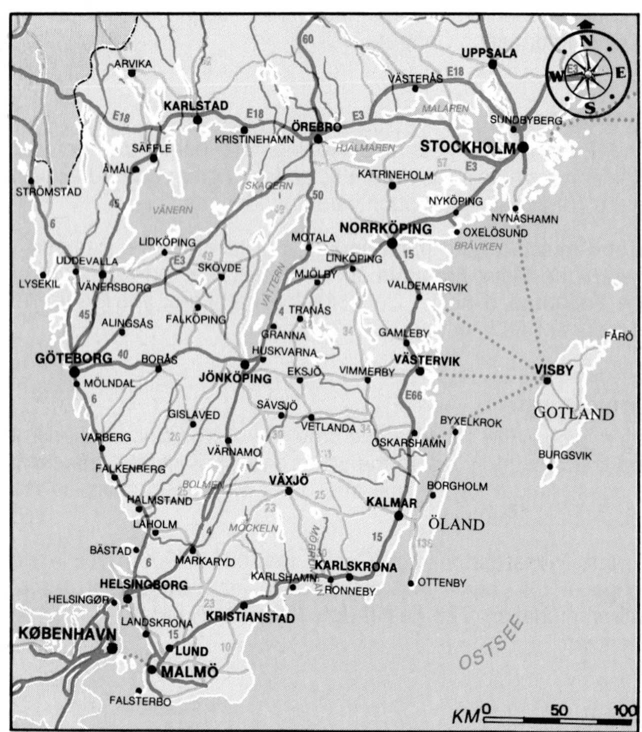

Kalmar

The strategic importance of the Kalmar Fort is evident at first sight. It dominates the Kalmar Straits, it commands the town entrance and its water sources. For centuries Kalmar was the site of major historic events, crucial to the whole of Scandinavia.

Kalmar was the first seat of the Riksdag (the Swedish Parliament),

Kalmar's Town Hall

The Fort of Kalmar

which met there for the first time in 1397 to sanction the Kalmar Union between Denmark and Sweden. In 1523 King Gustavus Vasa, having seceded from the Danish empire, took residence in the Kalmar Fortress. In the last three centuries, after the Roskilde Treaty, by which Sweden won back its southern regions, Kalmar lost much of its strategic value, and changed gradually into a prosperous tourist and commerical centre.

The Tourist Information Centre (tel. 0480-28270) is opposite the railway station.

The famous fortress (**Kalmar Slott**) is the first step in your visit. To reach it, cut through the public park and the defensive ditch that surround it, crossing the drawbridge; the ditch is still full of water, and you'll probably see some members of its population of swans gliding leisurely upon its waters. As you will recognize at once, the fort really dominates the whole town and its maritime gates. Eleven times, in the course of several centuries, the fortress found itself under siege — but it was never conquered. Its ramparts were never breached, discounting King Johan II, who dismantled the fortress defences in the 16th century in order to reinforce them.

Turn back toward the centre of town, to Stortorget Square. Here you'll see the **Rådhus** (City Hall) and the elegant **Kalmar Cathedral**, that was built at the end of the 17th century by Tessin the Elder (who designed also the City Hall building).

The narrow meandering alleys of the Old City will lead you to the city walls, to the water reservoir and to the town's green belt. Near the harbour, on Skeppbrogatan Street, stands the **Regional Museum**, whose "pièce de resistence" is the **Kronan**, a gigantic 17th century ship that sank with all hands on board in 1676, and was refloated in 1980, with all its fabulous treasures.

Food and accommodation

Kalmar's hotels often offer summer bargains. The best is probably the *Slottshotellet* (Stortorget 14, tel. 0480-88260); the *Villa Angö* near the harbour, tel. 0480-85415) is relatively inexpensive. At the Tourist Information Centre, at the hostel (tel. 0480-12928) or at the camp site you'll also find lists of rooms in private residences. The hostel and the camp sites are conveniently situated at Angö, not far from the Öland Island bridge.

The Italian and Greek restaurants of the centre are moderately priced.

Öland

A 6 km long bridge connects the island of Öland to the mainland, not far from Kalmar. Having crossed the bridge, you will immediately catch sight of its everpresent windmills (400 in all), which provide the island with all its electricity requirements.

On the island you'll see an attractive park, a chain of some 20 5th century forts, several ancient burial grounds and quite a few very attractive beaches.

A half an hour ride on bus 101 or 106 will take you to **Borgholm**, the capital of the island. It's a model tourist resort, whose parallel avenues are lined with private residences, gardens and orchards. The yacht marina and a modest amusement park are the main local attractions. The **Borgholm Slott**, with its unusual ramparts, throughly blackened by the 1806 fire that gutted its interiors, stands guard over the town from the heights of a rather modest hill. The fort has never been restored, but it is nevertheless open to visitors, who will find in it a good example of the characteristic defensive Scandinavian structures — so staunch, so dark, so bleak.

At the Tourist Information Centre (tel. 0485-12340), business as usual.

Gotland

This island has belonged to Sweden for many centuries and is the traditional resort to which well-to-do Swedes stream every summer by the thousands: its climate is temperate, and while it is so close, its insularity ensures its visitors the fullest possible relaxation from the bustle and hustle of their daily life.

A series of archaeological digs started almost a century ago proved beyond the shadow of a doubt the presence in the island of Mycenean merchants as far back as the 2nd millennium B.C., and later of Greek and Roman traders. Yet later, in the 6th century of our era, the Vikings left here their imprint. For several centuries the island remained independent, until the Hanseatic League made of its capital, Visby, one of their major northern trading centres.

The island became richer and richer, as witnessed by its remarkable palaces, residential villas and rose gardens, and year after year, for no less than three centuries, all the Who's

One of Visby's picturesque alleys

Who in Sweden have crossed over, summer after summer, to spend at least one leisurely month in Gotland.

Visby

During the summer, several motorboats regularly ferry across the strait between the mainland and Visby. Upon your arrival,

A Dutch Symbol in the Heart of Swedish Öland

you'll find yourself immersed in a unique atmosphere — a mixture of ancient history, of leisure and prosperity, of relaxed security. This is the ideal spot for a bicycle tour, and there are several bicycle-hire agencies in town; the tariff is 25SEK a day.

How to get there
From Stockholm, at the Nynäshamn pier, there are three daily

ferry runs (5 hours); from Oskarshamn, two daily crossings (4 hours); from Västervik one daily crossing (3 and a half hours); from Grankullavik, one daily crossing (3 hours).

Tourist services

There are two Tourist Information Centres; the first is at the harbour (tel. 0498-19010) and the other at the city walls (tel. 0498-10982); the *Gotland Card* costs 80SEK and is valid for three whole days; very convenient, especially for those who want to get around a lot.

Food and accommodation

Visby is the best overnight spot in the island.
Luxury Hotels:
Visby Hotel: Strandgatan 6, tel. 0498-11925.
Villa Borgen: Adelsgatan 11, tel. 0498-71170.

Tourist Class Hotels:
Solhelm: central, tel. 0498-79070.
Toftagården: at the beach, tel. 0498-65400.

There are two hostels: the *Hultmans* (tel. 0498-18400) and another one, rather far from town, at tel. 0498-16933; there is also a camp site (tel. 0498-12157), as well as rooms in private residences (double occupancy for 180SEK).

There are scores of restaurants and simpler eateries. Some are very central, situated in old palaces; stop at their door to look for the *Dagen Ratt* sign, that will assure you of a full meal at moderate prices.

What to see

If you wish to see it all, use the Tourist Information Centre maps and pamphlets. Otherwise, just wander around. We'll recommend the "churches circuit", with St. Nicholas, St. Clemens, the Holy Ghost, St. Katherine and others. You should set aside at least one hour for the city walls circuit (3 km); the walls were erected by the city fathers in the 14th century to keep the poor apart from the rich. As fate wills, in 1361, when the Danes invaded the island, the city fathers locked the gates, and the rich could watch, from the top of the walls, the slaughter of hundreds of innocent peasants at the hands of the invading Danish army.

Recent digs have uncovered a common burial ditch, with the remains of thousands of victims of a mass slaying — mostly of women and children. When the city fathers finally surrendered, after a months long siege, the Danes made exhorbitant demands, which could not be met by the people of Visby; hence the slaughter.

In the so-called **Jungfrutornet** (the Maiden's Tower), the angered Visbians hung a young girl, accused of having betrayed her town to the Danes.

Behind the tower are the **Botanic Gardens**. The **Fornsal Museum** documents the events of the 1361 siege and the age of the Vikings; it has also a splendid collection of stained glass windows. The **St. Mary Domkyrkan** (St. Mary Cathedral) was built in the 13th century, and repeatedly restored in later times. Its splendid towers rise well above those of the other 16 churches, and on Sundays the Cathedral is the most popular attraction in town.

Coming to Visby in July or August, inquire about the exact date of the *Petrus de Dacia* pagan pageant, which takes place at the St. Nicholas ruins (entrance 40SEK). It is simply an unforgettable experience.

There are several night spots, bars and discos. The Visby Carnival, a mixed Swedish-Brazilian style affair, takes place at the end of June.

Outings

Gotland is full of historic sites and natural scenery: old churches, fishermen's villages, woods and meadows, shining white beaches. The island map (available, of course, at the Tourist Information Centre), will assist you in the planning of your visit according to your own tastes and means.

A few hints: don't neglect to visit **Lummelunde** (a stalagmite grotto, north of Visby), **Lärbro** (spectacular view) and **Fårö** (the shepherds' island).

Carry on to **Slite**, following the coastal road southward to **Åminne**, **Dalhem** (12th century Gothic style church) and **Ljugarn** (splendid and never too crowded white beaches — and a hostel, tel. 0498-93124).

Return to Visby from the south, passing through **När**, **Hemse** and **Klintehamn**.

From Kalmar to Malmö

The E66 leaves Kalmar southward, crossing **Blekinge**, an attractive sea resort, full of gardens.

An old Malmö Residence

Karlskrona

The regional capital, **Karlskrona**, is 100 km south of Kalmar. It owes its name to its founder, King Carl VI, who built it to serve as the Swedish Navy's headquarters. Even the main streets of the centre were named after famous Swedish admirals. The town spreads over thirty islets, joined to each other by a bridge net. The local Tourist Information Centre (tel. 0455-83490) will provide ample details of all there is to see in this interesting town. At the Fisketorget (the fishermen's pier), short motorboat tours will take you for a brief visit to all the major islands. Facing the **Kungliga Amiralitetskyrkan** (the Admirals' Church — a wooden structure built in 1685) you'll see the statue of a shipyard worker, who froze to his death in a winter night, while begging for alms at the church door after a work accident. The Sea Museum and the Regional Museum are not far from the church.

The main square, Stortorget, is framed by two churches designed by Tessin the Younger. The first, **Trefaldighetskyrkan**, was built in 1709 for the Hanseatic League in Romanesque style; the second, **Fredrikskyrkan**, is in Baroque style and was built a few years later. There are guided visits to the Bronze Age graffiti that was discovered east of town, at Hästhallen and at the village of Kristeanopel, a modest resort whose walls date from the time of the wars between Sweden and Denmark. Inside the walls you'll find several cafés, restaurants, hostels and camp sites.

The E66 leaves Karlskrona side by side with the railway, turning westward to **Ronneby**, **Karlshamn** and **Sölvesborg**.

Kristianstad

Kristianstad, one of the main centres of the Skåne region, is also on the E66. For many generation the Skåne was a Danish province; Kristianstad itself bears the name of the Architect King (Christian IV of Denmark); several neighbouring hamlets are among the most picturesque Medieval villages in Sweden. The palaces of downtown Kristianstad reflect the Renaissance style that Christian IV loved so dearly. The splendid **Trefaldighetskyrkan** is considered one of the best examples of its style in Northern Europe. Built in 1628, this church is in the heart of an exclusive residential quarter, whose elegant villas were unusually built out of stone. In the main hall of the **Cinema Museum** there are frequent showings of classic films, including a 1909 production made with the machinery on show at the museum itself.

At the Tourist Information Centre (tel. 044-121988) there are bicycles for hire, maps of the town and whatever else you may need to know. The **Bäcksaskog** fort, a summer residence of King Carl XV, is 10 km east of town, and may be easily reached by bike.

The camp sites (tel. 044-110767) also has several family rooms and accommodation.

Ystad

The E66 proceeds to Lund and Malmö, but if you can take the time, you won't regret leaving it for Road 10 to **Ystad**, a very attractive little Medieval town; at the local Tourist Information Centre (tel. 0411-77279) you'll be offered a town map and a useful tourist itinerary.

The itinerary goes through 22 sites, including the Art Museum (with a monumental 50 square metres oil painting), an avenue of old wooden residences, all the main squares, the gardens and a selection of palaces of various epochs — from the 12th to the 20th century.

As for accommodation, make your own choice:
Hotel Prince Carl: Hamngatan 8, tel. 0411-10035.
Ystad Soltsjöbad: at the seaside, tel. 0411-13630.
The hostel: tel. 0411-77297.
You may also turn to the local Tourist Information Centre, and ask for a list of private residence rooms.

Malmö

The E6 (coming from north), the E66 and the E14 — and also three different railway lines — join together at Malmö, the third largest city in Sweden and the regional capital of the Skåne district. Malmö is a miniature metropolis, characterised by its Danish past, its dynamic harbour, its importance as a main road and railway junction — and its 250,000 people. It is a city of endless variety. Less than 50 metres from the modern industrial seaport you'll find yourself within the labyrinthine alleys of a Medieval burg, complete with its centuries old wooden residences. The main square will remind you of Copenhagen, and within the radius of less than one kilometre you'll be able to visit (using the *Malmö Card*, on sale at the Tourist Information Centre — tel. 040-341270 — for 30, 40 or 80SEK, respectively valid for 1, 2 or 7 days) scores of historic sites and museums, without having to spend a penny on transportation or entrance tickets.

The Old City is protected on both sides by canals. The main Stortorget Square is four centuries old, but its statue of Carl V dates from 1658. Around the square there are several majestic buildings, crowned by the **Rådhus** (City Hall — 1546), that was repeatedly restored in the Renaissance style. Behind City Hall, in the middle of a charming meadows, stands **St. Peter**, a 14th century church in Baltic-Gothic style, with Teutonic architectural undertones.

But the section of town best loved by its people is around **Lilla Torget**, an elegant square designed toward the end of the 16th century in harmonious Renaissance style. The square is particularly attractive after dusk, when its old-fashined street-lamps light up. In summer nights Lilla Torget is crowded with people, leisurely strolling or stopping to enjoy the tunes of many casual street musicians. On the south side of the square, an old wooden structure houses the **Centre of Industrial Design**. On its north side there is a roofed market.

Food and accommodation

Luxury hotels:
Savoy: Norra Vallgatan 62, tel. 040-70230.
Garden: Baltzarsgatan 20, tel. 040-104000.
Tourist class hotels:
Strand: Strandgatan 50, tel. 040-162030.

At the Tourist Information Centre you'll find a long list of private residence rooms, and some very convenient package deals at the best and most central hotels.

The hostel (Dalhemsgatan 5, tel. 040-118585) is open only during the summer; free limousine service is provided from the Kyrkogatan 3b Railway Office.

A second hostel (tel. 040-82220) is 5 km out of town. The camp site (bus line 41b; tel. 040-155165) stays open throughout the year.

There are scores of restaurants, and all the major cuisines are well represented. We recommend *Casa Mia* (Södergatan 12), just off the railway station. If money counts, try the *Oversten* (Regementsgatan 52, tel. 040-919100); you won't regret it. The *Stortorget* is very central, just opposite City Hall, and the *Fagel Fenix* (tel. 040-110059) is a recommended vegetarian restaurant.

Like anywhere else, youll find in Malmö quite a number of pizza and sausage counters and other fast-food spots.

Lund

A 15 minutes train run — or a 20 minutes car ride — will take you to **Lund**, Uppsala's rival in the Swedish college world — not unlike Britain's Oxford and Cambridge. Its ancient stone-paved

Lund's Cathedral

alleys, its bleak stone buildings may put you off at first, but the characteristic pulse of student life will soon make you feel more at home. The **Domkyrkan** (Cathedral) is one of the most beautiful churches in Scandinavia. Erected in 1145 in the Romanesque style, it was repeatedly expanded and restored. Its two slender and tall towers are a 19th century addition, and they make of it a reference mark clearly visible from anywhere in town. Within the cathedral there are several great works of art, and north of the main gate you'll see a most interesting astronomical clock.

Probably the best way to visit Lund is by bike — bicycles are on hire at the local Tourist Information Centre (tel. 046-124590), where you'll also find a *Lund Card* on sale and various free information material.

In this garden city there are several interesting churches. Not far from the Cathedral you'll find the vast complex of the **Kulturen Museet**, which houses several collections of handicrafts and architectural designs.

The list of private residence rooms is long and attractive. Among the hotels, we recommend the *Ahlsträm* (tel. 046-110174), very central and not too expensive. Ask for available discounts and package deals. The hostel (tel. 046-124084) is open only during the summer and is 2 km out of town.

Leaving Lund behind, you'll probably go on northward to Göteborg and end your visit in Sweden at the Norwegian border — at Stromstad.

Helsingborg

Helsingborg was built as a defensive fortress overlooking the Kattegat Strait. It was already settled well before the end of the first millennium, at the days of King Knud of Denmark. Its twin bastions of **Kärnan** and **Krönberg** are a reminder of the strategic value of the site.

Helsingborg is, of course, also the main junction between Denmark and Sweden, and the strait is always crowded with ferries and other vessels crossing its waters. It takes but 20 minutes — and 20SEK (bicycle included) or 120SEK (car included) — to cross from side to side.

At the ferries pier stands the neo-Gothic styled City Hall palace, the **Rådhuset**, with the local Tourist Information Centre. The *Helsingborg Card* costs 35SEK and is valid for three days.

Helsingborg is an industrial town of about 100,000 people, and is certainly worth a few hours' stopover.

The first site to see is the **Kärnan Fort**. We know is that it was already there as early as 1320. Its massive walls are 4 metres high. It's open to the public 9am-6pm (in winter only until 3pm). Entrance 5SEK (students 2SEK).

Now go on to **St. Mary**, a church dedicated to the Patron Saint of fishermen since 1100. The wooden building has been repeatedly restored and improved, but its original lines are still recognizable. Within the church you'll find a precious collection of religious silver objects. The collection is open to visitors Mon.-Fri., 9am-3pm; the church is open daily, 9am-6pm.

The **Fredriksal** is a vast open-air museum, surrounded by splendid botanic gardens with more than 400 variety of roses. The woodland that surrounds the complex is rich of attractive meadows, ideal in sunny weather for a romantic siesta or a family picnic. The museum is open from May to October, 10am-6pm, but of course the roses are in flower only until mid July.

The *Grand Hotel* (Stortorget 8, tel. 042-120170) is a luxury establishment; the Högvakten (Högvakten 14, tel. 042-120390) is an inexpensive pension.

There are two hostels (one of them is out of town), and a camp site, situated 5 km from the centre.

Sofiero

Some 5 km north of Helsingborg you'll find the majestic royal villa of **Sofiero**, which was presented in 1974 by King Gustav Adolf VI to the people and the city of Helsingborg. The villa was built by King Oskar II for his wife Sophia. Gustav Adolf and his Queen Margrete transformed the residence and its grounds in a real terrestrial paradise of rose gardens, woodland and meadows; later the old guardhouse was transformed into a café restaurant, and the stables into a museum. Some of the greatest personalities of the world honoured Sofiero with their visit: among them two US Presidents — Eisenhower and Johnson — , Soviet Premier Kossigin, Indira Gandhi, and British Prime Ministers MacMillan and Wilson. In the summer there are frequent open-air concerts and other cultural programmes. Sofiero is open to the public from May to August, 10am-6pm.

North of Helsingborg

The distance between Helsingborg and Göteborg is 230 km, quickly covered by the E6 that crosses the fertile plain of **Halland**, with its picturesque rural villages and isolated farms. It might be pleasant to stop on your way north to visit some of the most attractive little towns and to rest for a while at a charming café or on one of the beckoning beaches.

Båstad is a popular summer resort, famous for its tennis courts and tournaments: it is the major site of the Swedish Open, an event that attracts in July thousands of fans from all Sweden as well as from abroad.

Falkenberg is another attractive tourist centre, famous for its splendid beaches, for the salmon rich waters of the Ätran, and for its interesting Old City, with its wooden houses and the 14th century St **Laurentie** church.

Varberg is the landing port of the Grena (Denmark) ferries; it has a monumental castle, surrounded by water — the harbour and the castle ditches — and towering high above the whole town. Within the castle there are a museum, a hostel and a restaurant.

Göteborg

Göteborg is Sweden's major seaport and the centre of the country's maritime trade. The harbour cranes and the ships' funnels and masts form an integral part of the city's skyline, together with its high rise office and residential buildings, its spacious avenues and its many canals.

Göteborg has a population of almost half a million people. It was founded in 1621 by King Gustav Adolf, to provide Sweden with its own seaport, free of the the exorbitant taxes imposed by Denmark upon all sea traffic crossing the Kattegat straits. In 1659 the new city had achieved such status, that King Carl V made it the new seat of his Parliament. The harbour and the hectic life of the commercial centre attracted thousands of immigrants from Scotland, Britain and Germany.

The new Trollhätte Canal, connecting Göteborg with Lake Vänern, was inaugurated at the beginning of the 19th century, introducing Sweden's major port to the wood industry. Then came the era of the great new shipyards, and finally that of the Volvo complex. Today Göteborg is the unrivalled industrial capital of Sweden.

How to get there

By sea: Göteborg's piers are frequented by several regular ferry

GÖTEBORG

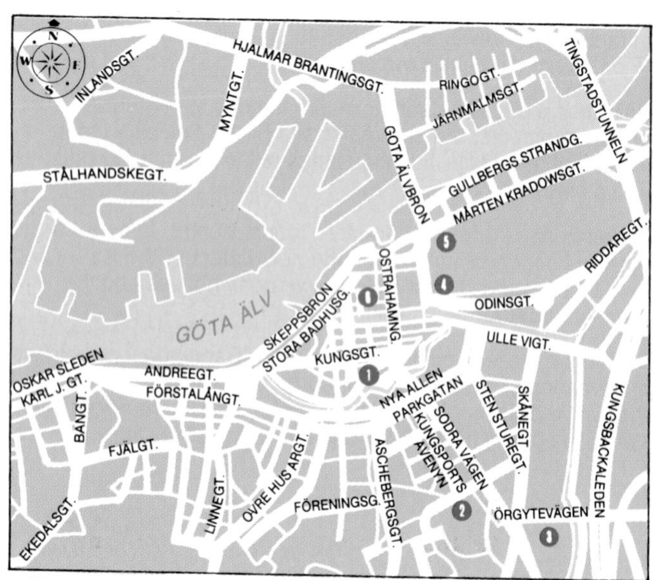

Index
1. Tourist Information Centre
2. Götaplasten Square
3. Liseberg
4. The Railway Station
5. The Bus Terminal
6. The History Museum

---

lines coming from the British Islands and from other foreign and Scandinavian ports. Buses leave the port for the city every few minutes (price 20SEK per hour).

By rail: Several international (and national) trains stop at the Göteborg railway station. Naturally the station is connected by several bus lines to the harbour and to all parts of town.

Göteborg's Fountain

By bus: The central bus station for all interurban lines is on Nils Ericson Plats, by the railway station.

By air: The **Landvetter** Airport connects Göteborg with many European capitals. The *Flygbuss* bus line connects the airport with the railway station (18 km, 30SEK).

The telephone prefix for Göteborg is 031.

Tourist services

Göteborg has two Tourist Information Centres: the main office offers lots of written material and has hotel booking services, lists of other accommodation and guided tours of the city and its region. It is situated at the corner of Ostra Hamngatan with the canal, on Basargatan 10, tel. 100740 (open Mon.-Fri., 9am-5pm; on Saturday 10am-2pm; during the summer, 9am-6pm). Its other branch is situated at the Nordstan commercial centre, at the corner of Götgatan and Postgatan streets (open Mon.-Fri. 9.30am-6pm, on Saturday only until 3pm). Both offices have on sale cumulative tickets for all urban lines (30SEK per diem), and the *Göteborg Card* (free transportation, museum entrances and ferry discounts — 70SEK for one day, 120SEK for two, 165SEK for three and 200SEK for four days; children cards are about 40% cheaper).

The Göteborg *tourist bargain* includes, to holders of the Göteborg Card, bed and breakfast in a hotel for one night (prices vary between 200 and 360SEK, according to hotel categories).

Food and accommodation

Hotels:
Ekoxen: Hamngatan 38, tel. 805080. Very expensive.
Poseidon: Storgatan 33, tel. 100550. Moderate.
Royal: Drottninggatan 67, tel. 170100. Modest.

A list of rooms in private residences awaits you at the Tourist Information Centre; the price will be around 90SEK (150 for double occupancy), plus a 20SEK registration fee.

The most convenient accommodation is at the hostels, which is, however, rather far from town.

Nordengärden: Stockholmsgatan 14, tel. 196631: 40SEK for a dormitory bed, 60SEK ina four-bed room; showers and kitchen service. Trolley line 1 and 3; open from May to September.
Ostkupan: tel. 401050; bus 64; open from June to August.
Partille: tel. 446163; 15 km far in the hinterland, open all year. Bus 503 from Heden.

There are three camp sites; the most attractive is the *Kärralunds* (tel. 252761); open all year, 5 km out of town.

The best (and most expensive) restaurants are at the luxury hotels. Also very costly are the restaurants situated along the roofed pedestrian mall. For cheaper eats there is little more than the usual pizza and sausage counters.

In most restaurants you will be able to choose between three menu types: the cheapest (spaghetti or *smörgasbörd* — at most 60SEK per person); the fish menus (never above 140SEK); and a rich selection of meats (as high as 200SEK).

Attaglas is an attractive eatery situated on a barge anchored by the Tourist Information Centre.

Hunters (Ostra Hamngatan 30) is a very popular pizza eatery (with cabbage side dish, 50SEK).

There are several dine-and-dance night spots; we'll mention *Nefertiti* (Hvitfplatsen), *Jazzclubben* (Esperanto Platsen) and *Kären* (Göteborgtstaten — frequented mostly by students).

What to see

Weather permitting, you'll be able to see most of the town and its major sites in a single full day. Then, in the late afternoon, it will be time for tea and relaxation at Liseberg.

Moving from the Tourist Information Centre, follow Kungsportsavenyen Avenue, crossing the canal to **Götaplatsen** Square, with its Neptun Fountain by Miles. Along the avenue you'll find yourself stopping to admire some of the most attractive shopwindows in town; you'll be able to visit the **Museum of Theatre History** (on your left) and the **Röhsska Museet** (Museum of arts and crafts — on your right). Also on your left, spread along the canal bank, are the **Botanic Gardens of Trädsgardsföreningen**.

East of the square is the **Liseberg**, a vast park combining a small Disneyland with a Tivoli: marionet theatres, amusement park, restaurants and cafés inside a very beautiful park. Entrance 15 SEK, but a combined ticket for all programmes may cost as much as 225SEK. Open from April to September, 10am-12pm; trolley line 5.

Turn back toward the Tourist Information Centre, and follow Ostra Hamngatan to the Tourist Information Centre branch of Nordstan, the roofed shopping mall with its scores of boutiques, department stores, cafés, cinemas etc.

The tourist motorboats of the harbour will take you for a tour of the harbour; the best time is sunrise, with the inimitable aura and smells of the fish market.

The boat tour (*Padden Boats*, 35SEK per person) will also bring you close to the **Gustav Adolfs Torg** and to the **Exchange Building**, giving you a very attractive view of the city skyline. The **Nya Elfsborg Slott** boat tours will take you to the islet where that fortress was built, in the middle of the harbour; after a visit to the fort's museum, you might find a pleasant seat at the fort's café to enjoy the panoramic view of the city, situated proudly all around its harbour. The motorboats run from 10am-6pm, from May to September. Other boats run to some of the neighbouring islands.

The cruise along the Göta Canal has already been described

The Lysekil Marina

The Tjorn Suspension Bridge

in a previous chapter. Another itinerary goes to **Tanum**, with its prehistoric graffiti.

From Göteborg to the Norwegian Border

Leave Göteborg northward, following the arrows indicating the direction for Oslo. After few minutes you'll find yourself in the Bohuslän district, a coastal strip between the E6 and the sea, covered with woodland and furrowed with small fjords. Along the coast you'll see many islets, semi-submerged rocks and rocky reefs. You are in the most popular seaside region in Western Sweden. Travelling by car, you may leave the E6 at one of its many exits, and you'll be immediately in the very heart of the region. Coming by rail, stop at the **Uddevalla** station, and continue by bus or by ferry to a location of your choice (selected from one of the Tourist Information Centre maps and pamphlets).

Leaving the E6 for Road 160 — a very panoramic route indeed — you'll reach the island of **Tjorn**, where you'll find an excellent camping. Now take Road 161 to **Lysekil**, crossing (freely) the fjord by ferry. Lysekil is like a picture from a childhood fable, with behind it one of the most beautiful beaches in Sweden: shining sands and a rocky cove, with its own hidden sailboat anchorage.

Other local roads branch from the E6 to **Marstrand** (an ancient 13th century burg), to **Smögen** and to **Strömstad**, where you can pick up an island ferry.

The E6 proceeds northward to Oslo and Norway. The border post is at the majestic **Svinesund** Bridge, that crosses the omonimous fjord.

The Lakes

North-east of Göteborg there is a region of thousands of small lakes, and the two great lakes of Vänern and Vättern.

The Göta Canal runs through them on its long route, exploiting them and connecting them while it proceeds on its way from the Kattegat to the Baltic Sea, south of Stockholm.

In the lake region one finds several signs of ancient settlements dating from the third and fourth millenium B.C. According to many scientists, this region is the homeland of the Gotes, the famous tribe that caused Rome, in its later imperial days, such headaches. It is one of the most densely peopled regions in

Sweden, and many consider it the very birthplace of the Swedish nation.

The itinerary we suggest starts from Lidköping, crossing Jönköping (at the southern end of the Vättern) to Vadstena and to Karlstad, to follow Road 45 along the western coast of the Vänern.

Västergötland

The name means, in Swedish, "Land of the Gotes"; and archeology has recently confirmed this surmise.

Lidköping is the district capital, and it boasts a very good Tourist Information Centre (tel. 0510-83500), comfortably situated within the Town Hall. The most impressive building is that of the **Court**; in former times, this was the residence of a princely Swedish merchant, Gabriele de la Gargie.

The northern road leads to the picturesque peninsula of **Kelland**, with the **Läckö Castle** and its Regional Museum.

You might also enjoy e visit to **Kinnekulle**, a table-topped hill that one million years ago must have been on the bottom of the sea.

South-east of Lidköping is the ancient burg of **Skara**, whose wooden buildings were destroyed by fire, while its 12th century Romanesque church survived, though bearing the signs of several successive restoration works. The name of Skara was mentioned in the regional chronicles as early as the year 829.

16 kilometres east of Skara is the church of the **Vernhem Monastery**, a splendid 13th century building and the burial site of several kings of Sweden.

Östergötland is the region surrounding Lake Vättern, whose eastern coast is quite interesting.

Gränna is a small centre, birthplace of the famous polar explorer André, who lost his life not far from the North Pole. **Visingsö** is the island site of a former great prison; today it's a summer resort, where tourists ride on horse carriage tours to the isolated farms and old ruins scattered on the island.

Vadstena is a picturesque burg, famous for its embroidery and the birthplace of St. Brigid, who died in Rome in 1373 on her return from a pilgrimage to Jerusalem. Her remains are buried in the local church, not far from one of Gustavus Vasa's monumental castles.

Värmland is the birthplace of Selma Lagerlöf, the great writer who brought to life the magic aura of this region. **Karlstad**, the district capital, is an important iron mining centre and a good starting point for walks and tours in this spectacular region. The Tourist Information Centre is on Södra Kyrkogatan (tel. 054-102160), and has lists of accommodation and booking services for various motorboat lake cruises. A motorboat cruise to the **Fryken Vale** or a car ride along Road 234 to **Sunne** and to **Mårbacka** (with the Lagerlöf home, now a personal museum) is an excellent way to spend a sunny morning. Three kilometres south of Sunne are the magnificent **Rotteneros** gardens.

NORWAY

Norway, known for its hundreds of fjords, its ancient Viking culture and its long arctic nights and midnight sun, is a highly attractive tourist destination.

With its mountain tops, lakes, fjords and ancient burgs, its glaciers and snowfields; its mountain roads that climb up and down from peak to precipice; its modern highways and railways that connect to each other even the remotest corners of the country, Norway is one of the most desirable summertime paradises.

Add to all this the incomparable qualities of the Norwegians, and you have all the ingredients necessary for the best holiday ever.

History

The topographical structure of the country has often influenced much of its history. Until 15,000 years ago the whole western side of Norway was frozen solid. Then at the end of the last Ice Age, man made his first appearance — and his conquests — at first only along the southern coast, and later, slowly but surely, he advanced northward along the sea, until he reached the world's end on the shores of the Arctic Ocean.

During the second millennium B.C., several small nomadic tribes began hunting beyond the Arctic Circle, evidenced by burial sites, bones, stone arrowheads, and hundreds of perfectly preserved drawings of animals, hunting scenes, ships and gods.

By the end of the 8th century A.D. those tribes had merged into a single, new, quasi-national entity: the Vikings.

At the end of the 9th century, King Harald Håfagra (the Blond) ruled the whole of Norway, and his mighty ships mastered the seas as far as the western coasts of the Atlantic Ocean. Their seaward expansion brought the Vikings into contact with Christianity at a time when the new faith was rapidly spreading beyond the borders of the old Roman Empire. After King Harald's death, and following a period of protracted internecine quarreling among his potential successors, King Olav I was able to rally most of the country under his rule and to adopt the Catholic faith for himself and all his subjects. His repeated attempts to free Southern Norway from the Danes failed again and again, and finally, in the course of his last expedition, King Olav lost his life in battle.

His son, Olav II, was able to gradually recover most of the territories that had been lost by his father. He completed his father's missionary work, only to follow in his father's steps, launching a campaign for the conquest of Denmark. Defeated in battle in 1028, Olav II was forced to surrender. Unwilling to pay homage to Knud, King of Denmark and Britain, Olav II fled to Sweden and to Russia. Less than two years after his defeat he attempted a final comeback but fell prey to an an alliance of barons and peasants and was killed at the battle of Sticklested. A few decades later, Olav was canonized by the Roman Church, and became the Patron Saint of Norway.

After the death of King Knud, in 1035, the whole of Scandinavia was thrown into a two centuries of anarchy and bloodshed.

In 1240 King Haakon IV of Norway signed a treaty with the Hanseatic League. This achievement brought Norway a long period of peace and prosperity. Free from their more urgent defensive functions, the Norwegian army and navy launched several successful campaigns overseas, reaching as far as the Hebrides, Iceland and Greenland.

In 1349 the Black Plague devastated the whole of Scandinavia, killing almost one third of its population. In a very weakened Norway, the German merchants of the Hanseatic League strengthened their hegemony, taking full charge of local and foreign affairs in most Norwegian seaports.

In an attempt to win the friendship of his stronger neighbour, Denmark, some years later, King Haakon V moved his court to Oslo and encouraged his son — who was later to become King Haakon VI — to join in marriage with Princess Margrete, the direct heir to the Danish throne. Haakon died long before his wife, and Margrete became the sole ruler and Queen of Denmark and Norway. Not much later, in 1397, the Union of Kalmar ratifed the union of all Scandinavia — Denmark, Norway and Sweden — under the Danish rule. While Sweden regained its independence in 1523, Norway was destined to remain a Danish province for more than four centuries.

During that period Norway practically lost its national identity. Its major towns were administered by Danish barons, appointed by the Crown as regional or local governors. Maritime trade was strictly controlled by the Danish navy. However, Norway also enjoyed the effects of Danish prosperity. King Christian IV, the Architect King, was in more than one sense the father of the new capital city of Norway, Oslo.

Finally, at the beginning of the 19th century, Denmark, blinded by Napoleon's early military triumphs, allied itself with France against the rest of Europe. Defeated by Sweden, who had joined the ranks of the anti-Napoleonic alliance, Denmark found itself reduced to the status of a tiny provincial kingdom, devoid of its former military importance, and Norway passed from Danish to Swedish hands.

During most of the 19th century, a long series of anti-Swedish rebellions were repeatedly repressed. The wave of liberalism that exploded through Europe in 1848 reached Norway in 1851, and after a long struggle, in 1881 the Norwegian Parliament was able to force the Danish Crown to concede at least a certain measure of self-rule to its Norwegian province. Then, in 1905, the Parliament established its own Norwegian representatives in most of the world's capitals and called for a referendum, whose results called for full independence of Norway from Sweden. The Danish Prince Carl was called to the Norwegian throne and crowned as King Haakon VII of Norway.

During the First World War Norway remained strictly neutral (while its navy, serving the cause of the Entente Cordiale, lost many of its ships to the treacherous attacks of German submarines in the Atlantic. Nevertheless, neutrality brought with it increasing prosperity and industrial growth. The severe economic crisis of the end of the 20's caused very difficult times also in Norway. At the beginning of the 30's unemployement soared to an unprecedented 30%. The parties of the left won power, and their policies brought the country dangerously close to anarchy and bolshevism.

During that same period between the two World Wars, Norway annexed several formerly German arctic territories and islands.

At the beginning of the Second World War, in 1939, Norway resumed its neutrality once again. However, in April 1940, the Nazis blitzed the whole country in a matter of weeks, and while several resistance fighters continued their struggle against Germany until the end of the war, the Germans retained firm control of the coastal strip until Hitler's final surrender, in May 1945. On the eve of their flight, the German occupation forces set fire to all major Norwegian strongholds, leaving a scorched country behind them.

After the war, Norway recovered swiftly; its merchant navy grew rapidly. By 1965 it was the second largest navy in the world.

NORWAY

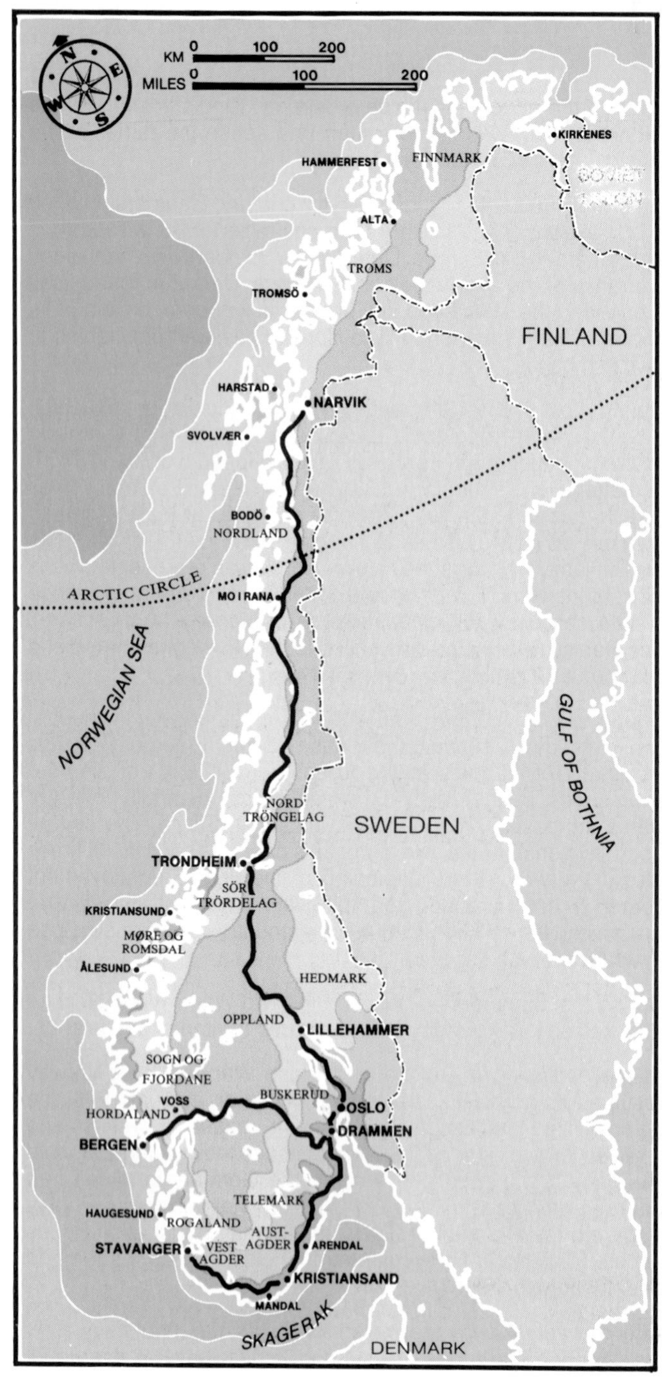

N
E
S
W
KM
0
100
200
MILES
0
100
200
KIRKENES
HAMMERFEST
FINNMARK
ALTA
TROMS
TROMSÖ
FINLAND
HARSTAD
NARVIK
SVOLVÆR
BODÖ
NORDLAND
ARCTIC CIRCLE
MO I RANA
NORWEGIAN SEA
GULF OF BOTHNIA
NORD
TRÖNGELAG
SWEDEN
TRONDHEIM
SÖR
TRÖRDELAG
KRISTIANSUND
MØRE OG
ROMSDAL
ÅLESUND
HEDMARK
OPPLAND
LILLEHAMMER
SOGN OG
FJORDANE
VOSS
BUSKERUD
HORDALAND
OSLO
DRAMMEN
BERGEN
TELEMARK
HAUGESUND
ROGALAND
AUST-
AGDER
STAVANGER
VEST
AGDER
ARENDAL
KRISTIANSAND
MANDAL
SKAGERAK
DENMARK

In 1949 Norway was granted full membership within the NATO alliance.

In recent years Norway has become a very prosperous country, not far behind the high Scandinavian standards of the Swedish welfare state.

Geography

Norway is a long and narrow coastal strip along the length of the Scandinavian peninsula. Its maritime borders are the Skagerrak and Kattegat Straits, the North Sea, the Northern Atlantic and the Arctic Ocean — respectively on its south, west and north sides. Its eastern neighbours are Russia (at the extreme north), Finland and Sweden.

Norway covers a total area of 324,000 km^2, a maximum length of 1770 km; its width varies from 63 to 430 km. Thanks to its many fjords, its coastal line reaches the phenomenal length of 28,000 km. The Sognefjord cuts 183 km inland. Norway has no less than 200,000 lakes; the largest, Lake Mjosa, covers an area of 227 km^2 and reaches a depth of 444 m. The highest mountain is the Glittertind (2481 m). The Jostedalsbreen is the largest glacier in Europe (815 km^2) and reaches a height of 2084 m. The most important river, the Glomma, is 556 km long. There are about 150,000 islands; the largest, Hinnøy, covers an area of 1366 km^2.

The whole of Scandinavia, including Norway, belongs to one of the most ancient land masses on Earth — more than a billion years old. Its lakes, fjords, chasms and coastal archipelagoes were formed during the Ice Ages, the last of which ended only 15,000 years ago.

Climate

Norway owes its considerably mild climate to the influence of the Gulf Stream, whose relatively warm waters reach from the Gulf of Mexico and the Equatorial Atlantic to the Norwegian coast. Norway's latitude is similar to that of Alaska or Siberia — yet most Norwegian ports remain open to shipping even in the dead of winter. Norway's average annual temperature is 7°C.

Nevertheless, Norwegian weather is often stormy and wet: along the coast annual precipitation is over 2,000 mm (1,000 in the inland).

Flora and fauna

Norway is rich in woodland: there are several types of conifers as well as hundreds of other (mostly deciduous) trees. There is also a very rich undergrowth of ferns, evergreens, berries, strawberries and scores of (edible and poisonous) mushrooms.

A large part of Norway is covered by arctic and sub-arctic tundras, and populated with typical arctic wildlife: reindeers and other members of the deer family, bears, wolves, foxes and other small carnivores.

Fjords and fresh water rivers are blessed with plenty of fish — especially cod and herring at sea, and salmon and trout in freshwater lakes and streams (get your fishing lines and permits ready!). In the summer the coastal regions, and especially the islands, are swamped with hundreds of thousands of migrating birds that, having wintered in Northern Africa and in other Mediterranean lands, return to their summer nests on Norway's rocky islets and fjords.

The people

Norway has a population of about 4 million people. Norwegians have the white skin, tall stature, blond hair and blue eyes that they inherited from their Viking forefathers, along with the other Scandinavians.

Only 65% of the population lives in the major urban centres. The rest live in small hamlets of a few hundred people. Urbanization and emigration (mainly to Northern American countries) are two rather common trends.

The birthrate is quite low — 18 births per thousand people — but the death rate is even lower.

Religion

In Norway there is complete freedom of religion. 96% of the people belong to the Lutheran Church, and the King is also the head of the Norwegian Church. There are about 9,000 Catholics and 1,500 Jews.

Norwegian churches are often rather singularly shaped; their ornaments have a distinct "pagan" character. This is particularly true for the more ancient, "stave" (wooden) churches, that date from the late Middle Ages. In those "stave churches" you'll discover graven images of dragons and other mythical monsters side by side with the traditional Christian symbols.

Government

Norway is a democratic constitutional monarchy. The crown is passed on from father to the first born son. The three main branches of power — the judiciary, the executive and the legislative branches — are strictly separate. The legislature — the Parliament or *Storting* — is composed of 150 members, elected for a four year term in national democratic, multiparty proportional elections.

Economy

Today the Norwegian economy, once based mainly upon its merchant navy and fisheries, is that of a modern industrial nation.

Norway is not a country endowed with many natural resources, except for the sea and the recently discovered oil fields in the North Sea. Norwegian industry imports great bulk quantities of the raw material they require; however, Norway also exports the majority of its industrial produce throughout the world, and Norway's GNP is among the highest in the world.

Agriculture: During the six last decades the growing rate of urbanization has often put at risk Norwegian agriculture, and vast farmland areas have gradually been abandoned. However, thanks to government intervention, the trend has recently been reversed, and agriculture has resumed its main function of supplying the country with most of its food requirements — except for cereals and citrus fruit. Forestry and the wood industry have become one of the main branches of the national economy, and several thousand workers are regularly employed in a vast spectrum of wood-related industries. About two thirds of Norwegian forests are on privately owned land, and great afforestation projects have recently been launched throughout the country, to save and protect this vital resource, second only, to water.

Fisheries: Fishing is still the main occupation in the small towns and villages of Northern Norway. While the output of the Norwegian fisheries is simply staggering and more than 75%

of the total is consumed locally; the rest is exported, frozen or processed.

Minerals: The mineral industries are, like elsewhere, often in crisis, with the only exception of magnesium and aluminium. Norway's otheral mineral resources — coal, quartz, nickel, iron etc — are only marginally exploited. Nevertheless, the mining industries, which employ just 5% of the national manpower, produce about 20% of Norway's exports.

Energy: Norway is the world's greatest producer of hydroelectric energy per capita. Electricity prices are among the lowest in the world, and this, of course, is of great help to the energy-consuming industries whose products can be sold in the international market at very competitive prices.

Oil: Since sixties, Norway has become a decidedly oil-rich country thanks to its share of North Sea oil. Oil production has stimulated the development of several related industries.

The Merchant Navy: Norway was, in the 19th century, the Queen of the Northern Seas. Its merchant fleet, however, was severely damaged by two World Wars; nevertheless, it still counts more than 1,300 ships (including 600 oil tankers), commanded by Norwegian officers, but manned mostly by foreign crews.

The language

Norwegian is an Indo-European language, with some 250 dialects which may be classified into the Bokmål and the Nynorsk languages.

Bokmål is the mothertongue of about 80% of the population, and is therefore the main national language. The Ministry of Education, however, has recently promoted the teaching of both languages in all Norwegian schools.

Like all Scandinavian languages, Norwegian has many dyphthongs and consonant groups; here is a brief list.
oe — pronounced like "e" in "bell"
ø — pronounced like "i" in "bird"
å, øy — pronounced "o"
The letters c, q, w and z do not belong to the Norwegian alphabet, and are pronounced as in most latin languages;
gi, gy, ei — pronounced like "ee" in "sheep"
rs, ski, sji, sky, sjy — pronounced "she"
hv — pronounced v

lj, hj, gj, j — pronounced like "ee" in "sheep"
k before i, y, j — pronounced like "h" in "home".

When to come

Norwegians travel freely throughout the country any time of the year. What's good for the Norwegians, however, is not necessarily good for you. The most picturesque season is, without doubt, late spring — from April to June, when nature throws off its white blanket of snow and dresses up in the thousand colours of its flowers.

Summer is also very pleasant, though crowded. If you plan to visit in July or August, don't neglect to book your accommodation as early as possible.

When fall approaches, most tourists pack up and have, leaving the beautiful scenery for you to enjoy the colours of autumn, so spectacular in the deciduous forests. But don't forget to take your warm sweater, because cold weather is on it's way!

Winter is for winter sports: from November to March all Norwegians become ski-experts and meadows change into ski-slopes, well equipped, well manned and often not too costly (at least by Scandinavian standards!).

Both in winter and in summer you can enjoy *Cross Country* walks, ski-routes and climbs, along hundreds of kilometres of the most spectacular itineraries in the Norwegian Alps.

Holidays
New Year
Epiphany
Easter
Ascension Day
Ash Wednesday
5 June — Constitution Day
Christmas

How long to stay;

How much does it cost

Norway is a land of many facets; it's perhaps better not to come at all, if you can't give it at the very least a week. The Oslo-

Bergen route requires one full week; the Fjord Region demands even more. The far north needs yet another week — and the far south too.

The cost of living is a delicate question, despite attempts by the Norwegian Tourist Administration to attract mass tourism. Almost everywhere, and in every season, you'll be offered attractive deals, including transportation, tours and accommodation. The details of many such bargains are available at your travel agent's.

If you travel by rail on a rather strict budget using a *EuRailPass*, you'll still have to spend from 100 to 240NOK (Norwegian Krone) a day: 50-100 for a hostel bed or camping roof, 30-50 for food (sandwiches and pizzas), and 20-60 for entrance tickets to tourist sites.

A young couple travelling by car, and staying in B&Bs or private residence rooms, will need 350-750NOK a day: 150-250 for accommodation; the same for food, 50-100 for fuel and 50-100 for entrance tickets.

In the following chapters you'll find many details that will help you decide where to visit, how long to spend there, and how much to pay for food and accommodation.

Norway's Gates

Norway's three major gatewayes are Oslo, Bergen and Stavanger.

By air: Each gateway has its own international airport; all three are frequented by international and national *SAS* lines and by several other airline flights. The local and Scandinavian *SAS* flights reach practically all Norwegian airports.

By sea: Many ferry lines connect Norway with Danish ports. From **Frederikshavn** there are lines to Oslo, Moss, Tønsberg and Larvik; from **Hitshals** one may ferry to Oslo, Kristiansand, Stavenger and Bergen; there is also a regular Copenhagen-Oslo run. Prices vary according to distance and class. The two most popular lines are the Fredrikshavn-Oslo and the Hitsholm-Kristiansand. Travelling by car, it may be convenient to ferry from Helsingør (in Denmark) to Helsingborg (in Sweden), and then follow the E6 northward to Oslo.

Coming from Great Britain, there are two very convenient ferry lines, Newcastle-Stavanger and Newcastle-Bergen.

NORWAY

By rail: Two daily trains connect Oslo with Stockholm. Three trains connect Oslo with Copenhagen. Sweden and Norway are connected by several latitudinal rail lines, ending at Trondheim and at Narvik. The London-Oslo train crosses the Channel and Holland, into north-western Germany and the Danish Jutland, to Copenhagen, Sweden and finally Oslo; it's a 34 hour crossing. Another great European train line is the Rome-Milan-Zurich-Köln-Hamburg-Copenhagen-Göteborg-Oslo.

EuRail passes are valid for all those (and many other) lines.

By bus: International bus lines are somewhat less comfortable, more costly and slower than their railways alternatives.

By car: The E6, as we have mentioned, reaches Oslo from the south. The E18 crosses over from Stockholm; Road 75 connects Stockholm with Trondheim; Road 70 runs from Kiruna to Narvik; and Road 4 crosses Lappland to Hammerfest.

Tourist services

In each and every town you'll find a good Tourist Information Centre, where you'll be able to communicate in English, and find a vast selection of written information, specifically maps, tour itineraries and accommodation lists. It's highly recommended to begin your daily rounds at the local Tourist Information Centre.

Don't forget to ask for the *kortet* (a bargain at its price), a card valid for free entrance to all major local sites and museums that also offers several sizable tourist discounts.

The roads

A word of warning: while the road system is vast, modern and often spectacular — with its mountain tunnels and daring bridges spanning deep fjords — topography and climate in Northern Norway often create very difficult road conditions, especially along the northern coastline. If the road is covered with a thin crust of ice, and if you are not a practiced winter-driver and have no chains for your tyres, forget about that car trip and step into a nice warm pub!

Trains

All Norwegian railway lines, a network of about 4,500 km, belong to the *NSB*, which has overcome Norway's topographical problems, but at very considerable cost.

The southern railway ends at Bergen. From Bergen, one will find very good bus connections to Narvik, where the next railway segment proceeds northward to Bodö. North of that point, there are two alternative transportation means: bus lines and the *Hurtigruten* coastal navigation line.

Railway travel is very expensive, unless you have the advantage of special discounted tickets or package deals; don't ever buy a regular ticket, unless you have explored other alternatives at the Tourist Information Centre or at the station's ticket counters. For longer trips, especially in high season, seats should be booked in advance.

Buses

North of Narvik and in all the Fjord Region, buses will often be the one and only available means of transportation. *EuRail* passes entitle you to considerable discounts (as high as 50% in some cases). Timetables are not as rigid as with the trains, but they are still reliable, check all details in advance, especially before undertaking a daring expedition to the far north.

The *Nord-Norge Bussen* (Northern Norway Bus Line) is a regular bus line from Fauske (the railways northern terminus) to Kirkenes, at the Russian border.

Ferries

Ferries are an integral component of the Norwegian transportation system. In the Fjord Region, for instance, ferries are simply essential.

Ferries are not very expensive, but you could find yourself stranded for several hours beside an empty ferry landing, if you don't check timetables before you start out. Adventurous and stubborn hitchhikers will find the ferry landings the ideal spot to make new friends.

The ships of the **Hurtigruten** Line leave Bergen daily at noon, and after their 11 day cruise northward they reach the Kirkenes terminus. Other coastal navigation lines go from Oslo to Arendal and from Bergen to Stavanger.

By car

Travelling by car, with or without a trailer, is the best way to visit Norway, and specially its Fjord Region. It's not always easy,

A Pastoral Scene

because while roads are on the whole good, the topography often requires considerable driving skills. There are frequent steep and narrow winding hairpin turns and mountain tunnels. Headlights are compulsory day and night, and seat belts too, in city traffic as well as on highways. Before leaving town, you'd do well to check your car, especially your brakes and clutch or automatic gears. Driving along inland roads, beware of reindeer or bear crossings. Driving under "the influence" is a very serious offence, and a pint of ale could bring your alcohol level above the legal maximum. Plan your itinerary in advance and you might be able to keep down your expenses.

Maximum speeds are 50 kph within city limits and 100 kph on interurban arteries; with a trailer, only 80 kph is allowed. Fines can go as high as $200! For car emergencies, call tel. 22 42 94 00 or 22 60 90 60 (Oslo) and tel. 55 29 22 22 or 55 32 62 00 (Bergen).

Norway has two types of interurban roads: the international highways belonging to the continental system (the "E" roads) and the regional roads (we shall indicate them as "R" roads), that are generally a single, two-way ribbon of asphalt, that in the most difficult segments (hairpins, tunnels and bridges) become one-way.

Hitchhiking: This can be a successful way to travel in the Fjord Region, thanks to the frequent ferry crossings, camp sites and observatories. Hitchhiking is not recommended on rainy days, or in winter. Outside the Fjord Region, chances are that you will often have to wait for several hours before catching a ride.

Taxis: *Drosje* in Norwegian, may be flagged down, or booked by phone. The main price of an Oslo *drosje* ride is 20-40NOK.

National flights: With a length of 1,770 km, Norway is certainly big enough to require a regular internal air-flight service. In recent years, discounted tickets have become available for almost everybody: students and senior citizens (50%), family groups and tourist tours (off-season, 35%). Travelling by air has become increasingly popular. The *SAFE* offers very convenient cumulative tickets, valid for four (or more) flights in the south of the country. For details, ask at any Travel Agency.

Car hire: All major international agencies have several branches in Norway; the Oslo and Bergen branches offer often also some good campers and trailers.

Bicycles: Norway is not the ideal country for bicycling, except in the Oslo plain and in the extreme north. The tariff is 30NOK per day, and slightly less for longer hires of not less than a week.

Accommodation

In Norway all hotels and pensions come under the strictest supervision of the Ministry of Tourism; therefore they are very expensive but also very well serviced and comfortable. The same is true of hostels and camp sites. Even after a 50% discount, accommodation will remain probably the highest single component of your Norwegian budget.

Hotels: Bed and breakfast for two — in a double-bed room — will cost you 300 to 1,800NOK.

SAS owns an hotel chain, through which you'll probably be able to obtain relatively unexpensive package deals, including flights and accommodation.

Pensions: (*pensjonat* in Norwegian) are relatively cheaper: B&B for two, 200 to 500NOK.

Private residence lodgings: are let for not less than one week; 150-400NOK per day for a whole furnished flat.

Rooms: (*hytter*) in private homes; the lists are available at the local Tourist Information Centres. There are some excellent double rooms for as little as 150-250NOK per night, breakfast included. Booking by phone in advance will save you, during the high season, from standing lengthy queues at the Tourist Information Centre.

Hostels: Norway has 80 hostels, scattered throughout the country. They are very well equipped, and the cost of a bed is 50-60NOK per night. In several hostels you'll find also double-bed rooms and family units. Some hostels offer also a breakfast service. The International Youth Hostel membership card will entitle you to discounted prices. The *NUH* (National Hostels Association, Dronnigensgade 26, Oslo, tel. 22 42 14 10) publishes and distributes regularly updated lists and details of all hostels.

Rorbu (old stone bungalows): In past times the Crown required all northern fishermen's villages to build and upkeep a number of stone bungalows, to be used as temporary shelters for transiting fishermen in distress. Where such bungalows still exist, they are often offered as hostel accommodation to transiting tourists.

Camp sites: In many cases Norwegian camp sites offer a variety of options. The Camping Card is on sale at all camp sites and costs 10NOK. Camping rates go from 20-30NOK (for a sleeping-bag), to 50-70 for a tent or camper; 100-170 for a bungalow and 120-300 for a *hytter*.

Norwegian cuisine

The Norwegian cooking is practically indistinguishable from other Scandinavian cuisines. The same is true of its prices. Breakfast includes a rich selection of cold cuts, smoked fish, cheese, fresh vegetables, fruit juices, different types of breads and buns, and lots of (mediocre) coffee. Price: 20-50NOK.

At lunch time, Norwegian *Smørbrød* is an unforgettable experience: Ten metre long tables covered with plates of shrimps, seafood, cold cuts, fish, cheese, salads, drinks and dozens of different breads and buns.

Beware of dinner! Finding a good restaurant is easy. But the prices, the prices... It's not uncommon to spend 280NOK for a single meal. Fish (except for salmon, of course!) is somewhat cheaper, and in most tourist restaurants you'll be able to enjoy a good fish dinner for not more than 150NOK.

Chinese, Middle Eastern, Italian and vegetarian restaurants are less expensive, and a meal for two will cost you 140 to 300NOK.

If you really want to economize, walk to the closest fish market, and buy your own selection of ready to eat seafood, sold by weight in a paper-bag.

Drinks — Beware: the anti-alcoholism campaign has made the price of drinks skyrocket. A bottle of ale costs 35NOK — and a bottle of wine 350! The enterprising Norwegian overcomes this by distilling at home his own *drum* and *akvavit*.

What to order
Restaurant menus will often mention at least some of the following tongue-twisting dishes:

Fish
Lutefisk: dried codfish.
Nedlagt Sild: salted herrings in tomato sauce.
Fiskecabaret: a mixed fish and seafood plate, with vegetables.
Rakorret: pickled trout.
Rokelaks: smoked salmon cold cuts with spinach.
Gravetlaks: pickled salmon in brandy sauce.

Meat
Farikal: roast lamb with cabbage.
Kjottaler: meatballs (in a secret Norwegian sauce).
Fenalar: Smoked lamb feet on eggs, ale and akvavit.
Dyrestek: roast deer in white sauce.

Deserts
Tilslorte Bondepiker: roast apples with cream.
Flotelapper: omelet with cream, jam and sugar.
Riskrem: rice pudding.

Breads, buns and cakes
Grahambrød: Norwegian wholemeal bread.
Havrekjeks: light oats biscuits, excellent for cheese sandwiches.
Kransekake: almond and egg pie.
Blotkake: various regional cream cake recipes.
Vafler: a waffle.

It's not difficult to eat well in Norway. *Kros* (cafeterias) and pizza counters will be of help. You'll often find even at the best restaurants a *tilbud* (the reduced price "specials"). Sausage counters and *smørbørd* lunches are also not too expensive.

A picturesque Fjord Cruise

Finally, one may buy food at a supermarket, and find a pleasant sunny corner in the square for a relaxed and pleasant meal.

Tips

Norway's other name is No-tip-land, because service is always included, though you can round your bill up if you feel like it. One exception only: hotel and night-spot porters will expect a small tip.

General information

Currency

The Norwegian currency is the *krone* (NOK), subdivided in 100 øre. Its approximate course is US$1 = 7NOK.

Currency is changed at bank branches, railway stations, airports, post offices and Tourist Information Centres (for a small fee). Credit cards (*Visa, American Express, Diners, Eurocard* and *Mastercard*) are welcome at all the best shops, hotels and restaurants in the larger urban centres.

Office and shopping hours

Shopping: Mon.-Fri., 9am-4pm; Saturday 9am-1pm. In the smaller centres, there might be a lunch break.
Posts: Mon.-Fri., 8am-5pm; Saturday 9am-1pm.
Banks: Mon.-Fri., 8.15am-3.30pm.

Shopping

Norway is famous for its furs, fabrics, silverware, crystal glass and china. In many cases, you might receive a VAT refund by mail, and have to present your receipts at the customs desk at the airport.

Post and telecommunication

All public phones display clear instructions in English. The phones accept 1NOK and 5NOK coins; the cost of a local call is 2NOK, but not all phones return your change.

For further details, ask the operator, free of charge. Public phones accept international calls.

Medical services

A pharmacy is an *apotek*; if you find it closed, the list and addresses of all local emergency *apoteken* will be posted.

In case of emergency, ask your hotel or hostel personnel to assist you. These are the phone numbers of the Red Cross' 24 hour service:
Oslo — 22 20 10 90.
Stavanger — 51 53 83 33.
Bergen — 55 32 11 20.
Tromsø — 77 68 30 30.
Trondheim — 73 59 88 00.

For details of services for the handicapped, call Nils Hansen, Norges Handikapforbund, Vei 2, Oslo 6, 0667 Norway.

Entertainment

The Tourist Information Centre publishes a list of all art and culture programmes in the country. Norwegian folklore is displayed in hundreds of conventions, fairs and local festivals. Besides concerts of Grieg's music and Ibsen's plays, hundreds of concerts and spectacles by many other composers and authors are presented regularly.

Films are shown in their original language.

There are many night clubs, discos and cafés-concerts, especially in the university towns.

Suggested itineraries for Norway

The outstanding tourist sites are the Fjord Region with its capital (Bergen), Oslo and its district, Trondheim and the extreme north. In the following chapters we shall trace some itineraries through those regions and along the main national arteries. The Tourist Information Centres and the *DNT*, which organizes many cross-country mountains tours, will be of great assistance.

Most visits to Norway begin at the capital, Oslo. Bergen and the Fjord Region will also claim much of your time; the extreme north remains a tempting option for those who have an additional week.

Four main arteries connect Oslo with Bergen:

— The coastal E18 to Stavenger, followed by the net of inland roads through the southern fjord district.
— The E76, through the Telemark to Haugesund and on to Bergen.
— The R7, along the route of the Oslo-Bergan railway line.

A Bergen Fishery Stall

— The northern route, first to Lillehammer and Otta on the E6, then cross-country to the Geiranger Fjord and finally the R15 to Bergen.

From Bergen, crossing the northern fjord district, you'll reach Trondheim, the Lofoten Archipelago, the island of Vesterålen,

A Norwegian stave church

Harstad, Tromsø, Alta, Hammerfest, and finally, at the Russian border, Kirkenes.

The Maps: Norwegian cartography is of the highest standards. The *Cappelens* maps divide the country into 5 (1:325,000) road maps; should you wish to purchase more detailed topographical maps, you'll find a series of outstanding 1:20,000 maps in most book shops.

Oslo

Oslo is situated at the northern end of an omonimous fjord, and it covers the surrounding hillsides to a distance of several kilometres. It gives the impression of being an almost endless village, that grew out of a little Renaissance burg, crowded with blocks of majestic palaces, well spaced between wide avenues. Oslo has a population of almost half a million people.

History

Oslo is Scandinavia's most ancient capital; it was founded at the beginning of the 11th century by Harald the Blond. For close to four centuries, Oslo remained a small province town, slowly growing around the **Akershus** castle, which dominated its sea approaches. It was fought over, sieged and conquered again and again in the course of the centuries old struggle for supremacy between Denmark and Sweden. Then, in 1624, it was almost completely gutted by fire. Almost all of today's palaces and residences date from after 1624, the most impressive product of the building fever of Christian IV of Denmark, the Architect King.

The next two centuries were a period of increased economic prosperity, with Norway remaining a province within the Danish empire. After the Danish defeat in the Napoleonic Wars, the whole of Norway came under Swedish domain; Oslo continued to grow, and the Swedish period is marked by the Royal Palace, the Storting and the new Karl Johans Street.

When Norway finally regained its independence in 1905, Oslo began to grow even faster, and today it is the capital of a modern industrial state and the pride of its people, admired by all its visitors.

How to get there

By air: Oslo has two airports: The main one, Fornebu, is only 9 km out of town; Gardermoen, 50 km inland, is frequented by charter flights coming from many European countries. The city terminal is just across the street from the Central Railway Station; the *SAS* bus ride from the airport to the terminal costs 20NOK. Gardermoen is connected to the same Oslo terminal by the *Flybussen* line (price of ride 50NOK).

By rail: The Oslo Sentralstasjonen (Central Station) is situated at the east end of the centre; the only lines that use the Oslo Vestbane (Oslo West) station are the Stavanger and Larvik lines. For further details, ask at the Central Station information desks.

By bus: International buses alight at Oslo S. (Sentralstasjonen) and at Gronlands Torg.

By ferry: All ferries land at the Akershus Castle pier, not far from Oslo S.; only the Kiel ferry lands at Oslo V.; that pier is connected to the centre by trolley no. 9.

By car: Oslo is a main junction, where most international and Scandinavian highways (and by many other national roads) meet.

Tourist services

The Main Tourist Information Centre is situated within the magnificent City Hall Palace (Rådhus), and is open May to September, Mon.-Fri. 9am-6pm, Sat. 9am-4pm, Sun. 9am-3pm; tel. 22 83 00 50. Its personnel will be happy to assist you in all your queries, and to present you with maps, a tourist guide of the city and additional written information on tours, accommodation, etc. The *Oslo Kortet* (Oslo Card) is on sale for 70NOK (valid 24 hours), 100NOK (48 hours) or 130NOK (three days). It entitles you to unlimited urban transportation, free entrance to all museums and several shopping discounts. The Kortet is on sale also at the major tourist hotels.

There is a branch of the Tourist Information Centre at Oslo S. (open all year, 8am-11pm; tel. 22 17 11 24); it specializes in booking of all sort of accommodation.

Youth: For information on cheap lodgings and other services, call Akersgate 57, tel. 22 11 04 09.

Public Transportation

The Oslo transportation network is managed by the *Oslo Sporveier* (Dronningensgate 27); it consists of bus lines, trolleys, ferries and the Underground. The bus and trolley terminus is near the National Theatre. A single ticket costs 10NOK, a short-run ticket 5NOK.

COLOSSEUM
VIGELANDS
MONOLITTEN
MAJORSTUEN
ST. DOM.
KIRKE
KIRKEVEIEN
FROGNER
PARKEN
AMALDUS
NIELSENS
PLASS
INDUSTRI GATA
FROGNER
VIGELANDS
MUSEET
16
HALVDAN SVARTES GATE
GYLDENLØVES
FROGNERVEIEN
LØVENSKIOLDS
E18
BYGDØY
ELISENBERGVEIEN
ALLE
NIELS JUELS
STANGS GATE
THOMAS HEFTYES GATE
FREDERIK
JUELS GATE
FROGNERSTRANDA
FROGNERKILEN
SKILLEBEKK
NIELS
MUNKEDAMS
BYGDØY
KONGEN
FILIPSTADVEIEN
DRONNINGEN
11
14
12
13
15

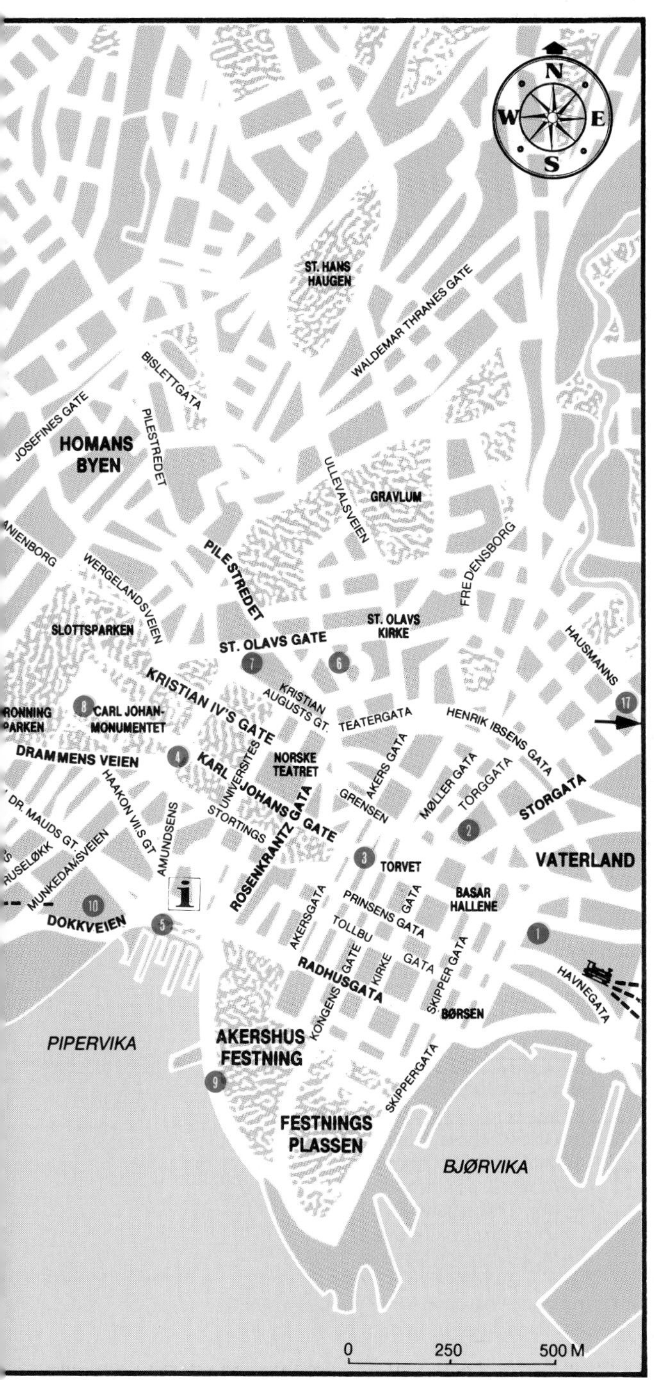
N
W
E
S
ST. HANS HAUGEN
WALDEMAR THRANES GATE
BISLETTGATA
JOSEFINES GATE
HOMANS BYEN
PILESTREDET
ULLEVALSVEIEN
GRAVLUM
FREDENSBORG
WERGELANDSVEIEN
PILESTREDET
SLOTTSPARKEN
ST. OLAVS GATE
ST. OLAVS KIRKE
HAUSMANNS
KRISTIAN IV'S GATE
KRISTIAN AUGUSTS GT.
TEATERGATA
HENRIK IBSENS GATA
CARL JOHAN-MONUMENTET
DRAMMENS VEIEN
NORSKE TEATRET
KARL JOHANS GATE
UNIVERSITETS
AKERS GATA
MØLLER GATA
TORGGATA
STORGATA
GRENSEN
HAAKON VII'S GT
AMUNDSENS
STORTINGS
DR. MAUDS GT.
MUNKEDAMSVEIEN
ROSENKRANTZ GATA
TORVET
VATERLAND
BASAR HALLENE
PRINSENS GATA
AKERSGATA
TOLLBU GATA
DOKKVEIEN
KONGENS GATE
KIRKE GATA
SKIPPER GATA
RADHUSGATA
HAVNEGATA
BØRSEN
PIPERVIKA
AKERSHUS FESTNING
SKIPPERGATA
FESTNINGS PLASSEN
BJØRVIKA
0
250
500 M

The **Tunnelbanen** (Underground): There are two lines: the first is west of the National Theatre; the second east of Jernbanetorget not far from Oslo S. The two lines cross each other, allowing free transfer at the crossing; tickets cost 10NOK and are valid for 60 minutes. Tourists will probably use mostly the Holmenkollen line.

Taxis: Taxis are very expensive; they may be flagged down on the street or booked by phone (tel. 22 38 80 96) or at their Oslo S. parking lot. Minimum price: 20NOK.

Bicycles: The Tourist Information Centre has, on demand, a list of several bicycle hire agencies in town. The rate is 40NOK per day, plus a 200NOK returnable deposit. In the suburbs, bicycle riding may be physically taxing.

Index

1. The Oslo S. Railway Station
2. The Cathedral
3. Parliament House
4. The National Theatre
5. City Hall and the Tourist Information Centre
6. The National Gallery
7. The History Museum
8. The Royal Palace
9. The Museum of the Partisan Struggle
10. The Oslo V. Railway Station
11. The Museum of Norwegian Folklore
12. The Arctic Ships Museum
13. The Kon-Tiki Museum
14. The Museum of Viking Ships
15. The Museum of the Norwegian Seas
16. The Vigeland Museum
17. The Munch Museum
18. The Homenkollen Chain

Accommodation

Like all Scandinavian capitals, Oslo has many hotels in a wide range of classes — all except economy class. The only cheap accommodation to be found are available through the Oslo S. Tourist Information Centre, or at the hostels and camp sites in the suburbs.

The *Oslo Guide* contains a list of all hotels, classified by various categories. The *Oslo Kortet* may sometimes help keep prices down. There are four main hotel categories: luxury, tourist, moderate and inexpensive. Most are downtown, and breakfast is included in the basic price.

Luxury Hotels (800-1800NOK)
Bristol: Kristian IV's Gate, tel. 22 41 58 40; quiet, two restaurants, dancing hall and bar.
Continental: Stortingsgate 24-26, tel. 22 41 90 60; very central, across the square from the National Theatre and the Royal Palace. Exquisite restaurant, dancing halls, billiard. On the ground floor is the *Theatercafeen*, a high-class, bohemian spot.
Grand: Karl Johansgate 31, tel. 22 42 93 90. Facing the Oslo S.; restaurants and first class bar.
Ambassadeur: Camilla Collettsvei 15, tel. 22 44 18 35. Near the Royal Palace; swimming pool and sauna.

Tourist Hotels (550-1000NOK)
Sara: Gunnerusgate 11-13, tel. 22 33 64 70. Very large, situated near the Oslo S. Restaurant and Nightclub.
Astoria: Akersgate 21, tel. 22 42 00 10. Near the Korting Palace; has a good restaurant.
InterNor Savoy: Universitetgate 11, tel. 22 20 26 55, near the National Gallery.

Moderate Hotels (400-900NOK)
Europa: St. Olavsgate 31, tel. 22 20 99 90. Excellent location; discounts for children.
Stefan: Rosenkrantzgate 1, tel. 22 42 92 50. Popular restaurant, recommended for dinner.

Inexpensive (300-500NOK)
Gyldenløve: Bogstadveien 20, tel. 22 60 10 90. B&B; take trolley 1.
Cocks Pensjonat: Parkveien 25, tel. 22 60 48 36. Near the Royal Palace.
Ansgar: Mollergate 26, tel. 22 20 47 35; quite central.

Anker: Storgate 55, tel. 22 11 40 05. Central; restaurant; rooms with kitchenette; May to August.

Rooms: are booked at the Oslo S. (7am-11pm). In summer the early bird wins; prices from 110 to 300NOK (180-500 for doubles). Bookings also for the "expensive" hotels (registration 10NOK).

Hostels: The best is the *YMCA* (Mollergate 1, tel. 22 42 10 66), not far from Oslo S. Open mid-June to mid-August, 7.30am-11pm and 5pm-12pm. Price 55NOK per person. The *NOH* Hostel (Haraldsheim, tel. 22 22 29 65) closes for Christmas week; take trolley 1 or 7 from Storgate to the Singen terminus, or Grefsen local train. Price 105NOK.

Camp sites
Bogstad: tel. 22 50 76 80, bus 41 to Bogstad, open all year, with rooms and restaurant.
Ekeberg: tel. 22 19 85 68. Summer only, buses 24 and 72.
Stubljan: tel. 22 61 27 06. Line 75 from Oslo S.

Rooms to let
Den Norske Hyttenformidling AS.: tel. 22 35 67 10, Mon.-Fri., 9am-5pm.
Valdres Hytteutleie: tel. 61 36 04 00.

Food

There is practically an endless choice of eateries, every possible cuisine at every possible price — except cheap prices. With a meager purse, the only choices are pizza and sausage counters and some delicatessen.

The *Smørbrød* lunch is a real bargain; you'll find it along Karl Johansgate, at several *McDonalds*, at the two *Wenches* (Rådhusgate — and not far from Christiania Torv) and at the *Helios* (across from the National Gallery) — and it costs 20-50NOK.

Here is a list of restaurants:

Luxury (200-400NOK for two)
Blom: Karl Johansgate 41, tel. 22 42 73 00. Norwegian and international cuisine.
Ludvik: Torgate 16, tel. 22 42 88 80. Mostly fish.

loderate (150-300NOK for two)

iamla Rådhus: Nedre Slottsgate, tel. 22 42 01 07. Within City all; mostly fish.

ladon: Dronningensgate 2, tel. 22 61 95 71; North-African uisine.

egetarian (100-200NOK for two)

'egeta Vertshus: Munkedamsveien 3b, tel. 22 83 42 32.

let Grynne Kjokken: Grensen 9a, tel. 22 42 15 61.

'urbadets: Akersgate 47, tel. 22 20 64 14.

izza

eppe's Pizza is a vast national net of eateries, with scores branches (and imitators) throughout the country. Oslo's *eppes* are at Solli Plass (tel. 22 44 77 38), Frognerveien 54 el. 22 56 51 40) and Konghellegate 3 (tel. 22 35 67 34).

he Itineraries

efore setting out, it will be worth your while to verify the opening ours of most sites; do this at the Tourist Information Centre or ith the help of the *Oslo Guide*.

slo is a vast city that covers both side of the fjord and a series of ales and hills, meadows and woodland. Certain neighbourhoods re as far as 15 km from downtown Oslo. There are about 20 useums, and many of them are also far from the centre.

he centre is located around two main crossings: **Karl Johans ate**, a 1.5 km long street that goes from the Royal Palace to slo S; and **Universitets Gate**, from the Rådhuset (City Hall, ith inside it the Tourist Information Centre) almost up to the rts Museum. Most of Karl Johans Gate is a pedestrian mall, ch in elegant shop windows, restaurants and cafés.

oving from Oslo S., back up Karl Johans Gate to the **Domkirken athedral**, you'll see it on your right, with its 17th century front cing the statue of King Christian IV of Denmark, builder of odern Oslo. The vast restoration works of the last century are asily recognizable. Behind the cathedral, on the site of an old pen market, there is an interesting Art Centre.

he pedestrian mall begins here. On your right you'll see the **tortorgate**, the springtime Flower Market. After a few steps, on our left, you'll find the **Stortinget** (Parliament House, open to sitors only in summer), surrounded by elegant gardens. Further n, on your left, there are several open-air cafés. On holidays and week-ends this area becomes the site of open-air spectacl and handmade jewellery stands. At the corner of **Universite Gate** you'll see on your left the **National Theatre** (Stortingate 1 that dates from the end of the 19th century; its winter reperto is in almost exclusively in Norwegian; the theatre closes f the summer. Follow Universitets Gate toward the harbour ur you reach the **Rådhuset**, a red brick palace sided by two tw towers. Its halls have often been criticized for their unabash luxury; the entrance is from Fridtjof Nansen square (open visitors 11am-2pm). The Tourist Information Centre is on th other side of City Hall. You are now almost at the harbour, ar along its piers you'll see several vendors of fresh seafood. Th corner of Karl Johans Gate and Universitets Gate is the ide spot for a short midday rest at one of the inviting open-air caf or on one of the sidewalk benches, enjoying the sunshine ar observing the passers-by.

Turn into Universitets Gate, and at no. 13 you'll find the **Nation Gallery** (established 1836). Its collection includes more th 4,000 works of art; 3,000 of them are by Norwegian artists. Th gallery is open to visitors Mon.-Sat. 10am-4pm, Sunday 12an 3pm. Free entrance.

The ground floor is dedicated to classic and modern Norwegi art. The right hand hall contains a collection of ancient Egyptia Greek and Roman statues (most of them reproductions). Th halls on the right of the first floor display the works of mode Norwegian artists; the left hand halls contain impressionist ar post-impressionist European art. The second floor is exclusive dedicated to Norwegian works. The museum's most famou exhibit is Edvard Munch's painting *The Shriek*, showing heartrending, open-mouthed cry by a quasi-autistic figure, whic was stolen in February 1994.

At the corner of Fredriksgate you'll find the **Histo Museum** (Fredriksgate 2, 11am-3pm; closed on Monda entrance free), with the **University Museum** on its upper floo The ground floor contains a Viking Era exhibition — arms, jewel coins and fabrics — and a collection of Medieval art. One of th first floor halls displays a collection of ethnography.

Turn back to the junction of Universitets Gate and Karl Johar Gate. At the west corner stands the **Slottet** (**Royal Palace**). I steps lead to a plaza with the statue of King Karl Johan, th Swedish ruler of Norway. The palace is not open to visitors, ar is guarded by impressive, statuesque sentinels. The ceremor of the Changing of the Guard is at 1.30pm; if the ceremony accompanied by military band music, you'll know that the kir is in residence. Generally from May to October the royal fami lives at the Bygdoy Summer Palace. The palace is sided by two statues: on its west, that of Queen Maud, mother of King Olav and daughter of the British King Edward VII; to the east, that of King Haakon VII (1905-1957). The gardens are open to the public, and when the weather is good, they are crowded with people.

Metropolitan Oslo

The Tourist Information Centre has a rich selection of guided walking tours of the city. The tours leave from City Hall or from Oslo S. If you prefer to design your own routes, we recommend purchasing an **Oslo Card** first; it will offer you, very considerable savings in transportation tickets and museum entrances.

The Akershus Castle

This towering structure dominates the city skyline and the harbour. Built by Haakon III around the year 1300, it was frequently fought over for more than three centuries. The Old City, nesting south of the castle, was utterly gutted by fire in 1624, and King Christian IV, not content just to rebuild the old city, (modestly renaming it "Christiania"), expanded it north of the castle, where he built some of the most impressive Renaissance style palaces. In later years, the southern side also recovered some of its former splendour. The castle is perched at the very centre of downtown Oslo. Not surprisingly, in the dark years of German occupation during the Second World War, the castle was used by the Nazis as their General Headquarters. Today it houses the **Museum of the Resistance**, which immortalizes the heroic struggle of the Norwegian freedom fighters during the Nazi occupation.

The castle entrance opens on Festningplassen; the little park perched on that hillock commands an exceptional view of the fjord and the Bygdøy Peninsula. The Museum is open April to September, 10am-4pm; entrance fee is 5NOK.

The Bygdøy Peninsula

The little Bygdøy Peninsula forms the western arm of Oslo's harbour. It contains 5 interesting museums, four of which are related to the Norwegians' special love affair with the sea. Bus 30 leaves the National Theatre Square for the peninsula and all its museums. During the summer there are also motorboat crossings, starting at the City Hall pier. Great savings with the Oslo Card!!

A short climb will take you from the pier to the **Norsk**

Open Air Chessboard on Karl Johans Gate

Folkemuseum, a museum of urban and rural folklore in ancient Norway. The museum is composed of no less than 170 structures, including a 13th century stave church, several Sami huts, Viking dwellings etc. Open 10am-6pm, 15NOK.

The second stop will be at the **Vikingskiphuset** (Viking Ship Museum). The two most spectacular ships are the *Osberg* and the *Gokstad*, which were retrieved at the end of the 19th century from the Vestfjord shallows. The ships have been restored, manned with a crew of mummified Vikings, reclaimed from the fjordside burial grounds. Open 11am-5pm, 10NOK.

The third stop is at the **Kon-Tiki Museum**, dedicated to Thor Heyerdahl and his life's work, especially his trans-oceanic voyages on the famous Kon-Tiki raft, designed to test the feasibility of the conjectured Inca expeditions from Peru to Indonesia and Oceania. Later, in 1970, Heyerdahl also crossed the Atlantic Ocean on one of his rafts. Open 10am-6pm, 10NOK.

The **Framhuset** (Museum of Polar Discovery) is just across from the Kon-Tiki Museum, on the bridge of the *Fram*, the very ship that was involved, in a series of polar expeditions, from 1893 to 1912 culminating with Roald Amundsen's discovery of the South Pole (1912). Open May to August, 10am-5pm, 7NOK.

The Parliament House Entrance

The fifth and last museum on the peninsula is the **Norsk Sjøfartsmuseum** (Museum of the Seas of Norway), with a mediocre collection of ships, a model of a shipyard and a small exhibition of naval objects and instruments; open 10am-5pm, 7NOK.

The Munch Museum

The **Munch Museum** is situated north of downtown Oslo (Tøyengate 53, open Tues.-Sat. 10am-8pm, Sunday 12am-8pm, bus 29 from the Stortinget), and Norway's first ranking art museum.

The Norwegian Edvard Munch (1864-1944) lived a long, intense and tragic life. After his studies in Paris with the great Impressionist masters, he settled in Berlin; there his work was not immediately successful, and the young, impoverished painter wandered from town to town, seeking recognition and his livelihood. Today Munch is considered the father of the Expressionist School of painting. Munch was a very productive artist, and the paintings exhibited in this museum are but a fraction of his work. When he died, Munch willed all his work to the City of Oslo. The museum's collection includes a number of oil paintings, sketches and drawings, and hundreds of prints and photographs.

The Vigeland/Frogner Park

Trolleys 1 and 2 from the National Theatre and bus 2 from the Munch Museum go to the Vigeland Park, an open-air museum built in honour of Gustav Vigeland and his work.

The entrance is majestic: a wrought-iron gate opens onto a bridge decorated with bronze statues, leading to a splendid fountain and to a 15 metre granite obelisk decorated with 121 engraved figures. The surrounding parkland, peopled by the artist's work, is in itself one of Vigeland's masterworks. South of the park there is a small museum of the great artist's life and work. Open 12am-7pm, closed on Monday. In the park there is also a pleasant café-restaurant.

Walk back to the centre along Gyldenløversgate, and climb the Eilert Sundts for one of the best views of the city. Following the Vranienborgveien, you'll find yourself in downtown Oslo.

The Sonja Onstad Art Centre

This modern Art Study Centre was presented to the city by Sonja and Nils Onstad. The Centre is surrounded by a splendid park and statuary. Inside the Centre are a permanent exhibition, some transient exhibitions, a library, a convention hall and a café.

The Holmenkollen Hill

The Holmenkollen Hill is clearly visible from the harbour and from downtown. Its name ("Mount of the Jump") is due to the towering wintersports springboard on its top. If the weather is good, ride the local train from the National Theatre to Frogerseter, then climb (not more than a 15 minutes walk) to the lift, and finally to the observation platform. At the foot of the observatory you'll see the beginning lane — and the jump.

The springboard attracts thousands of fans, especially during the March championships. Off season, you can stop by the deserted springboard to visit the **Wintersports Museum**, where you'll see a large collection of wintersport equipment, and the actual skis, boots and other paraphernalia worn by Nansen and Amundsen during their polar expeditions. At the top there is a hotel with several cafés and restaurants. The restaurant is situated below the hotel itself and is not too expensive, and below the restaurant you'll find the train stop for your ride back downtown.

Oslo's two "musts" are the Munch Museum and the Vigeland Park.

Entertainment

A listing of all current cultural, artistic and social pragrammes may be found in the *Oslo Guide* and in the *Oslo This Week*.

Theatre: Practically all plays are in Norwegian. However, if this doesn't discourage you, inquire at tel. 22 44 76 77.

Concerts: The Oslo Philarmonic Orchestra has a vast repertory and is one of the best in Europe. Its summer concerts are held at the Ruseløkveien **Konserthuset**, at the Sonja Onstad Centre, at the Munch Museum, at the Vigeland Park and elsewhere. For details, ask at the Tourist Information Centre or call tel. 22209333.

Opera and ballet: The *Den Norsk Opera Theatre* (Storgate 23c, tel. 22 42 94 75) has a repertory of classical dance and operas. The shows begin at 19.30; for tickets and information, call the *Billettsentralen*, tel. 22 42 76 77.

Folklore: Norwegian folklore is very developed, and several groups give frequent performances around Oslo; there are two regular weekly programmes at the Munkedamsveien 14 hall. Others are held at the Bygdøy Museum of Folklore.

Jazz: Oslo is a well known centre of European jazz. The most popular spot is the *Guldfisken* (Rådhusgate 2, tel. 22 41 14 89). Other excellent bands play at *Jazz Alive* (Observatoriegate 2, tel. 22 44 07 45) and at *Jeppe's Kro* (Vinderen). Names and addresses of other clubs are reported in the *Oslo Guide*.

Rock and disco: Mass rock events are held at the sports stadium and in other sites (consult *Oslo This Week*). Most discos are downtown, along Karl Johans Gate. During the summer you may be lucky enough to find some of the world's best rock music groups in Oslo.

Cinema: There are about 30 cinemas, and films are never dubbed. The local papers publish a complete list of all regular shows.

Shopping

Foreign tourists are exempt from VAT if the goods are purchased at authorized shops and amount to more than 300NOK. Keep your receipts and hand them to the customs officers at the port of

The Viking Ship Museum

exit. Oslo's main shopping centres are near the Cathedral and the Stortinget. Another good shopping centre is at Hegaehaugsvn-Bogstadvn.

Handicrafts — Ceramics, fabrics, embroideries, prints and

Vigeland Park — a Fountain

drawings are on sale at the *Domkirken* Bazaar, just behind the cathedral, and at the *Norway Designudi* of Stortingsgate 28.

Copper, ceramics and crystal art objects — are on sale at *Tinnboden* (Tordenskjoldsgate 7) and at *Christiania* (Stortorget 10).

At *Heimen* you'll find a splendid collection of high fashion knits and **pullovers**; if you like furs, don't miss the shopwindows of Slottsgate 8 and 14.

The flea-market is at Trondheimsveien 13; open Mon.-Fri. 12am-5pm and Saturday 10am-2pm.

Important addresses and phone numbers

Police — tel. 002 or 22 66 90 50.
Red Cross — tel. 003 or 22 20 10 90.
Falken (garage) — tel. 22 23 25 85.
Dentist — tel. 22 67 48 46.
Pharmacy — Jernbanetorget 4, tel. 22 41 24 82.
Lost and Found — tel. 22 66 98 65.
Central Post Office — Droningensgate 15. Mon.-Fri., 8am-8pm, Saturday 9am-3pm, tel. 22 40 78 23.
International calls prefix — tel. 0115 or 0181.
Laundry — Theresesgate 25, tel. 22 69 43 17.
Telex — tel. 0153.
SAS — Fornebuun 40, tel. 67 59 60 50.

Embassies

United States: Drammenveien 18, tel. 22 44 85 50.
Britain: Ths. Heftyesgate 8, tel. 22 55 24 00.
Australia: info office at Jernbanetorget 2, tel. 22 41 44 33.

Southern Norway

From Oslo to Bergen

There are several Oslo-Bergen routes, all pleasant and interesting; on the whole they give a complete picture of Southern Norway.

Leave Oslo on R68, an artery which turns north after a few kilometers, following the coast of Lake Tyrifjorden to **Honefoss**. From this town, the railway cuts directly to Geilo, Voss and Bergen, while the R68 turns to follow the charming coast of **Lake Krøderen**, and enters the beautiful **Hallingsdal Valley**. The beauty of this lake gave birth to several romantic legends. Here, in the little village of **Krodsherad**, lived the famous storyteller Jorgen Moe, whose fables are often told at the foot of the "Charmed Castle" or the "Millennary Oak"; it's quite possible that on your way you'll meet the the original prototypes of both... In summer, a little old steam train goes from the village of Krøderen to Vikersud and to the main railway line.

This is the zone of **Viker Sund**, one of Southern Norway's major ski resorts, with the highest ski jump in Europe. At the crossing, take the R287 to the town of **Sigdal**, a very charming little resort surrounded by 125 little lakes.

Proceed now along R7, passing through a series of picturesque hamlets and old farms. The camp sites of this area, during the summer, are usually full; in winter they are sought by young Norwegians, wintersports enthusiasts and incurable skiers. If you are planning to stay overnight, you are advised to make advance bookings. You might try booking at the **Nesbyen** (tel. 32 07 01 70), conveniently close to a Centre of Nature Studies and a Museum of Folklore; or at the **Gol** (tel. 32 07 42 41), with its beautiful waterpark and an old stave church; or at the **Hemsdel** (tel. 32078156), only 30 km away from one of the best ski slopes in the region.

The railway, the highway and the valley itself cut through the land westward, and after crossing Torpo and Aol they come to **Geilo**, the centre of the **Hardangervidda** plateau. Here the railraod continues on its way, while the highway delves deep into one of Norway's most beautiful Alpine regions.

Hardangervidda

Perhaps "plateau" is not the right term to describe the Hardangervidda; it is more than just a plateau. It's a region of some 7,500 km^2, at a mean height of 1000-1200 metres, enclosed between the Hardanger Fjord on its west side, the Bergen railway on the north side, the E67 on its south side, and an imaginary line going from Geilo to Amot on its east side. It's a region of many lakes, connected to each other by mountain streams.

There are only rare signs of human habitation: at most, you might get a glimpse of an apparently abandoned vehicle along the road. Its occupants are probably wandering around, absorbed in the scenery or in the study of some unusual specimen of the local flora.

Geologically, this is a very ancient plateau, whose higher strata are composed mainly of marble and granite. It provides an ideal ecological infrastructure for the growth of a unique and very complex flora. Many of the 450 species growing here have never been found anywhere else at this latitude. The plateau is in fact a vast prairie, attracting a great number of herbivorous animals, including several species of deers, bovines and equines. The region was known to the hunting tribes seven thousand years ago, who left their imprint in the many graffitis discovered on several rocky walls.

The *DNT* (Association of Norwegian Alpinists) has prepared detailed tour maps of the area, based on ancient paths crisscrossing the plateau. The whole complex has recently been declared a National Park. The maps (as well as other details) are available at all the main Tourist Information Centres.

Along those routes you'll find frequent road signs and arrows, and at the feet of the major peaks there are several (rather primitive) Alpine shelters.

At the western rim of the plateau the road snakes down very steeply, challenging the drivers' skills and expertise, and forcing them to disregard the attraction of the majestic views: waterfalls, mountain rivers, ravines. Even the lake that appears as if by magic at the foot of the plateau must be viewed with a measure of caution, after having stopped the car at one of the

SOUTHERN NORWAY

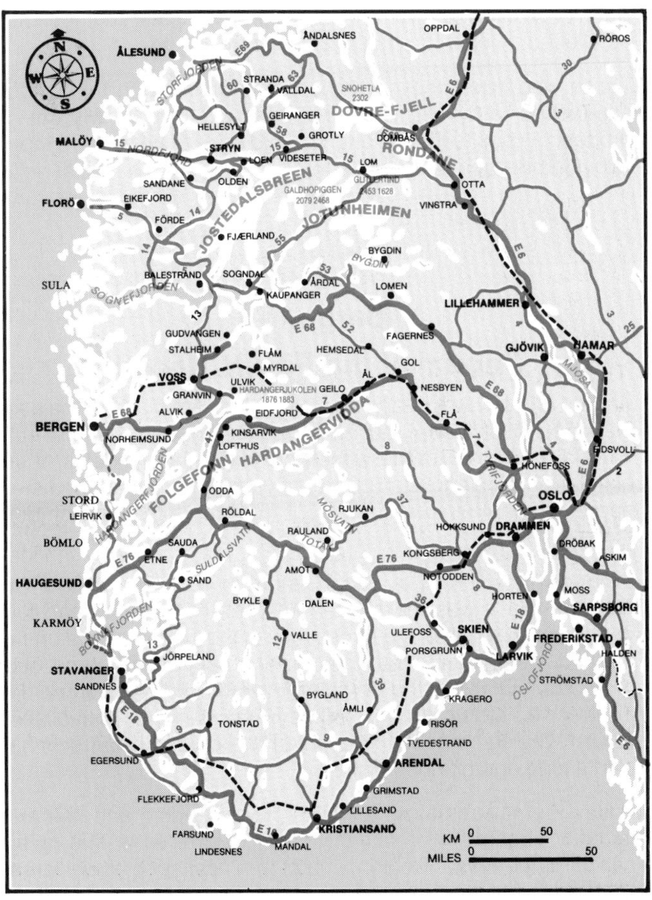

frequent observation points. Those who appear to have remained indifferent to the appeal of the lake and its meadows, will find at **Eidfjord**, a small village that seems to have been taken from the illustrations of an old story-book, relaxing and pleasant if modest accommodation.

Eldfjord is the ideal base for a visit to the Hardanger Fjord (see "The Fjord region"). You are now less than 50 km from Bergen. But please don't hurry: the road is so spectacular that it should be allotted at least four hours of leisurely driving.

Those who have chosen to travel by rail, missing this unique experience, may still save their day alighting at **Myrdal**, to proceed by bus to **Flåm** along the fjord bank to **Voss**. Here they'll rejoin the Bergen railway.

Bergen — Capital of the Fjords Region

Bergen is Norway's second city. It nestles amid a very majestic background of fjords and Alpine peaks, that surround it from three sides, while on the west it blends with the islands of the coastal archipelago. Its unique, savage charm is immediately apparent, whether one reaches it from the hinterland or from the sea.

Bergen was founded by King Olav III in 1070; for most of the 13th century it was the capital of Norway. For more than four centuries it remained the largest city in the kingdom, and one of the principal maritime trade and fishing centres in Europe, seat of the Main Office of the Bryggen Anseatic League. Bergen has a renowned old university, and its *Bergen Theatre* (established 1850) is the first theatre in Norway. The Bergen Philarmonic has also a long and glorious history.

Today, Bergen remains Norway's major seaport, and has also recently become a prominent tourist centre, as is due to the capital of the Fjords Region, one of the most spectacular areas in Norway.

How to get there

By air: There are regular *SAS* and other flights landing at the Flesland International Airport (19 km south of town) from several Scandinavian and European cities. The airport is connected to the city by a regular bus service.

By rail: The Oslo-Voss-Myrdal-Bergen line (6-8 hours) has several daily trains. Other trains go from Bergen to Voss.

By bus: A daily bus connects Bergen with Oslo, running along the R7 and E68 route; it's a 13 hour trip, much longer but more spectacular than the train ride. Three daily buses go from Bergen to Voss via Norheimsund (4 hours); the Trondheim bus leaves once a day, in the early morning, for its 15 hour trip.

By sea: Many motorboats link Bergen with other Norwegian and European ports; there are 2-3 daily crossings to Stavanger (4 hours); for detailed information on coastal cruises, ask at the Travel Agencies or at the Tourist Information Centre.

Bergen is also the southern terminus of the *Hurtigruten* cruises, that links all the major seaports of Northern Norway (up to Kirkenes, at the Russian border), with the Kingdom's "western capital", Bergen. The whole cruise takes at least 11 days, and sometimes even longer. The line offers the tourist various opportunities; the best is probably a 21 day cruise (2,400NOK, but only 1,300 under the age of 26). If you can afford it — in cash and in time — you'll be able to get well acquainted with the northern coast of Norway and all its major centres. Meals are not included in the price of the cruise (it's a matter of 40NOK for breakfast and 100NOK for supper — or for making your own provisions at the pierside supermarkets and fish markets at some of the longer stops).

For further details, see "The Bewitching Hurtigruten Cruise" below.

The Newcastle-Bergen ferry crosses over twice a week (May to September only, 21 hours); there are daily ferries for the Shetlands, the Faeroe Islands and for Iceland (June to September, 41 hours).

Tourist services

At the Torgalmenning Tourist Information Centre you'll probably find answers to all your questions, and you'll also be offered a city map and a copy of the *Bergen Guide*. The currency change desk remains open long after regular banking hours. The accommodation list is impressive: it includes scores of hotels, pensions and B&Bs, and hundreds of rooms in private residences. The office opens May to September 9am-10pm; the rest of the year 10am-3pm; tel. 55 32 14 80 and fax. 42394. The *Bergen card* is valid for 48 hours and costs 35NOK.

Car hire: All major car-hire agencies have a Bergen branch; some of them have also an airport branch. The *Avis* and *Hertz* branches are at Lars Hillesgate, nos. 18 and 15 respectively.

NORWAY

BERGEN

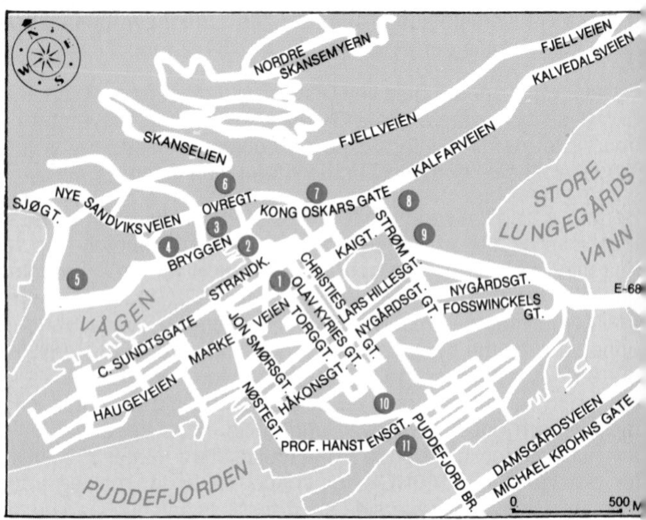

Index
1. Tourist Information Centre
2. The Fisheries
3. The Anseatic Museum
4. The Bryggens Museum
5. The Rosenkrantz Tower
6. The Cable Car Terminal
7. The Cathedral
8. The Railway Station
9. The Bus Terminal
10. The University
11. The Hurtigruten Pier

Telecommunications

The international public phones are at the Byparken Telegraph Office, open daily 8am-9pm.

The Central Post Office opens Mon.-Fri., 8am-5pm; Thursday until 7pm and Saturday 9am-1pm.

Public Transportation

Buses: Line numbers and terminuses are clearly indicated on

Bergen, Capital of the Fjord Region

all buses. Tickets cost 9NOK and are valid for 60 m; you can see how convenient the *Bergen Card* is!

Motorboats: The ferry line across the gulf functions on all workdays; tickets cost 5NOK (3 for children).

Taxis: may be hailed or called at tel. 55 99 09 90.

Accommodation

There are many choices, but this won't necessarily solve all your problems. If you have arrived without prior bookings, refer to the Tourist Information Centre, in person or by phone. They most probably will be able to help you find at least some private residence rooms.

Luxury Hotels

Norge: Ole Bulls Plass 4, tel. 55 21 01 00; 12 suites, 8 restaurants, etc.
SAS Hotel: tel. 55 54 30 00; very new.

Tourist Hotels
Orion: Bradbenken 3, tel. 55 31 80 80.
Rica: Vestre Torgate 20a, tel. 55 31 96 66.

Economy Class
Park: Hårfagrest 35, tel. 55 32 09 60.
Skogens: Håkangsgate 27, tel. 55 23 20 28.
Strand: Strandkaien 2-4, tel. 55 31 08 15.

The price of a private residence room ranges from 100NOK (singles), to 180NOK (doubles) and 220 (three or four beds).

Hostels
Montana: Johan Blydtsveien 30, tel. 55 29 29 00, 5 km out of town, 250 beds in 50 rooms, open May 10 to October 12; bus 20 from the Central Post Office.

YMCA: Kalfarveien 8, tel. 55 31 06 70; open July 15 to August 15; bus 3 from downtown Bergen.

Camp sites
Lone: tel. 55 24 08 20; 20 km out of town, on E68; open all year
Bergenshallens: tel. 55 28 28 40; open June 15 to August 15; bus 3 from downtown Bergen.

Food

There is never enough said about the dearth of restaurant prices in Norway. But you'll have in Bergen at least a rich selection of international cuisine. Nevertheless, to fully appreciate Bergen's food, one should give at least a first and second chance to Norwegian cuisine. Three restaurants compete for the title of "Number One": the *Norge Hotel* restaurant, the *SAS Hotel* restaurant, and the *Bellevue* (Bellevuebakiken 9, tel. 55 31 02 40). Slightly behind those three (also in prices) are the *Bryggen Tracteursted* (where you may even bring your own, market fresh fish, and hand it over in person to the chef), and the *Holbergstuen* (Torvalmenning 6; here you'll only be allowed to make your selection from the restaurant's fresh fish supply). At the *Wesselstuen* (Engen 14) there are also very good fish menus.

Peppe's Pizzas are present in Bergen too; a family-size pizza costs 110-150NOK.

The *Mekka* (Skostredet) offers very convenient dinners for 40-

50NOK; there are several other eateries in the same price range; seek them in the *Bergen Guide* lists.

The Students' mess at Parkveien 1 has a fixed menu dinner for as little as 30NOK.

Vegetarian restaurants are also rather inexpensive (a full meal will cost about 50NOK); such as the *Kornelia Spisestedal* (Fosswinckelgate 9), the *Santana* (Morkens Gate 4-6) and the Indian vegetarian restaurant *Taj Mahal.*

What to see

Bergen is one of many cities in the world that claim to have been built upon "seven hills". It lacks none of the components that make Norway one of the most spectacular touring countries: sea, mountains, and fjords.

The **Torget** includes the port and the fisheries and is situated at the far end of the *Vagen* (the commercial harbour). Facing the port at the fishery pier, you'll see the Old City of **Bryggen**, on your right with its Medieval alleys. The wooden structures, with their moss-covered walls, are used today as warehouses. At the extreme right, you'll recognize the skyline of the New City.

Mount Fløyen towers above the centre, and if the weather is clear it will be well worth your while to ride the local train up to its top. The trains start at the Cablecar Terminus; a return ticket costs 22NOK, and the view from the top is simply breathtaking.

You'll start your walk at the Torget (fisheries open 8am-3pm). The pyramidal warehouses on your right are the so-called *German Barracks*, that used to belong to the Anseatic League. Here, in **Bryggen**, the city began to grow and prosper six centuries ago, when the German merchants of the League undertook the gigantic task of selling and transporting practically all Norway's fish, and in return the fishermen, burghers and peasants were supplied with grain, flour and beer imported by the Anseatic fleet from the League's southern centres in Germany and other countries. From these barracks — or rather their original version, later damaged and finally destroyed by fire in the 18th century — the Anseatic Merchants ruled the city as they ruled most of the other seaports of Norway, for close to two centuries.

The **Hanseatic Museum** is lodged within one of those barracks; its furniture dates from the 16th century, and its shows document the trade life of Anseatic Bergen (open June-August, 10am-4pm,

The Old City of Bergen

and the rest of the year 11am-2pm; closed on winter Tuesdays, Thursdays and Saturdays).

The harbour section is enclosed within a perimetral lane, that ends at the **Rosenkrantz Tower**, built in 1560 for Eric Rosenkrantz, one of the major city notables of his times. Near the tower you'll see the **Høkonshallen**, a 14th century palace built by King Høkon as his official Ceremonial Hall. Both tower and palace were seriously damaged in 1944, when a German ammunition ship blew up in the harbour. They have since been restored, and they are open to visitors May-September, 10am-4pm; in winter only on Sunday, 12am-3pm.

Turn back toward the centre, stopping briefly at the **Bryggen Museum**, which houses the many ancient objects recovered at the local 1955-72 archeologic digs. The museum is open May-August 10am-4pm (Tuesdays until 8pm) and the rest of the year daily, 11am-3pm.

Øvergaten Street marked the Bergen city limits for many centuries. Cross to **Lilla Øvergaten**, a characteristic shopping lane of many antiques shops, that leads to the **Domkirke**, a cathedral that in spite of its recent restoration has little to offer.

The majority of the 26 museums and art galleries of Bergen are too specialized to be of great interest to the lay visitor: let's see, for instance, who would be interested in a visit to the Museum of Leprosy? Be as it may, all museums and galleries are duly listed in the *Bergen Guide*.

The Suburbs

The tours organized by the Tourist Information Centre reach all the major suburbian sites. One of the most popular tours is the pilgrimage to the residence of the greatest son of Bergen, the world famous composer Edvard Grieg, and to the wooden Medieval church of **Fantoft**. Grieg's house is today a personal museum of the composer's life and work, furnished with original objects that belonged to his family. Open May-September, 10.30am-1pm and 2.30-5.30pm. The Fantoft church was built in the 12th century in the Sognefjord, and was transported here at the end of the 19th century; the Viking dragons that decorate its front give it a pagoda-like, almost pagan countenance.

Wishing to visit those sites by car, in spite of the advantages of a guided group tour, you'll find all the necessary information at the Tourist Information Centre, and also clear signs and arrows along your route.

Entertainment

Bergen is rightly proud of its bicentennial Philarmonic Orchestra. The philarmonic season lasts from September to June; its concerts are held at the Grieg Hall on Thursday (programmes and tickets at the Tourist Information Centre). Bergen cinemas present their programmes in the original languages, non-stop from 11am to 11pm. On Sundays, you'll often find at the Bryggen Museum some interesting folklore programmes.

There are several night-clubs and discos, frequented mostly by young students. The *Hulen* (Nygardsparken) is a Saturday night disco, with frequent weekdays folklore programmes.

Shopping

Should you make some purchase at one of the many *tax free* shops, easily recognizable by their window or door signs, you'll be able to demand a refund of your VAT payments at the customs desk of the exit port; the refund will be forwarded to you by mail at your home address. The best furs outlet is probably the *Motepels*; for silverware, try the *Theodor Olsen*.

Addresses
Laundry: Lille Ovregate 17, tel. 55 32 55 04.
Bicycle Hire: Fjøsangerveien 30b, tel. 55 29 78 30.
Police: tel. 002.
Firemen: tel. 001.
Red Cross: tel. 003.

From Oslo to Stavanger

Two main arteries connect Oslo to Stavanger: the E18, a coastal route, and a "shortcut", that climbs daringly up to Amot and Röldal. In between the two routes there are several interesting sites.

The coastal route

Following the signs of the Oslo road signs, you will easily find the E18 exit for Drammen. However, slightly before reaching Drammen itself, exit on your right to **Spiraltoppen**, a spiral road that circles the mount six times, climbing gradually to a spectacular observatory, with a pleasant open-air restaurant beside it.

Drammen is the capital of the Buskerud region. It has a remarkable open-air museum, dedicated to local history and traditions. The Town Hall dates from 1872; its architect won first prize for "the best architectural reconstruction in Europe".

Drammen is situated at the northern end of the Drammen Fjord, which forms the Hurun peninsula, site of the omonimous **Hurun** town. On midsummer week-ends the beaches and tiny villages of the peninsula attract thousands of Oslonians. At the Holmsbu Art Gallery you'll find several works by Henrik Sorensen.

Lier, a garden town (it's also known as "Eastern Norway's Garden"), is only a few kilometres north of Drammen. In the spring its orchards bloom with thousands of white and rose coloured flowers. Toward the end of summer its woods and meadows fill with wild berries of all types — and once again an endless stream of Oslonians come to harvest them, armed with tins, baskets and containers. West of Drammen is **Nedre Eiker**, an old renowned centre of salmon fishing.

This region is only 40 km away from the capital. This is probably the reason why it lacks suitable local accommodation. There are only a few hotels at Drammen and at Hurun; on the other side, there are several attractive camp sites. Drammen has also a hostel (Korsvegen 62) and a Tourist Information Centre (tel. 32 80 62 10).

The E18 proceeds, alongside the railway, to **Larvik** and to **Skien**, Ibsen's home town. Skien is also a good starting point for tours of the Telemark; itineraries, maps and other information is available at the Tourist Information Centre (tel. 35 52 82 27).

Today the **Ibsen House** is a cultural centre; it has a good library and holds several mobile exhibitions and theatre shows. The **Gjerpen** church (12th century) and the **Måhlum** church (18th century) are two interesting contemporary reconstructions.

Ibsen's Venstop, an old farm where Ibsen lived in his youth, is today a private museum.

The *Victoria* motorboat sails daily at 8.30am from Skien, following the Bandak Canal to Dalen, crossing several lakes, watercourses and locks. The motorboat's slow progress will introduce you gradually to the unique pastoral atmosphere of the Telemark; it's a day long cruise. To save a few hours, you might board the boat at its half-way stop, at **Ulefoss**.

Back to Skien, proceed now south-westward on the E18 to **Kragerø**.

In this picturesque little town there is much to see: you'l enjoy its ancient alleys, its coastal islets, and the town museum, dedicated to the history of ancient agricultural settlements. At the hostel (tel. 35 68 18 66) and at the Tourist Information Centre (tel. 35 98 23 30), ask about tour routes in the surrounding area.

There are several colourful little seaside villages, easily reached from the E18 exits: **Risør**, **Lyngør** and **Tvedestrand**. Risør has a Tourist Information Centre (tel. 37 15 22 70); it is, also, one of the stops of the Oslo-Arendal motorboat line.

Arendal

The many canals that criss-cross most of this town's neighborhoods have earned the name of "The Little Venice

A characteristic little Alpin lake

of the North". Arendal's neighborhoods have a specious and sophisticated tourist resort, full of luxury hotels and restaurants. The assistance of the Tourist Information Centre personnel (tel. 37 02 21 93) is vital here: they will help you to avoid the most expensive accommodation, and direct you to pleasant short tours of the town and of the gulf islands.

Observe the architectural structure of the centre, with its unusually pretentious pot-pourri of private villas and residential condos, of modern hotels and Renaissance-style palaces. The most popular tours go to the islands of **Merdogård** and **Tromöya**, and at the little islet of **Faro**, nicknamed "the Guardian of the Gulf".

Follow the E18 to **Grimstad**, where Ibsen made his fateful decision to abandon his former chemist's career to dedicate his life to literature. Here too you'll find several hotels and a hostel (tel. 37 04 03 00), a modest museum and some ancient burial.

Lillesand's attractive beaches will try to lure you to a refreshing stop on the way to Kristiansand, capital of the Vest Agder region.

Kristiansand

Kristiansand is of course yet another of Christian IV's creations, built by the Danish Architect King, in the course of the 17th entury (to be precise, in 1641). Many regular ferry lines land at ristiansand, from the British Islands, from Denmark and from ther Norwegian ports. Its beaches, its modern resort hotels and ne elegance of its buildings make Kristiansand a very popular easide resort. Downtown Kristiansand, with its Old City quarter, s situated between the Otra river and the sea. At its northern end borders with a splendid public park. The pastoral character of ne Old City vanishes when you come to the harbour, a small ut bustling and very modern seaport, which looks more like a entral European port than a provincial Norwegian town. The ourist Information Centre (Werselandsgade 17, tel. 38 02 60 65) s open from June to August 8am-7pm, and the rest of the year, rom Mon.-Fri., 8am-4pm.

ood and accommodation

s one might expect, being in Norway as well as in a luxury ummer resort, prices are rather steep. However, in summer nere are also some interesting "bargains" for family and tourist roups. The *Savoy* hotel (Kr. Ivsgate 1, tel. 38 02 41 75) is ot among the most expensive; the *Ernst* (Rådhurstgate 2, tel. 8021400) is one of the best, but also very expensive. The hostel el. 38 09 49 47) and the camp sites (tel. 38 09 47 59) are open lay to September and are 3 km out of town, on the other side f the Otra.

you are on a limited budget, avoid the restaurants; at *eppe's Pizza* (Gyldenlovesgate 7) you'll be able to satisfy your unger at a relatively low cost.

Vhat to see

he downtown streets will remind you of some little country own in Denmark; however, you'll find them much more rowded. The elegant cathedral dates from the last century. he **Kristianholm** Castle, which rises high above the town on he eastern slopes of the gulf, was built in 1674. It is very well reserved and contains a modest art museum.

here are three regular motorboat tours. The first sails from ier 6 to Lillesand (3 hours, 70NOK); the second sails from the ishermen's Pier to the gulf islands (2 hours, 50NOK); the third oes from Hallen to the island of N.Y. Helsund (1 hour, 25NOK).

ristiansand's major attraction is the **Zoo** and its surrounding arkland. It spreads along the E18, about 11 km out of town; eside its thousands of animal species, it also has the best musement park in Norway.

he **Ruvenlanden** Park is a very attractive site, crossed by fascinating paths and dotted with refreshing cafés. It's not far from downtown Kristiansand, easily reached on foot.

Touring the region

The *Steamtrain*, a last relic of the *Setesdalbanen* railways, offers a refreshing experience: it's a narrow-gauge line, with an almost centenarian engine, that runs from Grovane (20 km out of town) for not more than 5 km (30NOK, 20 for children).

Another pleasant tour goes to the **Gimla Estate** Arts Museum, situated on the E18, halfway to the Zoo.

The **Vest Agder Museum**, situated in the same zone, is an open-air museum with about 30 ancient structures documenting four centuries of local history; you'll find particularly interesting the epoch furniture of most residences and churches.

Kristiansand is also the starting point of one of the Southern Fjords Region itineraries: the tour of the Setesdal Valley.

Setesdal

This valley remains to this day a geologist's nightmare: for reasons yet unknown, its inimitably grey soil is furrowed by crater-lakes and watercourses, whose formation defies all standard geologic models. Be as it may, it's a feast for the tourist's eye.

Road 12 goes up the Otra course to **Byglandsfjord**. Further on you'll make the acquaintance with one of the miracles of Norwegian engineering: the daring tunnel that has delivered the valley from long centuries of complete isolation. Continue to the little town of **Valle**; from here on you'll walk. Valle is surrounded by a number of old, picturesque farms, and its people often wear the characteristic costumes of their forefathers. You'll enjoy the Sunday functions, when the majority of the population dresses up for church. At the Tourist Information Centre (tel. 37 93 73 12) you'll find details of eventual tours, as well as some written information on local old customs and traditions.

One of the next routes follows the ancient *Skins' Route*, a path that for centuries was followed by a stream of farmers and hunters, carrying on their back skins and other tributes to the regional customs office, as bulk payment of their tax dues. This route (3 km long) climbs up to an Alpine shelter, where you'll enjoy a splendid view of the valley and its lakes. A second path goes first to the Bossbu shelter, and after 10 km reaches the village of **Bykle**, with a regular bus line back to Valle.

Road 45 to Dalen (see the following chapter) will take you to the Telemark. However, we'd like you to make a detour from Valle to Bykle, along a route that at times becomes quite demanding. Specially spectacular, if not unique, is the sight of the famous *Byklestigen Ladder*, undoubtedly one of the most daring examples of modern Norwegian road building.

Road 12 will take you to your next stop, **Hovden**, an excellent strategic point for the tour of the valley. Hovden is also the bus terminus; details of timetables are available at the Tourist Information Centre (tel. 37 93 96 30) or at the hostel (summers only).

R12 then joins the E76 to Roldal, to Odda and to the Fjords Region.

Mandal

Mandal (the "White City") is situated at the southern end of Norway (at a latitude of 58 degrees) and it owes its name to the shining white beaches, its homes and its old, picturesque alleys. It is well worth an afternoon's visit.

The main street, that was recently reconstructed with the utmost care, is a shopping mall leading to the **Mandal Church**, a monumental wooden church in the Empire style of 1821. Proceed then to the Museum, situated near the incomparable **Sjosanden** beach, that is one of the most popular haunts of Norwegian sun-worshippers.

There are a number of hotels and B&Bs, a Tourist Information Centre (tel. 38 26 08 20) and a hostel (tel. 38 26 15 01).

The E18 to Stavanger has several inviting exits. About 8 km from Mandal, the R460 branches off to **Lindesnes**, the southernmost lighthouse in Norway. The bird-flight distance from here to Norway's northern tip is 1,770 km.

The E18 then crosses **Lyngdal** and **Farsund**. In this area there are many ancient burial sites and other archaeological sites, dating from the Stone Age to the days of the Vikings. For details or guidance, call the Farsund Tourist Information Centre (tel. 38 39 08 39).

Another E18 exit turns northward, crossing **Hægebostad** to lake Eiken, an attractive resort situated near the ruins of old Viking settlements. Then the road joins the R9 to **Tonstad**. From Tonstad, the spectacular R468 snakes on to Sivekrok and to **Lysebotn**.

If you want to save some time, you should decide to remain on the E18 to Stavanger, you will still see some very interesting views. The two centres of **Kvinesdal** and **Flekkefjord** provide an excellent introduction to the island of **Hidra**, known as the "Pearl of the South" (R469 from Flekkesfjord).

Travelling by rail, you'll miss the views we have just described; however, even the train ride offers some spectacular sights, and we strongly advise against taking a night train.

Egersund

Egersund (Tourist Information Centre at tel. 51 49 08 19) is yet another characteristic "white town": shining beaches, whitewashed walls and spotless pavements. The harbour, well protected by the gulf arms and the Egerøya Island, is the terminus of the Hantsholm (Denmark) ferries.

Travelling by car to Stavanger, you should opt for the R44, that follows the railway route crossing Jæren, a village famous for its spectacular glacial perpendicular cliffs.

Stavanger

Stavanger is the strategic base of the North Sea oil fields, and an important centre of ancillary oil industries. With its 100,000 people, it is the major town and regional capital of the Rogeland; it's also the best strategic starting point for the tour of the Southern Fjords. There are signs of human settlement dating as far back as the 11th century B.C. — a clear sign that Scavanger's strategic importance had been recognized long before the oil age of today.

The town of Stavanger itself was founded in the 12th century, and has been for many centuries an important maritime trade centre. A visit to Stavanger is simply a must.

How to get there

Stavanger is much more than a strategically-sited seaport; it is also a road and railway junction, and it is highly accessible from all parts of Norway, and indeed from all-over Europe.

There are 3-4 Oslo-Kristiansand-Stavanger trains (9 hours).

The ultramodern *Hurtigbut* motorvessel makes three regular daily crossings from Stavanger to Haugesund (4-5 hours).

By sea, Stavanger is connected by ferry to Newcastle (May to September, once or twice a week, 17 hours) and to Hantsholm (2 weekly crossings, 11 hours).

Food and accommodation

The town and its suburbs are dotted with hotels, B&Bs and hostels of all types. The most renowned, and most expensive hotel is the *SAS* (Løkkevn 26); the *Havley* (Valbergate 1, tel. 51 53 31 14) and the *Rogalandsheimen* (Musegate 18, tel. 51 52 01 88) are two relatively modest B&Bs. The *Mosvangen* hostel (tel. 51 52 75 60) is rather far and not inexpensive; the *YMCA* hostel (Rektor Berntsensgate 7, tel. 51 53 28 88), which is more convenient, is open only for the month of July. There are two camp sites, the first near the hostel and the other at Raege (tel. 51 53 29 71).

There are quite a few restaurants. For a limited budget dinner, it's a matter of choosing between restaurant fish menus, pizza counters or chinese food. The *Straen* (fish, Strandgate 15), the *Peking* (chinese, Skagenkaien 10) and the *Moon House* (chinese) are three good options.

What to see

Viewed from the sea, Stavanger will look like a typical modern industrial town. After your landing, things change and become gradually more exciting. **Gamla Stavanger** (the Old City), is a complex of 130 buildings accurately restored into an open-air museum. In one of its buildings you'll find the **Cunning Museum** (0vre Strandgate 88), an authentic reconstruction of the first tinned-sardine plant in town.

Øvre Strandgate leaves the Old City and ends in **Torget**, the vegetable market square. Along the pier, at sunrise, the fishermen (and other fishmongers) sell their daily catche at the fishery stands. Across the pier, in front of the fisheries, stands the **Cathedral**, a 13th century church that has so often been restored, that its original Norman style has been almost completely obliterated in later styles. The **Stavanger Museum** (Musegate 16) documents 8 centuries of cultural and trade life.

The **Valberg Tower** was built at the beginning of the 19th century to serve as a fire-alarm observatory; today it is a sightseeing platform, open to visitors 10am-4pm.

On the western arm of the Gulf (Vagen), along Skagen Street, you'll find the Stavanger's main Shopping Centre, the Tourist

Information Centre (tel. 51 89 62 00, June to August 9am-6pm and the rest of the year Mon.-Fri. 9am-4pm and Saturday 9am-1pm) and the railway station. The *Stavanger Card* is on sale at the Tourist Information Centre for 20NOK.

Neighbouring sites

Just above the Tourist Information Centre is the Touring Office (tel. 51 52 75 66, Mon.-Fri. 9-11am), with several attractive offers of daily tours to the Rogeland and to other areas.

One of the most attractive is the **Lysefjord** tour, that climbs up to the **Altar Peak**, a perpendicular 610 m high table. The tour starts from the Fiskepiren (fishermen's pier), with a motorboat crossing to Tab; then it proceeds by bus to Jørpeland, and finally there is a two hour climb on foot. The tour price is about 200NOK. The climb is not too steep, and the view from the top is more than spectacular.

The **Månafoss Waterfall** is one of the most beautiful in Norway. It's reached south-eastward along the E18, turning onto the R45 to Gilja and to the Frafjorden vehicle parking areas. The waterfall itself is at the end of a 30 minute walk along a pleasant pathway.

The "Discovery Route"

This itinerary will take you to **Ryfylke**, a spectacular little centre in Northern Rogeland, surrounded by miniature little fjords, lakes and islets connected to each other by a net of tunnels, bridges and ferry crossings. Also very interesting is the gigantic hydro-electric complex, that exploits each and every lock for the production of scores of megawatts. The motorboats sail from Stavanger to **Jelsa**, at the mouth of the Sandsfjord; from there a bus climbs along the R41. **Sand**, a little resort situated along the R41, is a very good base for walking tours in the area.

From Oslo to Haugesund — on E76

The E76 is a modern highway, fast and exciting, running across some very spectacular sceneries. It goes through a series of tunnels (the longest, Haukeli, is 5.7 km long) and crosses hundreds of bridges. There are several lookout parking spots, with restaurants, toilets and gas stations etc.

The Buskerud

Leaving Oslo on the E18 to Drammen, look for the arrow indicating the exit for the E76 to Hokksund and, through the Buskerud, to **Kongsberg**, the silver mining centre. The Kongsberg mines are the only ones in the world, where silver is mined as pure metal, and not as a mineral ore. Nevertheless, the mining complex is only a tourist attraction today. At the entrance to the mines is the **Silver Museum** (summers only, 10am-4pm). In town there are three other museums: the Museum of Mining, the Folklore Museum and the Wintersports Museum. The Jazz Festival (end of June) attracts thousands of jazz-lovers to Kongsberg. The **Kongsberg Church** is a monumental 18th century building in High Barock style, witness of the great prosperity that its silver mines brought to 18th century Kongsberg.

Next, we suggest a short break along R8. After only 6 km you'll reach a crossing. Take the right-hand branch, following the railway route and crossing the silver mines area to the Hardangervidda Plateau. The road climbs along the **Numedal Valley**, crossing from side to side of the Lågen stream. At **Flesberg** we suggest you stop for a brief visit to the Dåset village-museum (16 carefully restored 17th and 18th century houses). At **Rollag** you'll find an ancient stave church. Still higher up, at **Nore** and **Uvdal**, you'll see two other stave churches. The zone is a chain of contrasts between its savage alpine scenery, its decrepit isolated hamlets and its ultra-modern hydroelectric plants.

Rødberg is the railway terminus; this railway line is used by thousands of tourists and hundreds of alpinists, eager to start on the famous **Blefjell Trail** route (see "Backpacking through Norway"). At the Tourist Information Centre (tel. 32 74 13 90) and at the hostel (tel. 32 73 20 24) you'll find all the information you need.

Proceed now to **Notodden** (Tourist Information Centre, tel. 35012022). After 3 more kilometres, at Heddel, you'll come to the largest wooden Medieval church in Norway. Then, at the **Bø** crossing, turn left toward the E76 to Seljord. Near this crossing, a few hundred metres southward on the R360, you'll come to a spectacular lookout point, high above the Lefjell hotel. Bø has a Tourist Information Centre (tel. 35951880), some hotels and a hostel. The R36 now joins with the E76 near **Seljord** (another stave church), and then to **Kviteseid**, where you will sail on the *Victoria* ferryboat, to Dalen.

Dalen is probably the best strategic starting point for Telemark tours; it has several hotels and a good hostel (tel. 35 07 71 00). The main neighbouring attractions include the vast hydroelectric plants, Lake Bandak and its surrounding mountains. In town you'll find yet another old stave church and a little museum, whose "pièce de resistence" is the oldest washing machine in history, the invention of a local peasant.

Several tourist routes and four main roads branch off the Dalen junction. The R38 runs northward and reaches the E76 near **Amot**. The R37 crosses the Tokko hydroelectric plant, fed by the majestic **Hyllandfoss** waterfalls, and reaches **Rauland**, with its Tourist Information Centre (tel. 35 07 11 17), the stepping stone of several Telemark and Hardangervidda routes. Rauland was the home town of the famous artist Dyre Vaa, creator of the Swans Fountain, which you may have seen back in Oslo, on the City Hall square.

Rjukan

The R37 climbs on north-eastward to the Telemark peaks, but we shall first take a short timeout for a brief historic digression.

As you know, late in the course of the Second World War Germany was forced to conclude that its only hope of victory was through the invention and use of a new, revolutionary, spectacular weapon: the atom bomb. This is how the Reichstag embarked upon its "heavy water" project, intended to provide the Third Reich with the prime material for the production of such a bomb. The plants were built at the bottom of a deep gorge, just below the little village of **Vemork**. But one of the scientists, in a crises of conscience, betrayed the project and its aims to the local arm of the British Intelligence, and in a freezing winter night a group of Norwegian freedom fighters took the German garrison by surprise and blew up the whole works. This heroic action was later dramatized in the famous film **The Heroes of the Telemark**. Now let's get on board again and speed on.

The R37 follows the coast of Lake Møsvatn to Rjukan. The bus stops briefly at the Skinnedru dam; the driver will invite you to step into the local tourist curio shop. He will probably inform you that the business belongs to one of the actual heroes of the Telemark mission. Then the bus will move on, climbing slowly to the **Vemork Observatory**, where you'll see also a field reconstruction of the Telemark mission. After this second stop, the bus hairpins cautiously down to **Rjukan**, at the foot of Mount Gausta (1850 m).

Haugesund's Shipyards

Rjukan has several hotels, a hostel (tel. 35 00 95 27) and a Tourist Information Centre (tel. 35 09 15 11). At Rjukan you'll find the Vestfjord and Mael train, which crosses Lake Tinusjø by ferry, to proceed to Notboden. Travelling by car along the R37, you'll first reach the lake following its shore eastward to Kongsberg.

The E76 carries on westward, joining with the E12 after Amot, and climbing down to Kristiansand. This segment of the E76 is one of the most spectacular in the region, not only because of the rugged beauty of its mountains and ravines, but also because of the daring of the route itself, that will often leave you breathless

From **Roldal**, a town we have already mentioned, start several Hardangervidda routes. 9 km south-west of Roldal, the E76 crosses the R46 to Stavanger. Here the E76 turns north-westward, following the course of the Sørdalen river to Akrefjord (one of the most beautiful in the entire Fjord Region), and the spectacular Longfoss Waterfall.

Then the E76 climbs down, crossing **Etne** and **Ølen**, two splendid little towns on the banks of the Hardangerfjord.

Haugesund

The main urban centre of the Rogeland is situated on the western bank of the fjord, protected by the islet of Karmøy. Haugesund is one of the major folklore centres in Norway, and is easily accessible by car on the E76 and the R14, or by the motorboats of the fast Stavanger-Haugesund-Bergen line.

Haugesund was first settled by the Vikings, and the stormy life of its first few centuries is largely documented by the findings of several archeologic digs. 3 km north of the town you'll see the **Haraldshaugen**, an obelisk erected in honour of King Harald Håfagre (the Bearded), who according to a legend had vowed never to shave his beard unless he succeeded in his effort to win the whole of Norway under his rule. After his great victory at Hafrsfjord, in 872, he finally was able to shave. The obelisk was erected in 1872, on the occasion of the celebrations for the thousand anniversary of the first Norwegian union.

At the **Haugesund Museum** you'll find the documentation of the legendary life of King Harold, and a cursory exhibition of eight centuries of fishing and maritime trade. At the Tourist Information Centre (tel. 52725055), ask for the town map and the map of the area. The **Church of St. Olav** was built by King Haakon IV in 1250. In the harbour, you'll see the shipyard and other ancillary structures of the North Sea oil rigs.

Then, following the instructions obtained at the Tourist Information Centre or at the hostel (Skeisvannsveien 20, tel. 52712146), you'll be able to visit the Karmøy Island Viking burial sites and the Karmsund bridge monolites.

The Haugesund hotels are very expensive, with the only exception of the *IMI* (Strandgate 192, tel. 52723699). At Sandue, on the Karmøy island, you'll find a hostel (tel. 52820191) and two camp sites.

From Haugesund you may select one of several Fjord Region routes (see "Backpack Trails"). The R14 crosses all the Fjords region, connecting Haugesund to Bergen.

Western Norway — The Fjord Region

Bergen is the capital of the Fjord Region; whatever route you take, there'll be something worth seeing. And, as any Norwegian will tell you about fjords, never think that "if you've seen one, you've seen them all". This is never the case: each fjord has its own unique personality. How then can we write a single chapter for the whole Fjord Region? It would be more adequate to write a whole volume on each fjord...

Having said this and putting our conscience at rest, we'll continue to outline some itineraries through this unique region in a short chapter; we shall try to follow two simple principles: the first, that it would be presumptuous to pretend to show you everything; the second is, that we'll be guided by two conditions: time and accessibility. Our routes are suitable for every tourist allowing for a measure of rest and relaxation; they let you stop from time to time at a suitable spot, just to look at the sights and enjoy. Given the topography of the region, it is often necessary to switch from one means of transportation to another, from bus to motorboat, to train, and even, for shorter distances, to your own mountain boots.

The Fjord Region can be divided into three areas:

— South of Bergen, around the Hardangerfjord, with its many tributaries.

— Not far North of Bergen is the complex of the Sognefjord, which cuts deep into the hinterland for more than 160 km, between almost perpendicular mountain walls that often reach as high as 2,000 m, amidst frequent summer waterfalls and winter avalanches.

— Farther North, the incomparable trio of the Nordfjord, the Geiranger and the Romsdal fjords.

To simplify your route even more, we have traced four different routes; but we'll begin with some brief introductory notes.

The Birth of the Fjords

During the last Ice Age, the Norwegian Alps were practically

The Eidfjord

buried under a thick mantle of ice and snow. Toward the end of this Age, it occasionally defrosted and sometimes froze. This caused a relatively fast deepening of these ancient valleys, so suddenly exposed to extreme temperature changes and consequent irresistible lateral pressures. When our present Temperate Era got under way, the sea level rose gradually, bringing the sea deep into those alpine gorges, and transforming the ancient valleys into today's fjords.

Homo Fjordensis?

During your visit, you'll often be surprised by the sight of some isolated old farm, down in the deep shadow of the fjord bank or perched high on top of a small plateau, hugged by its small orchards and vegetable gardens, and with its little motorboat roped to a wooden jetty. And you'll probably ask yourself: what are these people doing here? Don't they miss the rest of mankind? You will have met one of the unique types of Norwegian individualism, an expression of the intimate lien that links man to a personal piece of soil. Almost a case of symbiotic existence of man and nature. Homo Fjordensis?

Hardangerfjord

Leave Bergen on the E68 toward Voss, following the road signs that lead southward, on the R14, to **Halhjem**. Here you'll switch to the **Sandvikvåg** motorboat (45 minutes, 100NOK). Then, on **Stord** island, follow the R14 to **Leirvik**. South of Leirvik you'll begin your second motorboat crossing (30m, 70NOK) to **Utbjoa**. Now the R543 will take you to **Ølen**, and the R46 to **Ropeid**. A third motorboat crossing (10 m, 40NOK) and you'll be at **Sand**. Proceed now up the course of the **Suldalslägen**, a salmon rich mountain stream, to follow the coasts of **Lake Suldal** to **Nesflaten**.

Here the road climbs up the Brattslandal Valley until it joins the E76 (the Oslo-Bergen highway that cuts through the Telemark). The road snakes on and on toward the north-west, crossing Seljestad and then **Odda**. On the way you'll find several spots too breathtakingly beautiful not to stop for a good look and for a well earned rest. At Odda you'll find accommodation, restaurants, cafés, a hostel and a Tourist Information Centre (tel. 53 64 12 99).

Leaving Odda behind, drive northward until you reach a crossing, that gives you the choice between the western and the eastern bank of the Sørfjorden. Turning to the left, on R550, you'll come to **Åga**, a hamlet of 9 (nine) peasant families. The village exists since times immemorial (almost seven centuries), and its houses have been declared a national monument. The road — and it is often little more than a single lane of asphalt ribbon — cuts through a land of vegetable gardens and orchards that in the spring bloom in white and pink flowers.

At **Utne** the Sørfjorden flows into the Hardangerfjorden; this is the ideal place for an overnight stop. Here the fjord is 3 km wide, and its waters are 800 m deep. North of Utne the **Oksen** plateau rises to 1241 m, forming a divide between the Eidfjord and the Granvinfjord. Until the 17th century the fjords were the only link between the various regions of the Norwegian hinterland, and Utne was a relatively important junction. In fact Utne's historic hotel was founded in 1722 (and for the last two centuries it has remained in the hands of the same family). Go in, and you'll find yourself in the 18th century; however, its spacious rooms cannot be rented for less than 600NOK per night. Near the hotel you'll see the local museum, dedicated to the history and customs of Utne.

From Utne you may proceed by boat to Kranndal or to Kinsarvik, or by road to **Jondal**, for a splendid view of the **Folgefonna** glacier.

Having crossed the fjord to Kinsarvik, you'll find yourself at the foot of the Kisko valley, that climbs down from the Hardangervidda plateau, creating four spectacular waterfalls. Kisko is an ancient village, with a 12th century church — one of the rare stone churches of that time; many of its houses are also more than five centuries old. Proceeding southward you'll come to **Lofthus**, a tiny village on a valley bed peppered with ancient farms. Grieg lived in one of these farms for several years: his piano and some of his other furniture are exhibited in the Ullensuag hotel lobby.

Eidfjord

The R47 will take you to Eidfjord, an attractive village situated at the fjord end of the omonimous watercourse. From Eidfjord (Tourist Information Centre tel. 53 66 51 77), the road follows the coast of the fjord to Sima and to Kjeåsen.

Sima is a powerful hydro-electric complex, whose main installations are open to visitors. **Kjeåsen** is an isolated farm, perched high above the fjord, at almost 600 m of height. According to an old legend, the farm buildings were erected by a stubborn farmer, who had to carry all building materials, logs, floorboards and all the rest, by hand along a narrow path that

THE FJORDS REGION — THE SOUTHERN DISTRICT

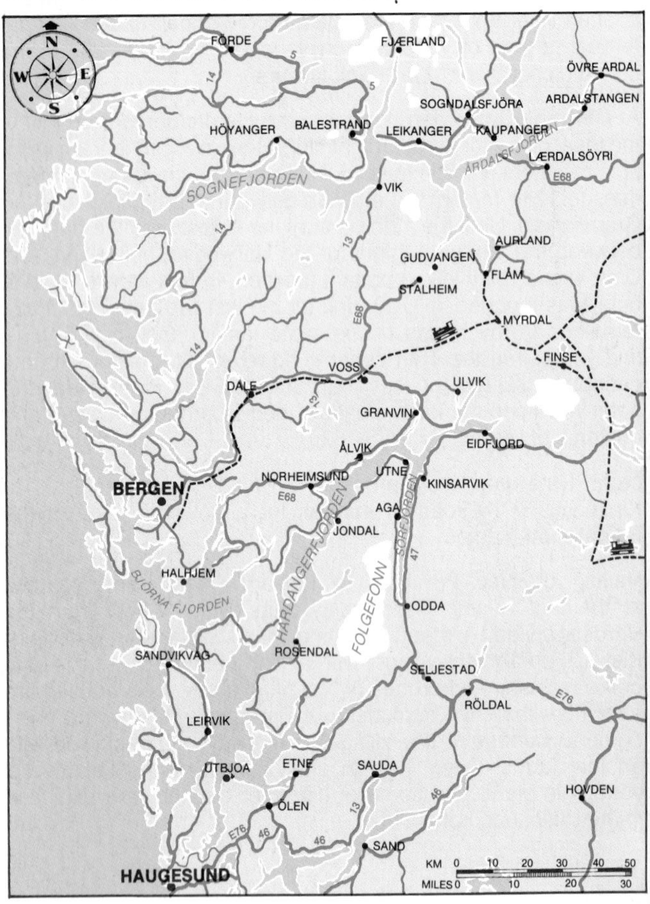

climbed from the jetty to the overhanging plateau. Thirty years of Sisyphean labour. Another legend describes the singular custom of the Kjeåsen farmers, who used to go around on their chores all day long with their younger children firmly tied to their back, to avoid their wandering close to the perpendicular walls of the plateau.

A characteristic fjord-like valley

All along the R7 you'll have the opportunity to admire the massive dams of the **Vøringsfossen** hydroelectric complex. The Vøringsfossen waterfall is the most spectacular in Norway: it's a 14 cubic meter per second stream, falling down from the mountainside to a depth of 182 m.

Back to Bergen

The R7 goes from Ejdfjord to Brimnes, crosses the fjord by ferry to Vallavik, goes through the longest tunnel in Norway (8.3 km) and joins the E68 soon after the tunnel exit. If you disapprove of tunnels, whatever your reason, you'll find colse to its mouth the R572, a side road that crosses **Ulvik** and **Granvin**, to rejoin, together with the R7, the E68.

Near **Porsmyr** the **Fykesund** fjord cuts through the village of **Botnem**, a hamlet of only three families, whose sole connection with the outside world (except for telephones) is a biweekly motorboat (summers only!) along their fjord.

The E68 now turns westward to **Norheimsund**. At the local Tourist Information Centre you'll have the personal attention of the last exponent of one of the village's most ancient families, Mr. Geismund Nes.

The Sognefjord

Voss

This itinerary does not start off at the banks of the fjord, but at a more convenient point, easily accessible by car and by rail, **Voss**. It's a 14,000 people township, scattered along the coasts of a mountain lake, halfway between the two major fjord complexes of the region and surrounded by eternal snows. The Church of Voss is more than 7 centuries old, and is one of the most ancient stone chorches in Norway. The church walls are two metres thick.

Voss is one of the most popular winter sports resorts in Norway. Its Tourist Information Centre (at the Town Hall, in front of the church, tel. 56 51 17 16) is open June to August, Mon.-Sat. 9am-7pm, Sundays 2-6pm; the rest of the year Mon.-Fri., 9am-4pm. It distributes a *Voss Guide* in English and *Norway in a Nutshell*, a timetable and guidebook for one of the most spectacular routes in Norway.

As for accommodation, there is a relatively wide choice. You have the more expensive *Fleischer* (tel. 56 51 11 55) and *Kringsjå* (tel. 56 51 16 27) hotels; then you have the more modest *Noøring* (tel. 56 51 12 11) and *Rondo* (tel. 56 51 19 80). Inquire whether their saunas are functioning. Near the lake you'll find a very good hostel (tel. 56 51 20 17, closed November and December), with a very pleasant eatery. There are two campings: the first, very central, is the *Voss Camping*; the second, the *Tvind Camping*, is north of the town.

"Norway in a Nutshell"

"Norway in a Nutshell" is a popular standardized itinerary, aimed at presenting the tourist with a taste of all Norway's major attractions. The price of this unusual guided group tour is 250NOK per person. It starts and ends at Bergen, but it's also possible to join at **Myrdal**.

Myrdal is in fact little more than a little railway station surrounded by a few houses. If you wish to leave the train at Myrdal, don't forget to inform the conductor in advance. The first Myrdal train leaves Bergen at 9.15am; the line goes through the 5 km long Gravahalsen tunnel and reaches Myrdal. Here the tour changes trains and proceeds to **Flåm** (a 40 minute zigzag miracle of Norwegian railway engineering, descending from an elevation of more than 1,000 m to the fjord coast (which naturally is at sea level). The whole length of this route is not more than 12 km, and even from your comfortable train seat you'll get a long series of breathtaking views. Flåm has a Tourist Information Centre (tel. 57632106), B&B accommodation, a hostel (April to September) and a camp site.

Next comes the motorboat crossing from Flåm to **Gudvangen** along the Nærøfjord, a chasm often narrower than 500 m, locked between 1,000 m high perpendicular mountain walls. The final, and most spectacular part of this tour is the bus ride from Gudvangen to the **Stalheim Hotel**, along a vertiginous road; if you could only keep your eyes open on that fearful hairpin climb, you'll see some sights you'll never forget.

The Stalheim Hotel was originally a vast wooden building; it was destroyed by fire, reconstructed in wood and redestroyed, it has finally been rebuilt in stone. At the hotel you'll find a bus, waiting to take you back to Voss. End of the "Norway in a Nutshell" tour.

The Sognefjord Branches

The R13 leaves Voss in a northerly direction, reaching the spectacular observatory of **Vik**, with a magnificent 12th century

One of the Sognefjord Branches

wooden structure, of the Hopperstad Church at its side. After Vik comes **Vangsnes**, the motorboat terminus, at the junction of the six main branches of the Sognefjord. The southernmost branch, the Aurlandsfjord, has already been mentioned.

Following the fjord coast to Hella, take the R5 to **Sogndal**, **Kaupanger** and **Amla**. Here you'll switch once more to a motorboat, crossing to **Revsnes**, and then to the Aurlandsfjord and back to Flåm. **Lærdal** is on another branch of the fjord; its 13th century wooden Bourgund Church is one of the most interesting of its times, with harmoniously integrated Christian and pagan ornaments and reliefs.

The next branch takes you to **Øvre Årdal**, a little village accessible from the west only by water. Near Øvre Årdal the fjord was blocked by the fall of an enormous glacier head, that barred the access road, creating, just above the village a vast, icy

freshwater lake. Above the lake are the **Jotumheim** Mountains, with the beautiful **Lake Tyin** hidden deep among their peaks. Here too, the 1000 m drop from the lake to the fjord has been exploited in a daring hydroelectric plant, that provides the vast metalworks of the region with electricity.

The main branch of the Sognefjord is the **Lusterfjord**, whose end reaches as far as **Urnes** (yet another old stave church, 1070). Not far from the Lusterfjord is the **Nigard Glacier** (climbing is absolutely forbidden without a qualified guide!!!).

The fifth branch takes you back to **Sogndal** and to **Kaupanger** (with yet another old stave church).

The last branch of the Sognefjord is the **Fjærland**, and the beginning of your next itinerary. Here you'll see the fjordside resort of **Balestrand**, where at the turn of the century Kaiser

Wilhelm II of Germany used to spend at least part of his summers. The local Tourist Information Centre (tel. 57 69 12 55) is open May to September 8.30am-0.30pm and 3-6pm. There is a hotel (the *Kringsja*, tel. 57 69 13 03), a hostel (tel. 57 69 13 03) and a camp site (tel. 57 69 12 23).

Fjærland

For many centuries the only connection between Fjærland and the rest of the country was by ferry; finally, in 1986, a new roadway has been cut into the **Jostedal** glacier, crossing it through a 6.5 km tunnel.

The view of this miniature village, situated at the very end of a forlorn little valley, is simply magnificent. An icy mountain stream runs along the bottom of the valley, fed by a spectacular waterfall. Behind the village, the deep green of the wooded mountain sides blends with the bleak wall of a gigantic glacier. Below the glacier, the stream waters turn white ("glacier's milk", according to local slang), so rich in minerals. And, strange as it may seem, while the "glacier's milk" turns off most fresh-water fish, salmon included, herrings are wildly attracted to it.

The people of Fjærland are mostly farmers and peasants, but there are also a few families of fishermen (herring fishermen, of course). Thanks to the combined influence of the fjord and the glacier, the climate is perfect for fruit-growing and for cattle.

There are two hotels: the *Mundall* (tel. 57 69 31 01) and the more modest *Fjærlandfjord* (tel. 57 69 31 61). Both hotels hold folklore activities, organize mountain walks and offer boats for hire. The *Mundall* has also a small Museum of Glaciers.

Ice-alpinists will find a splendid base for an attack on the **Jostedalsbreen**, or the much closer Supphellebreen and Bøyabreen glaciers. But even the most experienced climbers should not think of approaching these glaciers unaccompanied by an authorized guide. The guide lives at the foot of the glacier, and he may be chartered for shorter or longer ascents — from 3 hour bagatelles to 3 day enterprises. To join in those daring exploits, one must put down his name and queue at the Tourist Information Centre or at the hostel. For further details, see "Backpacking through Norway".

Nordfjord

The Northfjord is perhaps the most picturesque of all the great fjords: this is due to the changing hues of its waters and to the pervading presence of the great mass of the Jostedal Glacier. Starting from the last part of the former itinerary, follow, the exit of the Fjærland tunnel, the road to Stryn — or cross the Jotunheimen Pass on the R55 to **Lom**, and then the R15 to Grotli. By sea, the fjord entrance is at **Måløy**.

The Northfjord has three main branches, that cut deep into the hinterland for more than 100 km. The central branch splits into three branches of its own, the **Stryn**, the **Loen** and the **Olden**, whose valleys reach as far as the north-western rim of the great Jostedalbreen (breen = glacier).

The Jostedal is the largest glacier in Europe: it covers an area of 800 square kilometres. The Nordfjord was, during the last Ice Age, one of its branches.

For a tourist tour of the glacier, turn to the Bergen Tourist Information Centre.

Stryn

The village of Stryn gave its name to the omonimous fjord branch. The village itself is a relatively important road and trade junction. Most of its people grow orchards or herd cattle; a sizable minority, however, is employed in the tourist industry. The Tourist Information Centre (tel. 57 87 23 32) and the hostel (tel. 57 87 11 06) will cater to most of your tourist needs. The hostel is quite close to the R15, but it is open only June to August.

Loen, an agricultural settlement situated on the omonimous fjord branch, is 12 km east of Stryn. It has a church and a small community centre. Its history goes back as far as the Bronze Age. The mountain stream that flows into the fjord waters is the **Lo**, yet another member of the "glacier milk" white water family. The road follows the coast of Lake Loen to the foot of the Kjenndals Glacier (one of the branches of the great Jostedal). The mountain tops reach as high as 1500 m. An authorized guide is a must, from here upward, should one wish to climb the ice. During the first half of our century there have been several fatal accidents here; the greatest tragedy took place in 1903, when a sudden avalanche crushed part of the village, killing 61 persons and devastating the local marina.

Loen is often crowded with mountain-climbers, and therefore it is well equipped with hotels and other accommoaation. The *Alexandra* (tel. 57 87 76 60) is one of the best; the *Loen* (tel. 57 87 76 24) is one of the cheapest; there are several B&Bs along the lake, side by side with restaurants and open-air cafés.

THE FJORDS REGION — THE NORTHERN DISTRICT

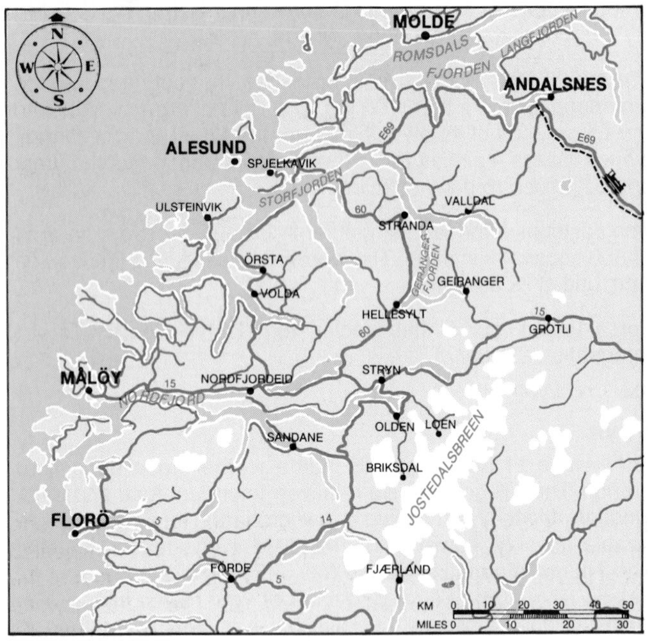

There is a boat-hire agency, and a Tourist Information Centre (tel. 57 87 76 77).

Olden is situated at the southern end of the fjord, only 20 km from the Jostedal, whose perpendicular walls rise to a height of 1700 m. The Olden Valley stream crosses the two little lakes of Olden and Floen, creating a series of waterfalls on its way, clearly visible from the bottom of the valley. The Olden Church (built 1759) is built on the foundations of an ancient stave church.

The route to the relatively small **Briksdal** glacier, starts from Olden passing by the more impressive **Melkevollsbre**. This is also home to the great *Fjordings*, the powerful work horses bred

The Stryn Camp Site

in this region. You might also have the opportunity to ride on one of their two wheel *Stolkjerrer*, the characteristic two-wheeled local tourist carriage. The glacier route climbs to the foot of the Melkevollsbre, then turns left to the Briksdal. Then, after only one kilometre, it's time either for walking or for the *stolkjerrer* and its *fjording*. Finally you'll come to an obervatory, situated at the very edge of the ice. As we have already pointed out, without an authorized guide this is the end of the road; even last century's old "cattle path" is definitely out of bounds to unguided tourists.

The Olden Tourist Information Centre (tel. 57 87 31 26) organises several tours of the area and has all the usual details regarding accommodation: hotels, B&Bs, and lakeside camp sites. A regular bus line connects Olden to Stryn and to Loen. The R15 exits Stryn eastward, following the course of the stream, whose waters, teem with salmon in season.

The Hjelledal Valley

Having left behind Lake Stryn, you will arrive at the crossing located 12 km further east, here you should decide whether to turn northward along the R15, tunnelling through the mountains, or to rise to the challenge of the hairpin turns of the older side road. Having taken the second alternative, from the height of the pass, on top of the **Videseter Hotel** terrace, you'll have a clear view of the whole Stryn Valley. The old road then proceeds through the stunning lunar scenery of the Hjelledal Valley: summer snows, Alpine lakes, rocky meadows; the majesty of the view is yet unspoiled by man: the only humans in the area are the occasional botanists, immersed in the study of the unique flora of the valley. Fill your fuel tank before entering: There are no fuel pumps until Grotli!

This is the end of the itinerary, not far from the starting point of the next, that continues to the Geirangerfjord.

The Geirangerfjord

One of the most striking aspects of the Fjord Region is the frequent contrast of climates, sceneries and hues. The sudden changes never fail to catch unaware not only the novice, but also the most inured addict. The frequency and variety of these "stage tricks" are characteristic of the Geirangerfjord.

The Geirangerfjord branches eastward from the **Storfjord**, which cuts eastward for 40 km before turning in a great arch toward the south, sending frequent branches out in all directions. The view from the height of the **Eidsvol** Observatory (on R58) is simply fantastic.

The fjord ends at the village of **Geiranger**, where the Tourist Information Centre (tel. 70 26 30 99) specializes in the visit of the fjord and its surroundings. It will even assist you in the planning of a motorboat visit to several other spectacular fjordside observatories. There are also two hotels: the *Union*, tel. 70 26 30 00 is more expensive, and the *Geiranger*, tel. 70 26 30 05, is very pleasant and more convenient.

There is also a motorboat line from **Hellesylt** to Geiranger — through the Geirangerfjord from one end to another; the route is splendid; it lasts two hours and costs 20NOK.

Hellesylt itself is a tourist resort (Tourist Information Centre tel. 70 26 50 52), with a hostel (summers only, tel. 70 26 51 28) and a camp site (2 km away, with boats for hire and fishing permits, tel. 70 26 50 79). One thousand years ago Hellesylt was a nest of Viking pirates, well hidden and protected in the depth of its fjord.

Geiranger is also an important regional junction: the R60 and R15 go to **Nordfjordeid**, and the R14 crosses **Byrkjelo**, **Skei**, **Førde** and **Sandane** to **Lavik**; here it crosses the Sognefjord by ferry to **Brekke**, ending at **Knarvik**, where you'll find regular sea passage to Bergen.

One might also leave Geiranger northward to **Eidsdal**, and then cross the Linge by ferry. On arrival at Valldal, climb along the R63 to the **Trollstigvegen Pass** (852 m). Here the view is so exciting, that you will just have to pause, feasting your eyes until you absorb all its beauty: the little town of Åndalsnes, perched between fjord and lake, the 1800 m high mountain peaks, the hairpin windings of the road, and an unbelievable 180 m high waterfall. Much of the area is never touched by the sun; even in high summer, you'll find the air chillingly cold.

Åndalsnes

This sleepy little town lies in the shadow of some of Norway's highest peaks. The town wakes only in winter, with the invasion of endless hordes of wintersports fans. There is a Tourist Information Centre (tel. 71 22 16 22), a hostel (tel. 71 22 13 82) and a camp site (tel. 71 22 16 29). Åndalsnes is on the Ålesund-Dombås E69 latitudinal route, that meets at Dombås with the E6 from Oslo to Trondheim.

Among the local B&Bs, we recommend the *Rauma* (tel. 71 22 12 33), which also has a modest but very good little restaurant.

From Hellesylt to Ålesund

The R60 goes from Hellesylt to **Stranda**, a dynamic industrial town (textiles, food products, and furniture). Stranda is also fast becoming a first rate tourist resort; for information, call the local Tourist Information Centre (tel. 70 26 00 44).

Ålesund

Ålesund is an interesting town with a very long history. There are clear signs of prehistoric settlement dating as far back as the end of the last Ice Age, and several ruins and fragments dating from the Stone Age to the days of the Vikings. In 1904 a sudden fire razed the whole town to the ground. In less than three years, with the help of Kaiser Wilhelm II of Germany, a great lover of the Fjord Region, the town was completely rebuilt.

The town presents therefore an unusual *Art Nouveau* façade, rich local and foreign components that form a surprisingly harmonious mixture: floral ornaments and dragons, human figures and monsters, human statues and allegoric motives.

The Tourist Information Centre is at the Town Hall (tel. 70121202; open Mon.-Sat. 9am-4pm). Beside the regular services, it also hires out fishing lines and other equipment. The *Ålesund Card* costs 40NOK; the town map and guide are free.

The Moonlike Hjelledal Valley

The Geirangerfjord

After a pleasant walk through the town, it may be worth your while to visit the Town Museum (Rasmus Rønnebergsgate 16; open 11am-3pm), its neighbouring public Park and the new Ålesund Church.

The return trip to Bergen may be made on board the Hurtigruten Cruise ship.

Food and accommodation
Ålesund is famous for its restaurants: the *Astoria* (Røysegate 15) is very expensive, while the *Peppermållen* (Kirkgate, at the bridge), is hardly less exquisite but more reasonably priced. The *Skatefluol* (on the Skagerake 1 pier) and the *Cafena* (Kongensgate 25) have very enticing menus and prices. The best hotels often offer interesting bargains (a double-bed room for 500NOK). At the B&Bs, a double room costs 280NOK; such as the *Centrum Hospitis* (Størgate 24, tel. 70 12 17 09) and the *Havely* (near the museum, tel. 70 12 49 60). The *Prisen Strandcamping* (tel. 70 13 52 04) is a camp site with a fishing permit desk, tent-spaces, campers and bungalows.

Around Ålesund

At the Ålesund piers you'll find motorboat ferries to the many islands of the Gulf. For their timetables, call the Tourist Information Centre. **Giske** is a 40 km^2 island, with a population of 4100 commuters. The scenery is pleasant, and thousands of tourists visit its ancient ruins and its aviary reserves. There are also many tourist accommodations, from luxury hotels to private residential rooms. Don't miss the 7th century burial sites and the 13th century marble church.

Herøy is a group of eight islands connected by a bridge net. **Runde** is a nesting ground for millions of birds, and its Aviary Rock is a very popular attraction. Herøy too is well equipped with tourist accommodation.

Also interesting are the islands of Skodje, Ulstein and Ørskog.

Romsdalfjord

At the northern end of the Fjords Region we find the Romsdalfjord, a world of difference from its bleaker southern brethren.

Åndalsnes, a little town easily reached by rail or by road from Oslo and Bergen, is most conveniently situated in the middle of a very spectacular area, but it has little to offer.

Molde is a sleepy village, immersed in deep slumber for 11 and a half months a year. It wakes briefly at the end of July for its world-famous Jazz Festival. The Hurtigruten vessels stop regularly at its pier.

Kristiansund

Yet another Hurtigruten stop, this little harbour was once famous for its local dried codfish industry: practically all local housewives used to hang their codfish on their courtyard laundry lines. Picturesque, if rather smelly; now gone forever, thanks to more modern and efficient methods, less offensive to tourists' noses. The R16 connects Kristiansund with the E6 Oslo-Trondheim route. Like several other Norwegian towns, Kristiansund was built on several islands, interconnected by bridges and ferries; its ultra-modern appearance is due to the vast restoration works of the fifties, after the Nazis burned everything in 1944.

All necessary information about lodgings will be found at the Tourist Information Centre (tel. 71 67 72 11); there are also several restaurants, cafés and a hostel (tel. 71 67 10 40).

The Grip islet was inhabited for several centuries by small groups of fishermen. However, it was frequently destroyed by the sea, and today it has been completely abandoned; the only signs of its past settlements are the ruins of an old stave church and some fragments of stone dragon-heads scattered on the island moors.

From Oslo to Trondheim

The Oslo-Trondheim northward route of the E6 is often the scene of a mass exodus of Norwegian tourists; it's particularly crowded during week-ends. Many of them travel leisurely along the route, enjoying every moment of the ride and stopping here and there for a good view of the mountains — the Dovrefjell, the Rondane or the Jotunheimen; others follow in the steps of Peer Gynt; others speed through it in their great hurry, anxious to reach the far north.

For this itinerary we shall adopt the leisurely approach. The first stop will be at **Eidsvoll**, a little town 40 km north of Oslo, where in 1814 the National Assembly convened to proclaim Norway's independence. Eidsvoll is on Lake Mjøsa, the largest lake in Norway.

A sedate ferry service, on board the century old *Skibladner*, crosses the lake daily to **Hamar**, where you'll find hotel accommodation, a hostel (tel. 62 52 36 41) and the ruins of an old 12th century cathedral.

The old *Skibladner* then sails on to **Gjøvik**, an industrial centre, also equipped with several hotels and a hostel (tel. 61 17 10 11), deep at the northern tip of the lake and at the mouth of the Lågen river, which flows from the Gudbransdal valley, passing through the regional capital, Lillehammer.

Lillehammer

The Oppland capital is a modern (founded 1827) town of 24,000 people. It lies on the E6 and on the northward railway route and has also several interurban bus connections.

The town itself is certainly worth a visit. **Maihaugen** is the largest open-air museum in Northern Europe: it has several Medieval stave churches, transported here from all parts of the country, 120 old residences and 30,000 ancient art objects. Summers only, 10am-4pm.

The **Gallery** (Størtorget Square, 11am-4pm; closed on Sunday) contains one of the most important art collections in Norway. The **Museum of Motor Vehicles** is a must for all car buffs.

Children and troll lovers will surely enjoy visiting the **Troll Park**, a lovely amusement park, and the huge troll statue weighing about 70 tons. Another pleasant place to visit is **Lilliputhammer**, a model of the town's main street.

In February 1994 Lillehammer hosted the seventeenth Olympic Winter Games, during which about 150,000 visitors, including 2,000 athletes, swarmed to this small town for a sixteen day celebration of sport and fun.

Finding a good place to stay in is no problem here, since many rooms were built in anticipation of the guests coming for the Olympic Games. The best — and of course most expensive — hotel in Lillehammer is the *Rica Victoria* (Storget 82-4, tel. 61250049); Two nice moderately priced hotels are the *Bellevue* (tel. 61250400) and the *Dølheimen* (tel. 61250430). Sleeping in suburbian farms is also a pleasant possibility, and there are several camp sites around the town as well. Information on lodgings and tourist brochures can be obtained from the Tourist Information Centre (tel. 61259299).

The E6 leaves Lillehammer north-westward; one of its exits, almost 20 km from Lillehammer, leads to **Aulestad**, not far from **Follebu**, home of the great poet and writer Bjørnstjern Bjørnson, who was awarded the Nobel Prize for literature in 1903.

The Aulestad road goes on to the **Gudbrandsdalen Valley**, while the E6 and the railway proceed along the river to **Vinstra**, where the legendary Peer Gynt (of Ibsenian memory) is said to have found his final rest.

You are now at the gate pof the "Peer Gynt Route", an itinerary full of spectacular views. It starts at the mouth of the valley, climbs up from the crowded E6 toward **Otta**, passing through some remote little hamlets and forlorn old farms until it reconnects with the E6 at Vinstra.

The Peer Gynt Legend

The hero of all main versions of this popular lore is a clever and adventurous peasant, who, after a brief adulterous affair with a young local matron was forced to rather hurriedly leave his native abode. Having found at first shelter in the woods, he was welcomed by the local gnomes, who wanted to adopt him as one of their own. Having rejected their generous offer, our hero found himself once again on the run. This time he turned eastward. In the Far East, Peer Gynt made his first fortune, and lived happily among his new friends and with his beloved Anytra. Somehow, by chance, Peer Gynt came to learn of his own royal extraction;

the news was too much for the lad, who lost his mind and ended up in a mental asylum. After a daring escape, once more on the run, he fled back to his native village. Having finally reached the end of his Odissey, he found his true love, Solweg, with whom he lived happily ever after till the end of his days.

Otta

Otta is the starting point for a visit to the **Rondane** massif, situated between the Gudbrandsdal and the Østerdal Valleys, an area of spectacular mountain peaks as high as 2,200 m, and scores of Alpine lakes, created by the intense glacial action of the region. The whole area has been declared a National Park.

Its freezing winters and its arctic vegetation have given this area a bleak and forbidding aspect, which never lacks to impress even the most accomplished alpinist. Scores of narrow mountain paths climb to several *DNT* shelters. At the foothill villages of Dombås, Folldal, Hjerkinn, Otta and others you'll find lodgings and Tourist Information Centres. The region is accessible not only by the E6, but also by rail (three daily trains). For further details, see "Backpacking through Norway".

Wishing to reach the Fjords Region, take the R16 to Lom and the Geiranger. The R16 passes by the **Jutundeimen Massif**, which, with its 2,400 m high mountain tops and its 60 glaciers, is rightly the pride of most Norwegians. Its precipitous Alpine faces and ice challenges are met year after year by growing numbers of daring alpinists.

This savage and spectacular massif is bounded by the valleys of Ottadal and Sjodalen on its northern and eastern sides, by the Tyin, Bygdin and Vonstervatn Lakes on its southern side, and on its west side it borders with the Sognefjord. The watercourses that criss-cross it in all directions form scores of deep gullies and spectacular waterfalls. The *DNT* has traced, on its excellent 1:50,000 and 1:100,000 maps, hundreds of paths and tourist routes. The R51 and R55 cross the massif longitudinally, reconnecting north and south with the main latitudinal arteries that run eastward and westward. Coming from Bergen, you may board the **Leikanger** ferry, and then proceed by bus to Sogndal. Another route goes from Bergen to Ardalstangen by boat, and then to Øre Årdel by bus. On arriving from Oslo by rail we recommend alighting at Otta, to continue by bus to Randverk and Gjendesheim, and then Bøverdalen and the Sognefjell shelters. There is a bus line from Fagerness, on the E68, to Bygdin and Gjendesheim (for further details, see "Backpacking through Norway").

Dombås

Both the railway and the E6 take the route from Otta to Dombås, where they meet the E69 to Andalsnes, at the northern end of the Fjords Region. We advise you to follow the E6, crossing the **Dovrefjell Massif**, which also attracts hundreds of backpackers. Soon you'll reach Oppdal, a wintersports resort, which "hibernates" comfortably through the rest of the year. From this point both railway and E6 climb swiftly down toward Trondheim, running across one of the widest agricultural regions in the country.

At Dombås (tel. 61 24 14 44) and at Oppdal (tel. 72 42 17 60) you'll find regular Tourist Information Centres, hotels (some of which are open also for the summer) and two hostels.

The *Dombås* Hotel (tel. 61 24 10 00) offers substantial winter discounts; the hostel (tel. 61 21 20 64) is modest but convenient.

The *Oppdal* Hotel (tel. 72 42 11 11) and the Oppdal hostel (tel. 72 42 13 30) are similar to their Dombås counterparts.

Trondheim

The capital of the Trødelag is more than one thousand years old. As early as the first millennium it was a major strategic bastion of the Viking tribes. King Olav proclaimed it his own official capital, christening it Nidaros, and building a vast Royal Palace in its centre. A large part of the troubled life of that monarch remains a mystery; however, it's clear that after his flight to Sweden and Russia, in 1028 he was able to win back his kingdom, only to be killed in the battle of Stiklestad, barely two years later. His remains are buried in Trondheim. After his canonization by the Catholic Church, his tomb became a Holy Site, visited yearly by thousands of pilgrims. In 1070 the great **Nidaros Cathedral** was built, and in its hallowed grounds rest the remains of many Norwegian kings. Since the beginning of the 18th century all the official Coronation ceremonies have taken place in this Cathedral. The Norwegian Parliament has one of its official seats in Trondheim.

Ancient Trondheim was built almost exclusively in wood, and its old alleys were very narrow. A small fire was enough to endanger the whole town, which indeed was repeatedly destroyed, until, after the great 1681 conflagration, General de Ciclgnon was put in charge of vast reconstruction works. He designed a new urban plan, based on a network of large city blocks, separated by a network of wide open avenues. The results are visible to this day. De Cicignon also built the Kristiansten Castle, a landmark visible from anywhere in town or in the suburbs. The only original remains of Old Trondheim are on the island of Munkholmen — and, of course, in the Cathedral.

Trondheim is an important college town. The most famous of its schools, the University of Trondheim, is one of the largest and most renowned in Norway. Trondheim is also an important trade centre and market town. Even now, great building projects are under way: residential condos, office buildings and shopping centres that will become some of the best and most modern in Norway.

How to get there

By air: The Værnes Airport is only a few kilometres north of the centre, and is serviced by several *SAS* and other national flights. The airport bus leaves on the hour; the city terminus is at Earling Skakkesgate 40.

By rail: There are three daily trains for Oslo via Dombås (7 hours) and two via Röros (9 hours); two trains for Stockholm (12 hours), and two for the far north, to Mo-i-Rana and Bodö (11 hours). The railway station is on the far bank of the waterway, near Nidarbru.

By bus: There is one daily run to Bergen (15 hours), and one daily run to Molde and Ålesund (8 hours).

By sea: The northbound Hurtigruten vessels reach Trondheim daily at noon; the southbound vessels at 11am.

Tourist services

The Tourist Information Centre is on Torvet square (tel. 73 92 94 00, open June-August 8.30am-8pm and the rest of the year Mon.-Fri., 9am-4pm, Saturday 9am-1pm). The *Trondheim Card* sells for 30NOK (valid for 24 hours only).

Public transportation

A net of buses and trolleys covers both centre and suburbs; you'll find all line numbers and routes indicated clearly in the Tourist Information Centre city maps.

Taxis may be booked at tel. 73 52 78 00.

TRONDHEIM

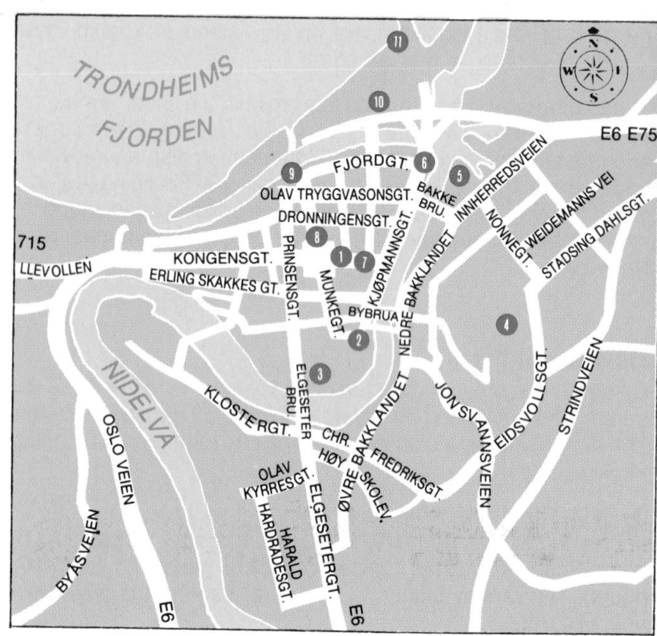

Index
1. Tourist Information Centre
2. The Nidaros Cathedral
3. The Archbishopric
4. The Kristiansten Fort
5. The Nedre Elvehavn Project
6. The Museum of the Sea
7. The Vur Frue Church
8. The Stiftsgården Royal Residence
9. The Fisheries
10. The Railway Station
11. The Hurtigruten Pier

Food and accommodation

Luxury Hotels

Prinsen: Konengsgate 30, tel. 73 53 06 50.
Ambassadeur: Elvegate 18, tel. 73 52 70 50.
Royal Garden Hotel: Kjøppmansgate 7, tel. 73 52 11 00.

Economy Class

Singsaker: Rogersgate 1, tel. 73 52 00 92.
Dronningen: Dronningensgate 26, tel. 73 52 43 66.

The Trondheim Cathedral

Private residence lodgings are available through the Tourist Information Centre (180-200NOK per double-bed room).

The hostel (Weidemannsveien 41, tel. 73 53 04 90) disposes also of some family rooms (280NOK, breakfast included); bus 9.

Camp Sites
Flak: tel. 72 83 58 00, on the R715, 10 km from town.
Sandmoen: tel. 72 88 61 35, on the E6, 10 km south of town; with rooms, fishing permits desk and campers.

The best restaurants are at the luxury hotels; a full dinner will cost you 200-500NOK per person. At the *Bajazzo Rica* (Søndregate, tel. 73525760), at the *Kunstnerknen* (Prinsengate 38, tel. 73521880) or at the *Landlord Pub* (Prinsengate 40, tel. 73522515) you'll be able to buy a good dinner for two for not more than 200NOK.

There are also *Peppe's Pizzas* (tel. 73 53 29 20), whose only competitor, as prices go, is the restaurant of the Kongensgate *IMI* Hotel. For even stricter budgets, there are always the supermarket and the fishery stalls.

What to see

Trondheim offers very little challenge. And at the Torvet square Tourist Information Centre you'll find a good map of the city.

Facing the Tourist Information Centre, stands the statue of St. Olav, in front of the Cathedral and with the **Ravnkloa** (fishery) behind it. The Nidelva river and the port form a triangular circuit around the centre of town. Leaving the square along Munkegate, you'll come to the **Nidaros Domkirke**, that was built on the site of St. Olav's sepulchre. The cathedral is the largest surviving Medieval building in Norway. In 1153, when the Norwegian Church won its independence, the Cathedral became an Archbishopric seat, and the main religious centre of the country. In 1585 the Reformation revoked all the Cathedral's traditional privileges, and its religious supremacy came to an end. Today the old cathedral is little more than a parochial church, frequented by a community of not more than 5,000 souls. Its last surviving privilege is that of the Coronation ceremonies.

A few fragments of its structure date from 1130, but the present Cathedral was built in 1869.

The church is open to visitors (guided visits on demand, for details inquire at the Tourist Information Centre) throughout the year, it also hosts frequent organ concerts.

The **Erkebispegården** (Archbishopric) was built at the beginning of the 12th century at the Cathedral's side, to serve as the residence of Archbishop Oystein. Later it became the seat of the Danish Governor, and after the end of the Danish rule it was transformed in an Armoury.

On the other side of Prinsengate there is an interesting Synagogue, frequented every Friday night by the small local Jewish community.

Turn back toward the centre along Kjøpmannsgate, and you'll see the last authentic remains of Old Trondheim: a series of wooden warehouses, not unlike their Bergen counterparts. The western ones have been restored and are in use for various trade and shopping purposes. At No. 19 you'll see a rather expensive fish restaurant, and at No. 25 you'll find the local branch of *Peppe's Pizzas*.

Turn back at the **Bakkabru** bridge, until you come to the singular *Royal Garden Hotel Hothouses*. The new residential and shopping neighbourhood of *Nedre Elvehavn* will be erected on this site. The little Maritime Museum has little to offer.

Next turn now onto Olav Tryggvasongate, where, at the corner of Nordregate and Cicignon, the street changes into an interesting pedestrian mall.

Across the street from a long line of cafés you'll see the **Vår**

Frue Church, a 13th century building, extensively restored in 1739.

Back on Torvet Square, go on to Munkegate Street. On your right you'll have the **Stiftsgarden**, the only survivor of the many ancient fires that martyred the city (open to visitors 11am-2pm, 5NOK). It's vast enough to be considered the largest wooden building in Europe. It was built well after the era of the great fires, in 1778, and is today an occasional summer residence of the Royal Family.

The street ends at the fishery pier and at the landing of the **Munkholmen Island** ferries (20NOK). For centuries the island was the official site of hundreds of hangings and beheadings. At the beginning of the 11th century the Benedictine Order built a proud Monastery on that island, which was transformed after six centuries into a prison, and later into a Customs warehouse and office. Today the island is the most popular summer resort in town.

Entertainment

Trondheim's "night life" begins and ends at the downtown restaurants and cafés, which after dinner often change into rather sedate discos. Trondheim's students prefer the *Studentersamfunnet* (near the Elgeseter Bridge, or the *Ritz*, up on the Skansen, with its frequent visiting and local jazz bands.

The Trøndelag

Trondheim is the capital of the Trøndelag Region, a vast and fertile plain, crisscrossed by little fjords, lakes and watercourses. This plain was the site of many past battles; in the most famous of them all, the 1030 Battle of **Stiklestad**, King Olav found his death. The epic of the legendary king, that later became St. Olav, patron of all Norway, is sung year after year on the occasion of the anniversary of the great battle, July 29. For details, ask at the Trondheim or Levanger Tourist Information Centres.

Proceeding southwards, you'll come to Røros, a small town not far from the Swedish border.

Røros

This mountain town (it's the highest town in Norway) was for three centuries the major copper mining centre in Northern Europe. When its mines were finally abandoned, little more than

The old warehouses along the Nid

Rørøs — A town of copper mines

20 years ago, Røros changed quickly into an attractive tourist centre (active both in summer and in winter), as well as a growing centre of the Norwegian adolescent film-industries. The tourist boom brought about even the restoration of the Old City. For all details of lodgings, tours and guided visits of the copper mines (10 km out of town), ask at the local Tourist Information Centre (tel. 72 41 11 65).

The **Røros Church** reflects the great riches of the Røros Copper Era.

The *Røros Hotel* (tel. 72 41 10 11), the hostel (tel. 72 41 10 89) and the camp sites are modern and well equipped, and they are open throughout the year.

Northern Norway

The Nordland

Northern Norway is subdivided into three different sections: the Nordland, the Troms and the Finnmark (with the Nordkapp at its northern tip). The Nordland is a coastal belt of islands, fjords, valleys and glaciers. The Ocean is its source of life, and it owes its relatively temperate climate to the influence of the Gulf Stream. Its plentiful fishing grounds, which for centuries have been the main source of subsistance of its population, are yet another gracious gift of the benevolent Gulf Stream. The Nordlanders live mostly on the islands and along the well protected mouth of their fjords. The tourists, on the other hand, are attracted mainly to its mountains, its valleys, its Alpine lakes and its glaciers.

The main communication route is the E6, that runs through the Nordland from north to south. It's an outstanding highway, built for speed, but it certainly is not a panoramic route. We might even say that it is rather monotonous. The most spectacular option, of course, is to push northwards by sea, on bord the *Hurtigruten* motor ships (see "The Bewitching Hurtigruten Cruise"); the second option is to abandon the E6 at **Grong**, in favour of the R17, which crosses the monumental Folda Bridge and zigzags leisurely along the coastline, pushing stubbornly northward, slowly but surely. Sometimes, as if for the sake of variety, it crosses over to one of the Helgeland isles. If, wishing for some reason "to get to Nordland as fast as possible", keep on the E6 beyond the Grong exit, you'll be able to avoid its monotony. If you turn onto the R73, that runs inland through **Trofors**, Hattfjelldal and its National Park. Then, when the R73 crosses into Sweden, you'll switch to the R806, via Lake Røssvatnet to turn back to the E6 a few kilometres away from Mo-i-Rana.

Mo-i-Rana

This little and rather sleepy town is the ideal starting point for several outings toward the hinterland and the Swedish border. The main attraction of this area is the great **Svartisen** (Black Ice) glacier, one of whose offshoots ends at the spectacular Lake Svartisvatnet. This breathtakingly beautiful valley is only 30 km away from Mo (this is how Mo-i-Rana is affectionately called by its people). The Svartisen route ends at the **Ronnli Grottos**. For further details, ask at Mo's Tourist Information Centre (tel. 75 15 04 21).

There are two hotels (both rather expensive, as usual), a few reasonably priced B&Bs, the *Fagerason* hostel (tel. 75 15 09 63) and a camp site (with hostel rooms at 150NOK per person); the last two are situated slightly south of the centre. Both the railway and the E6 run on north of Mo, crossing the Arctic Circle after a few kilometres; the passage is clearly indicated: on the E6, by an inviting roadside café and on the train, by the engineer's powerful whistle.

Fauske, the last train stop before the Bodø terminus, is a road junction, with connections to the Rago and Pajelanta Parks and the R830 to the mines and museum of **Sulitjelma**, a little hamlet perched at the feet of the mountains.

Bodø

Bodø is not only the railway's northern terminus, but also the capital of the Nordland. For the last century Bodø has been the major northern home port of the Norwegian herring fishing fleet. In 1940 the town was razed to the ground by the invading Germans. By the mid-50's it had already been fully restored, and today it is a busy centre of 35,000 people, still mostly employed in the fishing industry and its ancillary enterprises. Its harbour welcomes daily the northbound and southbound *Hurtigruten* ships and the Lofoten Islands ferries. The **Budin** church dates from the 12th century, but the purity of its lines was later compromised by cumbersome Barock style additions (1670). The Nordland Museum is focussed mainly on the history of herring fishing.

On a clear day the **Rørvik** peak is a spectacular observatory. The view from its top spreads from the sea and islands and to the icy peaks of the hinterland.

Don't miss (even if you don't care to much for herring) the little **Saltstraumann** fjord, 33 km east of Bodø and not far from Fauske. Its unique, tides cause such fast currents that at the turn of the tide millions of herrings may often be left stranded on dry land. It goes without saying that the major ebb tides are, on new moon and full moon days and nights. At the local camp site (tel. 75 58 75 60) you'll also find a spacious parking lot.

Also interesting is the **Kjerringøy** tour. The Kjerringøy is an open-air museum: 15 old buildings dedicated to the daily life

THE NORDLAND

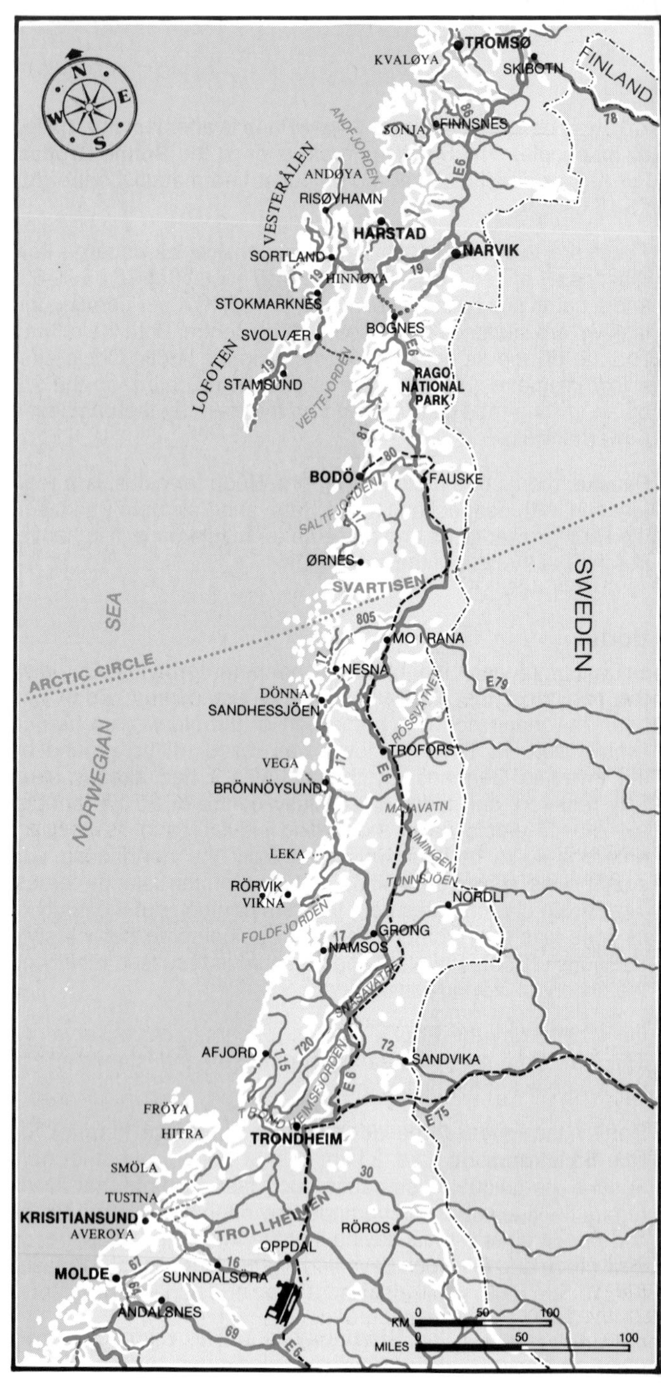

A Picturesque Nordland Scene

and customs of past centuries. Guided tours leave shortly after noon from the Bodø Tourist Information Centre (tel. 75 52 60 00).

High class lodgings are available at the *SAS Hotel* (Storgatan 2, tel. 75 52 41 00). The *Grand* (Storgatan 3, tel. 75 52 00 00) and the *Centrum* (Storgatan 39, tel. 75 52 74 89) are more moderately priced. There are also a hostel (tel. 75 52 12 40) and a camp site (tel. 75 52 29 62).

There are two northbound routes from Bodø to Narvik: along the E6, which is surprisingly interesting in this part, or the Lofoten Islands ferry, with its Narvik road connections.

In either case, the next destination is Narvik. You'll be surprised to see a number of empty cars along the highway in late summer; don't worry, they are not stranded; their owners are simply busy at the edge of the forest, a few steps off the road, filling their baskets to the brim with strawberries, blackberries and perhaps even mushrooms.

Narvik

Narvik is a modern seaport, built toward the end of the last century in an outstanding natural harbour. It is well protected from the bitter arctic weather, and serves as the main outlet of the Kiruna (Sweden) iron mines. Its modern and sophisticated equipment gives the town a striking appearance, especially on a clear day, when the snowy mountain peaks in the background provide the harbour, nestled between the gulf and the town itself, with a spectacular frame.

The railway connection with Sweden (and its iron mines) spurred the town onto its present boom; the powerful, modern engines of its cargo trains have become an integral part of the daily routine and folklore, as witnessed in the already traditional *Winter Festival*, held in honour of the builders of this daring railway line.

Narvik is the main sea and land connection with the Lofoten Islands and the far north of the country. The wintersports facilities, including the spectacular cablecar to the mountain slopes, 600 m above sea level, also operate during the summer.

The **War Museum** is situated near the harbour. It documents Narvik's life and struggle during the Second World War. Narvik's war victims are buried in the Monumental Cemetery, at the southern gates of the town.

The Tourist Information Centre (tel. 76 94 33 09) is on the ground floor of the *Breidabblikk* Pension (Tore Handsgate 41, tel. 76 94 14 18; double rooms for 230NOK). The *Grand Royal* Hotel (Kongensgate 64, tel. 76 94 15 00) is the best in town (double rooms for 650NOK). At the *Nordstjernen* Hotel, B&B prices are somewhat lower (450NOK). Even the camp site, situated slightly north of the town, is rather expensive (double rooms for 300NOK), but at least it has a fishing permits desk; the southern hostel (tel. 76 94 25 98) is open June to September.

The *Café Rosa*is a sailors' haunt — café, restaurant and dancing. The most expensive restaurant is in the most expensive hotel (*Grand Royal*, see above); next door to the hostel you'll find the attractive *Havnecafé* (closed on Sunday).

The railway line from Sweden goes by the name of **Ofoten Line**. It was inaugurated in 1903, and its route crosses some of the most spectacular regions in the Norwegian Alps.

The Lofoten Archipelago

There are clear indications that the Lofoten Islands were inhabited as far back as 4,000 years ago. The Gulf Stream is largely responsible for the islands' relatively temperate climate — and for the rich fishing grounds of the Vestfjord waters, which from January to April teem with thousands and thousands of codfish. Hundreds of boats of all types join the frenzied fishing expedition, whose climax is the traditional Lofoten Carnival (for details, ask at the Tourist Information Centre).

Arriving in Lofoten from the south, at first sight one cannot miss the famous "Lofoten Barrier", a mountain chain that seems to rise from the sea, with its peaks spattered here and there with snow. Then, coming closer, at the foot of the mountain one sees the first isolated hamlets, perched on the mountainside and surrounded by orchards and gardens; and finally you can view the islands' coves, with their little harbours, marinas and fishing ships at anchor. Along the rocky coastline you'll also see several **rorbus** — ancient stone bungalows erected as fishermen's shelters all along the coast by King Oystein in the 12th century. Today the surviving rorbus serve as tourist shelters and some of them are rented out to tourists by the week.

There are six major Lofoten Islands, and the R19 crosses them all. The Lofoten capital, **Svolvær**, is situated on the main island, **Austvågøy**. Svolvær is also a cultural centre and a tourist resort, well equipped for the exploration of the islands.

Its hotels are very highly priced; two of them are: the *Lofoten Nordic* (tel. 76 07 12 00) and the slightly more moderately priced *Lofoten Motel* (tel. 76 07 07 77). The hostel (tel. 76 07 03 16) and the *Svolvær Sjohuscamping* (tel. 76 07 03 36) are well equipped and considerably cheaper.

An overnight stop at **Kabelvåg**, a fishermen's village 5 km from the capital, will provide an interesting experience. Kabelvag was built on the ruins of the ancient village of Vagas, and one of its major attractions is the **Lofoten Museum** (summers only, Mon.-Fri. 9am-3pm, Sat.-Sun. 11am-3pm, entrance 10NOK).

The second largest island is the **Vestvågøy**, whose main centre is the picturesque seaport of **Stamsund** (one of the *Hurtigruten* stops). The local hostel (tel. 76 08 91 66) is but a collection of rorbus dispersed along the coast of that splendid gulf. The hostel doubles up as a Tourist Information Centre, with lots of information on the Lofoten Islands and their itineraries, and in general on all Northern Norway.

At the hostel you'll also find all the necessary equipment for a fishing expedition — boats, permits and lines.

There are even some bicycles for hire (40NOK per day); and in fact, the bike is the best transportation for a tour of the island. Beside the hostel, Stamsund is also graced by the *Lofoten* Hotel (tel. 76 08 93 00); along the coasts of Vestvåagøy you'll find quite a few camp sites. The **Vestvågøy Museum** is at Fygle, not far from Leknes, and its main subject is the history of local fishing.

The next island, **Flakstadøya**, is reached by ferry. At its capital, **Ramberg**, you'll see an 18th century church. Along the island coasts many rorbus are found; the most interesting ones are around the **Nusfjord** fishing village.

The island of **Moskenesøya** is also accessible by ferry, but at its southern tip there is also a convenient bridge. The open-air museum of **Å** is a pretty reconstruction of a 19th century fishermen's village.

The two smaller islands of **Væroy** and **Røst** are accessible only by motorboat. They are the natural nesting grounds of thousands of seabirds; in the summer their peaks are covered with *Puffins* (a sort of sea parrot), and the local hostels are crowded with birdwatching tourists.

Vesterålen

Where the Lofoten Archipelago ends, the Vesterålen begins. Its two major islands, Melbu and Fiskebøl, are connected to each other by a regular ferry (30 m) and by the *Hurtigruten* ships. A series of bridges creates a network between all the Vesterålen islands. While the Lofoten are rather popular resorts, often crowded with tourists, the Vesterålen's fame has not yet reached most travel agencies, and their occasional visitors are welcomed by a surprisingly peaceful, pastoral atmosphere. The **Trollfjord** (the strait that separates the Lofoten from the Vesterålen, is crossed by a regular ferry (from Svolvær to Stokmarknes), from whose bridge you'll enjoy splendid views of both archipelagoes.

Sortland

The best starting point for a tour of the Vesterålen is **Sortland**; its Tourist Information Centre (tel. 76 12 15 55) has lots of details on guided tours and other tourist programmes and a list of rorbu lodgings. There is accommodation also at the *Sortland* hotel and at the camp sites (tel. 76 12 25 78). The *Hurtigruten* ships also land here, and if the sea is rough, an overnight stop might be a good idea.

The Troms

After the relative solitude of this island tour, you will probably welcome the Troms' lively cultural undertones. You will find here, a unique human environment and an intense cultural and economic life, at the feet of some of the most spectacular Alps.

NORTHERN NORWAY

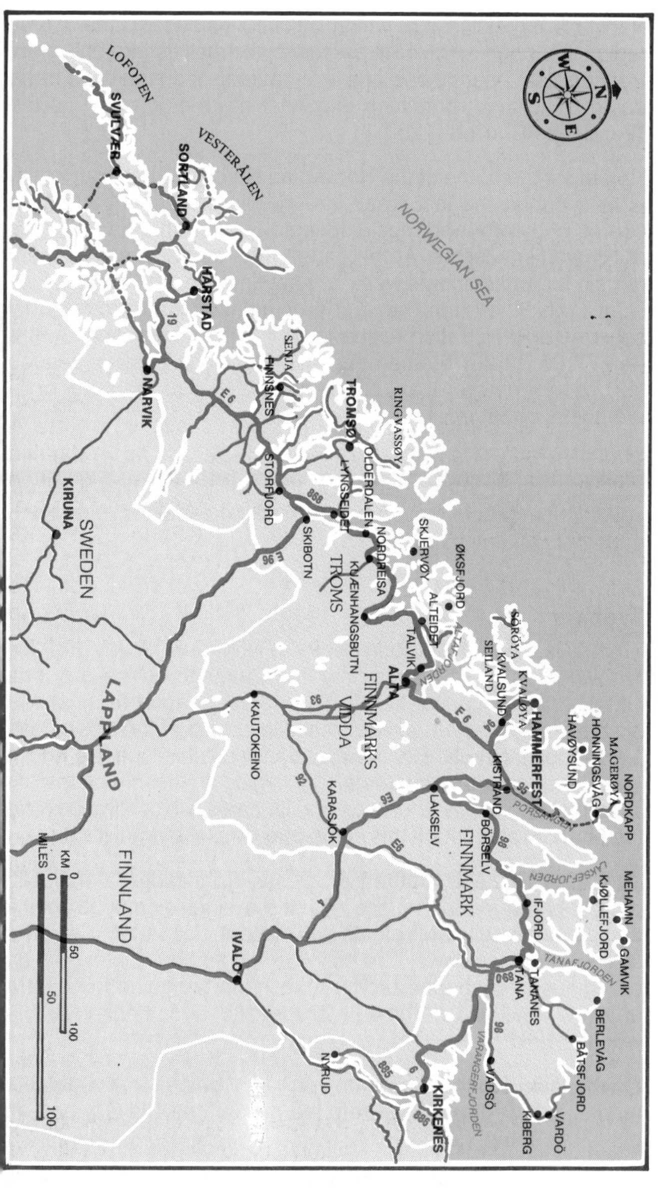

Harstad

Harstad is situated near the north-western end of **Hinnøya**, Norway's largest island, which officially belongs to the Troms region. Founded in the 13th century by a small fishermen's clan, Harstad has recently become a remarkable industrial and trade centre. The only remaining exponent of its olden days is the **Trondenes Church** (1250).

Harstad is the home of the Norwegian Nordic Art Festival, which is held during the last week in June. Its programmes include scores of theatre and music spectacles, and attract thousands of Norwegian visitors. At the end of the Festival, many of them remain for an additional week, to participate in the "Biggest Fish Hunt", which attracts hundreds of amateur and professional fishermen. Registration at the local Tourist Information Centre (tel. 77 06 32 35). Remember that during the Festival season early bookings are absolutely a must, either at the hotel or at the hostel or camp site.

The Harstad church is a classic example of a 12th century fortified church. After the visit to the capital's medieval alleys, you might appreciate an outing to the **Biarkøy Island**, birthplace of one of St. Olav's opponents.

Tromsø

Tromsø is the largest urban centre in Northern Norway. It has a renowned university, a distillery that claims to be the only one situated in this part of the world, and the seaport from whose piers Nansen and Amundsen sailed in search of the North Pole. It's a young city, which boasts sophisticated elegance and a quasi-cosmopolitan character. Its night life, its museums, its students' haunts, its churches and its cafés will confirm beyond the shadow of a doubt: this is the true Capital of the North.

The **Arctic Ocean Cathedral**, whose front faces a majestic bridge, is the symbol of the city. It's a singular modern glass and concrete building, solemn and elegant, decorated with large stained glass windows. The main component of its interior is an enormous ship-shaped organ. Across the bridge, in the centre of town, you'll find an older, more traditional cathedral, built in wood in 1861.

On the main Stortorget Square you'll find the fruit and vegetable market, a few steps away from the ruins of the Old City and an old 13th century castle.

A tour of the museums will take you several hours. The **Tromsø Museum**, inside the Customs Palace, side by side with the

Arctic Ocean cathedral, is open 11am-3pm. The **North Pole Museum** will interest at least those who plan to proceed to the country's far north. The **Tromsø Arts Museum** (open 9am-6pm) contains several interesting works of art and dedicates a special hall to Sami life and art. It's on Strandveien, a half hour walk or a short no. 21 bus ride from the centre.

At the Tourist Information Centre (tel. 77 61 00 00) you'll find, beside all the usual details, a *Tromsø Card* (24 hours free transportation and museum entrances for 25NOK).

At most hotels there are considerable summer discounts, that bring prices down to a very reasonable 250NOK for a double-room. B&B and private residence lodging prices are more or less the same. We recommend the *Skipperhuset* (tel. 77 68 16 60), the *Park* (tel. 77 68 22 08), the hostel (summers only, tel. 77 68 53 19) and the camp site (tel. 77 63 51 57).

Most restaurants and cafés are situated around the Storgate. The *Theaterkafeen* is frequented by many local Bohemians; students prefer the *Samfunnskafeen*. The *Prelaten* is a jazz club; there are two other night spots at Storgate 4 and 51.

The Finnmark

The Finnmark region occupies the far north of Norway; its latitude is that of Alaska or of Novaya Zemlya; but the scenery is quite different, and again this is due to the caressing waters of the Gulf Stream. The Finnmark coastal waters only freeze up in the middle of winter. All along its fjords and even on its coastal heights there are several fishermen and farmer vilages. In summer there are days when the temperature climbs as high as 30°C; in winter it may plummet down to -50°C. For more than two months — from mid-May to the end of July — the sun never sets. And from the end of November to the end of January it never rises. The twilight hues and splendid moonlight of its sunless winter are simply stunning. Sunrise, at the beginning of spring, is a great occasion for man and nature to celebrate the rebirth of light; and with the thawing of the winter snow the land becomes a multicoloured blanket of wild flowers, and tourists flock in their thousands to enjoy the spectacle.

The **northern lights** are a phenomenon whose origins are still controversial. It appears as a sudden "explosion" of brightly coloured changing lights, that after a few moments may disappear without a sign. According to one school of thought, the lights are caused by the influence of the Earth's Magnetic

Tromsø's Arctic Cathedral

Pole on the solar rays, which in certain critic conditions, at given solar angles, results in an explosion of brillantly coloured lights.

In 1925, a clamorous discovery revealed traces of prehistoric human presence in this region: according to those findings this was the hunting ground of the roaming nomad tribe of the *Kosma* 10.000 years ago. Much later, at the very beginnings of our Era, several *Sami* clans also settled in this area.

After the end of the 10th century the Vikings made their first appearance here, and only a few years later waves of other Norwegian tribes, mostly agricultural settlers, expanded northward from the Finnmark's southern reaches.

After the 16th century, the Sami lost their predominance, bequeathing a rich cultural and folkloristic heritage to their Norwegian successors.

European civilization gradually infiltrated the Finnmark at the beginning of the last century, introducing improved fishing techniques, electricity, roadbuilding and heating; thus the Finnmark changed little by little into a modern Norwegian region.

In 1944 the occupying German troups, forced to withdraw, left behind them a completely scorched land. After the war, massive reconstruction projects had to be carried out, which turned the Finnmark into a model industrial centre and a well equipped tourist resort.

The Finnmark is very vast, and not always pleasant to drive through; an attractive alternative is that of the **Nord Norge Bussen** (Northern Norwegian Bus Line). Its southern terminus is at **Nordskjosbotn**, 75 km south of Tromsø on the E6. The bus stops overnight at Alta, and on the next day it proceeds to Tana, Bru Lakslev, Karasjøk and Kirkenes. The second alternative is the *Hurtigruten* line, from Harstad northward. The return trip to Kirkenes requires 5-6 days.

Alta

The capital of the Finnmark, Alta, has a population of 14,000 people. It's situated at the end of the formidable fjord. The R96, that turns toward the hinterland, Sweden and Finnish Lappland, and the E6 coming from the south, make Alta an important road junction.

The **Hjemmelutt** graffiti, the largest and most picturesque in Europe, are 3-6,000 years old. They are perfectly preserved, and they represent various aspects of daily human life, several local animal species and ships and boats of their times. They are easy to find, thanks to the frequent roadside arrows that indicate the way, starting from the hostel to the final footpath turnoff that leads (1 km) to the graffiti walls. The site is open to visitors June to August, 8.30am-10.30pm; entrance 10NOK.

The **Alta Museum**, while it boasts no great rarities, will give you a good idea of the extreme North; this will suffice for most, but the daring few will carry their way to the Nordkapp, whatever the cost.

There is a Tourist Information Centre (tel. 78 43 77 70); there is the very expensive *Alta Hotel* (tel. 78 43 53 11), and a second hotel, the *Alta Gestue*, (tel. 78 43 53 36), slightly cheaper and with a good restaurant. There is a summer hostel (tel. 78 43 44 09) with an information desk for northern itineraries, and a camp site (with double rooms, tel. 78 43 52 26), not far from the Hjemmelutt graffiti.

For details of excursions and outings, see "Backpacking through Norway". For other details (fishing, ski, skiing etc.) call the Tourist Information Centre. Wintersports are very popular here; there is a good and not too difficult descent from **Mount Haldde** (about 900 m). This spectacular four hour route begins at Kafjord and ends at a splendid mountain observatory.

Another pleasant outing goes to the splendid canyon of **Sautso**. Starting from Alta, it turns south for 26 km to **Gargia** (map and details at the Gargia *Fjellstue*), where following the frequent arrows an 11 km footpath leads to the canyon mouth.

South of Alta

Kautokeino and **Karasjok** are two Sami villages on the **Finnmarksvidda** plateau.

Kautokeino is easily reached from Alta (R93, 130 km) and from Finland (45 km). In summer it attracts thousands of tourists, who swarm to the local sites — the red stave church and the **Sami Museum** — and the Sami handicraft markets.

There are two hotels: the *Kautokeino* (tel. 78 48 62 05) and the hostel-like *Alfred Kro* (tel. 78 48 61 18); you may also inquire about private residence lodgings at the hostel.

Karasjok

Karsjok is a little town of 2,700 people, crossed by the R6. It's one of the main Sami culture centres, as witnessed by its vast **Sami Museum**, situated next door to the bus station. Beside its art and craft exhibitions, it has also a very attractive sales centre. The **Karasjok Church** (1807) is the oldest in the region, and the only building to have survived the 1944 scorched land disaster. The **Sami Library** contains a vast literary collection translated into different languages and a series of modern ethnological studies.

At the Tourist Information Centre (tel. 78 46 73 60) you'll be able to book seats for several interesting guided tours. Karasjok is one of the stops of the *Nord Norge Bussen.*

If you would like to stay overnight, you'll find the *SAS Hotel* (tel. 78 46 68 02), a motel (tel. 78 46 64 46) and a hostel (tel. 78 46 64 6).

Toward Kirkenes

Lakselv means "salmon stream"; later the name was also passed on to the little town built on the Porsanger Fjord, 175 km east of Alta, on the E6. From here the R98 goes on to Kirkenes, while the E6 turns south to Karasjok. The Silfarfossen Canyon, not far from Lakselv, is enormous; the Stabbursdalen National Park is full of little streams and mountain rivers — naturally full of salmon — and crisscrossed by hundreds of foot paths.

The Lakselv Tourist Information Centre (tel. 78 46 21 45) will provide you with detailed information on local outings and lodgings. There are two hotels: the *Banak* (tel. 78 46 13 77) and the *Lakselv*; the camp site and hostel phone number is tel. 78 46 14 76.

Tana Bru is a town of 3,300 people, on the Kirkenes road, at the R98 turnoff from the E6. It's situated on the river, the third longest in Norway, that marks the border with Finland. At Tana Bru you'll find a regional museum and a Tourist Information Centre (tel. 78 92 82 81), with details of frequent tours organised by the neighbouring hotels.

Kirkenes

Kirkenes is the northern terminus of the *Hurtigruten* cruise and of the *Nord Norge Bussen*. It's only 16 km from the Russian border. It's a mining centre, and at the beginning of the Second World War it was frequently bombed by the German Luftwaffe. Then, four years later, the retreating German troops set fire to the whole town. Today's Kirkenes is less than 50 years old.

The *Hurtigruten* ships only stop for two hours, and then sail back on their return trip to the south. But two hours may suffice to get a fair idea of the town. However, at the Tourist Information Centre (tel. 78 99 25 01) you'll find also details of available accommodation in town.

There are the *Kirkenes Rica* (expensive, tel. 78 99 14 91) and the *Rica Gjestehus* (moderate, also tel. 78 99 14 91) hotels; not far from them, you'll find an outstanding restaurant, the *Grillstua*.

The Varangerhalovøya Peninsula

Bugøynes, north of Kirkenes, is an ancient fishermen's village, which survived the scourge of the Second World War without damage. The local language is Finnish. There are motorboats sailing from the pier to **Ranvik**, a birds' Island 90 minute-sail away. Bugøynes is on the Varangefjord, across the water from

A Reindeer Herd and its Sami shepherd

Vadsø. The *Hurtigruten* ships land at Bugøynes, at Vadsø, at Vardø, at Båtsfjord and at Beverlåg. **Vadsø** has a population of 6,000, almost equally divided in a Finn and a Norwegian community. It has a good library and a museum of local history. The Zeppelins of the Amundsen-Nobile expedition took off from the **Luftskipmasia** (Airship Mast), situated on an islet just off the town coast. There is a Tourist Information Centre (tel. 78951839), which has detailed information on hotel and camping accommodation.

Vardø, on the northern side of the Varangefjord mouth, is the only Norwegian town with a real arctic climate. The castle was built by King Christian V in 1739, and it's open to visitors. Within the castle you'll find a modest museum. You are now at the northernmost and easternmost tip of Norway. In the whole town only one tree survives the year after year bitter winters; it grows inside the castle walls.

Båtsfjord has 2,600 people and is one of the most renowned fishermen's villages in Norway. It has two major attractions: the **Hamningberg** open-air museum, set as a living memorial on the grounds of a village destroyed by the Germans toward the end of the Second World War, and the Birds' Rock, an islet situated at the port gates. There is only one hotel, which organises frequent outings and fishing expeditions.

Berlevåg has 1,400 people, a history museum and the Tanahorn Hill (269 m), where the Sami used to offer their gods their human sacrifices.

The Nordkapp

The Nordkapp (Cape North) is a popular tourist destination; it's easily accessible both by sea and by land, along the route briefly described below.

The starting point is **Hammerfest**, a town that claims to be the northernmost city on Earth. Curiously, it holds a second record: it was the first European town to adopt electric street lighting. Destroyed by fire in 1891, the town was rapidly rebuilt — and redestroyed in 1944 by the Germans. Today's town is therefore very modern. It has a Tourist Information Centre (tel. 78 41 21 85) and two motels (*Rica*, tel. 78 41 13 33, and *Hammerfest*).

The main street has attractive shopwindows and several pleasant cafés, as well as two interesting churches. The **Meridianstøotten** (Meridian's Monument) and the **Civic Museum** (also known as the "Royal and Ancient Polar Bear Society", summers only, 8am-6pm).

The motorboat to the Nordkapp stops also at **Havøysund**, the capital of Masøy, a region of more than 300 islands. Half an hour will suffice to enjoy a hot cuppa or a short walk to the local museum.

The next stop is **Honningsvåg**, a town that tried to rob Hammerfest of one of its two records: it is 80 km north of the incumbent "Northern Champion". However, Hammerfest was wide awake, and did not surrender its title: after a brief but tempestive administrative campaign, Honningsvåg was demoted to the rank of "village", and Hammerfest could thus legitimately retain its title.

The R95 branches off the E6 northward and after 75 km it reaches the landing of the Kafjord ferry for Honningsvåg. This fishermens' "village" has a church and a **Polar Museum**. The Tourist Information Centre (tel. 78 47 25 99) will assist you with available outings and boat-hire, and even with possible hitchhiking lifts.

The Nordkapp bus makes several daily runs, but one may also elect to spend the night at the *Nordkapp* hotel (tel. 78 47 23 33) or at the relatively cheaper *Valanbu* (tel. 78 47 30 26).

A last effort will finally take you to the end of the line — Cape

North, 34 km from the village itself. Along the road, with a little luck, you'll see the reindeer herds with their Sami shepherds, who often spread their handicraft fares along the road. Then, from the 307 m height of the Cape, the view of the Arctic Ocean will leave you breathless and speechless.

On top of the Cape you will see several monuments: the stone memorial of King Oskar's royal visit in 1873; another memorial of Louis Philippe d'Orléans' visit in 1755. There is no memento of Sir Richard Chandler's discovery of the Cape itself in 1553, during his unsuccessful search for the "North-Eastern Passage to China".

Not far from these memorials, you'll probably be glad to find a café-restaurant. It sells souvenirs and Nordkapp illustrated postcards, that may be stamped and posted on the spot, at the local miniature post-office.

Backpacking Through Norway

Faithful to their traditional passion for backpacking abroad, the Norwegians have also created, in their own country, an excellent network of services for foreign and local backpackers. One of these services, the *DNT*, has designed a whole catalogue of itineraries for you, covering all the major tourist destinations in Norway. The itineraries are outined clearly not only on the *DNT* maps, but also on the spot, with a series of pathside arrows, that make it practically impossible for any hiker to lose his way on route. Today the *DNT* is also responsible for the upkeep of all Alpine shelters in Norway.

The Shelters — The great distances through sparsely populated areas, along a chain of pretty high Alps, in a climate liable to suddenly reach very unpleasant extremes, required a network of Alpine shelters of three different categories:

— hostel-type shelters, with lodgings, service personnel and auxilliary hygienic and kitchen facilites.
— dormitory-shelters, equipped with beds, toilets, heating and kitchen facilities.
— basic shelters, equipped only with vital overnight requirements.

The maximum stay in any of these shelter is three days. Beds may be booked in advance only at the first-type shelters; you can book either through one of the neighbouring Tourist Information Centres or directly, by phone. In all shelters you'll find clear instructions (in Norwegian and in English). It's the *DNT*'s policy never to let anybody spend the night in the open.

The *DNT* itineraries are marked with a large red "T"; you'll recognize them easily at all crossings, turnoffs and road exits. Distances are mostly indicated in walking hours from shelter to shelter.

In the following pages we'll briefly describe some of the most popular itineraries. Some of them may only be morning walks, while others may even be two-week enterprises. At least for the longer routes, you'll do well to come equipped with a reliable compass and with the 1:50,000 (0r 1:100,000) maps of the whole route (available at the Tourist Information Centres and at the *DNT* branches). Our routes follow the Norwegian Alps northward; the areas they cover have already been described in earlier chapters. Advance with caution, making sure to be able to reach your planned overnight lodgings well before dark.

Equipment
It's almost inevitable that during your walk you'll have to cross some mountain brooks or swampy lowlands; come well prepared with a pair of good galoshes and some extra socks. Inquire in advance as to the type of the shelters you'll find on your way, and equip yourself with everything you'll need, but nothing extra.

Åseral-Bykle — Setedalsheiene (5-8 days)

The greyish hues of the Setedal are a challenge to modern geologists. The topographic structure of this plateau, with its sudden falls and precipices, is unequalled anywhere on Earth.

Maps: Austad, Kuifjorden, Rjuven, Bossvatnet.

Start: Bus from Krinstiansand to Åseral and second bus to Ljoslandshytta.

Route: Moving from the Lake Langevatn Dam, the route proceeds along a series of little mountain lakes and through vales, reindeer reserves and old, abandoned farms. You'll cross lots of muddy ground, then climb to a height of 1370 m, to the "Skins's Route"; overnight at the Bossbu Shelter and down to **Valle**. After a lengthy lakeside walk, the route proceeds down the Grjotadal Valley, then climbs again to a height of 1250 m, to cross the Ljosøni Bridge and ends, after a last climb through a deep conifer forest, to the final plateau, at whose northern end the R12 runs down to **Bykle**, on your right.

Bolkesjø — Imingfjell — the "Blefjell Route" (6-8 days)

The route covers the area south of the Hardangervidda. An area singularly rich not in flora, but in unusual quartz crystals. The route has been popular for centuries.

Maps: 1:50,000: Notodden, Tinnsjø, Nore, Tessungdalen. The whole series of the route maps is on sale at the best bookshops and at most Tourist Information Centres.

Start: By rail from Oslo to Kongsberg (90 minutes), then by bus to Bolkesjø (30 minutes).

Route: The path begins 1 km west of the village, turns toward

Mount Bletoppen (weather permitting, one may climb to its 1341 m high top). Then, through a series of mountain lakes of various sizes, the route reaches the winter reindeer reserves and the Nansen Shelter. Almost all shelters along this route are of the third category, so come prepared. The route crosses two main arteries: the *Nordmannslepa* to the Fjords Region and the *Uvdal-Tessungdal.* The route ends by the Imingfjell Dam.

Hardangervidda: from Finse to Haukeliseter (9-10 days)

The Hardangervidda Plateau attracts thousands of visitors: in summer, mostly hikers, in winter, mostly skiers. Our route is one of many; if you wish, with the help of a good map and some prior experience, you may improvise your own route with the help of an expert.

Maps: The 1:200,000 map of the plateau will be sufficient. You'll most probably be glad to have a reference book or handbook with you that will help classify the plateau birdlife and flora.

Start: From the Finse railway station, on the Oslo-Bergen line.

Route: Follow the ancient route to the eastern tip of Lake Finsavatn and its dam. Then the path follows the rim of the Hardangerjøken Glacier, through mountain lakes and passes, to the highest Hardangervidda peak (1476 m). Then it climbs down to the Madobal Observatory and to the **Vøringfoss Waterfall** (182 m high).

At the waterfall one may stay at the shelter overnight or board the bus to Eidsfjord. Then the route climbs again among lakes, vales and woodland, to end at **Haukeliseter**, a village situated on the E76 route. Form here one may travel to Haugesund (5 hours) or to **Bø** (3 hours), and there board the Oslo train (2 hours). Most shelters are of the first category; hence you'll be able to travel light.

Another splendid route starts from **Finse**: a 4-5 day northern itinerary to **Aurland** (on the Sognefjord). This is the beloved route of many Norwegians, who for some reason have nicknamed it "The English Route". It crosses several minor glaciers, climbing to some of the most spectacular views in the country. The final descent follows the river course, along its frequent waterfalls and the great hydroelectric plants of the valley. On the way back, the most interesting itinerary follows the line of the little Flåm Railway.

The Route of the Giants — from Gjendesheim to Hjelle (12 days)

According to the *DNT* the Jotunheimen Chain is to Norway what the Yosemite Park is to the USA or the Lochaber Region to Scotland. Mountains, valleys, lakes, glaciers, waterfalls; its 60 glaciers and 250 peaks above 1,900 m definitely make it a "Route of the Giants", and a paradise of mountaineering, especially in spring.

Maps: 1:50,000: Glittertinden, Gjende, Sygnefjell, Tyin, Hurrungane.

Start: By rail or by bus from Oslo to Otta (4 hours), then by bus to Gjendesheim (2.5 hours).

Route: The path zigzags first to a first alp (1195 m), then descends to the valley where Peer Gynt fell to the bottom. Then up again to the highest peaks (2200 m) with their precipitous canyons. Then by boat across Lake Gjende, and deep into the valley to the shelter. After a good night's rest, it's time to climb the **Glittertind** (2481 m) for an amazing view of all the lakes and glaciers far down below. The route ends at **Hjelle**, after crossing several mountain streams with their narrows and waterfalls. On your arrival (on foot or by bus) to **Øvre Årdal** you'll board the bus to Årdalstangen, and then the ferry to Bergen (6-8 hours) or the pullman to Fagernes (3.5 hours) — and finally the Oslo train (4 hours).

A word of caution to the wise: this route is rather demanding, and sometimes even dangerous; it requires therefore at least some prior experience and training.

The Jostedal from Fjærland to Tølster (2 days)

The Jostedalbreen (Jostedal Glacier) is to be treated with considerable respect. Its complex spreads through an area of 815 km^2. It's the largest glacier in Europe, reaches a height of 2083 m and is more than 300 m deep. It has no less than 24 branches: the Tunsbergdalsbreen is the longest, and the Austerdalsbreen is the most spectacular. The ice moves at a rate of about more than one foot a day. The Jostedal's most expert guide lives in the little farm at the foot of the Bøyabreen; he may be reached through the Fjærland Tourist Information Centre services, or courtesy of the local *Mundall Hotel.*

Maps: 1:50,000: Fjærland and Brigsdalsbreen. Maps and

equipment are available at the village, on the evening before your tour.

Start: Fjærland is accessible by boat from Hella or by car from Skei.

Route: The path moves northward from Fjærland to the waterfall and then to the Bøyum farm; it follows the arrows to the top, for an unforgettable view of the Flatbre Glacier, with its Suphelle tongue high above the chasm. Then comes the crossing of the ice, following cautiously in the guide's steps. The descent ends at the Stardalen Valley, which reaches the R14 from **Stryn** in the North to Bergen in the South. Coming from the opposite side of the Jostedal, not far from Olden and Loen, one may climb to the glacier top on foot or by the fabulous reindeer sleds.

From Rondane to Hjerkinn (8 days)

The Rondane Massif, one of the most striking in the country, was declared in 1970 a National Park. Its geologic structure, its fauna, the variety of its flora and its splendid lakes put it in a class of its own.

The itinerary we suggest is relatively simple. It goes from peak to peak, crossing the most spectacular sections of the region. A word of warning: the entire itinerary has to be taken — or not at all.

Maps: 1:100,000: Rondane; or 1:50,000: Rondane, Solnkletten, Hjerkinn.

Start: Alighting from the Oslo train at Alvdal (5 hours), carry on to Follandsvangen on foot (4 hours) or by taxi.

Route: Beginning from the north-eastern tip of the massif, the path climbs to the observatory and crosses a chain of vales and montain lakes to Straumbu. Here, assisted by some local expert, one must wade the Etna stream. This is more or less the half-way point of no return on the way to the Rondane National Park. The path climbs the Høgronden (2114 m), and then descends toward Lake Rondvatnet to reach Otta (on the Oslo-Trondheim railway). Further on to the north-west there is the railway station of Hjerkinn, also on the same railway line.

East of Rondane are **Femundsmarka** and **Gutuilia**, two villages situated on **Lake Femund**. The whole area is a botanic and zoological garden, crisscrossed by reindeer paths and meadows among a spattering of mountain lakes. The starting points are **Tynset** or **Røros** (on R30). Another popular route crosses into Sweden, to the Jamtland and to the village of Funasdalen.

Backpacking up the Jotunheimen

Mo-i-Rana (5-6 days)

Mo lies between the two Alpine masses of **Borgefjell** to its South and **Okstindan** to its North. The Borgefjell Park may be reached on foot from Majavatn (45 km South of Trofors). The route starts from Susendalen, a village accessible from the R804 or from the south, by means of the Namsvassgarden ferry across Lake Namsvatnet. The park is also accessible from Sweden. The park flora counts 295 endemic species as well as several unique animal species. At Fagerneset, near Lake Namsvatan, three old Sami families live the life and customs of several centuries ago.

Maps: 1:100,000: Borgefjell, Namsvatnet (neither of them is up to the usual Norwegian standards).

Start: The Mo bus to **Umbukta** reaches the **Okstindan** in about one hour.

Route: The path begins at the local camp site and crosses Lake Akersvatn toward the Swedish border. Then, from Leirbotnhytla or from Grafjelhytta one may climb up to the glacier. The route ends at **Korgen** and then by bus back to Mo.

Not far from here is the **Svartisen** (Black Ice); but this itinerary must be taken with a certified Alpine guide; for details, call the Tourist Information Centre.

Sulitjelma and the Saltfjellet Massif (4-6 days)

The copper mines of the region, discovered by chance by a passing farmer, have been recently abandoned, but the massif itself remains one of the most popular challenges sought by thousands of mountaineers. The captivating charm of its vales and its glaciers brings them back again and again, year after year. But don't worry, the route we suggest will not be beyond the scope of the average tourist.

Maps: 1:100,000: Saltdal, Junkerdalen, Beiardalen.

Start: By bus from Fauske to Sulitjelma, then by bus or taxi to **Tjorvihytta**.

Route: The path (clearly marked with large rockpiles), turns off the shore of Lake Balvatnet, climbing to the divide only to descend, after crossing a wooden bridge, along the opposite mountainside. Then the route proceeds to Beiarn, where one may board the Fauske bus.

North of Fauske is the **Rago Park**, adjacent to the great parks of Sweden. The mountain paths ignore such nonentities as national borderlines, zigzagging between countries at the call of the local topography. The park is accessible from the Trengal bridge and from Lakshola, on the E6.

Yet farther north, not far from Narvik, east of the E6 and south-east of Tysfjord, rise the peaks of another striking massif, whose streams are unusually rich trout (fishing permits available at the Tysfjord hostel). On this massif there are no shelters.

The areas of **Narvik**, the **Lofoten Islands** and the **Vesterålen Islands** are thick with tourists throughout the year. One of the most popular routes follows the **Ofoten** railway line to the mountains and to the iron mines.

The Skjomen route starts at the Katterat stop. It's a three day tour through several snowy peaks and minor glaciers. It's rather lengthy, and we'll suggest a shortcut from Beisfjord to Lake Losivatn.

We've already described some of the Lofoten Island routes, most of them short half day walks through rather difficult terrain. For information, equipment and guides, call the Svolvær or the Stamsund Tourist Information Centre.

The "Border Route" of Troms (8 days)

This is a region of great contrasts: the majesty of the Arctic

Ocean, the dark austerity of its many fjords, the lure of its hundred lakes, the foreboding shadow of its peaks — and the crisscrossing network of its dark green valleys.

Start: Alight from the Skibotn bus to Finland just 1 km before the border, on the E78. The path entrance is marked with a rockpile; the path turns westward, through the forest and far above it, following the course of the valley, between lakes and mountaintops. The views, on both sides of the border, are sometimes simply staggering.

The route ends at Innset, where one may board the bus to Narvik or to Tromsø.

North of Tromsø, on the **Senja Island**, is the **Ånderdalen** National Park. The lake, enclosed among dark conifer forests, was for centuries a summer pasture frequented by large reindeer herds and their Sami shepherds. Today the Park offers his visitors its majestic silences, its changing hues of green, blue and gold, and (if you have been able to obtain a valid fishing permit), some of the best fishing you've ever dreamed of.

Finnmarksvidda—Alta—Karasjok (4 days)

The Finnmark Plateau, once one of the most popular reindeer grazing lands, has a very special appeal for winter skiers and for spring salmon fishers.

Maps: 1:100,000: Alta.

Start: Ravnastua, which may be reached by boat or by road from Karasjok (4-6 hours).

Route: The path climbs up to the plateau, crossing vales and watercourses, through bridges or by rowboat, to end at Tverrelvaden, terminus of the Alta bus.

The Finnmark is a land crisscrossed by scores of paths, which may at times just seem to go nowhere at all, while in other cases they lead straight to the great National Parks of the region, like for instance the **Øvere Pasvik**, which spreads on both sides of the Norwegian-Russian borderline.

Another interesting park is the **Stabbursdalen**, famous for its conifer forests (the northernmost of their type on Earth) and for its deep chasms and great glaciers. It's situated east of the Porsangen Fjord and west of Alta, and may be easily reached from the E6.

The Bewitching Hurtigruten Cruise

The Norwegian Coastal Navigation Bergen-Kirkenes line was established almost hunderd years ago and functions like clockwork, 365 days a year (366 in leap-years...). It provides the basic trade and tourist communication element along the longitudinal axis of the country. The immensely indented coasts of Norway make it possible for ships to land at scores of seaports situated on island shores, at fjord mouths or deep within the natural gulfs of the Arctic Ocean. All this makes the line a spectacular tourist cruise, unequalled to any other sea route on Earth. Tickets are bought on a daily basis; there are scores of possible routes, with almost endless possibilities for stopovers at any of the regular boat landings, reembarking the next day on either direction.

The ships leave Bergen daily at sunset toward the north. At the opposite terminus, Kirkenes, they sail daily southward at noon sharp. The ships of the line are seasoned, strong and reliable vessels, suitably equipped for their often stormy passage. There are luxury staterooms, tourist cabins and day-beds and sleeping-bags for the economic class deck-passengers. The traditional atmosphere of relaxed social interaction has no equal on board any other cruise ships. There are in all 36 stops along the line; at all stops there is sufficient time for a refreshing walk, a cuppa and eventually some quick souvenir shopping along the pier. It's also possible to stop here again for an overnight rest, only to resume the voyage on the next-day's ship. Having enjoyed the experience, many return year after year for new experiences and new variations of the Hurtigruten cruise.

The timing of the cruise is of great importance. There are various aspects to consider: the midnight sun during a high summer cruise; the long twilight hours of the autumn and spring; the blinding white of the winter snows — and, with a little luck, the caleidoscopic instants of the Northern Lights; in spring, the view of the many-coloured meadows along the coast and on the islands, and in summer, thousands and thousands of seabirds nesting on the rocky islets. Can you make your choice or just enjoy what there is at the time of your visit.

The ship company are not unlike the personnel of a mobile Tourist Information Centre; they know the route like the palm of their hand; they will be glad to advise you on your choice of stopovers, the views you'll find anywhere along the line, the best restaurants and hotels, as well as the best fishing grounds... Many passengers travel with their own bike (no extra fee); some of the more modern ships are equipped also for vehicle ferrying services.

All Tourist Information Centres have detailed data on the *Hurtigruten* line, its timetables, its ships, its tariffs etc. Sometimes there may even be some interesting bargains: be sure to inquire before buying your ticket!

We have mentioned the *Hurtigruten* cruise several times throughout the book, but we have never described its route.

The first stop after Bergen is Florø; then Måløy, Torvik and Ålesund. Then we have Molde — town of the roses — and Kristiansund. Next comes the Trondheimsfjorden and Trondheim itself. From the height of the bridge you'll have the opportunity to follow the flight of great clouds of seabirds, planing above their summer nests perched on the rock of the coastal archipelago and of the fjord mouth.

After Trondheim the ship crosses the Helgeland Archipelago, stopping at Rørvik and at Brønnøysund. Ask to be shown the Torghatten Massif, with its remarkable hole, which according to legend is to be attributed to an arrow, shot at the mountainface by a local hero. Geologists, however, claim that the hole is the effect to the corroding action of great prehistoric waves and tides, when the sea level was considerably higher than today. Not far from here the ship will cross the Arctic Circle (the passage will be duly announced by the ship's horn), entering the area of the "midnight sun" (in June and July). The next stop is Bodø (the northern railway terminus); if you've been told about the "Vortex Fjord" and wish to see it in person, you'll have to spend the night here.

Then the ship reaches the Vestfjord and the Lofoten Islands.

The Vestfjord

The fjord waters are crowded, during the winter, with hundreds of fishermens' boats: it's the time of the great Lofoten Fishing Competition. But the straits are crowded at any time of the year. North of the islands, the weather cools at once; the Gulf Stream loses much of its life-force, and is replaced by the icy waters of the Arctic Ocean. Harstad and Tromsø are the next stops; suitable for a short walk, or for refilling your food reserves.

Now the course turns eastward. The ship stops at Hammerfest, a modern arctic town, with very good connections for the Cape North. Its people will welcome you warmly, cheering the ship, cheering your passage, cheering the midnight sun, cheering the Cape North, cheering.

After three hours, the ship will move on to Honningsvåg; and after several brief stops at a series of fishermen's villages, you'll see Vardø and its Medieval castle, then Vadsø, and finally Kirkenes, the end of the line.

Ski in Norway

Norwegians are said to be born "with a pair of skis". For the sake of their mothers, let's hope it's just an allegoric motto; nevertheless, a non-skiing Norwegian is probably the equivalent of a non-biking Dane... Skis in Norway are first of all, a daily transportation means, which in winter are used for cross-country wintersports.

At the same time, skis are also the most popular sport in Norway. There are scores of national and international events — cross-country, descents, slaloms, jumps and lots of other sports, which the common southern has probably never heard of. But what matters is that on those frequent occasions, even non-skiers may take advantage of very convenient tourist discounts and bargain deals.

The winter season never ends before May, either on the Alp slopes or along the hinterland plains, beside the everpresent fjords or along the frequent Alpine waterfalls or above some brightly flowering spring meadow.

Here is a short list of some of the more popular wintersport resorts in Norway.

Geilo

A small town on the banks of the Ustedalsfjord, one of the fjords whose waters freeze over in winter. There are ski tracks on either side of the fjord. Excellent for beginners. Not less than 16 ski lifts and 26 km of descents. Several hotels, B&Bs, restaurants and night-clubs.

Voss

On the bank of Lake Vangsvatnet; the ski tracks are open until the end of April. An outstanding ski-school, and descents of various levels, from beginners' class to experts' challenges. Outstanding cross-country to the Telemark. Voss is on the Oslo-Bergen railway line, and is very well equipped: 9 ski lifts and 32 km of descents.

Beitostole

Situated on the southern slope of the Jotunheim, 200 km from

Oslo. All classes of ski tracks, including a "children's track" and a professionists' track, with a 30% gradient. Very well equipped for ski, sled and walks. Several jumpboards, 7 ski lifts, 100 km of cross-country. Hotels, saunas, night clubs, restaurants and other sports.

Hemsdel

Hemsdel is one of the most popular wintersports resorts in Norway. 100 km of cross-country, 12 ski lifts, 4 km of descent with a 16% gradient).

Oppdal

Oppdal is the official skiing capital of Norway; it was the site of the 1984 and 1988 world slalom championships. 26 descents, 184 km of tracks and 14 ski lifts.

Trysil

This is the largest wintersports resort in Norway, is situated only at 220 km from Oslo, not far from the Swedish border. Two main tracks, with 30 km of cross-country, 29 descents and scores of jumping-boards; 12 ski lifts. Open from the end of November to the end of April. Lots of additional activities, a wide choice of accommodation and a hectic night life.

FINLAND

Finland, or rather *Suomi* (in the language of the country, "Land of the Thousand Lakes") is quite different from the other Scandinavian countries. This is true in a wide range of fields: geography, history, language, climate... For many centuries Finland has been a frequent battlefield in scores of conflicts between its two more powerful neighbours: Sweden to the west and Russia to the east. From time to time other European powers were only too happy to join the struggle on finnish soil. As if the scourge of war were not enough, Mother Nature contributed a long list of additional disasters of her own: droughts, floods, ice; yet Finland's cup was not full, and man added his own breed of Armageddon: the Black Death, and civil war, and fire.

But probably the most unique aspect that sets Finland apart as a Scandinavian "freak" is the language: 93% of Finns speak a tongue of quite a different race: not an Indo-European but an Ugaro-Finnic language. 7% of Finns (mostly in the South-Western regions of the country) speak Swedish. This was enough for Finland to declare itself a bilingual state, where the country itself, its towns, its regions, its mountains and its lake have always (at least) two official names: one is in Finnish and the other in Swedish.

History

At the end of the last Ice Age, when the land was beginning to thaw, Finland was mainly populated by polar bears and other nordic species. Man made his first appearance more or less 10,000 years ago, when the first Baltic hunting tribes took to following the great herbivorous herds toward the new pastures of the north in spring.

The first more or less permanent human settlements date from the Third Millennium B.C., and soon the new communities established some forms of trade relations among neighbouring villages and clans.

The forefathers of today's Finns represent a much later wave of nomadic, bellicose tribes, who reached Finland from the East

— from the foothills of the Urals and the Valley of the Volga. Their coming was mentioned by Tacitus, the Roman historian, who wrote of them as the "Finns". The "natives" were gradually forced to seek safety in the far north, and their survivors formed the ethnic group known today as the *Sami* (or Laps), a tribe of reindeer shepherds who live to this day in the frozen tundras of northern Finland, Sweden and Norway.

The first Finnish townships were founded, not unnaturally, on the seashore. There they came into (often traumatic) contact with the Vikings, whose frequent incursions forced the local tribes to fortify their seaports and to seek shelter in new towns, built along the many watercourses and lakes of the hinterland.

The Swedish wave of conquest reached Finland toward the end of the first millennium, bringing in its wake the new Catholic faith, which slowly replaced most of the old idolatrous traditions.

The conquest of Finland brought the Swedes in direct contact with Russia, a great empire which had many good reasons to view the Swedish expansion with the utmost concern: Sweden was catholic; Russia was Orthodox; Sweden wanted to rule the whole of the Baltic Sea — and Russia wanted a free Atlantic outlet through the Baltic. The result was a long series of wars, that were very often fought on Finnish soil.

In the course of the next two centuries, Sweden gradually conquered most of Finland. A charter gave the Finns citizenship rights; Swedish became the official language of the land, and most of the population was "encouraged" to adopt the Catholic faith.

Toward the end of the 14th century, when the Union of Kalmar sanctioned the supremacy of Denmark over the whole Scandinavian peninsula, King Eric Tott also claimed for himself the crown of Finland, and built a powerful border fortress in Turku. (The Russians reciprocated, by erecting their own new Castle of Olavinlinna in the East.)

In 1555 Russia invaded Finland, but its armies were defeated by the Finns, who exploited their victory to obtain a measure of autonomy from Sweden. King Gustavus Vasa of Sweden granted that request, and gave his own son Johan the title of Duke of Finland. Johan, however, had other designs, and turning against his father's armies, after a series of skirmishes, won for himself the throne of Sweden.

In 1637 Sweden appointed a new Governor of Finland, Per Brahe. Brahe introduced a whole series of new regulations, making the use of the Finnish language and reawakening dormant velleities of Finnish independence compulsory.

Then came the terrible drought of 1696, when hundreds of thousands of Finns were left by their Swedish masters to die of hunger in their wasteland. This was enough to raise the bellicose spirits of the Finns, who, under the leadership of Daniel Juslenius, ousted their Swedish oppressors from their land.

In 1711 Peter the Great, Czar of all Russias, conquered Viipuri. The local Finnish barons fled to Stockholm. Then, after ten years of strife, Russia and Sweden signed a treaty (1721), which left to Russia only a narrow belt of Finnish soil along the south-western borders of Finland, while the bulk of the country remained in Swedish hands.

The next Russo-Swedish war began in 1741, and it too was fought mainly on Finnish soil. It was a no-win situation, with the Finns as the main losers, and toward the end of the 18th century the two great empires were forced to adopt a sort of armed truce, which recognized two spheres of influence in Finland, the Russian sphere in Karelia and in the vast north-eastern regions, and the Swedish sphere in the richer, if smaller South-West and along the coasts of the Gulf of Bothnia. During the Napoleonic Wars, in order to avoid the danger of an additional front, the Russian Czar offered the Finns a form of autonomous rule (as Grand Duchy of Finland), within the imperial frame of "All Russias".

In 1812 Viipuri was officially annexed to the Grand Duchy of Finland, and the Grand Duke himself transferred his Court from Turku to his new capital, Helsinki. Finland gradually became more intimately connected with Russia, and a Finnish contingent fought side by side with the Russian armies in a series of 19th centuries wars, in Poland, in Turkey and in the Crimean Peninsula.

At the same time, Finnish freedom fighters continued their struggle for the recognition of the Finnish language. The great saga of the *Kalevala* (by Elias Lönnrot), published in 1835, became the national credo, almost a call to arms for all Finnish patriots.

In 1899 the Russian Czar Nicholas II took administrative steps for the russification of Finland. Russian was declared the only official language of the country, and the ruble became the only valid currency.

In 1905 the Finns launched a week long general strike, which forced the Czar (who by that time had considerable troubles of

FINLAND

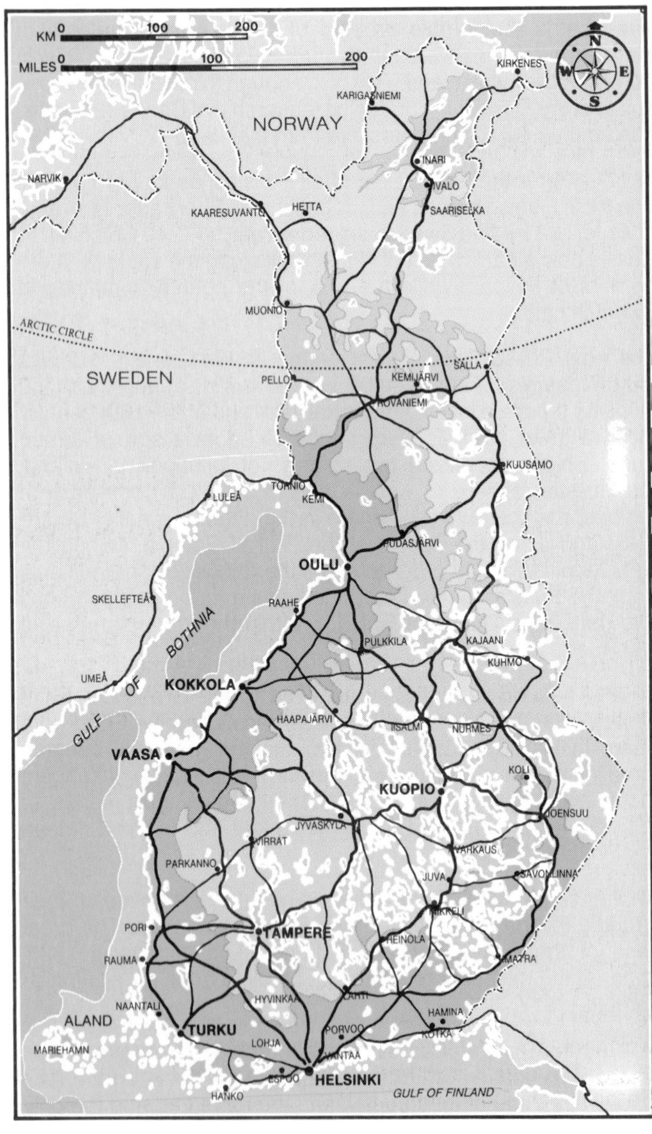

KM 0 100 200
MILES 0 100 200
N
S
W
E
KIRKENES
KARIGASNIEMI
NORWAY
INARI
IVALO
SAARISELKA
NARVIK
KAARESUVANTO
HETTA
MUONIO
ARCTIC CIRCLE
SALLA
SWEDEN
PELLO
KEMIJÄRVI
ROVANIEMI
KUUSAMO
LULEÅ
TORNIO
KEMI
PUDASJÄRVI
OULU
SKELLEFTEÅ
RAAHE
BOTHNIA
PULKKILA
KAJAANI
KUHMO
UMEÅ
OF
KOKKOLA
HAAPAJÄRVI
IISALMI
NURMES
GULF
VAASA
KOLI
KUOPIO
JOENSUU
JYVÄSKYLÄ
VIRRAT
VARKAUS
PARKANNO
JUVA
SAVONLINNA
MIKKELI
PORI
TAMPERE
HEINOLA
RAUMA
IMATRA
NAANTALI
HYVINKAA
LAHTI
ALAND
HAMINA
TURKU
PORVOO
KOTKA
MARIEHAMN
LOHJA
VANTAA
ESPOO
HELSINKI
HANKO
GULF OF FINLAND

his own at home), to revoke most of his recent unpopular edicts. When Russia was clamorously and ignominiously defeated by Japan, Finland took the opportunity (1906) to set up its own democratically elected (by the whole adult population, men and women alike!) Parliament.

Belated attempts of the Czar to turn back the clock of history were not destined to follow their complete course: Europe was quickly ripening for its first World War.

In 1917 the defeated Russian armies were forced to sign an armistice with the Central European Empires of Germany and Austro-Hungary. Only weeks later the first Socialist Revolution, led by Kerensky's Menshevik Party, broke the ground for the final debacle of the Czarist Regime, overthrown by Lenin's Bolshevik Party October Revolution. The new Russian Sovietic Republic, and its Red Army, brought the Czarist White Army to its knees, and the Soviet Union came into being on all the territories that had belonged to the great Russian Empire.

In December 1917 Finland was declared an independent state. The new state was immediately plunged into a bitter civil war between the (Soviet supported) "Reds" and **Mannerheim**'s "Whites". General Mannerheim, in a brilliant blitz, conquered Helsinki and captured more than 80,000 "Red" prisoners. That war was fought by both sides with such cruelty, that in several cases hundreds of innocent victims, many of them women and children, were brutally and casually slain by armed bands on either side; 8,000 of Mannerheim's "Red" prisoners were put to death, and 9,000 more died of hunger and persecutions during their imprisonment.

By the end of 1919 Mannerheim's "Whites" had won the civil war. Finland became a democratic republic, with Kaarlo Juho Ståhlberg as its first President. In 1921, the Society of Nations assigned the archipelago of the Åland Islands to Finland, at the expense of Sweden.

In November 1939 the Red Army invaded Karelia, a vital land corridor situated between the Gulf of Finland and Lake Ladoga. After an early series of Finnish victories, Stalin brought in vast reinforcements, and Finland was forced to call for an armistice, which robbed it of almost 10% of its national territory, in a region of great strategic importance, due to its vicinity to the great Russian city of St. Petersburg (then Leningrad).

In 1941 the Finnish Army, with the help of a German Army Corps, reconquered Karelia, and thus embroiled Finland in the Second World War, at the side of the Axis Powers, Germany, Italy and

Japan. Then, in 1944, Finland signed a separate armistice with the Allies, pledging to oust the whole German garrison from its territory. The Germans fled to Lapland, in the extreme north, setting fire on their way to all the towns and villages they crossed and leaving behind a scorched land, both in Finland and in occupied Norway.

Today Finland is an integral part of the European economy, and at the same times it maintains very close and friendly relations with its Russian neighbour.

Geography

The nickname "Land of a Thousand Lakes" is probably the understatement of the century: Finland's lakes number not 1000, but 187,888! They cover an area of more than 12% of the whole national territory.

The total area of Finland is 338,000 km^2. Its maximum north-south length is 1160 km; its east-west maximum width is 540 km. Approximately 2/3 of its area are woodland; agricultural soil amounts to only 8% of the territory. The total number of Finland's islands is 179,584 (more than half of them are fresh-water islands).

Climate

Finland's climate varies according to its latitude. In general, the influence of its waters (its seas and lakes), creates conditions considerably more temperate than one would expect at Finland's latitudes. Summer temperatures vary from Helsinki's 18°C to 15°C in Central Finland and to 13°C in Lapland. The winter averages range respectively from -5°C to -10°C and to -14°C in the far north. From December to April, practically the whole of Finland rests under a deep blanket of snow (in Lapland, snow reigns for seven months, from November to May).

Flora and fauna

Finland's ecology is a function of Finland's climate. In the northern tundras there are practically no full-grown trees. During the summer, the thawing snows create endless swamplands, where several species of mosquitoes reign supreme, attacking, and often even killing, even the largest animal species who dare enter their kingdom. Even the great reindeer herds, the arctic rabbits in their warrens and the endemic carnivores (mostly brown bears, foxes and wolves), are often threatened by great clouds of blood-thirsty mosquitoes. In the northern lakes small communities of otters prosper, and share the local fish resources with bands of fishing birds of prey. Carnivores are frequently found also in Central Finland, while in the more densely populated regions of the South they are practically extinct.

Population

Finland's population amounts approximately to 5 million people. About two thirds of them live in the five major urban centres: Helsinki, Tampere, Turku, Lahti and Oulu. The average population density is of 16.2 persons per square kilometre.

The Finns form three main ethnic groups, also distinguished by their own different languages: 93.6% are Finnish speaking Finns; 6.1% are Swedish speaking Swedes, and little more than 2000 are Sami speaking Samis.

About 90% of the population belongs to the Luteran Church; the largest religious minority is that of the Russian Orthodox.

The Sauna: In Finland, saunas are a fundamental socio-cultural element of daily life. Even the smallest hamlet, even an isolated farm, will have at least one working sauna, frequented by the whole local population of men and women, babies, children, adults and seniors, at least six days a week, in summer as in winter. According to Finns, the sauna has multiple functions, all conducive to good health and welfare of body and spirit of each and every person and also of larger community groups and social units. There is no better means than the local sauna, either to recover your strength after a long, tiring and stressful day of intense touring, or to get acquainted with the local people, not to mention grasping the nature of the national spirit of the Finns. But you should never try to emulate the Finns on their home ground: you'll see them climbing up to the very hottest steps, close to the ceiling of the small scorching hot chamber of the sauna, only to jump straight into the icy waters of an open air basin or a lake — and back again. Be prudent: keep to the lower steps, limit yourself to few minutes at a time, and don't feel obliged to plunge with the natives into those forbiddingly ice-cold waters just outside; the fresh air will be sufficient to cool off for a few minutes; and don't repeat this sequence for more than two or three times, even at the cost of cutting short your interesting conversations with your hosts. After the first two or three visits, you'll have found your own most suitable range of roasting; and you'll be well advised to keep within that range, even if soon you'll feel the urge to emulate your betters.

Economy

Finland is in the throes of a frenzied process of industrialization. For centuries most of its people had been living off its great forests; while timber remains the major single component of the national economy, today wood is increasingly processed and exploited locally, in a wide range of auxilliary industries, with an increasingly successful furniture industry among them.

About 40% of all manpower is employed in industrial branches; 8% in agriculture; more than 10% are unemployed — and the rest forms a wide, efficient and sophisticated network of human services.

The major industrial branches, beside wood related industries, are mining (copper, tin, zinc, silver and gold) and metallurgy.

A considerable portion of Finland's exports finds its way eastward to Russia.

Architecture

The first impression one gets at arrival, either at Helsinki or anywhere else, is of harmony, neatness, order and wide free spaces, even in the main streets of the larger urban centres. The buildings, the street dimensions, and the people themselves, seem to have been built in a considerably larger than elsewhere. This sense of awe and majesty, is enhanced by the fact that even at the peak of rush hours, it never gets really crowded, not even with tourists.

For many centuries the most common building material was, not surprisingly, timber. Wooden buildings and cold winters are a sure formula for a very short building life, even for the grandest palaces. Indeed, for many centuries every few years great sudden fires destroyed whole neighbourhoods and sometimes even whole cities. Only here and there, where the strategic requirements indicated it, great castles and defensive churches were built in local granite stone, and have therefore survived, more or less untouched, to this day. Sometimes, by chance, a rare wooden 17th or 18th century church or palatial residence also survived; this is, for instance, the lucky case of the great Soomenlinna Villa (1748), built on an island at the gates of the Helsinki harbour.

In 1816, after one of the bitterest fires in history, the great German architect Karl Ludwig Engel was appointed by the Russian Governor as Helsinki's city planner. He designed and built a great part of the present monumental centre of the capital.

Later Art Nouveau also left its imprint in Helsinki, and toward the end of the 19th century several four great Finnish architects added new trends to Helsinki's new image: Gesellius, Lindgren, Saarinen and Sonek.

Alvar Aalto, with his own unique style, whose elegance stems from functionality and simplicity, dominates the 20th century architectural scene throughout the major urban centres in Finland. His work is easily recognized thanks to his unusual choice of building materials and his original creative solutions, which harmonize uncannily with the topography of the background scenery.

After the 60's new trends tend to turn to older, traditional approaches; this is apparent at least in some of the newer high-rises and churches of the capital.

The language

As we have already pointed out, Finnish is not an Indo-European language; it comes from the smaller Ugaritic trunk. As is often the case with "minor" languages, a large majority of Finns has at least some command of English. Nevertheless, if only to be understood when asking for directions, one must have at least an inkling of the fundamentals of Finnish phonetics. The first peculiarity is that most words, even the longest, are accented on their first syllable.

The consonants f, q, w, x and z, as well as the vowel å have been only recently introduced into Finnish, and they appear exclusively in recently "imported" words.

j — is pronounced like ee in "bee".
np — is pronounced "m".
ö — is pronounced like oo in "moon"
ä — is pronounced like e in "red".

Finland has two official languages: Finnish and Swedish; all its road signs are bilingual.

Government

Today the Republic of Finland, after 70 years of growing pains, is a solid, staunchly democratic and reliably efficient administration.

The *Eduskuntatalo* (Parliament) has 200 members, with a four year term of tenure. The President of the Republic is elected fo a 6 year term; his functions are mainly ceremonial.

General information

When to come

The best touring season is spring, at the time of the thawin of the snows, when Finland's plains and lakeside meadows ar covered in blankets of wild flowers. It goes without saying tha coming between May and August, one should take care to boo accommodation in advance.

Holidays
New Year Day
Epiphany
Easter
May Day
Ascension Day
Ash Wednesday
Summer Festival (24-5 June)
All Saints Day
Independence Day (6 December)
Christmas

How long to stay; How much does it cost

A week-long visit will be adequate to get a fairly good idea of the country as a whole; if Lapland is to be included, 4-5 day should be added.

On the whole, Finland is not less expensive than the rest of Scandinavia. However, in the summer one will often find some very interesting package deals, with considerable travel and hotel discounts. A modest couple will be able to cope with as little as US$ 80-180 per day; a lone backpacker will manage on US$ 40-60 .

How to get there

By air: Finland has its own *Finnair* Airline, which works very closely with *SAS*. Finland's airfields are connected by frequent daily flights to all the major centres in Scandinavia. There may be seasonal discounts, and special rates for students and for senior citizens; inquire at a reliable Travel Agency.

FINLAND

By sea: Two regular lines, the *Silja* and the *Viking*, connect Helsinki with Stockholm daily. There are several ferry lines across the Gulf of Bothnia, from Finland to Sweden. In some of the longer crossings, the ferries are often equipped with restaurants, cabins and even Duty-Free shops.

EuRail Pass and *Nordturist* cards are valid also for Sweden-Finland ferry crossings.

By land: The Eastern coastal Swedish railway line to the northern end of the Gulf of Bothnia crosses over into Finland, and together with its parallel highway, the E4, it connects with the national Finnish communications network. Another highway crosses into the north of Finland from Karasjok (in Norway). The railway and those two highways provide good daily overland connections (by bus as well as by train) between Sweden, Norway and Finland.

Private cars may cross into Finland along the same routes, or by ferry, from one of the Swedish ports.

There are two daily Helsinki-St. Petersburg (formerly Leningrad) trains (10 hours), one of them continues to Moscow (6 additional hours).

Domestic transportation

The Finnish road network is the busiest and most modern in Scandinavia. The railway network is also very vast. In spite of Finland's everpresent lakes, ferry crossings may generally be avoided. There is, nevertheless, a 4,000 km long network of privately owned inland cruise lines.

Inland flights: *Finnair* has an adequate network of daily inland flights; frequent fliers should inquire about attractively discounted multiple flight tickets. The "Holiday Ticket", for instance, costs 600FIM (Finn Markkas) and is valid for 15 days of flying on all *Finnair* national routes. Discounted tickets are available to youth, seniors, handicapped, family groups — and, off-season, also to just anybody. Inquire at any Travel Agency.

Trains and buses: The *VR* (National Railways) is the most attractive form of transportation for the longer, North-South routes. Most bus lines are privately owned, and they serve as back up transportation for the railway. Tariffs are more or less the same for trains and buses (c. 40FIM per 100 km); however, tourists equipped with *EuRail Pass* or other similar cards will find the railways decidedly more convenient.

Inland navigation: There are no regular public transportation waterway lines; private cruise lines are comfortable and entertaining, but at their prices they also suitable only for the most affluent tourist, for whom money doesn't count.

Taxi: In the south of the country, taxis are common and their tariffs are reasonable; in the north, however, they are rare and very expensive. The Helsinki tariff is 10FIM, plus 15FIM per km. Night and week-end tariffs are higher.

Car hire: In Finland you'll find all the international car-hire agencies; international driving permits are valid and mandatory; drivers must be above the age of 20 and have at least a year of prior driving experience. The regular category A tariff is 110-160FIM per day.

In Finland it's not difficult to find camping equipment, trailers, minibuses, yachts or even airplanes for hire. Advance bookings are mandatory; inquiries about special discounts are recommended.

Bicycle hire: Bicycle hire facilities may be found at many Tourist Information Centres, hostels, camp sites and also at certain hotels. The tariff is 20FIM per day (or 80FIM per week).

Hitchhiking: Finns are often sympathetic to hitchhikers. However, the most elementary caution requires that hitchhiking should be avoided from autumn to the early spring, and the rest of the year, during the late afternoon or evening hours: even in high summer, nights may often be very cold, and are not to be spent in the open!

Accommodation

In view of the increasing importance of the tourist industry, Finland has promoted the development of the hotel industry that offers from the highest luxury class to the simplest hostels and camp sites. Most hotels are very modern and well equipped (with saunas too, it goes without saying!).

Not all hotels remain open throughout the year; there are quite a few summer-only establishments. In college towns, during the summer students' lodgings double up for the summer as conveniently priced tourists' accommodation.

Hotel tariffs generally also include a large buffet breakfast.

At many tourist-range hotels you'll find the use of the *Finncheque* very advantageous. This is a ticket card valid for single-night accommodation. Each ticket costs 140FIM, which may often offer a 30% discount on regular hotel tariffs. At the end of your stay should you have some superfluous left-over

Finncheques, their cost will be refunded to you in full at the original purchase agency (or its branch).

The main *Finncheque* office is at Helsinki: *Matka-Vesame Tours*, Fredrikinkatu 48a, 00100 Helsinki, tel. 90.694.8877.

The Farms: Travelling through rural Finland, look for the frequent *farm lodgings* sign, which offers very pleasant accommodation (with breakfast or half-pension) for as little as 80-250FIM per person. In all there are some 150 such farms, and they are classified in 5 different groups.

Cottages: Another attractive alternative, particularly common along Finland's southern seaside resorts, is provided by some 5000 "cottages" for hire. Their standards range from the simplest fishermen's bungalows to great luxury villas. They are fully furnished with fully equipped kitchens — but bring your own beddings. Prices start from 120FIM per night.

Camp sites: Finland has over 360 camp sites. 230 belong to a public national net (they are marked by a white "C" on a blue tent background). They are strictly supervised by the Camping Administration of the Ministry of Tourism, and their location is generally strategically situated at the gates of all main tourist centres. Several camp sites also offer tourist "cottages". Camping tariffs vary from 60 to 150FIM.

Camp sites are always equipped with tent and camper spaces, 220V electric current and toilets. Around wintersports resorts, most camp sites also offer fixed campers and bungalows.

Only rarely (never in the north) will a camp sites store be equipped with refill bottles for your kitchen-gas containers.

Camp sites are divided into three classes, and prices vary accordingly between 25 and 55FIM per person.

The International Campings Card is very useful, and may be purchased at the cash counter of all "C" camp sites.

For further information, call *FTA Camping Department*, Mikonkatu 25, Helsinki 00100, tel. 90.170.868, Fax. 122.619.

Hostels: There are about 160 hostels, often located in *farms* or in old city residences. They have 2, 4 and 5 bedrooms, and 10 or more dormitories. Only 50 of them are open throughout the year. They are divided into 4 categories. According to their location, they may have hiring services for bikes, skis or boats. Their tariffs vary from 25 to 70FIM per night. The International Students Card may sometimes entitle its bearer to small discounts.

In addition to the vast choice of traditional tourist accommodation, in Finland there are several Tourist Villages, International Study Centres and Permanent Seminars. Particularly interesting is the Viittakivi Village and Study Centre, not far from Hämeenlinna, which offers very interesting programmes of study throughout the year: short seminars on a wide range of subjects during the summer, and a 5 month "winter programme" of experiential studies. For detailed information write to *Viittakiven Opisto* 14700 Hauho, tel. 917.44911.

The Finnish cuisine

The Finnish cuisine has a lot in common with both the Swedish and the Russian traditions. In the western regions it will be predominantly Swedish; in the south-east, it is mostly Russian. The Sami kitchen, in the far north, is almost exclusively based on reindeer meat and milk. Most local dishes are not too sophisticated: meat, fish and milk products, invariably accompanied by potato side-dishes and a wide selection of interesting breads.

Meat is sometimes cooked but preferably roasted in a wood or coal oven. Fish is generally cheaper than meat. The most popular deserts are strawberries or other types of wild berries.

Many *ravintola* (restaurants) offer a *smörgåsbord* lunch, the classic Scandinavian fixed price cold meat, fish and cheese buffet. Cheaper eateries are called *kahvila* or *baari*.

Finland represents a welcome exception to Scandinavia's general approach to alcoholic beverages: here prices of beer, wine and most hard drinks, as a rule, do not exceed the regular European standards.

Tips: All hotel and restaurant bills include a service fee, but nobody will reject an occasional tip. Hotel porters will smile gratefully at a 5FIM coin.

Currency

The national currency is the *Markka* (FIM for short), subdivided in 100 *penniä*. There are 10, 50, 100, 500 and 1000FIM banknotes, and 5, 10, 20 and 50p, 1 and 5FIM coins.

Credit Cards are welcome almost anywhere. Change counters are found at all bank branches, railway stations, airports and Tourist Information Centres. The approximate value of the Markka is 5.9FIM = 1US$.

Shopping and office hours

Banking hours are Mon.-Fri. 9.30am-4pm. Shopping hours are Mon.-Fri. 9am-6pm and Saturday 9am-2pm. Department stores keep longer hours, and mostly keep open as late as 7.30pm.

Shopping

Finnish products are of the highest quality; prices are, of course, in the same high class. You'll be probably attracted to winter collections, traditional artifacts in wood and glass as well as to furs, jewels and ceramics.

Vodka, whisky and wines are often interestingly priced, either for local consumption or for the duration of your Scandinavian visit. Don't forget to keep your receipts, which might entitle you to tax and or tax refunds at your port of exit.

Telecommunication

All public phones are equipped to deal with international calls. The international prefix is 990; then as usual, will come the country and area codes, and finally the requested phone number. National interurban calls require the prefix "9", the area code, and the number. For further details, call the 09 operator (who most probably will speak reasonably good English).

The European postal charge is 2.50FIM. The *Poste Restante* address is Main Post Office, Mannerheiminte 11, Helsinki 00100 — or, in other towns, the local Main Post Office. Post Office hours are Mon.-Fri. 9am-5pm.

Medical services

In Finnish pharmacies are called *apteekki*. All hospitals have an emergency room. The charge for a doctor's call is 40-50FIM.

For further details, call tel. 90.735.001.
For dentist care, call tel. 90.736.166.
For emergencies, call tel. 000 or 008.
At your hotel desk you will find the addresses and phone numbers of additional services.

Entertainment

The (rather provincial) night life of Finland gravitates around downtown pubs, cafés and discos. There are frequent music programmes, theatre and folklore in the major towns; for a list of weekly programmes, ask at the local Tourist Information Centre

— or search through the pages of English dailies or local weekly foreign language publications.

Films are never dubbed; however, they are subtitled in both official languages of the country.

Suggested itineraries for Finland

Most tourists will begin their tour at Helsinki; others will reach Finland at Turku, and a small minority will start with Rovaniemi, the capital of Lapland. The tour of the southern regions will require 3-4 days; 2-3 additional days will give you a superficial first contact with the north. This is, more or less, the routine of those who view Finland as a minor chapter of their Scandinavian holiday.

We shall follow the mainstream, beginning with Helsinki and proceeding to the south-west, then the south-east, then Central Finland and finally Lapland and the extreme north.

Through the following pages we shall use the Finnish rather than the Swedish nomenclature, except for sites where the second is the most popular option.

FINLAND

Helsinki

Helsinki (Helsingsfors in Swedish) is a city of little more than half a million people. It is the political, cultural and economic capital of the country. It's a vast seaport, an important road and railway junction, and a natural link between Northern Europe and Russia. It's also the major (air and sea) gateway to Finland.

History

Helsinki became the capital of Finland in 1812, when the Russian Czar wished to bring the administration of its Grand Duchy under his rule, farther from the avid reach of Sweden (it had formerly been in Turku — Åbo in Swedish).

Helsinki was born in 1550, when Gustavus Vasa, King of Sweden, began to develop a small local fishermen's village into a strategic naval base, vital to his struggle with Russia. For two centuries Helsinki remained little more than that: a border fortress and naval base. But when, in 1808, a sudden fire incinerated the whole town, the Czar (and Grand Duke of Finland) invited the great German architect Karl Ludwig Engel, charging him with the construction of a model capital, whose granite palaces would survive the threat of any future fires. Engel's great project was completed in 1840, and its somewhat cumbersome neo-classic lines are easily recognizable in the wide avenues and impressive palaces of downtown Helsinki.

How to get there

By air: *Finnair*, *SAS* and several other international airlines have regular Helsinki flights. The **Seutula** international airport is 19 km from the centre, and a bus line connects it very conveniently with the railway station.

By sea: There are two daily ferries from Stockholm (15 hours); there are also daily crossings from Northern Germany. The landing pier is situated near the Market Square; the *Viking* ferries land at the pier's northern end, the *Silja* ferries at the southern end.

By rail: Dozens of trains leave Helsinki toward the norther hinterland, and along the western and the eastern coasts Southern Finland. The railway station is in the very centre town.

By bus: The interurban bus station is situated just outside th railway station; there are regular morning buses to Porvoo, Turku, to Lahti, to Mikkeli, to Tampere and to several other minc centres. Four major roads branch out from Helsinki: the R1 (westward and eastward), and the R12, R75 and E3, who branc off toward the north.

Tourist services

The main Tourist Information Centre is on Pohjosesplanadi 1 (Mon.-Fri. 8.30am-6pm; May-September also Saturday 8.30am 1pm — tel. 90.169.3757).

Ask for a map of the city, the *Helsinki Today* guidebook, an the *Helsinki this week* publication; there may be some othe useful sheets and pamphlets. The *Helsinki Card*, for free bu and trolley rides and museum entrances (there are no less tha 40 museums in Helsinki), costs 60FIM (valid 24 hours), 80FI (2 days) and 90FIM (3 days). At the Tourist Information Centr in *Helsinki this week* and at most Travel Agencies you'll find list of outings and tours in town and in the region.

For general information on the country, ask at the National Offic Unionkatu 26 (same hours as the Tourist Information Centre).

Public transportation

The urban network includes several bus and trolley lines a well as some local trains. Tickets cost 6FIM and are valid fo one hour. A ten ticket book costs 50FIM; a daily ticket, valid fo any numer of rides within 24 hours, costs 40FIM. Train ticke are sold at the station desks and vending machines; bus ticke are sold by the conductor or at the Tourist Information Centre.

Accommodation

The *Hotel Booking Centre* (Mon.-Fri. 9am-9pm, Saturday 9am 7pm and Sunday 10am-6pm — in winter only Mon.-Fri. 9am 6pm; tel. 90.171.133) has a complete list of all Helsinki touris hotels, and lots of detailed information on discounts availab and package deals.

FINLAND

Some of the best hotels offer frequent bargains, with as much as 75% discounts on their regular tariffs. Details are available at the Booking Centre, at the Tourist Information Centre and at the hotel lobbies.

Luxury Hotels
Hesperia: Mannerheimintie 50, tel. 43.101.
Inter-Continental: Mannerheimintie 46, tel. 40.551.
Marski: Mannerheimintie 10, tel. 641.717.

Tourist Hotels
Anna: Annankatu 1, tel. 648.011.
Helka: P. Rautatienkatu 23, tel. 440.581.
Martta: Uudenmaankatu 24, tel. 646.211.

Economy Class Hotels
Academica: Hietaniemenkatu 14, tel. 440.171.
Satakuntalu: Lapinrinne 1, tel. 694.0311.
Clairet: Teatterikatu 3, tel. 669.707.
Regina: Puistokatu 9, tel. 659.937.

Hostels
Kallion: Sturenkatu 11, tel. 753.2004. Trolley 3T, 3B, 8; summers only, pleasant and friendly.
Nuorisotomiston: tel. 709.9590, 2km from downtown, on the Espoo road.

Camp Sites
Rastila: Vuosaari, tel. 316.551.
Espoo Camping Oittaa: 02740 Espoo, tel. 862.585.

Food

Speaking of restaurants, Helsinki is not unlike the rest of Scandinavia: good quality and very high prices. Wines and beer may be cheaper, but the total will nevertheless be quite monumental.

The alternative may be found, as usual, in fixed price menus or Smörgåsbords for lunch, or at the pizza counters and vegetarian eateries. But at least for once, be daring and tackle one of the best Finnic or Russian restaurants. Do it on week-ends, when you'll find outstanding meals at bargain prices at some of the best places; in such cases, however, reservations are absolutely vital.

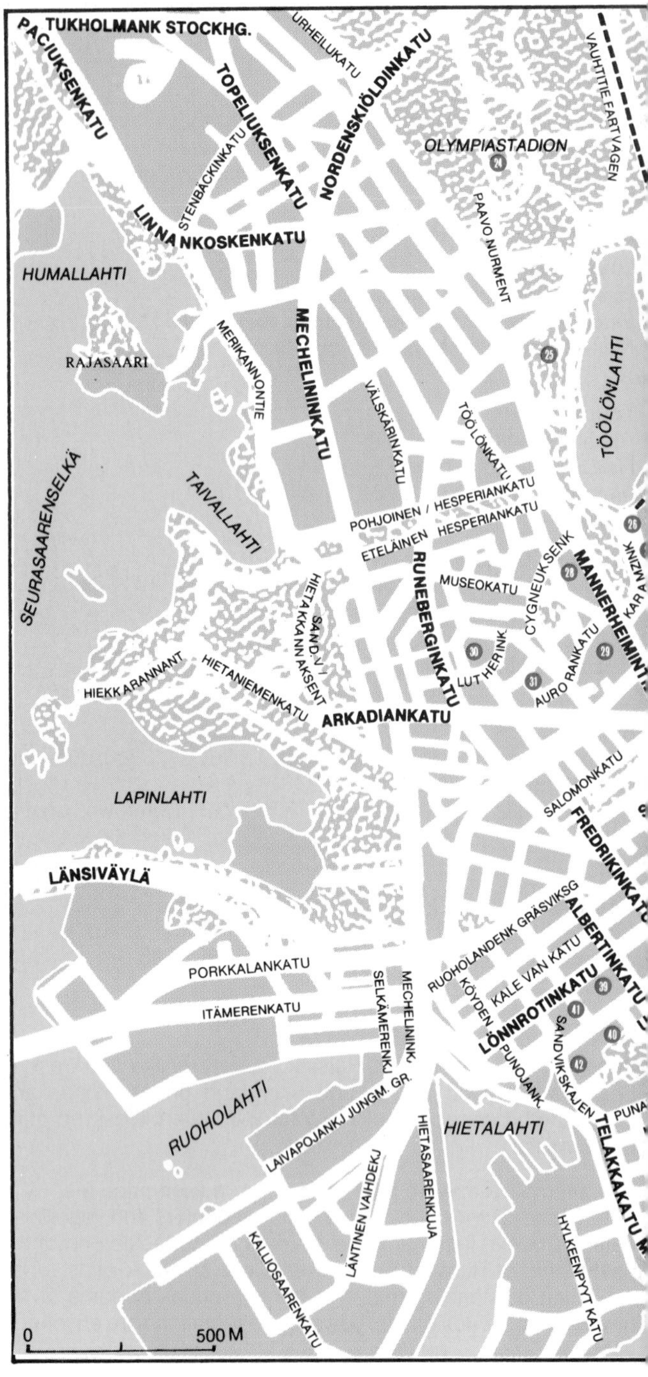
TUKHOLMANK STOCKHG.
PACIUKSENKATU
URHEILUKATU
TOPELIUKSENKATU
NORDENSKIÖLDINKATU
VAUHTITIE FART VÄGEN
OLYMPIASTADION
STENBACKINKATU
LINNANKOSKENKATU
PAAVO NURMENT
HUMALLAHTI
MECHELININKATU
MERIKANNONTIE
RAJASAARI
TÖÖLÖNLAHTI
VÄLSKÄRINKATU
TÖÖLÖNKATU
SEURASAARENSELKÄ
TAIVALLAHTI
POHJOINEN / HESPERIANKATU
ETELÄINEN HESPERIANKATU
RUNEBERGINKATU
CYGNEUKSENK
MANNERHEIMINT
MUSEOKATU
KARAMZINK
HIETAKKANNAKSENT
SAND. V.
LUTHERINK
AURORANKATU
HIEKKARANNANT
HIETANIEMENKATU
ARKADIANKATU
SALOMONKATU
LAPINLAHTI
FREDRIKINKATU
LÄNSIVÄYLÄ
RUOHOLANDENK GRÄSVIKSG
ALBERTINKATU
KALEVANKATU
PORKKALANKATU
MECHELININK
SELKÄMERENKJ
KÖYDENP
LÖNNROTINKATU
ITÄMERENKATU
SANDVIKSKAJEN
PUNOJANK
RUOHOLAHTI
JUNGM. GR.
LAIVAPOJANKJ
HIETALAHTI
PUNA
TELAKKAKATU
LÄNTINEN VAIHDEKJ
HIETASAARENKUJA
HYLKEENPYYT KATU
KALLIOSAARENKATU
0
500 M

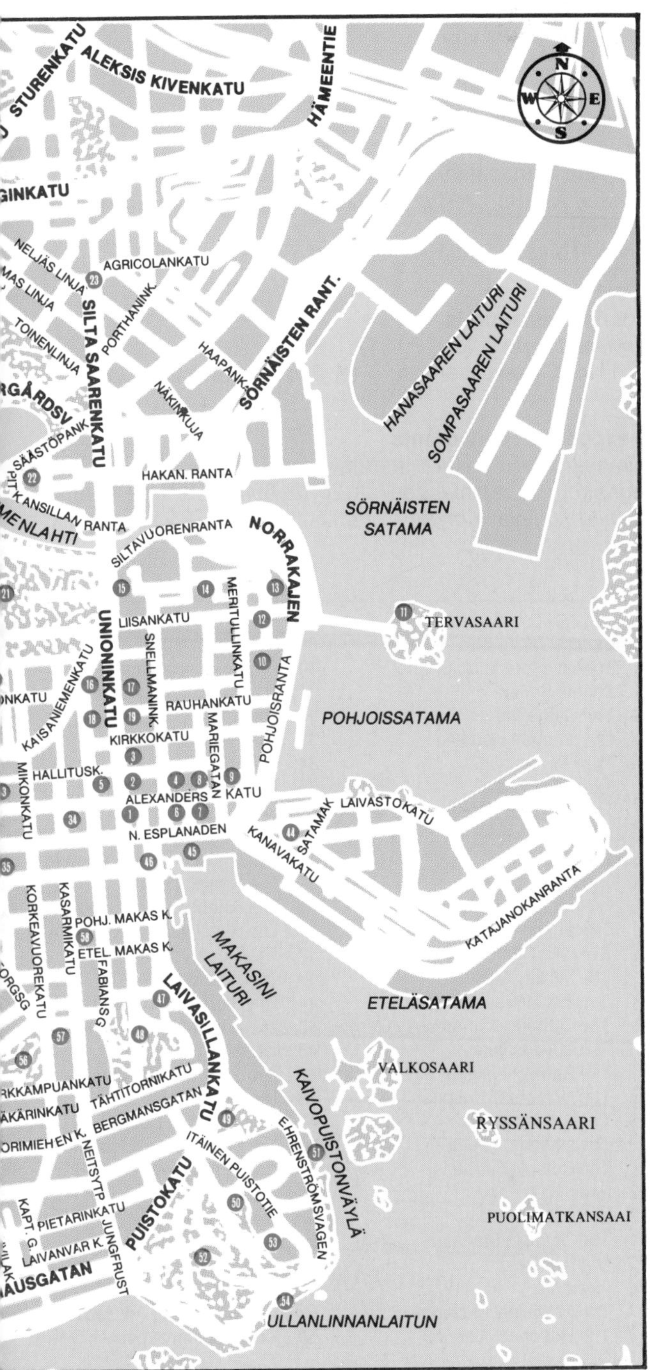

STURENKATU
ALEKSIS KIVENKATU
HÄMEENTIE
N
W
E
S
AGRICOLANKATU
SILTA SAARENKATU
PORTHANINK.
SÖRNÄISTEN RANT.
HAAPANK.
NÄKINKUJA
HANASAAREN LAITURI
SOMPASAAREN LAITURI
HAKAN. RANTA
SÖRNÄISTEN SATAMA
SILTAVUORENRANTA
NORRAKAJEN
MERITULLINKATU
LIISANKATU
UNIONINKATU
SNELLMANINK.
TERVASAARI
KAISANIEMENKATU
RAUHANKATU
POHJOISRANTA
POHJOISSATAMA
KIRKKOKATU
MARIEGATAN
MIKONKATU
HALLITUSK.
ALEXANDERS KATU
LAIVASTOKATU
SATAMAK.
N. ESPLANADEN
KANAVAKATU
KATAJANOKANRANTA
KORKEAVUOREKATU
KASARMIKATU
POHJ. MAKAS K.
ETEL. MAKAS K.
FABIANSG.
MAKASINI LAITURI
LAIVASILLANKATU
ETELÄSATAMA
VALKOSAARI
TÄHTITORNIKATU
BERGMANSGATAN
KAIVOPUISTONVÄYLÄ
RYSSÄNSAARI
ITÄINEN PUISTOTIE
EHRENSTRÖMSVÄGEN
NEITSYTP.
PUISTOKATU
PIETARINKATU
JUNGFRUST
PUOLIMATKANSAAI
ULLANLINNANLAITUN

FINLAND

Luxury Restaurants
Alexander Nevski: P. Esplanadi 17, tel. 639.610. Russian cuisine.
Bellevue: Rahapajankatu 3, tel. 179.560. Russian cuisine.
Piekka, Finnish Cuisine: Sibeliuksenkatu 2, tel. 493.591. Finnish cuisine.
Engel: Tehtaankatu 3, tel. 628.865. Finnish cuisine.

Tourist Restaurants
Esplanadikappeli: tel. 179.242.
Troikka: Caloniuksenkatu 3, tel. 225.229. Russian cuisine.

Inexpensive Restaurants
Timbuktu: tel. 175.041. International cuisine.
Aurinkotuuli: Lapinlahdenkatu 25, tel. 6942.563. Vegetarien food.
Kasvisravintola: Korkeavuorenkatu 3, tel. 179.212. Vegetarien food.

Index

1. Tourist Information Centre
2. Senate Square
3. The Cathedral
4. Government House
5. The University
6. Kiseleff House
7. The Municipal Museum
8. Noble House
9. The Customs
10. The Renaissance residential neighbourhood
11. Tervasaari Island
12. Svenska Clubben
13. The Military Museum
14. Burgher House
15. The Orthodox Community Centre
16. Forestry Institute
17. The Bank of Finland
18. The University Hospital
19. Trinity Church
20. The National Theatre
21. The Botanic Gardens
22. Paasivuori Park
23. Kallio Church
24. The Olympic Stadium
25. Opera House
26. Finlandia
27. The Municipal Museum
28. The National Museum
29. Parliament House
30. Tempelliankio Church
31. The Zoological Museum
32. The Railway Station
33. The Ateneum
34. Esplanadi Park
35. The Swedish Theatre
36. Stockmann's
37. The Customs and Forestry Office
38. The Otava Publishing House
39. The Finnish Opera
40. The Sinebrychoff Museum
41. The Hietalahti Market
42. The Sinebrychoff Distillery
43. Vanha Church
44. The Uspensky Cathedral
45. The Presidential Palace
46. Market Square
47. The German Church
48. The Planetarium
49. The Industrial Courts
50. The Mannerheim Museum
51. The Ancient Villa
52. Kaivopuisto Park
53. Embassy Row
54. Café Row
55. The Eira Quarter
56. St. John
57. The Museum of Applied Arts
58. The Museum of Finnish Design

You'll find several American-style fast-food eateries all along Mannerheim St., at the Forum, across the street from the *Stockmann's* department store and in the Kairopuisto Park neighbourhood.

What to see

The streets and palaces of Helsinki are an impressive sight; its museums are among the most interesting in Scandinavia. An updated, current timetable of all Helsinki museums is available at the Tourist Information Centre.

Downtown Helsinki is a single, harmonious and integrated architectural complex, built, as we have mentioned, less than two centuries ago by Karl Ludwig Engel, after the great 1808 fire. In our itineraries we shall point out the most important palaces; however, the Tourist Information Centre has various useful pamphlets and publications on the subject.

The Senate Square and the Kruununhaka

The Tourist Information Centre is at the corner of Unioninkatu and N. Esplanaden; and just opposite the Centre you'll find yourself on Senate Square, one of Engel's best architectoral projects.

If before the great fire this square was surrounded by a circle of wooden buildings, today it's framed by a series of majestic neo-classic palaces, and by the magnificent front of the **Toumiokkirko**, Engel's great cathedral, which was completed by Lorman after his death. The other palaces are the City Hall, several Ministries, a minor church and the National Academy.

The great cathedral is dedicated to St. Nicholas, patron of the Trade and the Seas, and at the same time to the infamous Russian Czar, to whose initiative Helsinki owes the whole great architectural complex.

Stop at the cathedral's steps, and look at the square. On your left you'll see the **Palace of the State Council** (another of Engel's works), which today serves as the seat of Finland's Government. The Prime Minister's office occupies the first floor, whose enormous main hall in Empire style is not open to visitors. On the right you'll see yet another Engel palace, that of the **University**, seat of the National Academy, which was transferred to Helsinki from Turku together with all major state institutions in 1812.

The Cathedral, the Government Palace and the Academy make this square one of the most impressive examples of early 19th century architecture in Europe. In the middle of the square you'll see a great statuary complex; the central figure represents the Russian Czar Alexander II, and is the work of Walter Ronberg (1894); the minor statues around the Czar are allegories of Faith, Law, Science, Peace and Labour. Across the square you'll see a series of minor buildings of the same epoch, which have been recently restored to form an elegant shopping centre, with luxury shops, cafés and a cinema. The two most impressive structures are the **Kiseleff Palace** (today subdivided into several fashionable little shops), and the **Sederholm Palace** (1757), which predates the rest of the square and even the great fire. The Sederholm houses the **City Museum**.

Beyond the gardens stands the **Ritarihuone (Noble House)** (1862), a structure in Neo-Gothic style, with its art galleries and a concert hall. On its left there is another pre-fire building, the Customs Palace (1765).

Now walk toward the pier, to Meritullintori square. The golden domes of the Orthodox Uspenski Basilica are clearly visible on the small **Katajanokka** Island, not far from the pier. Under the Basilica are the Army Barracks; the piers are used in the summer by the Finnish Navy icebreakers.

Follow the Pohjoisranta Pier to the left. Today this pier is one of the main arteries that lead out of town, toward the east. The Renaissance style **Presidential Palace** stands out just across the marina and the **Hylkysaari Island**, seat of the **Suomi Merimuseo** (Museum of the Seas, open 10am-3pm).

A wide bridge connects the little **Tervasari** island to the pier. Tervasari was, centuries ago, nothing more than a tar warehouse; today it is a pleasant open-air play-ground.

Further on, at the end of the Liisanpuistikko Park, is the **Svenska Klubben**, a palatial residence in English style, which houses a large luxury restaurant. East of Maurinkatu is the **Military Science Institute** and the **Army Museum**, which documents three centuries of Finnish military history. Cross the street into Kulmakatu, and walk along it to Kristiankatu. Here, at No. 12,

Helsinki — An arial view

are the oldest wooden buildings in the city. One of these, the **Burgomaster House**, hosts a section of the City Museum. The **Little School** next door has been brought over from Germany (1905). At the school the Kristiankatu becomes a pedestrian mall.

Carry on now along Oikokatu to Snellmanninkatu. On your right you'll see the **Orthodox Community House**, seat of the Orthodox Bishopric. Walk to the south, and after a right and a left turn you'll find yourself on Unionkatu. At the south-west corner stands the **Metsåtalo (Forest House)** (1939). On the opposite corner you'll see the **Bank of Finland**. Its palace was originally built as a hospital. The **University Hospital** (Engel, 1830) stands at the Rauhankatu corner, and, across the street, another Engel work, the **Trinity Church**. The interesting fountain between the hospital and the church is known as the **Raven's Nest** fountain, by Ayla Hiltonnen. The Bank of Finland is guarded by the statue of a popular hero of the Finnish students' movement at the beginning of our century. And now you are back again, on Senate Square.

The Lake Route

This itinerary begins at the railway station, follows Eläintarha St. and ends at the Töölö lakeside.

The **National Theatre** is a granite castle replica, built in 1902 in Romantic style. The statue that guards its entrance represents the writer Aleksis Kivi. The lobby walls are covered with frescoes; the marble inscription is in memory of a famous actress.

The **Kaisaniëmi Park** is always full of students, who also like to sit and browse at the lively café. Further on, following the lakeside lane to the right, you'll reach the Siltasaarenkatu bridge; at the end of the street, pause here to admire the **Kallio** church, whose carillon plays a tune by Sibelius. On your right you'll see the **Hakaniemi** square, with its open-air market (vegetable and fruit, fish and flowers). The covered market houses a few cafés and handicraft shops.

Turn left on Siltasaarenkatu and enter Paasivuori Park, with the **Fighters** statue. The granite palace you see north of the statue, with its pointed turrets, is the **Workers' Bank**.

The lakeside lane goes on to the **Torch Memorial**, dedicated to a national heroine. The **Timo Penttilä Municipal Theatre** (1967) is on Eläintarhantie.

Cross the bridge over the railway to Linnulaululuntie, a garden

Senate Square: the Cathedral

avenue that leads to Helsinginkatu; on your left you'll see **Lake Töölö**.

The **Olympic Stadium**, originally built to host the 1940 Olympic Games, which were postponed because of the war, may be seen north-west of the lake. The stadium was used, much later, for

lelsinki: the Railway Station

he 1952 Olympic Games. From the stadium tower (72 m high, open to visitors 9am-6pm) you'll have one of the best panoramic views of the city. Next door to the stadium is the **Sports Museum**, vith a statue of the famous Finnish runner, Paavo Nurmi.

Vest of Lake Töölö, at Hesperia Park, turn left to the beautiful **New Opera House**, with its halls and summer restaurant. Then, across the lake, perched on a modest hill, east of Mannerheim St., you'll see the statue of a popular Finnish singer.

The **Finlandia** complex towers above the lake; it's a cultural centre, equipped with theatre and convention halls, built in 1975 as the first stage of an ambitious project destined to revolutionize Helsinki's whole centre. After the construction of the Finlandia, however, the rest of the project was discarded.

At the **Villa Hakasalmi** (1846), not far from the Finlandia you'll find the **Helsingin Kaupunginmuseum (City Museum)** (open Mon.-Fri. 12am-4pm, Thursday until 8pm). The museum's main attraction is a model of 1870 Helsinki, which stresses the growth of the capital in the course of the last century.

Across Mannerheim St. you'll find the **Suomen Kansallismuseo (National Museum)**, with its art, archeology and ethnography wings. Next door to it you'll see the **Ostrobotnia**, the most popular haunt of Helsinki's younger generation.

Follow Mannerheim St. to the **Eduskuntatalo (Parliament House)** (1931), a monumental neo-classic palace with functional overtones, that has become a symbol of Finland. It's one of the last palaces built in Helsinki before the introduction of modern building technologies. Guided tours start at the Tourist Information Centre. The two statues that guard the palace gates represent two Finnish Presidents. Behind Parliament House you'll see the buildings of the **Sibelius Academy** and the **Zoologic Museum**.

Follow Arkadiankatu to Runeberginkatu, where you'll see one of the most beautiful churches in Scandinavia, the **Temppeliaukio Kirkko** (1969, open Mon.-Sat., 10am-9pm; Sunday 12.30am-2pm and 6-9pm). The structure was drilled within an enormous granite rock and covered with a great copper dome. The unique acoustic qualities of its interior are often exploited for frequent musical programmes.

Turn back to the Mannerheim-Arkadiankatu corner, easily recognizable by the equestrian statue of Mannerheim himself and by a second monument, the **Statue of East and West** (1980, in memory of President Paasikivi). On Postikatu you'll find, as its name suggests, the Central Post Office and the *Accommodation Booking Centre*. On Mannerheim St.'s right side stands the **Crystal Palace**, a complex with several cinema halls. Behind the Crystal Palace is the **Bus Station**.

On Kaivokatu you'll see one of the best known architectural complexes in Helsinki: the **Railway Station**. Around its enormous square you'll recognize all the major architectural trends of downtown Helsinki, from Romanticism to Neo-Classicism to functionalism. The Clock Tower is more than 45 m high; the clock itself has a 3 m wide face. The vast spaces of the square (designed by Lundgren), are enclosed by the station itself, and three other great palaces. On the eastern side is the **Ateneum** Arts Museum (by Höijer, 1887), dedicated to Finnish figurative art at the turn of the century. The other two places serve as offices and hotel buildings. The Kajsaniemenkatu, one of Helsinki's main shopping streets, begins on the Ateneum side.

From Esplanadi to Bulevardi

Start once more from the Tourist Information Centre and the **Esplanada** gardens. Stroll along the garden paths, the open-air cafés and the park's sunny benches. Next door to the Tourist Information Centre there are several specialized tourist services, which provide information (and sell maps and booklets) on Central and Northern Finland. The wide central garden plaza often hosts summer folklore programmes.

In the garden plaza you'll also see the statue of Finland's national poet, Ludvig Runeberg, by the poet's son Walter. The late-September Sculpture Festival is traditionally set at the foot of the statue. The great architect Höijer lived in this elegant and exclusive neighbourhood toward the end of the last century. The Phjoisesplanadi 31 residence is one of his works. West of the garden you'll see various statues dedicated to great Finnish writers. Beyond the gardens is the **Svenska Teatern** (Swedish Theatre). It was built in 1817 in wood, encased in stone in 1870, destroyed by fire in 1878 and rebuilt in 1886. Faithful to its name, the theatre is a Swedish language theatre. The statue that prides its front is of Victor Johnson.

Turn back to Mannerheim St. Walk for about 200 m and you'll come to **Stockmann's**, a towering department store built in 1830 and later repeatedly restored and expanded.

Turn south at the Mannerheim-Erottajankatu corner. Next door to a monumental office building stand the Customs and Forests House, one of the most impressive Höijer Palaces. Turn right onto Uudenmaankatu on the left within the small triangular garden you'll see the **Teilervo** statue, dedicated to the ancient Hunting Goddess. On the same side, a few steps further on, you'll come to the **Otava Publishing House**, one of the oldest Romantic style buildings in town. Across the street, on your right, is the Werner Söderström Publishing House. Annankatu, which begins at the next corner, is an interesting shopping street.

Turn right onto Fredrikinkatu to Bulevardi, a wide linden-sided avenue, lined with elegant palatial residences. Turn left, toward the gulf; the reddish stone building on your right is the **Finnic Opera House**, built in 1870 to serve as a recreation centre for the local Russian garrison. On its left stands the **Sinebrychoff Arts Museum**, with works by Dutch, Flemish and Swedish artists (open Mon.-Fri. 9am-5pm, week-ends 11am-5pm).

The Bulevardi ends at the **Hietalahti Market Square** (food and flowers), with its neighbouring roofed market. In the early morning hours, during the summer, the square hosts a colourful flea-market. The large building on the left side of the avenue belongs to the **Sinebrychoff Distillery** (1819, one of the oldest in Finland). The Sinebrychoffs, who gave their name to both museum and distillery, were an old family of great Russian merchants.

Turn back along Bulevardi to Mannerheim and to the old **Vanho Kirkko**, Helsinki's first Lutheran church, built by Engel in 1826. Its wooden structure, which was originally intended to be replaced by stone, has been left untouched to this day. Today it serves as a high society religious ceremonial centre, and as a concert

An attractive market stall

hall. The neighbouring park is a military cemetery for Finn and German victims of the Civil War. Follow Lönnrotinkatu and Mannerheim to Esplanadi Park.

From the Market to Kaivopuisto Park and to Eira: This walk begins at the Market Square, near the Marina (open 7am-2pm and 3.30-8pm). The market stands offer food and handicrafts; at the Marina you'll find the landings of the Suomenlinna and Korkeasaari Island ferries. The **Uspensky Cathedral**, with its golden onion-shaped domes, is not far from here, toward the east. The Uspensky is the largest Orthodox church in Scandinavia, and is dedicated to the Holy Virgin. Its interiors are no less elaborate than its front. Its ancient icons are an opulent marvel. Turn back, crossing the bridge to Esplanadi, and proceed to the **Presidential Palace** (built 1818 and restored by Engel in 1843 as an imperial residence for the Czar). After the birth of the Republic, in 1919, the palace became the official President's Residence. Not far from it are the Supreme Court Palace and the Swedish Embassy. Left of the Presidential Palace you'll see the **Czarina's Obelisk**, adorned with the double-headed eagle of the Romanoffs. In this case, however, the builder of the Obelisk (who if not Engel?) dedicated the eagle heads to the Czar Nicholas and his regal wife, the Czarina Alexandra. During the October revolution the eagle was summarily beheaded by the mob, to be restored only 55 years later, in 1972.

The **City Hall** (1833) is yet another Engel project, but only in 1913 it was purchased by the City founders, to serve as Helsinki's City Hall. Walk southward along Sodra Kajen and Etelränta, with the landing of the *Silja* Stockholm ferries. The eye-catching 1864 red brick structure belongs to the **German Church**. Behind the church, and slightly higher up, is the Engel **Planetarium**, which belongs to the Astronomy School of the Helsinki University.

Walk down Ullankatu. On your right you'll see the **Russian Embassy**, with the **Church of St. Henry** (1860) behind it, probably built in honour of the Catholic wife of the Russian Governor. Across the street from the embassy stands the **Industrial Courts** (Saarinen, 1916). The park that opens southwards is the **Kaivopuisto**, one of the most beautiful gardens in Helsinki, designed in the High Russian style of the mid-19th century.

Turn left toward the **Cygnaens Gallery**, with its rich collection of Finnish works of art. Further south, on Iso Puistoite St., you'll come across the Independence Tree and the **Bear-Fish Fountain**. Turn left onto Kalliolinnantie, near the **Mannerheim Museum**, set in the General's residence where he lived from 1924 to his death in 1951. It's a personal museum of the life and achievements of this controversial hero of Finnish independence.

Follow Ostra Allen St., a sort of "Embassy Row", with the embassies of the United States, France and Great Britain. It ends at the seaside lane, which runs along the gulf, lined with open-air cafés. Continue, along the luxury yacht Marina and the playgrounds, until you come to **Eira**, an exclusive residential neighbourhood of great luxury. Most of its villas are in the Art Nouveau style from the beginning of the century. Just stroll along its lanes, and enjoy their solemn elegance.

The most sumptuous villas are on Ehrensvardintie. Most probably any passer-by will be eager to tell you about the life and wonders of the most prominent owners. The Havsgatan is another very elegant avenue. Having reached Engelsplatsen, follow Fabriksgatan and cross over to Kaptensgatan. Here you'll see the **Church of St. John** (1893), whose spacious interiors (the largest in Helsinki) are often used for gala symphonic concerts. Next door to the church, on its right, stand the **Taideteollisuus Museo (Museum of Functional Art)** and the **Architecture Museum**. The first is dedicated to modern industrial design, the second to the great Finnish architects of the turn of the century (open 10am-4pm — both). Just in front of these museums you'll see a statue of a well-known Finnish writer in the garden. Turn right onto P. Roobertimkatu, and then left onto Kasarmikatu. On the right side of the square you'll see the **Museum of Industrial**

Design, with departments of furniture, home appliances, textiles and earthenware. The tour ends at the Esplanadi Park.

Around Helsinki

The Suomenlinna Castle: Toward the middle of the 18th century Sweden decided to strengthen the defences of the port of Helsinki. Using the natural barrier provided by the five islets that form Helsinki's natural harbour, they set up a powerful bulwark, whose walls crossed from island to island, and equipped with a series of outposts, turrets and artillery placements. Today Suomenlinna is one of Helsinki's major tourist attractions. During the summer there are daily guided visits from downtown to the castle (noon, 15FIM). Inside the complex you'll find several military collections and other exhibits.

Vantaa: Vantaa is a vast suburb, situated close to the omonimous airport. Its main attraction is the open-air museum, which reproduces 18th century Helsinki, grouped around an old (1494) granite church; at the village gate there is a small history museum.

Järvenpää: This is a small provincial town, situated 40 km from the capital, home (1904 to 1957) of Jan Sibelius, Finland's major composer and one of the biggest celebrities of his nation. Sibelius won international fame (and Finland's veneration) after the première of his great symphonic poem *Finland* (1899), which became the national anthem of enslaved Finland. Sibelius' home is **Ainola**, today a personal museum and a site of pilgrimage, visited by thousands of adults and schoolchildren from all over the country. The last years of the great composer, during which his Muse remained stubbornly mute, are known as *The Silence of Järvenpää.* Ainola is open to visitors 10am-6pm; closed on Monday.

Entertainment

Helsinki's entertainment world is rather provincial and old-fashioned. Weekly programmes are published in *Helsinki This Week*; they include museums timetables, cinemas, plays, concerts and folklore programmes, lectures and even a few "younger" opportunities.

Folklore: The **Seurasaani** open-air museum (tel. 484.712) offers three weekly folklore programmes. Bus 24 from Erottaja; entrance 20FIM.

Opera and ballet: The Opera House (Bulevardi 23-27, tel.

129.255) has quite interesting classic seasons. Detailed information at the Tourist Information Centre and in the English language weeklies.

Theatre: All programmes are in Finnish, except for those of the Swedish Theatre, which are in Swedish.

Cinema: All films are in their original language, with Finnish and Swedish subtitles. Programmes are found in the dailies and in the tourist bulletins. Ticket price, 25FIM.

Concerts: *Helsinki this week* has a *Venues* page, with the list of all musical programmes in town. There are several concert halls: in the cathedral, at the *Finlandia*, and in quite a few neighbourhood centres and churches.

There are hundreds of cafés, restaurants and bars with evening programmes. They are listed in the *City* monthly, a free publication available at all vendors, bookshops and hotels.

The *Groovy* night-club (Rvoholahdenkatu 4) is a very expensive jazz club.

Rock music lovers will find frequent good rock at the *Tavastia* (Kekkosenkatu 4-6).

All along the Mannerheimintie you'll find a long series of pubs and night-clubs.

Here is a short list of pleasant little pubs:
Richard's: Rikhardinkatu 4; frequented by the press.
St. Urhos: Museokatu 10; mostly students.
Jattutupa: Säästopankinranta; folklore.
Elite: Hesperiankatu 22; theatre buffs and artists.

Discos: *Ky-Exit* (Rautatiekatu), *Alibi* (Hietaniemenkatu 14), *Haralds (Kasarminkatu 40).*

For further details, try the Academica desks (see "accommodation").

Shopping

At the Tourist Information Centre you'll find a list of tax-free shops (11% VAT). Finnish wares are generally of the highest quality. *Stockmann's* department store has great choices of almost anything; and only a few paces away there is the *Aleksi 13* new shopping centre. The most spectacular shop windows are on Aleksanterinkatu and on Pohjoisesplanadi. Among the most sophisticated names are the *Arabia* (china and

A characteristic Eira lane

earthenware), *Nuutajärvi* (glass and crystal), *Marimekko* and *Vuokko* (fashions) and *Aarikka* (art objects and other knick-knacks). Between the Railway Station and Mannerheim there are several commercial galleries. The handicraft market is at the main vegetable and fruit market. The best Helsinki bookshop is the *Akateeminen Kirjakauupa* (Keskuskatu 1).

Important addresses and phone numbers

Medical services: tel. 008 and tel. 735.001.
Pharmacy: Mannerheimintie 96, tel. 415.778.
Emergency: tel. 000 or 4711.
Lost and Found: Mon.-Fri. 8am-3.15pm, tel. 1893.18
Police: Olavinkatu 1, tel. 9700.7700.
Central Post Office: Mannerheimintie 11, tel. 1955.1

Embassies
United States: Itäinen Puistotie 14, tel. 171.931.
Britain: Itäinen Puistotie 17, tel. 661293.

Southern Finland and the Gulf of Bothnia

The coasts of Finland, along the great Gulf of Bothnia, have always been the hub of Finnish cultural and social life; moreover, they are among the most densely populated zones in the whole country.

Centuries of foreign domination have left their imprint on all Finnish towns and villages. Along the south-western coasts, the influence of Sweden is obvious; east of the capital, along the Baltic, it's easy to recognize Russian overtones.

This is why we shall divide the coastal and southern regions in two: the Western and the Eastern region.

South-Western Finland

The E3 highway from Helsinki to Turku (167 km), the E79 from Helsinki to Tampere (176 km) and the E80 from Tampere to Turku form a triangle which practically encloses all the South-West.

We shall depart from this triangle only for a quick visit to Pori and to Rauma.

Espoo

Espoo is a relatively large urban centre (160,000 people), situated only 30 km west of Helsinki. The remains of ancient settlements were found dating from the 3rd millennium B.C. in its neighbourhood. The "New City" began to expand in the 15th century. The most famous of its five quarters is **Tapiola**, a residential "Garden City", very harmoniously framed by its natural background of green hills and woodland. At the local Tourist Information Centre (tel. 90.467.692) you'll find a selection of maps and pamphlets. Espoo owes its University campus buildings and its great cultural centre to the world famous Finnish architect Alvar Aalto.

Onward to Turku

Ekenäs is a modest sea resort, where Swedish is the mother tongue of 80% of the population. It has an interesting old quarter, with elegant 18th century homes and quite a few later buildings, in the characteristic Finnish Imperial style of the beginnings of the 19th century.

The southernmost town in Finland is **Hanko**, which was during the 19th century one of the most elegant summer resorts frequented by the Russian aristocracy. Hanko is Finland's one and only free port and its beaches are still very popular.

The E3 continues to hug the beaches, crossing **Pargas**, at the gates of the Turku Archipelago. In Pargas you'll find an old 14th century granite church; its lateral chapel is a 1690 addition. The local museum is dedicated to four centuries of agricultural life.

Turku

Turku (Åbu in Swedish) is situated at the mouth of the Aura river. It's a very dignified and opulent ancient miniature capital. Near the bus station (Brahankatu 17, tel. 312.557) you'll see a small but very elegant **Synagogue**.

The town began to expand as early as the 13th century, when the Pope made it the seat of a Bishopric. The Cathedral and the castle belong to that period.

Although Turku lost its privileged capital status in 1812, it remains the seat of the Luteran Archbishopric of Finland to this day. Turku was also the home of Finland's most ancient University (1640); however, after the 1808 fire, the campus was transferred to Helsinki. During the Second World War, Turku was bombed by the Allies, although not very severely damaged. Turku has always been one of the traditional centres of Finland's struggle for its independence from Sweden.

How to get there

By air: Turku's international airport is only 7 km out of town, and has very good connections with the centre.

By land: As we have already mentioned, both the E3 from Helsinki and the E80 from Tampere end at Turku. There are also similar parallel connections by railway; the railway station and the bus station are not far from one another, on the riverside.

By sea: The *Viking* and the *Tilja* ferries sail twice daily for

Stockholm from Turku and from the Naantali harbour, 16 km west of Turku.

Tourist services

The Tourist Information Centre (Käsityöläiskatu 3, summers only, 8am-5pm, tel. 921.336.366) offers also bicycle hire services.

Food and accommodation

The assistance of the Tourist Information Centre is particularly useful when looking for accommodation in town: the Centre is always very well informed regarding discounts, bargains and seasonal package deals offered by the best Turku hotels. For instance, a *Ritz* (Humalistonkatu 7, tel. 337.337) single bedroom is regularly priced at 600FIM; in August it often plummets to only 320FIM. Exceptionally attractive summer discounts are also offered by the *Astro* (tel. 511.800) and by the *Aura* (tel. 311.971), both in the vicinity of the Ritz.

The hostel (Linnankatu 79, tel. 16578, bus 1) is open all year long.

The most accessible camp site is at Ruissalo (tel. 306.649), an islet in the Turku Gulf (bus 8). Summers only.

There is a relatively wide choice of entertainment; details of actual programmes are available at the Tourist Information Centre. The heart of Turku night-life is along the riverside. Highbrow Turkuites mostly frequent the *Olavin Crouvi* (Hämeenkatu 28), while the younger generation prefers the *Students' House* (Rehtorinpellontie 3).

The night ferry to Stockholm (starting at 10pm) will save you the cost of an hotel night; your savings will suffice to pay for the excellent cuisine on board the ship.

The E3 turns northward from Turku to **Naantali**, one of the rare towns where most of the old wooden residences have survived the scourge of the frequent past fires. The **St. Birgit Church**, for instance, dates from 1443. Naantali is the landing port of the Öland (Sweden) ferries.

What to see

As usual, our route starts at the Tourist Information Centre. Turn toward the river, crossing the Skolgatan bridge. On your left, just beyond the corner, you'll find the **Wäinö Aaltoen Museo** (open Mon.-Fri. 10am-4pm and 6-8pm, Saturday only 10am-4pm).

TURKU

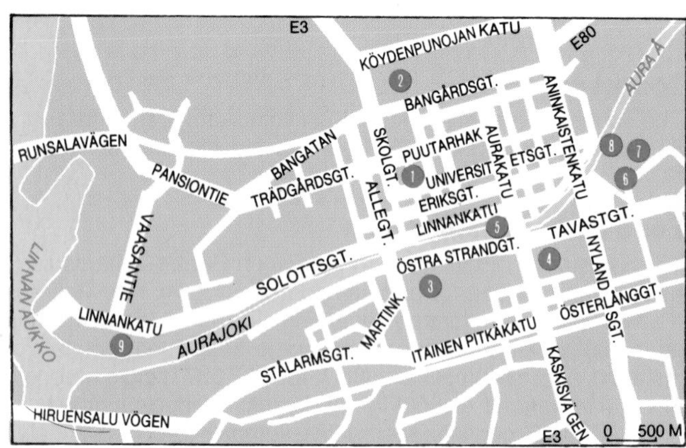

Index
1. Tourist Information Centre
2. The Railway Station
3. The Aaltoen Museum
4. The Open Air Museum
5. The Farmaceutics Museum
6. Tuomiokirkko Church
7. The Swedish Academy
8. The Sibelius Museum
9. The Turku Fort

Aaltoen is the most famous contemporary Finnish sculptor, and in this museum you'll be able to get acquainted with many of his most popular works.

Follow the Ostra Strandgatan along the riverside, and cross the Myllsilta Bridge to the **Museum of the Quensel Residence Pharmacy**, with a permanent exhibition of Finnish medicine. On top of the hill east of the bridge you'll see the Planetarium. Behind the Planetarium is the **Luostarinmäki Museo** (open 10am-6pm), the Old City open-air museum.

Turn back along the riverside, and carry on to the **Tuomiokkirko**, a 13th century cathedral with a spectacular belltower. The Cathedral was built by the Swedes, to serve as their strategic base for the Christian conquest of Finland. In front of the Cathedral stands the statue of Per Brahe, the Swedish Governor of Finland, who introduced the study of Finnish into all the schools of the country. South of the Cathedral is the campus of the **Åbo Akademi**, the last surviving Swedish language university in Finland. Down Henrikinkatu you'll find Turku's new university,

Turku, on both sides of the Aura

Turku's Open Air Museum

and not far from it, the **Sibelius Museum** (Sun.-Tues. 11am-3pm), whose halls echo with the subtle motives of the famous Finlandia symphonic poem. One of the halls of the museum is dedicated to the history of Finnish musical instruments.

The **Åbo Slott (Turku Castle)** is situated at the mouth of the river, about 1 km past the end of the Linnakatu riverside lane. It's a short ride on bus 1, or, if the weather is good, a pleasant and refreshing walk. The castle is open to visitors 10am-6pm. Its original 13th century bulk was repeatedly modified and restored, and you'll be able to recognize a long sequence of styles in its different sections. The modifications were not always due to war damages or to strategic requirements; more often they symbolized a "change of the guard" between the foreign masters of the city. The history of Finland , and in particular of Turku, is reflected in the walls and bastions of this great castle, and also in the permanent exhibitions that you'll see in its corridors and great halls.

Turn back to the city, and enjoy a well earned rest at one of its riverside cafés.

The Åland Islands

The Åland Archipelago is a group of more than 6,500 islands, most of them rocky and uninhabited. The total population of the archipelago amounts to 23,000 people. The islanders speak Swedish, and they are very proud of their autonomy. Half of them live in the main town of **Mariehamn**, a large village whose houses are grouped around two main streets: Esplanadgatan and Storagatan. The Tourist Information Centre (Storagatan 18, tel. 92.816.575) hands out information, hires bicycles and organizes island tours.

Today the Åland Islands are a popular summer resort, but they also have a long and stormy history. There are signs of very ancient, prehistoric settlements; later the Vikings used them as a foraging base; and the Bomarsund and Kastelholm forts date from the times of the great Scandinavian wars. The little local museum has an interesting collection of tools, fragments and art objects dating from all those different periods.

There are some quite good, but certainly not inexpensive hotels. The *Archipelag* (Storagatan 31, tel. 92.814.020) is the best. The *Pomnera* (Norragatan 10, tel. 92.815.555) is more modest. There are quite a few inexpensive B&Bs; the Tourist Information Centre has a fairly complete list.

The only hostel in the archipelago is at Eckerö (tel. 92.838.470); there are several camp sites.

North of Turku

The R196 (and the R194) follow the Finnish coast of the Gulf of Bothnia, pushing northward side by side with the railway to **Uusikaupunki**, a little town founded by King Gustavus Vasa in 1617. Repeatedly destroyed by fire during the 18th and 19th centuries, its name is famous mainly because of the Russo-Swedish treaty signed here in 1721, in which the two great northern powers traced a new map of their respective spheres of influence.

Rauma

Rauma, one of the most ancient town in Finland (1442) is only 45 km north of Turku, on the R196. For some reason, in 1550 the whole population of Rauma was forced to abandon their homes and resettle in the new town of Helsinki. Very soon, however, Rauma was prospering again, snugly growing around its little seaport. Its people are justly proud of their resilience, and also of the fact that, in spite of their geographic closeness to Sweden, their local dialect is clearly a Finnish, not a Swedish tongue.

The Old City, with its **History Museum** (Kauppakatu 13, 10am-4pm), is south of the waterway. The Tourist Information Centre is at Eteläkatu 7, tel. 93.822.4555.

The hostel and camp sites (summers only, tel. 93.822.4666) is 1 km out of town.

Pori

The next stop is **Pori**, 40 km north of Rauma. Pori's main attraction is its July Jazz Festival, frequented mostly by Finnish and other Scandinavian youth. Pori was founded in 1558, on the mouth of the Kokemäenjoki River. After the great fire of 1852, the town was rebuilt on a new site, 20 km from the rivermouth. The old port, however, survived, and its new industrial facilities are frequented by scores of merchant ships; in the neighbourhood of the harbour there are also several interesting museums and other tourist sites. There is a guided tour from the Tourist Information Centre (Antinkatu 5, tel. 93.933.5780) to the **Town Theatre** (Halituskatu 14), which dates from 1884, when the region was within the Russian sphere of influence. The rather minute inner hall (300 seats only) is not what one might expect a the sight of its monumental front. The **Town Hall** is situated nex door, in an 1895 palatial residence in Venetian style, purchase by the city fathers for its present use in 1962.

On the same street, at No. 11, you'll see the **Satakunta Museum** of local history. Two doors away, at No. 7, is Engel's **Court of Law** palace; the riverside lane is flanked by a series c elegant stone residences.

Food and accommodation

Rauma is a small town with a wide choice of lodging and eateries. It's advisable to inquire first at the Touris Information Centre. One of the best hotels is the very centra *Keskus* (Itäpuisto 13, tel. 93.918.447).

The hostel, which is also the site of the jazz festival, (Korventie 52, tel. 93.928.125) is 4 km out of town (buses 30-32 and 40-42).

There are quite a few pubs and night-clubs such as the *King's Road* (Itäpuisto 8), the *Casino* (Itäpuisto 13) and the *Jazz Café* (Eteläranta 6).

A rather long detour toward the east (115 km) will bring you to Tampere, the Lakeland City.

Tampere

Tampere was founded in 1779 by King Gustav III of Sweden who probably intended to use it as a lakeside summer resort pleasantly set on the beaches of its two great lakes, the Näsijärv and the Pyhäjärvi. Today Tampere is an important regiona centre, with a population of about 180,000 people. Toward the end of the last century, the Russian Czar Alexander II grantec Tampere a free-town status, preparing it for its industrial growth The first to exploit the advantageous conditions was the Scottish textile king Finlayson. Then came the days of the wood industries, then the paperworks and finally the new great metalworks. The economic growth brought the town great prosperity, and this was reflected in a richer cultural and social life, and a building boom of new museums, schools, theatre and concert halls, residential neighbourhoods, and a great, modern university campus.

The Tourist Information Centre (Verkatehtannkatu 2, tel. 93.112.6652) is open in summer Mon.-Fri. 8.30am-6pm, Saturday 8.30am-3pm and Sunday 12am-2pm; in winter Mon.-Fri. 8.30am-4pm. Near the railway station there is a second branch (summers only, 1-8pm). At the Centre you'll find free written material and a

'ampere, a centre of study and industry

'ampere Card, valid for local transportations and free entrance) Tampere's 14 museums (40FIM for 1 day, 60FIM for 2 and 0FIM for 3). A single day's brisk walk will take you through all ıe main museums and sites in town.

Vhat to see

owntown Tampere is easily covered on foot. The city planners ıade very good use of the Pyynikki Hill topography, and built splendid park, topped by an outstanding observatory, right in ıe middle of town. A second observatory is located on top of the 'äsineula Tower, with a magnificent view of the whole town, its ıdustries, and its two great lakes. Tampere is in fact a model ew town, a showcase of Finnish urban planning principles: a oung town, nestled within its natural scenery, emerging freely om the blocks of a modern town. Leave the Tourist Information entre toward the left, along the Hämeenkatu main street, and 'alk to the bridge, with its four elegant allegoric statues.

t the end of Hämeenkatu you'll see the **Cathedral**, and on ıe left, on Hämeenpuisto, the **Workers' Theatre** and **Lenin's luseum** (11am-4pm; closed on Monday). After the failure of the 'st Russian revolution, in 1905, Lenin was exiled to Tampere; om here, Lenin continued to write and even to keep a tight rein n the Russian workers' movement. The Lenin Museum is but a inor archive of Lenin's writings during the years of his exile.

At the Samakatu corner, turn right towards the park, th observatory and the Pyynikki open-air theatre. Now turn agai to your right, crossing the flower-beds and the parkland t **Amuri**, Finlayson's old industrial quarter, now seat of a moder hostel, and of two interesting museums: the **Amuri Workers Museum** (Makasiininkatu 12, summers only, 11am-4pm; close on Monday), dedicated to the daily life of the working classe — and the **Arts Museum** (Puutarhekatu 34), which is practicall across the street from the Workers' Museum.

Cross the railway, walking toward the shore of Lake Näsijärv and into **Laiturikatu Park**, which climbs to the **Sara Hilde Arts Museum** (open 11am-6pm). Next to the museum is th **Säräkanniemi** (10am-8pm), a sort of Tivoli cum planetarium panoramic observatory, aquarium and small zoo.

Turn back along Satakunnankatu to the centre, and afte crossing the waterway you'll find yourself beside the 190 **Tuomiokirkko** (Cathedral). Its frescoes caused a long and bitte controversy with the religious establishment, who found th painter's (Hugo Simberg) freedom of expression blasphemous The **Technological Museum** (12am-6pm, closed on Monday and the **Kalevan Kirkko** are the last two sites of this tour.

Food and accommodation

We'll never tire of recommending early consultation with the local Tourist Information Centre. The *Bookin Centre* (Puutarhakatu 1, tel. 93.133.155) will also be of grea help. One of the best hotels in town, the *Tampere* (Hämeenkat 1, tel. 93.121.980) offers clamorous summer discounts; th *Astrum* (Viinikankatu 22, tel. 93.135.317) is a very gooc moderately priced B&B.

Two hostels, the *YMCA* (Tuomiokirkkonkatu 12, tel. 93.135.900 summers only) and the *Vimahallinmaja* (Pirkankatu 10-12, te 93.129.460, all seasons) and the Härmälä camping (bus 1, te 93.165.1250) represent the least expensive lodging alternatives

The most sophisticated (and expensive) restaurants ar the *Hämeensilta* (Hämeenkatu 13, tel. 93.127.207) and th *Loterna* (Puutarhakatu 11, tel. 93.112.4005); both specialize i Russian cuisine; both have excellent bars and evening musica programmes. The *Merivosvo* (Särkanniemi, tel. 93.124.697 and the *Antika* (Väinölänkatu 1, tel. 93.111.1282) are tw considerably more modest fish restaurants. For those on a tigh budget, there are rather good pizzas and the students' mes — or bread, cheese and groceries from the supermarkets.

In summer time Tampere becomes a great jazz centre (details at the Tourist Information Centre); the Pyynikki Theatre has a summer repertory (mostly Finnish!). Along the main streets there are several friendly pubs (Hämeenkatu 10, 16, 18 and 25; Kalevanpuisto 7, 23).

From Tampere to Helsinki

Turning back south to Helsinki from Tampere, after 35 km you'll reach the gates of **Valkeakoski**, a town situated between the Mallasvesi and the Vanajavesi Lakes. In 1869 a waterway was cut through the narrow isthmus between the two, and around that canal the sleepy old village with its attractive waterfall soon grew into a prosperous and lively little town. In 1955 the waterway assumed new dimensions, and Valkeakovsi became a dynamic industrial centre (paperworks and pharmaceutics).

Next, either by motor-boat or along the E3, you'll go on to Hämeenlinna, a town founded by Per Brahe in 1639, on the site of a much older hamlet, to serve as the capital of the Häme district. But the town owes its fame to the fact that it gave birth to one of Finland's most revered sons, Jan Sibelius (whose place of birth is now a private museum). The **Hattula Church** (14th century), is the only survivor of the ancient village. Hämeenlinna is full of parks and gardens; its second attraction (after the Sibelius home) is a not too well preserved Swedish castle, which later served as a bleak women's prison.

On the way to Helsinki, along the E3, 15 km south of Hämeenlinna, is the little summer and wintersports resort town of **Hyvinkää**; its train Museum (Hyvinkäänkatu 9, 11am-4pm) is often crowded with youthful train-buffs of all ages.

Lohja

The summer steam-train from Hyvinkää to Lohja will take you to Finland's largest lake, 56 km from Helsinki. The majestic great Kirkniemi Villa (18th century) used to belong to General Mannerheim; it's well worth a visit; on its grounds is the seat of Finland's first fish-nursery.

South-Eastern Finland

As we have already mentioned, for many years Eastern Finland was under the influence of the Russian empire. Czarist Russia left its imprint on most towns and villages in that region.

Leaving Helsinki toward the east, along the coast you'll find a chain of pleasant little seaside resorts; then at Kotka, not far from the Russian border, the road turns northward, heading for Imatra, Parikkala and finally the ancient town of Savonlinna. After a visit to the lakes and to the regional capital of Kuopio, you'll cross Jyväskylä and Lahti on your way back to Helsinki.

Porvoo

Three main arteries leave Helsinki toward the east: the R6, the R7 and the E3, which turns north to Tampere. Porvoo is at little less than 50 km from the capital, on the banks of the infamous river. As early as 1346 King Magnus Ericson of Sweden granted Purvoo a free-town charter. In 1508 the town was razed to the ground by a marauding band of Danes, and remained barren for more than a century, until King Gustavus Vasa of Sweden decided to rebuild it. Today Porvoo is a remarkable arts and culture centre, seat of the great Werner Söderström Publishing House and home town of hundreds of artists and writers.

The Tourist Information Centre (Brahenkatu 12, tel. 98.238.475) distributes a good topographic map of the town and its suburbs. **Vanha Porvoo** (the Old City) is a very picturesque quarter of wooden residences and narrow, curving stone-paved alleys. The oldest buildings are the 16th century riverside warehouses. The **Tuumiokirkko** (Cathedral) that towers above the old city roofs dates from the 15th century. It's from this church that Alexander I, Czar of all Russias, proclaimed the establishment of the Grand Duchy of Finland, setting himself up as its first Grand Duke.

The **History Museum** (Kaivokatu 40, summers only, 11am-6pm) illustrates and documents the long history of Porvoo and of its region. Along Aleksanterinkatu you'll see many art galleries and miniature museums, dedicated to Porvoo's most celebrated children. For details, ask at the Tourist Information Centre.

At the **Arts Museum** (Välikatu 11, 11am-4pm), you'll find a collection of works by many local artists and a documented panorama of the regional arts.

One of the most pleasant hotels is the *Springhill* (Lohrentie 13b, tel. 91.514.5225). The hostel is at Linnankoskenkatu 1-3, tel. 91.513.0012. The Kokonniemi camp sites are 2 km out of town (tel. 91.517.1967).

Kotka

Kotka is the largest centre situated in the eastern most point of the Finnish Gulf, 115 km east of Helsinki. It's on the delta of the Kymi river and on the Kotka island. In 1795 Catherine II of Russia built the Ruotsinasalmi, a great defensive bastion, at the port entrance. The fort was completly destroyed by the British navy during the Crimean War, in 1855. Only its foundations remain, next to the Orthodox St. Nicolai Church.

The town was restored by Alexander II in 1878. Then his son Alexander III built his own personal summer residence here, perfectly situated for his fishing hobby. Today the imperial villa contains a museum (summers only, 10am-7pm).

Today Kotka, whose limits also include the village of Kymi, is a modern industrial seaport, well equipped for timber exports. Two interesting sites are the **Workers' House** (built by Eliel Saarinen) and the **Sunila Paperworks (by Alvar Aalto).**

Hamina is a strategically situated centre, 15 km east of Kotka, and only 35 km west of the Russian border. It was, on not less than 7 occasions, a bitter battleground between Russian and Swedish armies. Its concentric rings structure stresses its original defensive functions.

Imatra

Two highways leave Kotka toward north and north-east. The first goes to **Kouvola**, capital of the Kymi district, and the second — the R6 — reaches Imatra, capital of Finnish Karelia. Imatra, at a stone's throw from the Russian border, is a modern wintersports resort and a strategic starting point for guided tours to the **Imatrankoski** Rapids. The ultra-modern lines of the Alvar Aalto church harmonize perfectly with the architectural style of the town.US

Savonlinna

North of Imatra you'll find the regional capital of Savonlinna, an old Swedish garrison town built around the great **Olavinlinna** Castle (1475). The town began to grow during the 18th century, and was soon the recognized capital of the Savo district. It's also a fresh-water harbour, from whose piers several fascinating motor-boat cruises of beautiful Lake Saimaa begin.

The Tourist Information Centre is at Puistokatu 1 (tel. 95.713.492). You'll be offered a topographic map of town and district, the map of the lakes and the timetable of the motor-boat cruises. The **Olavinlinna** Castle is situated on an islet, south-east of the harbour; the castle cruise sails from Linnankatu. Olavinlinna is surprisingly well preserved, and in June it hosts a picturesque three week long opera festival. The **Savonlinna Museum** is on the pier and on board of the **Salama** vessel, and is almost exclusively dedicated to the region's lakes and their shipping (summers only, 10am-8pm).

The **Kerimäki Kirkko** is an interesting wooden church built in 1847, which claims to be the largest wooden church on Earth; you'll find it 25 km east of Savonlinna.

North of Savonlinna there are two pleasant and attractive towns: Varkaus and Joensuu.

Varhaus

Varhaus is 70 km north-east of Savonlinna, on the Taipale waterway, the main link between the lakes of the district. At the Tourist Information Centre (Ahlströminkatu 11, tel. 97.226.777) you'll find interesting details of the town and its lakes; there are also several pamphlets on the most interesting sites of the region, and specially the **New Valamo Monastery**, built after the October Revolution to provide shelter and a new home for the monks of the Medieval Valamo Monastery, situated within Russian territory, and from which they had been forced to flee. The New Valamo is on the R23 road to Joensuu, 60 km north-east of Varhaus.

Joensuu

Joensuu is at the extreme north of Finnish Karelia, on the banks of the Pielisjoki river. It was founded in 1848, and soon became the capital and main cultural centre of its district. The Town Hall building is by Eliel Saarinen. The **Museum of Northern Karelia** (Siltakatu 1, 10am-6pm) covers thirty centuries of local history, from the first prehistoric settlements to modern times.

In the summer months you might have the opportunity to embark on one of the three-weekly motor-boat cruises that sail from Joensuu along the western coast of Lake Pielisjärvi to **Koli** — one of Finland's rare mountain resorts (may also be reached by bus). From Koli there are quite a few backpack trails, (outings organised by the Tourist Information Centre, at the *Loma-Kali* camp sites, tel. 97.367.2241). Another bus line connects Koli to Nurmes, at the northernmost end of the Lake District.

The R17 connects Joensuu with **Outokumpu**, 45 km westward, Finland's foremost copper mining centre. Outokumpu is also an industrial centre (metalworks, textiles, polymers). The **Mining Museum** is at the entrance of an abandoned old mine (summers only, 10am-6pm).

Kuopio

Kuopio is the largest town in the Lake Region; it's an administrative, industrial and academic centre of more than 80,000 people. Founded by King Gustav III of Sweden in 1782, Kuopio was one of the main bastions of the western Swedish defensive line, close to the Russian border. It's a lively little town, elegant, modern and wide awake even at night time.

The Tourist Information Centre is at Haapaniemenkatu 17 (tel. 97.118.2584).

What to see

The main square, with its hectic market, is very picturesque. But we'd rather have you start at the **Kuopio Museum** (Kaupppakatu 23, summers only, 10am-4pm, Sunday 11am-7pm). The museum is situated inside a recently restored Medieval residence, and it exhibits the history and customs of the region. The **Arts Museum**, across the street, contains a collection of Finnish art works and frequent transient shows.

The **Open Air Museum** (Kirkkokatu 22, summers only, 10am-5pm) is a collection of original 18th century structures, furnished and decorated with period objects. The adjacent **Snellman House** (1843) is a museum dedicated to the famous national hero, who fought for the rebirth of the Finnish language from his headmaster's office, at one of the local high schools.

The most exciting museum is the **Museum of the Orthodox Church** (Karjalankatu 1, summers only, 10am-4pm; closed on Monday). It contains most of the original treasures and relics brought over from the ancient Valamo Monastery, in Russian Karelia.

The motorboats of the lake cruise lines sail from the Tulliportinkatu pier. Kuopio is a summer and wintersports resort,

Kuopio and its lakes

and has a wide choice of accommodation and entertainment venues.

The *Kuopio Card*, on sale at the Tourist Information Centre, costs 50FIM and is valid for 24 hours. It entitles youto unlimited public transportation, to free entrance at the local museums and to sizable restaurant and hotel discounts.

Food and accommodation

Like almost anywhere else in Finland, in the summer you'll find considerable discounts and attractive package deals at the best local hotels (for information, ask at the Tourist Information Centre). This is the case at the excellent *Kuopio* hotel (Haapaniemenkatu 20, tel. 97.112.4411) and at the *Atlas* next door (No. 22). There are also more modest hotels and B&Bs: the *Savonia* (Sammakkolammentie 2, tel. 97.1225.333), the *Puijo-Hovi* (Vuorikatu 35, tel. 97.111.4943) and the *Souvari* (Vuorikatu 42, tel. 97.1122.144).

The *Tekman* hostel is at Taivaanpankontie 14b (tel. 97.122.2925); the camp sites (tel. 97.1312.244) are 2 km south of town.

Restaurants are, as you may expect, very expensive. For an outlandish experience, try the roundabout restaurant on top of the *Puijon* skyscraper. On Kauppakatu you'll find some not too expensive eateries (with evening musical programmes) at *Henry's Pub* (No. 18), at the *Sampo* (No. 13) and at the *Traviata* (No. 40).

Kuopio has a theatre, a few cinemas, some concert and dancing halls and a number of pubs and night-clubs; the Tourist Information Centre has a full list on demand.

Around Kuopio

The Kuopio district is characteristic of the Central Finland hinterland: little hamlets, isolated farms, large tracts of woodland, lakes and vast prairies. At the Tourist Information Centre you may ask about guided tours (on foot, by motor-boat or by bus).

You might follow first the R5 and then the R14 to **Sillinjärvi**, with its archeological site of a 5th millennium settlement. Then you might carry on north-westward to **Mananinka**, a country hamlet surrounded by lakes and forests. Then you might turn toward the south-west, through woods and lakes, to **Tervo, Vesanto** and **Karttula**. This is where the road joins the E80 to the island village of **Vehmersalmi**, a popular stop for many lake cruises.

Follow the lakeside lane to **Tuusheimi**, where you might sail to the new Valamo Monastery, or pause to visit the local Museum of Musical Instruments. Then, proceeding northward, you'll reach **Kaavi**, the starting point of an adventurous canoe-ride along the rapids.

Yet farther north is **Juankoski**, a picturesque village, famous for the skill of its ironsmiths, and Nilsia, an ancient cultural and religious centre.

Alvar Aalto's Alma Mater is at **Jiväskylä**, a little town founded by Czar Nicolai I in 1834. The great architect's hand is recognizable on several of the university campus buildings, on the theatre and the Town Hall. Jiväskylä is on the R9, 145 km south-east of Kuopio.

The Tourist Information Centre is at Vapaudenkatu 38 (tel. 94.1294.083). Leaving it behind, walk to the **Aalto Museum**, at Seminaarinkatu 7, a well documented and detailed archive of the life and work of the great architect. Not far from it you'll find several other little museums.

The Kanpunginkirkko, opposite the Tourist Information Centre, is a 19th century cathedral.

The summer lake cruises through Lake **Päijänne** to Lahti sail from the Jyväskylä pier. It's a 10 hour crossing, and there are two daily cruises.

Mikkeli

Mikkeli is yet another town founded during the first half of the last century (in 1838) to serve as a new district capital (of the famous district). During the 1940 "Winter War" it served as General Mannerheim's Headquarters. At the local Tourist Information Centre (Hallituskatu 3a, tel. 95.5151.444) you'll be offered free entrance tickets to the **Mikkeli Club**, whose restaurant was frequently used by the General as well. The **Headquarters Museum** (Paamajankatu 1-3) is dedicated to Mannerheim's great military achievements. The **Arts Museum** (Ristimaenkatu 5a) has an important collection of Finnish impressionists, beautiful collections of antique furniture, objets-d'art and sculptures, and also space for transient art shows. The **Suur-Savo Museum** (Otavankatu 11) is an archeological museum; inside an old Gothic style mausoleum you'll find some 12th century tombstones and a few very ancient mummies.

The R5 goes on from Mikkeli to **Heinola**, a miniature town encircled by two great lakes and the Jyrängönvirta River, with an octagonal wooden church built in 1842.

Lahti

About 35 km from Mikkeli on the R5 you'll reach Lahti, a town of close to 100,000 people, 130 km from Helsinki. Lahti is an international wintersports resort, seat of the 1978, 1981 and 1989 world championships. Lahti is also a centre of the Finnish furniture industry; it has outstanding glass industries and an excellent distillery.

The **Ski Jump** which towers over the town from its west side is (weather permitting) an outstanding panoramic observatory. The regular Wednesday morning open markets of Lahti are picturesque and often very convenient.

There are a few interesting museums; ask for the list at the Tourist Information Centre (Torikatu 3b, tel. 91.818.2580). We'll mention the **Sports and Ski Centre**, 10 minutes from downtown. On the way to the centre you'll see the **Town Hall**, one of the characteristic Eliel Saarinen buildings, and the **Wireless Museum**, at the local Broadcasting Station.

We shall also mention the **Arts Museum** (Vesijävebkatu 11, 12am-4pm, closed on Monday), with works by Gallen, Kalleln and Edelfelt, and the **Poster Museum**.

Lahti is the last stop before reentering Helsinki, at the end of this long and rather exhausting itinerary.

Central Finland

The Gulf of Bothnia

Vaasa

Start from **Pori** (South-western Finland , on the coast of the Gulf of Bothnia) on the R8, and after 180 km you'll reach Vaasa. The port of Vaasa was founded in 1606 by King Carl V of Sweden. The city was consumed by fire in 1852, and rebuilt around its ancient harbour, according to plans drawn by the best architects of the time. Vaasa, which during the Civil War was one of the main strongholds of the "Whites", has a population which is 2/3 Finnish and 1/3 Swedish.

Its port is used by bulk merchant ships, which land here loaded mainly with imported cereals, by ferries and by other commercial ships. Trains arriving here from Sweden proceed from Vaasa to all parts of Finland.

The **Ostrobothnia Museum** (Museokatu 3) is dedicated to the history of the city. Old Vaasa is 6 km from today's centre; guided visits leave town regularly on the hour for a 3 hour tour.

From Vaasa to Oulu

Jakobstad, a little seaport 90 km north of Vaasa, was founded in 1625 by Ebba Brahe, the widow of General Jacob de la Gardia. The Skellefteå (Sweden) ferries land here. Jakobstad is known for its Strengberg tobacconists, and is the home town of Johan Ludvig Runeberg (born 1804), Finland's national poet. His little school, the **Westmansmors Stuga** has been turned into into a museum.

The R8 proceeds northward, crossing **Kokkola**, a town founded in 1620 by King Gustav Adolph II of Sweden. The town, which was for a century a busy seaport, has been left dry by the receding waters of the Gulf of Bothnia, and today is only a modest road junction, 5 km away from the sea. At the **Kokkola Park** you'll enjoy the unusual sight of a **British Warship** on dry land; it was forced to surrender after it had been left stranded in shallow water by the tides during the Crimean War. The ancient **Kaarlela** Church (1460) is only 2 km from town.

Further on along the R8 is **Raahe** (1649), a centre built by Queen Christine of Sweden. Around the middle of the last century, Raahe was famous for its great fleet of sail boats; today it is one of the major centres of the Finnish metalworks industries. Its Old City, with its 200 19th century buildings grouped around the old **Pekka** Square, is one of the most well preserved in Scandinavia. At the Tourist Information Centre (Brahenkatu 12), you'll be presented with an attractive map of the Old City.

Oulu

Oulo is 600 km away from Helsinki, and is the recognized capital of Central Finland. It has a population of more than 100,000 people. The port of Oulo, very well sheltered at the mouth of the river, is one of the most active in the region. It is Finland's main tar export centre. During the last century its tar installations were the largest and the most important on Earth, and Oulu was known all over the world as "Tarcity".

Towards the end of the 16th century King John III of Sweden had set up a modest coastal bastion here. In 1605 Carl IX, appreciating the strategic importance of the site, transformed the bastion into a vast fortress, and the new town was born around the fort. In 1822 the whole town burned to ashes, but it was rebuilt quickly and efficiently. Its neat new houses attracted many scientists and writers; the tar harbour changed gradually into a modern high technology complex, which includes today a university and several electronics and computer industries.

The Tourist Information Centre is at Torikatu 10 (tel. 98.1241.011) and is, as usual, very well manned and equipped.

What to see

Just across the square from the neo-Renaissance style Town Hall you'll see the **Tuomiokirkko**, a cathedral that went up in flames in 1882 and was restored according to plans drawn by Engel. Follow Linnankatu to the **Nord Ostrobothnia Museum**, deep inside the **Ainola** Park (open Mon.-Fri. 11am-6pm, Saturday 11am-3pm and Sunday 12am-6pm). The museum documents the production, transportation and trade of tar, throughout the history of the region. The Sami hall is one of the best of its kind.

The four little islands of the delta may be tackled with ease by bike (but also, of course, on foot). The hydro-electric plant on one of the islands was built by Alvar Aalto. On the islands you'll see the ruins of an old 16th century castle and an elegant artists' village, survivor of several great fires, with quite a few

Oulo in early spring

interesting galleries. In June the islands' traditional rock festival attracts thousands of young music lovers.

The island route goes on to the **university** and to its geology, zoology and botanics museums.

At the Tourist Information Centre you'll find details of several guided tours to the Turkansaari Open Air Museum, to the Sports Centre (rowboars, canoes and horseback riding) and to other entertainment sites.

For lodgings, turn again to the Tourist Information Centre; however, the best hotel is the *Vaakuna* (Hallitusakatu 1, tel. 98.1224.666); the *Turisti* (Asemakatu 24-26) is somewhat cheaper, and the hostel (Kajaanintie 36, tel. 98.1227.707) is even cheaper. The most accessible camp sites are on Mustassaari Island (4 km from the town) and on Hietasaari Island (tel. 98.1541.541).

Most restaurants and night-clubs are on Isokatu.

On to Sweden

Both the road and the railway proceed to **Kemi**, one of Finland's main centres of the timber industry, and to **Tornio**, right at the Swedish border. Tornio, which six centuries ago was already a sizable market town, is invaded daily by hordes of thirsty Swedish tourists, busily swilling the cheaper ales and beers of Finland. The Tourist Information Centre (Lukiokatu 10, tel. 98.040.048) has not only lists of the town's many, crowded pubs, but also a town and district map and a selection of routes and outings.

As for accommodation, there are the Heta (Saarenpäänkatu 39. tel. 98.040.897), the *Koivopuisto* (tel. 98.041.316), the hostel (tel. 98.040.146, 2 km out of town), and the camp sites (tel. 98.040.917), on the bank of the Torniojoki River.

The Interior

Kajaani

The capital of Central Finland's Lake Region, Kajaani, was built toward the middle of the 17th century, when the Swedish Governor Pietari Braho began the project of a new fortified town, to be built for the protection of the tar route. The town was destroyed by the Russians in 1716, and left in ruins for almost a century.

Kajaani is the home town of **Elias Lönnrot**, the famous folklore writer who published the monumental **Kalevala** in 1835, an anthology of old legends that was to become later the moving force behind the Finnish independence struggle.

After the construction of the railway line, at the turn of our century, Kajaani quickly grew into a lively railway and road junction.

The Tourist Information Centre is at Kauppakatu 24. Across the street you'll see a neo-Gothic style church; not far from here you'll recognize the characteristic lines of yet another Engel structure — the **Old Town Hall** palace. At the Asemkatu corner you'll find the **Kainuu Region Museum**.

Iisalmi

Iisalmi lies 50 km south-east of Kajaani. During the 1808-9 Finnish War, Sven Tuvva found himself, with a small contingent of Swedish troops, on guard at the strategically sited **Koljonvirta** bridge. In spite of the vast superiority of the Russian invaders, Sven Tuvva did not surrender, and his heroic stand resulted in the failure of the great Russian offensive. Today Iisalmi is an important road and waterway junction.

The **Regional Museum** is on the bank of the Palosvirta River (open 12am-6pm). The **Juhani Aho Museum**, dedicated also to the history of the region, is 5 km from town (open 11am-8pm). For further details, call the Kauppakatu Tourist Information Centre (tel. 97.724.611).

Lapland

In Lapland, man and nature are uniquely and intimately intertwined in a single entity. For centueries the endless tundras, the great dark forests and the thousand lakes of the short summer, and the uninterrupted snow fields of the long winter have controlled all forms of life, man included, by a very simple, explicit set of rules: fit in — or get out. And man, with his extraordinary adaptability, has been able to fit in for tousands of years, as witnessed by many signs of his presence, in the shape of Stone Age graffiti, clan burials and communal life. If we add the Roman, Arab and British coins that have been found in several Lapland sites, we may reach the conclusion that not only did man survive here, but that for some reason he was often attracted and drawn here — whether in a mood of conquest or a mood of exploration — or again, "because it was there".

Be as it may, the true origins of the small groups that for centuries have lived as they do today in the great Lapland wastes are not known. Their identity has absorbed now and again, from all their contacts with their neighbouring cultures, new facets and expressions, until today it holds on to its traditions while it gradually comes to accept beliefs and mores that once would have been spurned and rejected. Perhaps only their ancient pride remains; and remember, they are what they are: they are not "Laps"; they are the **Sami**.

The marvels of modern industrial and communication technologies have come into their lives. The reindeer, which for centuries was their only source of food and income, today is but one of their occupations, and around most of the Sami villages one finds many aspects of "modern civilization": telephones, post offices, museums, banks, hotels, supermarkets — and of course the picturesque handicraft shows and sales counters, either along the roads or at the gates of any settlement.

Our itinerary, one of many possible routes, will keep to the "Midnight Sun Zone", north of the Arctic Circle: from Rova to Kilpisjärvi, to Ivalo and to Inari.

Rovaniemi

Rovaniemi is the capital of Lapland, and for centuries has always

Welcome to Lapland's summer

been the main bartering and trading centre in the region. Just outside its present site clear signs of human occupation as far back as the 6th millennium B.C. were found. But today's Rovaniemi is a very modern town: all its buildings date from the second half of our century. The older buildings were razed to the ground by the Germans in 1944, on the eve of their flight. The reconstruction works involved some of the very best Finnish architects, as may be seen from the singular but proud profile of Alvar Aalto's **Lappia House**.

How to get there

By air: The local airport is only 9 km out of town, and it services several daily national flights, most of them from Helsinki.

By land: Rovaniemi is the main road junction in Lapland; it is crossed by north-south and by east-west arteries, which connect it with the rest of Finland and with Sweden, Norway and Russia. Rovaniemi is also accessible by rail; the trains follow the course of the Kemijoki river to the Gulf of Bothnia, where they join the main coastal line.

The Tourist Information Centre is at Allonkatu 2 (tel. 96.016.270); a second branch is at the railway station.

What to see
Rovaniemi is situated 10 km south of the Arctic Circle and is a good strategic base for excursions to the far north. Its museums will provide the best possible substitute to an actual northern trek, for those who for some reason don't have the time, the means or the itch to travel north in person. The foremost is the **Lapland Museum** (Lappia House, Hallituskatu 11, summers only, Tues.-Sat. 10am-6pm). Also inside Lappia House is the **Library**, with the richest collection of written material in several languages on Lapland and its people, the Sami.

Ten kilometres north of Rovaniemi, right at the (otherwise invisible) Arctic Circle, is the unforgettable attraction of the **Santa Claus Village** (summers only, 9am-10pm).

The **Pöykkölä** ethnographic museum is on the bank of the **Kemijoki** river, 35 km south of town; it's an open-air museum, with several 17th century northern farms and a village of reindeer shepherds, fishermen and farmers, all with homes perfectly furnished with period articles; summers only, 10am-5pm. The **Afforestation Museum** is in the same zone.

Food and accommodation
The two best restaurants are on Valtakatu: *Bel Giovanni* (No.34, tel. 96.016.406) and *Pinja* (No. 19, tel. 96.014.272).

On Koskikatu you'll find two B&Bs: *Aakenus* (No.47, tel. 96.022.051) and *Rovaniemi* (No. 27, tel. 96.022.066).

The Hallituskatu 16 hostel (tel. 96.014.644) is open throughout the year; the camp site (tel. 96.060.606) is 5 km out of town.

A Lapland Route

The region north of Rovaniemi is crisscrossed by tourist trails (see "Backpacking through Finland"). One of the most interesting routes leaves Rovaniemi, crosses Pello, Kolari, Kittilä, Muonio, Hetta, and after a brief breach into Norway turns back to Karigasniemi, Inari, Ivalo, Sodankylä and Kemijärvi.

The route is suitable for private cars (or for well equipped hitchhikers — tent and sleeping-bag are a must!). Buses are not too frequent, and their timetables rarely fit in with tourist requirements. If, in spite of this warning, you are planning such an outing by bus, ask at the Tourist Information Centre for detailed timetables of the bus lines, and plan your route accordingly.

The Finland-Sweden border follows the course of the **Muononjoki** river; the highway follows the same course, along the Finnish bank. Coming by car from **Tornio**, the border post on the Gulf of Bothnia, the R79 climbs up along the river, and after 70 km it reaches **Ylitornio**, with its spectacular **Aavasaksa** observatory of the midnight sun (June and July only!). The road goes on to **Pello**; on the way you might pause at the **Vihveä Pysäkki** parking, where you'll most probably find a Sami handicraft and herbs open-air market.

After Pello, the next stop is **Kolari**; a lateral road leads to the wintersports resort of **Ylläs Fell** and to **Kittilä**. The R79 proceeds along the border to **Muonio**; from this section, several paths lead northward to interesting routes (see "Backpacking through Finland").

Follow the R21 from Muonio to the **Hetta** turnoff (75 km). Now the R21 proceeds to **Kilpisjärvi**, to cross into Norway. Hetta is the main centre of reindeer growers.

Near the village you'll see Lake **Enontekio**; spring here is simply fascinating, when the snow first begins to melt. Most walks cross into Norway; having come so far, it's simply unthinkable not to cross over to **Karasjok** (the Lapland capital) and to **Kätokeino** (see Norway: "The Nordkapp Route").

The Inari Region

Crossing back into Finland near **Karigasniemi** you'll find yourself on the R4, coming from the northernmost tip of the country to **Inari**, a modest administrative centre not far from the **Inarijärvi** "Golden Lake", **Ivalo** and **Saariselkä**. It's a region of woodland, lakes and prairies. The lakes are peppered with little islands, and scores of limpid watercourses stream from the hills into Lake Inarijärvi or into some other lake. East of Lake Inarijärvi is the great **Lemmenjoki** natural park, which is rapidly becoming a popular tourist attraction.

A serious visit to the Lemmenjoki Park requires several days; there are no roofed shelters in the park, and it's absolutely vital to come equipped with tents and warm sleeping bags. The cruise motorboats follow the lake routes that during the last century were frequented by adventurous little groups of hopeful gold-diggers.

The **Urho Kekkonen** Park offers its visitors the luxury of some Alpine shelters, well marked on all topographic maps (available at the **Tankavaara** hostel or camp site.

A Sami summer tent

This is one of the main centres of the Sami; however, the Sami number much less than their reindeer...

At Inari you'll have the opportunity to visit the **Open Air Museum of Lapland**, which will give you a general idea of the daily life of the Finnish Sami.

The R4 leaves Ivalo and reaches first **Ivalo** (a road junction to Murmansk, in Russia) and to **Saariselkä**. The **Ivalo** Tourist Information Centre is at Piiskuntie 5, near the bus station. For lodgings, call ahead before coming (tel. 96.9712.521). Saariselkä is a summer and wintersports resort, with scores of exciting trails through the pastures and villages of the Sami. Ten kilometres south of Saariselkä you'll find the gigantic grotto of **Karhunpesäkivi** on your left, a product of lateral ice-pressures against the rocky hillside during the last Ice Age.

South of Rovaniemi

The ancient road to the south crosses **Vuotso**, a little town frequented during the last century by hundreds of feverish gold-diggers. Today it's a small tourist resort; one of its attractions is a gold-mine trek; period gold-digging equipment is available; gold, regrettably, is not. About 90 km farther south is **Sodankyla**, a little wintersports resort with a 17th century wooden church.

Kemijärvi, an administrative district centre 100 km north-east of Rovaniemi, is the last stop on this route. Kemijärvi owes its relatively peaceful existence in the course of more than five centuries to its strategic position on the Kemijoki River and on the shore of its namesake Lake Kemijärvi. The little town, surrounded as it is by a net of lakes, watercourses, and forest land, has always been an inland navigation junction of considerable importance. Near Kemijärvi is the splendid **Pyhätunturi** Park. Details on trails, routes and guided visits to the park are available at the local Tourist Information Centre (Luusuantie 15, tel. 96.9213.777).

Kemijärvi is connected to Helsinki by rail; in a hurry, and with updated flights information, one might also bus back to Rovaniemi, to reach the capital by air.

Backpacking through Finland

The Land of the Thousand Lakes, with its seemingly endless forests and prairies, its picturesque customs and peculiar languages, with its blue-eyed and blond-haired giants, has always attracted thousands of backpack addicts they flock northward from the more populated regions of the south, from other Scandinavian countries and from the rest of the world. The lay of the land favours mobility: there are only very rare steep climbing roads, and many backpackers take the opportunity to set out leisurely on their bikes. For detailed information on hundreds of routes through Finland — itineraries, maps, shelters, camp sites and hostels, Tourist Information Centre and other services, parks etc., write to *Office for National Parks*, National Board of Forestry, POB 233, Helsinki 00121.

The **best season** for backpacking is June to September. Do not forget to come equipped with a good, efficient insect repellant. The sun rises very early in this season, and it sets late at night; in high summer you'll have a daylight span of almost 18 hours!

Before leaving home, it's advisable to inquire at your closest embassy or consulate of Finland; you'll most probably be offered a selection of pamphlets and other information, and it might be worth your while to consult it before setting out.

Making your plans

You will find a wide selection of routes: from brief half-day outings to week-long expeditions; be guided by your preferences, your skill, your form and your goals.

Maps: Most newstands and bookshops have a vast selection of topographic and road maps on sale. However, before buying, consult the nearest Tourist Information Centre, or the *Kartta Keskus Espa*, Eteläesplanadi 10, Helsinki 00130 (tel. 90.1543.166).

Equipment: Two pairs of reliable walking shoes, and if possible a pair of galoshes. A raincoat, socks, socks and socks, a compass, a stove, a mountain tent, warm clothes and underwear, and a sleeping-bag. In Lapland, a good insect-repellant and a tent net are absolutely vital.

Road signs: Paths and tracks are generally indicated by road signs; in many cases, however, maps and compass will be your only guide.

Fires: No fires are allowed, except on specifically indicated sites.

Accommodation: All shelters and other facilities along the route are duly and clearly indicated. No camping is allowed on unauthorized sites.

An elementary backpacker's glossary

Telttailu — camp site.
Päivätupa — basic, unequipped shelter.
Autiotupa — basic shelter in Lapland.
Varaustupa — serviced shelter in Lapland; keys at Tourist Information Centre (upon payment of dues).
Kämppä — ancient forester's hut; authorization at Tourist Information Centre.
Kansallispuisto — National Park.
Luonnonpuisto — Nature Reserve.
Opastus — Outings Information Service.
Tunturi — Mountain.
Kuru — Valley.
Kero — Peak.

Itineraries

Here we have selected a sample of characteristic Finnish routes; we have included only those provided with camp sites and shelters.

Around Tampere

North of Tampere, a triangular area contained between **Parkano**, **Virrat** and **Kuru** is crisscrossed by several interesting routes. The most popular is known as **Pirkka's Trail**. Maps of the area are available at the *Matkailu Pirkkanman*, Aleksis Kive Katu 14b, 33210 Tampere, or at the Tourist Information Centres. The route may be subdivided into three sections:

The first segment (50 km) starts at **Kuru**'s camp site and ends at **Ruoves**. The path crosses woodland and prairies toward Lake Näsijärvi and the Lakes Region. For an exhilarating overview of the whole area, stop at the **Ruovesi** Observatory, by Lake Helvetinjärvi.

The second section (30 km) starts from **Toriseva**'s camp site (1.5 km south of Virrat). The path follows the coast of Lake

Toriseva, climbs up the hillside, crossing to the Lake Kangasjärv valley, where you may even happen to see one of the very rare surviving brown bears. The section ends at the former Sam school of Keuron, now the **Lapiranta** Tourist Information Centre

The third section (35 km) goes from **Ahtäri** to **Keurun**, crossing the northern section of the Lake Region. It goes from lake to lake and from wood to wood, with a few isolated farms here and there.

The Baron's Trail — (34 km), west of Pirkka's Route. The trail moves from Parkano, at the bottom of Kirveskatu, by the Tourist Information Centre. Woods, lakes, a few miniature settlements and the **Seitseminen** National Park.

South of Tampere — At the Aulanko camp site, north of **Hämeenlinna**, you will find maps and routes of some not too strenuous (4-9km) outings along the east side of the highway and around Lake Aulagonjärvi.

Mikkeli

The south-eastern Lakes District is full of interesting routes. Topographic maps are on sale at Hallituskatu 3. A bus service connects Mikkeli with Ristina and Anttola.

Ristina-Mikkeli (30 km) and **Anttola-Mikkeli** (34 km) are two woodland routes, which pass very close to the remains of ancient Iron Age settlements, an 1820 windmill and a nature reserve.

Hurissalo-Anttola (27 km) — Through forests, lakes and nature reserves.

Puumalu-Hurissalo (40 km) — A nature reserve and Stone Age ruins.

Ristina-Hurissalo (50 km) — Lakes of all sizes, the Astuvansalalmi graffiti, old farms and archaeological sites.

Central Finland

Kajaani-Nurmes-Koli-Joensuu — Northern Karelia routes often follow on the steps of invading Russian and Swedish armies, and come across frequent historic battlegrounds.

Approximately 70 km east of Joensuu, 4 km north of **Iiomantsi**, begins the so-called **Professional Trail** (26 km). The route is marked in orange on the map. Its major attraction is Lake Petkeljärvi, surrounded by woodland and meadows crisscrossed

'he colours of the Sami Fall

)y many little streams. It's an outstanding trail, either for summer valks or, in winter, for cross-country ski.

The Koli Routes

Koli is a popular centre for backpacking tourists, situated by one of the most beautiful lakes in this region, Lake Pielinen. At he *Loma-Koli* hotel, by the lake, you'll find on sale the maps of he region and lots of free detailed information. At 347 m above ea level, Koli is one of the highest spots in Southern Finland. 'he distances are not too long (3 to 28 km).

lurmes (28 km) — Start from the Mujejärvi School, 40 km north f Nurmes. The path is marked in red on the map, and it crosses steep canyon, on whose bottom a stream goes on from lake ɔ lake, until it ends at Lake Mujejärvi.

otkamo (18 km) — Start from the **Juurikkalahti** junction or from **'aokatti**; the path is marked in white, and crosses the Kainuu ills; the view from the top is simply magnificent.

aalu — The path cuts into the Rokou National Park, where a eries of arrows will lead you up the Rokuanvaara peaks.

lossa — You'll reach Hossa by bus from Kuusamo (80 km). At ıe local Tourist Information Centre, you'll find written information nd as well as assistance in finding the best possible route through one of the most spectacular regions in Central Finland: a splendid National Park, some of the most attractive lakes and mountain streams, woodland and good Alpine shelters. Hossa is an ancient Sami village, and most shelters in this district are in old abandoned Sami huts.

Lapland

The Arctic Circle may serve as an imaginary borderline between Central Finland and Lapland. In reality, nothing much indicates this momentous change on the ground. The only novelty, an exclusive right of the Far North in high summer, will be the crepuscolar light of the midnight sun.

The Lapland trails follow the traditional routes of reindeer herds and their shepherds.

Kuusamo — Approximately 25 km north of Kuusamo the **Bear's Trail** (55 km) begins; there are no bears whatsoever today, but wonderful scenery at each step.

Start at the **Rukatunturi** camp site (accessible by bus from Kuusamo). Your first stop will be at **Juuma** (unless you prefer to start your walk here, at the gate of the **Kiutaköngäs** National Park). This is a mountain trail, requiring skill, prior experience and good equipment. Inquire in advance, asking all the possible questions at the Kiutaköngäs Park office. In winter the route becomes quite a difficult cross-country ski trail.

Kemijärvi — A northward bus ride of approximately 50 km from Kemijärvi will take you to **Pyhätunturi**. Find the *Kultaker* hotel (not a difficult task in such a little village!), from which a 45 km pretty strenuous mountain trail starts, challenging but interesting both in summer and in winter (as a cross-country for professional skiers). The trail is marked with orange plastic strips. The route follows the Luostotunturi-Pyhätunturi divide, and ends at the Luosto winter ski lift.

Muonio — An 87 km trail goes from **Pallastunturi** to **Olostunturi** and **Akäslompolo**, three major Lapland tourist resorts. It's possible to take the trail in three 30 km steps starting from either of the three resorts. A bus ride will take you from Rovaniemi to Muonio; another will proceed to Akäslompolo where you'll find a hostel and some private residence lodgings.

Hetta — This is one of the most spectacular routes in Lapland both in summer and in winter. The trail starts at **Enontekiö**, by the lake, 400 m from the church. Cross the lake (with the help of some native passer-by or flagging the boat from the other side with the pier flag). The trail is clearly marked through all its 64 km; the scenery is simply spectacular: wild mountain peaks, deep ravines, swift alpine streams, prairies and lakes.

Inari — This is the famous **Church Outing** (15 km), which begins at the **Inari** Lapland Museum and ends at an old 1760 church, situated at the gates of the Pielppajärvi Sami village. By the church you'll find accommodation of sort, a little restaurant and one of the ubiquitous Sami handicraft markets.

Kilpisjärvi, at the Norwegian border, is the starting point of a lakeside trail to the **Malla** reserve and to the border junction between Sweden, Norway and Finland. An horizon of bleak tundras, arctic vegetation and endless, undisturbed silences.

Dictionary

English	Danish	Swedish	Norwegian	Finnish
yes	*ja*	*ja*	*ja*	*kyllä/joo*
no	*nej*	*nej*	*nei*	*ei*
please	*væ så venlig*	*så god*	*vær så god*	*olkaa hyvä*
thank you	*tak*	*tack*	*takk*	*kiitos*
pardon	*undskyld*	*ursäkta*	*unnskyld*	*anteeksi*
good morning	*godmorgen*	*god morgon*	*god morgen*	*hyvää huomenta*
good afternoon	*goddag*	*god middag*	*god dag*	*hyvää päivää*
good night	*godnat*	*god natt*	*god natt*	*hyvää yötä*
today	*i dag*	*i dag*	*i dag*	*tänään*
tomorrow	*i morgen*	*i morgon*	*i morgen*	*huomenna*
where?	*hvor er?*	*var är?*	*hvor?*	*missä on?*
when?	*hvornår?*	*när?*	*når?*	*koska/million?*
what?	*hvad?*	*vad?*	*hva?*	*mikä/mitä*
how much?	*hvor meget?*	*hur många?*	*hvor mye?*	*kuinka paljon?*
why?	*hvorfor?*	*varför?*	*hvorfor?*	*miksi?*
big	*stor*	*stor*	*stor*	*suuri*
small	*lille*	*liten*	*liten*	*pieni*
cheap	*billig*	*billig*	*billig*	*halpa*
expensive	*dyr*	*dyr*	*dyrt*	*kallis*
hot	*varm*	*varm*	*varm*	*kuuma*
cold	*kold*	*kall*	*kald*	*kylmä*
near	*er det nær*	*nära*	*i nærheten*	*lähellä*
far	*langt borte*	*avlägsen*	*langt borte*	*kaukana*
good	*god*	*bra*	*god*	*hyvä*
bad	*dårlig*	*dålig*	*dårlig*	*paha*
more	*mere*	*mer*	*mer*	*enemmän*
less	*mindre*	*mindre*	*mindre*	*vähemmän*
little	*lidt*	*lite*	*litt*	*hiukan*
much/many	*meget*	*en mängd*	*mye*	*paljon*
left	*venstre*	*vänster*	*venstre*	*vasemmalle*
right	*højre*	*höger*	*høyre*	*oikealle*
open	*åben*	*öppen, öppet*	*åpen*	*auki*
closed	*lukket*	*stängt*	*stengt*	*kiini*
pull	*træk*	*drag*	*trekk*	*vedä*
push	*skub*	*skjut*	*skyv*	*työnnä*
0	*nul*	*noll*	*null*	*nolla*
1	*en*	*ett*	*en*	*yksi*
2	*to*	*två*	*to*	*kaksi*
3	*tre*	*tre*	*tre*	*kolme*
4	*fire*	*fyra*	*fire*	*neljä*
5	*fem*	*fem*	*fem*	*viisi*
6	*seks*	*sex*	*seks*	*kuusi*
7	*syv*	*sju*	*sju*	*seitsemän*
8	*otte*	*åtta*	*åtte*	*kahdeksan*
9	*ni*	*nio*	*ni*	*yhdeksän*
10	*ti*	*tio*	*ti*	*kymmenen*
11	*elleve*	*elva*	*elleve*	*yksitoista*
12	*tolv*	*tolv*	*tolv*	*kaksitoista*

13	*tretten*	*tretton*	*tretten*	*kolmetoista*
14	*fjorten*	*fjorton*	*fjorten*	*neljätoista*
15	*femten*	*femton*	*femten*	*viisitoista*
16	*seksten*	*sexton*	*seksten*	*kuusitoista*
17	*sytten*	*sjutton*	*sytten*	*seitsemäntoista*
18	*atten*	*arton*	*atten*	*kahdeksantoista*
19	*nitten*	*nitton*	*nitten*	*yhdeksäntoista*
20	*tyve*	*tjugo*	*tjue*	*kaksikymmentä*
30	*tredive*	*trettio*	*tretti*	*kolmekymmentä*
40	*fyrre*	*fyrtio*	*førti*	*neljäkymmentä*
50	*halvtreds*	*femtio*	*femti*	*viisikymmentä*
60	*tres*	*sextio*	*seksti*	*kuusikymmentä*
70	*halvfjerds*	*sjuttio*	*sytti*	*seitsmänkymmentä*
80	*firs*	*åttio*	*åtti*	*kahdeksankymmentä*
90	*halvfems*	*nittio*	*nitti*	*yhdeksänkymmentä*
100	*hundrede*	*hundra*	*hundre*	*sata*
200	*to hundrede*	*tvåhundra*	*to hundre*	*kaksisataa*
1000	*tusind*	*tusen*	*tusen*	*tuhat*
Sunday	*søndag*	*söndag*	*søndag*	*sunnuntai*
Monday	*mandag*	*måndag*	*mandag*	*maanantai*
Tuesday	*tirsdag*	*tisdag*	*tirsdag*	*tiistai*
Wednesday	*onsdag*	*onsdag*	*onsdag*	*keskivikko*
Thursday	*torsdag*	*torsdag*	*torsdag*	*torstai*
Friday	*fredag*	*fredag*	*fredag*	*perjantai*
Saturday	*lørdag*	*lördag*	*lørdag*	*lauantai*

INDEX

INDEX

INDEX

INDEX

NOTES

NOTES

NOTES

NOTES

NOTES

NOTES

QUESTIONNAIRE

In our efforts to keep up with the pace and pulse of Scandinavia, we kindly ask your cooperation in sharing with us any information which you may have as well as your comments. We would greatly appreciate your completing and returning the following questionnaire. Feel free to add additional pages.

Our many thanks!

To: Inbal Travel Information (1983) Ltd.
18 Hayetzira Street
Ramat Gan 52521
Israel

Name: ____________________

Address: ____________________

____

Occupation: ____________________

Date of visit: ____________________

____

Purpose of trip (vacation, business, etc.): ____________________

____

____

Comments/Information: ____________________

____

____

____

____

____

____

____

____

____

____

____

____

INBAL Travel Information Ltd.
P.O.B. 1870 Ramat Gan
ISRAEL 52117